MW00800565

VOLUME 3, No. 1   SPRING 2009

COMING HOME

A SPECIAL ISSUE DEVOTED TO THE HISTORIC BUILT ENVIRONMENT
& LANDSCAPES OF BUTTE AND ANACONDA, MONTANA

A Joint Publication of the Montana Preservation Alliance & Drumlummon Institute

A Joint Publication of the Montana Preservation Alliance & Drumlummon Institute

*D*rumlummon Views is published irregularly by Drumlummon Institute, an educational and literary organization that seeks to foster a deeper understanding of the rich culture(s) of Montana and the broader American West. Drumlummon Institute is a 501 (c) (3) tax-exempt organization.

The editors welcome the submission of proposals for essays and reviews on cultural productions—including film/video, visual arts, literature, performing arts, scientific inquiry, food, architecture and design—created in Montana and the broader American West. Please send all queries and submissions to info@drumlummon.org.

We are not currently accepting unsolicited fiction, poetry, creative nonfiction, or portfolios of visual art.

ISBN 0-9769684-3-6

Printed by Artcraft Printers, Billings, Montana.

First edition.

10 9 8 7 6 5 4 3 2 1

Copyright 2009 Drumlummon Institute & Montana Preservation Alliance

Front Cover Image: *Lisa Wareham,* **Cruel Beauty (Mountain Con Mine),** *November 21, 2005, digital photograph.* © 2005 Lisa Wareham.

Frontispiece: *Lisa Wareham,* **Cruel Beauty (Mountain Con Mine),** *November 21, 2005, digital photograph.* © 2005 Lisa Wareham.

Back Cover Image: *Trestles from Main Street, Butte, 1920. Photographer unknown. Courtesy Butte–Silver Bow Public Archives, Butte (PH002-10).*

Drumlummon Institute is a proud member of

[clmp]

DRUMLUMMON Views

THE ONLINE JOURNAL OF MONTANA ARTS & CULTURE

Editor-in-Chief: Rick Newby
Art Director: Geoffrey Wyatt

Guest Editor: Patty Dean
    Consulting Editor: Chere Jiusto
    Copyeditor: Shana Harrington
    Editorial Intern: Angelina Martinez, Carroll College

Editorial Board for the Special Issue, Coming Home:
    Ellen Crain, Butte–Silver Bow Public Archives
    Chere Jiusto, Montana Preservation Alliance
    Laurie Mercier, Washington State University–Vancouver
    Mary Murphy, Montana State University, Bozeman
    Brian Shovers, Montana Historical Society
    Dori Skrukrud, Butte-Silver Bow Community Development
    Fredric Quivik, Philadelphia, Pennsylvania

Arthur Rothstein. The Original Mine operates in the heart of a Butte neighborhood, June 1939. Courtesy Library of Congress, Prints & Photographs Division, FSA/OWI Collection (LC-USF33-003115-M3).

Coming Home: A Special Issue Devoted to the Historic Built Environment and Landscapes of Butte and Anaconda, Montana, is a joint publication of the Montana Preservation Alliance & Drumlummon Institute.

Coming Home is made possible in part by a National Park Service Preserve America grant administered through the State Historic Preservation Office, Montana Historical Society.

Coming Home is also funded in part by a grant from Humanities Montana, an affiliate of the National Endowment for the Humanities.

The printed version of *Coming Home* was made possible through the generous support of the National Park Service Challenge Cost Share Program.

We are also grateful to the Montana State Historic Preservation Office and the Butte–Silver Bow Office of Community Development for their support and wise counsel.

Drumlummon Views
Volume 3, No. 1, Spring 2009

Coming Home

A Special Issue Devoted to the Historic Built Environment and Landscapes of Butte and Anaconda, Montana

TABLE OF CONTENTS

Foreword
Pat Williams

That summer evening in Butte, Montana, I was eight years old. Mom had tucked me into bed at my grandmother's house on West Woolman Street as she and her brother and sisters prepared for a Saturday night on the town. Two cars stopped outside the open bedroom windows, and laughter greeted my relatives as they crowded into the cars. I heard the sound of spinning gravel as they headed toward the adult wonderland that was downtown Butte.

The city's glow sliced through Grandmother's breeze-blown lace window curtains and neon danced on the bedroom ceiling as I longed to be in those cars bound for what was to me the unfathomable fun, mysteries, and joy of Butte's nightlife.

Perhaps it was a child's parochialism, but to me Butte was Boston, New York City, and Chicago combined in one loud, lovely, robust, generous, union-organized, ethnic, gritty, industrial Mecca. I really believed I lived in one of America's largest and most exciting cities. Einstein's theory of relativity being correct, I did.

The Butte of my childhood had many of the characteristics expected of great metropolitan cities: multiple languages, diverse architecture, ethnic neighborhoods, suburbs, and several newspapers—including ones in foreign languages. It was also the state's industrial and political potter's wheel. Butte, ironically, lacked one crucial attribute of a major urban city—Butte's population was only fifty thousand people.

The young Pat Williams on the streets of Butte. Courtesy of Pat & Carol Williams.

Decades earlier, of course, it had been one of the West's most populated cities, at nearly one hundred thousand people.

The author Bill Bevis once said this to me: "Unlike neighboring agriculture states, we had an international center. Butte was tied into the world and its politics. It was a city of strong individuals, of thinking intellectuals. In a state of wheat and cows, Butte was the exception—a center of excitement and ferment."

That round-the-clock activity, with its bustle, brawn, smells, and sounds, stuck to a kid's ribs: the shift-changing scream of the mine whistles every eight hours followed by the screech of the gallows frame's sheave wheels bringing worn miners to the surface and lowering the next shift; the constantly clattering wheels of the BA&P Railroad moving ore to the Anaconda Smelter; the enticing odors from the back-alley kitchens of the city's restaurants—The Chequamegon, Greens, Gamers, The Creamery, The Moxom, and The American Candy Shop.

My parents owned restaurants in Butte, and as a child I was allowed to stay until closing time on the occasional Saturday night. I remember Mom nudging me awake at 3:00 or 4:00 a.m. from the corner bed in our restaurant office on Park Street. The front doors had been closed to all except departing customers. World War II had ended a few years earlier, but Butte, naturally, had extended the celebration. As we left our restaurant, Dad would lock the doors behind us and then, by ritual, tightly hold one of my hands while Mom held the other to protect me from being knocked down or swept away by the crowds on Park Street—at 4:00 in the morning!

Downtown was my playground in the 1940s and '50s. I was enveloped by the Wurlitzer of it: the newsboys and street vendors, the circus parades, the forbidden dens on Mercury Street, the smoke, music, and one-armed bandits of the downtown's many bars—the Cheery lounge, the Atlantic, the Pacific, Cliffords, the U&I, the M & M, the Umpire Club, and the Crown—with their open gambling and the inevitable photo of FDR on each back bar wall.

I witnessed the hearty laughter and the vicious fights, the lucky winners and those down on their heels. Butte, in the words of the popular song, "I'm Just a Bartender": "saw all the sad faces, knew all the hard cases, and those with their backs to the wall." They were all there, the winners and the losers, between the streets bordered by Quartz and Mercury, by Main and Montana—perhaps the most tempestuous eleven square blocks in America.

In the early grades, I often walked to school from my grandmother's house across the street from the Original Mine. On my way I passed a stunning French chateau, once home of copper magnate William Clark's son Charlie but owned then by U.S. senator James

Murray. Its charming style complemented those of many other Butte buildings, assuring me that I lived in an important, worldly place, surrounded by the architectural delights of a cosmopolitan city. There was the Hennessy Building, with its gleaming marble stairways, solid oak counters, and magical pneumatic tubes whizzing receipts and cash throughout the building's many floors of merchandise. The state's then tallest building, the Finlen Hotel, with its stunning lobby and spacious downstairs ballroom, convinced me that surely all of Montana's political conventions and major dinners convened there. The City Hall, with its grand tower clock, and a dozen other imposing and beautiful buildings, including such churches as the extraordinary Church of the Immaculate Conception, the B'Nai Israel Synagogue, St. Paul's, St. Patrick's, and St. Mary's on North Main Street, served the faithful and bolstered the city's reputation as a rough mining city nestling lovely architectural structures.

During my late teens, I often danced the night away at the Columbia Gardens Pavilion. The Gardens, an oasis on the edge of a mining camp, was a magical place with hundreds of acres of gardens, lawns, and thrill rides. The Pavilion's dance floor—the largest west of the Mississippi—occupied fifteen thousand square feet. An evening in that elaborate pavilion, with its many windows opening to the hanging flower baskets and surrounding gardens, was a delight. One danced to the live music of Glenn Miller, Duke Ellington, Guy Lombardo, Benny Goodman, Tommy Dorsey, and Harry James. America's big bands were attracted to the nation's Mining City and to its antithesis, the green lawns and gleaming white buildings of the Columbia Gardens.

I attribute my belief in Butte as a singular city in part to my grandmother Elizabeth Keough, who, each year or so, would gather us grandchildren on the living room carpet around her chair and begin the ritual. She would carefully retrieve the shawl-wrapped bundle from "this very trunk that my Daddy and I brought with us to the United States from the old county on the good ship *Cedrick* of the White Star Line."

Laying her Irish medicine bundle at our feet, untying one knot and then the other, she would open the shawl's corners, revealing a concertina—a small accordion. "My Daddy played this on the boat," she would say. As we each gently touched the concertina, Grandmother would finish the story with words that imprinted Butte and its international importance on each of her grandchildren: "My Mommy saw Daddy and me off at the dock in Liverpool. She took this very shawl from her shoulders and wrapped it around mine, 'There you are Lizzie, in case you get cold on the boat.' Then, patting me on the head but looking sternly at my Daddy she demanded, 'Now don't forget, when you get to the new world, don't stop in America. You go straight to Butte, Montana.'"

Editor's Acknowledgments

Like the multi-layered levels of meaning and linkages that characterize the interdependence between the built environment and landscapes of Butte and Anaconda, Montana, so too exist myriad interconnections among the individuals and organizations who have collaborated to bring the Spring 2009 issue of *Drumlummon Views—Coming Home: A Special Issue Devoted to the Historic Built Environment and Landscapes of Butte and Anaconda, Montana*—to fruition.

The result of a partnership between the Montana Preservation Alliance (MPA; Chere Jiusto, Executive Director) and Drumlummon Institute (DI; Rick Newby, Executive Director), this special issue commemorates and complements achievements and events occurring in Butte and Anaconda in these final years of the twenty-first century's first decade. The successful creation of the nation's largest National Historic Landmark, the Butte-Anaconda Historic District, served as the initial impetus for this publication. It was a fourteen-year project undertaken by the MPA, Butte–Silver Bow Public Archives (Ellen Crain, Executive Director), and historian Derek Strahn with support from the National Park Service, Butte–Silver Bow Local Government, and the Montana State Historic Preservation Office.

Coming Home also complements upcoming preservation and heritage tourism initiatives such as the National Folk Festival (2008–2010) in Butte, the annual meeting of the Vernacular Architecture Forum in Butte (June 2009), and the establishment of "The Copperway: Mineyards to Smokestacks" tourism corridor in the Butte-Anaconda Historic District.

Special thanks are due to Maire O'Neill of the Montana State University School of Architecture and Rolene Schliesman of the Montana State Historic Preservation Office. They were the first to suggest the notion of a special online and print issue of *Drumlummon Views* devoted to the built environment of Butte and Anaconda, to coincide with the national meeting of the VAF in Butte. We hope that this special issue matches their original vision for a book offering a "richer perspective on locality than vernacular architecture and landscape alone . . . [presented in] a rich variety of formats (poetry, essays, photo essays, historical pieces, akin to Drumlummon's established practice)—A joy to read."

A "Preserve America" grant awarded by the Montana State Historic Preservation Office (SHPO) to the Butte–Silver Bow (BSB) Office of Community Development supplied critical funding early in this project, and a grant from Humanities Montana, an affiliate of the National Endowment for the Humanities, funded additional editorial and design work. Finally the extraordinarily generous support of a National Park Service "Challenge Cost Share Program" grant underwrote the printing of hard copies of the online journal and funded the remainder of the editorial work. Special appreciation is due to Lysa Wegman-French and Christine Whitacre of the NPS Heritage Partnerships program; to Roxann Lincoln, SHPO's Preservation Grants Manager; to SHPO's Mark Baumler and Rolene Schliesman; to Mark Sherouse, Kim Anderson, Ken Egan, and Clair Leonard of Humanities Montana; to Connie Ternes Daniels of the Anaconda–Deer Lodge Planning and Historic Preservation Office; and to Dori Skrukrud and Karen Byrnes of the BSB Office of Community Development, for their counsel and cooperation.

Given this project's abbreviated timeframe, much was asked of the essayists and artists whose contributions comprise this issue. Tellingly, their passion, commitment, and a desire to share their perspectives on Butte and Anaconda induced them to somehow shoehorn my request into already-straining schedules and agendas. My deep gratitude for their perseverance and continual good cheer is immeasurable. Contributors Jon Axline, Matthew Basso, Ellen Baumler, Joeann Daley, Edwin Dobb, Ron Fischer, Kate Hampton, Mary S. Hoffschwelle, Chere Jiusto, Dale Martin, Christopher W. Merritt, John Mihelich, Mary Murphy, Fredric Quivik, Dennice Scanlon, Brian Shovers, Benjamin Trigona-Harany, Nicholas Peterson Vrooman, Lisa Wareham, Carroll Van West, Roger Whitacre, and Pat Williams should be commended for abiding by the ambitious schedule, contributing exemplary work, and exhibiting great patience as I peppered them with last-minute e-mails and phone calls.

A substantial portion of this issue contains reprints or transcriptions of various primary sources, imbuing its content and appearance with a certain textural richness. Such quality is not easy to come by, and special gratitude is due to Drumlummon Institute editorial intern Angelina Martinez, of Carroll College, for her care and diligence in transcribing grainy newspaper text and microfilm (as well as for her proofreading of the entire issue). We are also deeply grateful to our copyeditor Shana Harrington, who did such a marvelous job in creating a clean and consistent final text. Deserving great thanks for their cooperation in providing digital scans and permission to publish the images in their care are Delores Morrow, Becca Kohl, Tom Ferris, and J. M. Cooper of the Montana Historical Society Photograph Archives; Lee Whitney of the Butte-Silver Bow Public Archives; Delores Cooney at the World Museum of Mining; and the staffs of the Glenbow Archives in Calgary, Alberta and of the K. Ross Toole Archives and Special Collections at The University of Montana.

Likewise, the especial care and sensitivity *Drumlummon Views* art director Geoffrey Wyatt shows in his design of every issue is in evidence with this one, as well.

Finally, I would like to thank DI's Rick Newby and MPA's Chere Jiusto, friends of long standing with common passions and interests, for entrusting me with the stewardship of this project and indulging my interest in all things Butte and Anaconda. I'm especially appreciative of their willingness to entertain and talk through the endless stream of ideas I trotted out to them on a continuing basis.

Patty Dean
Helena, Montana
Spring 2009

Coming Home to Butte and Anaconda: An Introduction

Patty Dean, Guest Editor

Perhaps the most scrutinized and documented of Montana's cities, Butte and Anaconda possess striking material and cultural incongruities that intrigue and beguile visitor and resident alike: pristine natural beauty, toxic waste Superfund sites, unrivaled riches, subsistence and poverty, ornate edifices, back alley hovels, a planned townscape, and higgledy-piggledy urban blocks punctuated by gullies and gallus frames. This snarled, complex history aligns well with the vision of the Drumlummon Institute, the publisher of *Drumlummon Views,* the online journal of Montana arts and culture: "We see ever more clearly that the origins of these [irrevocable] changes [in the American West] lie in our tangled history, a history that gets ever more complex the closer we look."

A joint venture by Drumlummon and the Montana Preservation Alliance, this special issue explores and revels in this tangled history. The project has been generously supported by organizations whose visionary and valiant efforts have done much to preserve, promote, and interpret these matchless Montana cities: the Montana State Historic Preservation Office, Butte-Silver Bow Local Government, Preserve America, Humanities Montana, and the National Park Service. We're especially pleased that, in addition to the regular online version of this issue of *Drumlummon Views,* we are able to offer a printed version, made possible by a generous grant from the National Park Service. Notice should also be accorded to the completion of an epic endeavor to expand the original Butte boundaries of the 1961 National Historic Landmark to encompass Anaconda, Walkerville, and the Butte, Anaconda and Pacific Railroad. As of 2005, this fourteen-year endeavor became a reality when the expansion was approved by the National Park Service, and now the Butte-Anaconda-Walkerville National Historic Landmark District—made up of nearly 10,000 acres containing just over 6,000 contributing resources of national significance—is the largest NHL in the United States.

From a personal perspective, I was especially delighted to serve as this volume's guest editor as a long-time member of the Vernacular Architecture Forum (VAF), an international organization dedicated "to encourage[ing] the study and preservation of all aspects of vernacular architecture and landscapes through interdisciplinary and multidisciplinary methods." After many years of effort by a number of VAF members with ties to Butte and Anaconda, we are especially happy that the organization's conference is convening in Butte this June of 2009.

In addition to the joy of collaborating on this

project with Rick Newby, Drumlummon Institute's Executive Director, and Chere Jiusto, Executive Director of the Montana Preservation Alliance, this project provided us all with the welcome opportunity to reconnect with people whose work we have long admired as well as to connect with others whose recent work expresses a similar enthrallment with the built environment and landscape of these cities. A particular priority of mine was to highlight under-utilized primary sources I had run across "looking for something else," a snare that entraps many a researcher.

Given how the old and the new are a constant dichotomy in the American West, the contributions and contributors to this volume demonstrate the perpetual fascination Butte and Anaconda has held for historians, visual artists, journalists, writers, and poets for more than 100 years.

The title of this publication, *Coming Home*, comes from Sister Joeann Daley's hand-tinted multi-frame etching of the 585-foot Anaconda Stack—a tower that would nearly equal two football fields stacked end zone to end zone. And, like the word "home" itself, the theme of "Coming Home" assumes many meanings and contexts for these authors and artists. For some of the contributors, Pat Williams, Edwin Dobb, John Mihelich, Dennice Scanlon, and Ron Fischer, Butte and Anaconda are their hometowns; they are natives. For others, such as Fred Quivik, Dale

Martin, Brian Shovers, and Mary Murphy, the Mining City is the much-beloved adopted hometown of their early professional careers, a magical place that shaped their intellectual interests and kindled an enduring camaraderie that lasts to this day.

Throughout this volume, "coming home" takes on various guises. Sometimes the homecoming is a return to a place well-known if not well-loved; in other instances it is new territory; other times, it is the house, as an actual physical structure; and yet other times it is the work place or a social club—"home away from home."

In his incisive opening essay, Carroll Van West delineates the landscape of power in southwest Montana as manifested by two of the region's monuments, the Washoe Stack in Anaconda, the sole survivor of a sprawling industrial complex, detoxified and now a Jack Nicklaus-designed golf course, and Butte's Berkeley Pit, an open-pit mine whose expansion gobbled up Meaderville, McQueen, and sections of Dublin Gulch and Finntown—these last two neighborhoods named after the residents' "old country" homes. Fredric Quivik's expansive "The Industrial Undergirding to the Vernacular Architecture of Butte and Anaconda" reminds us of the cities' very *raison d'être*, the mining industry, and the many ways it operated at cross-purposes with the communities built to support it. The mechanics and meanings of the gallus frame, a dominant feature of the Butte skyscape whose industrial tracery soars above clusters of hillside houses, is lucidly explained by John Mihelich in "What's Your Heritage Worth? Gallus Frames, Community and Experience in Butte, Montana." Dale Martin's "Maintenance Base for the Copper Conveyor: The Butte, Anaconda and Pacific Railway, its Roundhouse and Repair Shops, 1914" describes the Butte, Anaconda and Pacific Railway roundhouse and other West Anaconda shops, the workplace home for over 250 men, and the choreography necessary to transport the copper from the Richest Hill on Earth to the Anaconda smelter. Drawing on WPA writer Edward B. Reynolds' extraordinarily vivid essay on work at the Anaconda smelter, Matthew Basso discusses how the built environment shapes and informs an individual's sense of himself. A recent disclosure of Reynolds' ethnicity (as an African American) lends an additional complexity, especially in a workplace where work assignments were predicated on ethnic identity.

Edwin Dobb's "Dirty Old Town: Addiction and Betrayal in the Mining City" weighs the puzzling magnetism Butte has exerted on him over thousands of miles and throughout the stages of his life. Pat Williams' foreword evokes perhaps a less complicated but equally detailed picture of boyhood moments in the metropolis of Butte with its dazzling landmarks and teeming crowds. Ron Fischer's "The Tuna Fish Sandwich" posits the Montana of tourism brochures against the Montana of his boyhood in his hometown-smelter town of Anaconda while Dennice Scanlon's "Ballad for a Butte Miner" presents the grim work conditions her underground miner father and scores of others faced on a daily basis. Ron Fischer's harrowing story, "Manus Dugan," makes all too real the threats to life and limb encountered in the Butte mines.

But such dangerous and unhealthy prospects existed above ground in Butte, too. For thousands of new Butte residents, immigrants in particular, their new home in Silver Bow County more resembled Dante's *Inferno* than his *Paradiso*. The city's transformation from a mining "camp" to the largest city between Minneapolis and Seattle in only three decades' time exerted extraordinary demands on its nascent infrastructure and housing stock. Butte's most rapid growth coincided with the Progressive Era of the early twentieth century when the idea emerged that the morals and minds of citizenry could be improved by a beautiful and clean city. The "Report of Investigation of Sanitary Conditions in Mines, and. of the Conditions Under Which the Miners Live in Silver Bow County" documents in text and photographs the inadequacies—or even absence—of infrastructure, building codes, and planning that occurred in a city where the physical separation between home and workplace was often blurred or miniscule. Silver Bow

County health authorities were not the only ones to document shortcomings and prescribe improvements, however. Prolific Butte writer Helen Fitzgerald Sanders' "Redeeming the Ugliest Town on Earth," reprinted from a 1907 issue of *The Craftsman*, is introduced by Mary S. Hoffschwelle in a revelatory discussion of Butte's place on the national arts and crafts movement reform agenda.

Brian Shovers' "Housing on the Rocky Mountain Urban Frontier: Multi-Family Building Forms in Butte, Montana 1890-1916" examines the critical question of where some of the Mining City's most ubiquitous forms originated. A related inquiry—when, why and how did Butte workers furnish their homes—is taken up in my own essay, "Home Furnishing in the Mining City of Butte," which analyzes the furnishing purchases made by a wide range of credit customers at the city's most complete department store, circa 1910, and how these tied into socio-cultural trends of the time. Chere Jiusto's "Montana's Smallest National Historic Landmark: The Burton K. Wheeler House" illustrates how the appearance and context of his modest home contributed to and conveyed the persistent values and identity of Montana's most controversial U.S. senator.

As noted in a number of essays in this volume, Butte was home to a variety of ethnic groups in the early twentieth century, and reprints from a continuing feature in the *Anaconda Standard*, "Queer Spots In and About Butte," highlight how a few of these communities regarded Butte as their home. Christopher W. Merritt provides a brief history of the state's Chinese for two of the "Queer Spots" features, one on Butte's Chinatown—the largest in the state by 1890—and the other on their Chinese garden and "nursery." The surprising presence of a so-called "Assyrian Colony" in Butte and the complexities of Middle Eastern Christianity are revealed by Benjamin Trigona-Harany who identifies the colony as comprised of members of an Arabic-speaking Maronite population from Hadkit village in south Lebanon. Nicholas Peterson Vrooman uses the Queer Spots' "Cree Village" feature as the springboard for telling the story of the nation's first urban Indians. Traveling on foot with dog and horse travois, these refugees of Louis Riel's rebellion in Canada fruitlessly searched for a home throughout the cities and towns of central Montana before settling in Butte for a time.

The concept of "home" in the public sphere is addressed in essays describing homes-away-from-homes and social and/or recreational clubs of a sort. In "The End of the Line: Butte, Anaconda and the Landscape of Prostitution," Ellen Baumler details the domestic appearance of these euphemistic "female boarding houses" from the late nineteenth century to post-World War II days. Essays by Kate Hampton on the rustic Anaconda Saddle Club and my own on Butte's cosmopolitan Silver Bow Club document their respective clienteles and the cultural values that underlaid the clubs' designs. Mary Murphy's thoughtful and whimsical observations on fedora-wearing men describes their appearances as they strode about the Mining City while Jon Axline's "Extra Tasty and Fried the Way You Like It!: Butte's Historic Drive-In Restaurants" traces the history of food to-go, often consumed by travelers at nearby hotels or tourist camps.

The images of Butte's urban fabric as presented by photographer Lisa Wareham are such new viewpoints that even the native will wish to spend more time in this photographer's new home-town. Sister Joeann Daley's collages and prints from two suites, one produced in 1970 and the other in the mid 1980s, offer a capsule visual history of the Smelter City and its icons. Belying Anaconda's planned town origins, Sister

Joeann's prints present a visual cacophony of landmark church steeples, bar signs, and houses. Such exuberance is soberly balanced by other works that allude to the smelter's closing; "The Bus No Longer Stops Here," for example, depicts a smelter worker, lunchbox in hand, standing forlornly. Finally, veteran photographer Roger Whitacre presents straightforward views of the place of the final coming-home, the cemeteries of Butte and Anaconda.

Early twentieth-century essayist George Wesley Davis wrote of Butte: "There is tragedy and romance in the very look of the place and one's breath comes quickly." We hope that the contents of this issue will quicken the breath of readers for whom Butte and Anaconda are well-known territory and captivate those who are setting their virtual (or actual) footsteps there for the first time.

The Pit and the Stack: Decoding the Southwestern Montana Landscape
Carroll Van West

Many observers of the northern Rockies believe that the region's architecture has difficulty competing with the vastness and grandeur of the landscape itself. Those who write talk about the ruggedness of the mountains, the starkness of the plains, and the emptiness of endless space, but they have few words for the interplay of buildings, structures, and things within that environment unless they are like the forests and mountains themselves: writers wax eloquently about the mammoth "rustic" designs from Robert Reamer, Gilbert Underwood, and others in the nearby national parks but typically ignore the rest of the state's architecture, except when they throw out such descriptors as *quaint*, *picturesque*, and *abandoned*.[1]

In Montana, the space is so big that what residents built to control that space sometimes seems lost, even inconsequential. At the same time, for travelers close to the ground, the relative emptiness of the space means that buildings, districts, and structures have more prominence, begging for an explanation of how and why they got there.

A part of the answer is easy. Certainly much of the surviving historic architecture repeats patterns found in other eastern and midwestern states. Montana, after all, did not receive its first large batch

The Washoe Stack, Anaconda, Montana, 1942. Photograph by R. I. Nesmith. Courtesy Montana Historical Society Research Center Photograph Archives, Helena (Lot 19 A1a).

of permanent Euro-American residents until the 1860s and 1870s. The new residents brought along what they had in St. Paul, or St. Louis, or Detroit. But the larger part of the answer is much more difficult to discern today. In his recent study of Montana landscapes, geographer William Wyckoff admits "how difficult it is to make sense of the landscapes around us," especially since "the features that survive on the scene today are sometimes bare, always selective fragments of what happened in the place."[2] Nowhere is the tension between what is there now and what was there yesterday greater than in Butte and Anaconda.

At first encounter, the preserved and revitalized Butte and Anaconda are truly sights to see. A generation of work from committed and gifted preservationists, historians, artists, urban planners, and neighborhood activists has transformed the towns. Historic districts and successful renovations abound. The National Park Service designated the Butte-Anaconda National Historic Landmark in 2006.

Many important buildings, structures, and sites remain; there is a high integrity to the place, as preservationists like to say. Decades of meaningful preservation can take place here. Yet, the truth of Butte and Anaconda's past is far more difficult to see. The success of preservation can obscure the realities of unchecked industrial power on the western landscape.

Progress, prosperity, destruction, exploitation:

you can choose the terms of the debate, as writers did one hundred years ago. Past boosters chose the first two words—for example, Henry C. Freeman's *A Brief History of Butte, Montana* (1900) found Butte to be a cultural and economic marvel, a model of development for all of the Rockies. The mass media press was dominated by similar declarations of community stability, even beauty.[3]

Others who wrote found the landscape alien, even distasteful. In a postcard sent to a friend in 1908, Will Rogers wisecracked: "Beautiful scenery. there aint a tree in 10 miles."[4] A few years earlier, a youthful Mary MacLane was more graphic in communicating her disgust: "Butte and its immediate vicinity present as ugly an outlook as one could wish to see. It is so ugly indeed that it is near the perfection of ugliness."[5]

Dashiell Hammett, who fictionalized Butte and Anaconda, and probably a couple of other western abodes, into the town Personville in his novel *Red Harvest* (1929), wrote:

[The] city wasn't pretty. Most of its builders had gone in for gaudiness. Maybe they had been successful at first. Since then the smelters whose brick stacks stuck up tall against a gloomy mountain to the south had yellow-smoked everything into uniform dinginess. The result was an ugly city of

Meaderville and the Berkeley Pit, 1959. Photograph by Al Hooper, Butte, Montana. Courtesy of World Museum of Mining, Butte (Photo 5828A).

forty thousand people, set in an ugly notch between two ugly mountains that had been dirtied up by mining. Spread over this was a grimy sky that looked as if it had come out of the smelters' stacks.[6]

Thankfully, the air is much cleaner today, and reforestation and other environmental projects have reclaimed some of the damaged land. Butte and Silver Bow County in fact market themselves as part of the state's greater natural and recreational beauties. However, two structures in particular remain to convey a sense of historical reality, to remind anyone of what building the West was actually about. Butte and Anaconda's surrounding snow-capped mountains may take center stage—until the eyes see that great gash in the landscape (the Berkeley Pit) or that great finger of industrial capitalism (the Anaconda Stack) soaring skyward, surrounded by its mounds of industrial waste. Once burned into your eyes, the Pit and the Stack remain part of whatever architectural understanding you take away from this western place.

The Washoe Stack came first, built by the Alphonis Chimney Construction Company for the Anaconda Copper Mining Company in 1918. The stack is 585 feet high, 60 feet wide at the top with an interior diameter of 75 feet. Few industrial structures anywhere compare to it. The stack loomed over the company,

its workers, its region, and its state as the Anaconda company owned and ran Montana as "a commonwealth where one corporation ruled supreme."[7]

The company's power only continued to grow through the middle decades of the century; by the 1950s, it had decided to take its next great step—open pit mining—which destroyed thriving neighborhoods in Butte in exchange for another generation of work. The Berkeley Pit opened in 1955. By the end of its life, almost thirty years later, the Pit had grown to 7,000 feet long, 5,500 feet wide, and at least 1,800 feet deep. On a good day, miners and their mammoth machines dug out fifty thousand tons of rock and ore. As one local writer observed in 1988: "The Pit gave Butte an unique position in the history of American cities: the only town both created and then, in good part, actually physically destroyed by the industry that created it." The Pit eventually claimed the communities of Meaderville and McQueen along with portions of Finntown and Dublin Gulch.[8]

The Pit and the Stack are significant reminders of how industrial power shaped the landscape of and between Butte and Anaconda. Geographer Yi-Fu Tuan observed that "as a consequence of the Industrial Revolution, the scale of power was tipped in man's favor. He proceeded to outrage the land with coal dumps and urban sprawls."[9] The transformation first occurred in the English countryside and then, with particular brutality, in the New World landscape of the twentieth century, where new technology combined with modern consumer desires to create insatiable markets for natural resources. Nature might never be conquered, but the new machines could destroy it and replace it with a new, engineered landscape that experts could control.

The Pit and the Stack are among the West's most defining structures—corporate acts of will—that broke forever the scale of the Montana landscape, leaving no doubt that modern life could tame the West only by destroying it and creating in its stead huge machines capable of plundering its treasures.

To those who worked the mine and smelter, those landmarks governed their lives.[10] Historian Laurie Mercier spoke with Bob Vine, who believed that the Company and God were all the same in Anaconda: "Everybody would get up in the morning and they look and see if there was smoke coming out of that stack and if there was, God was in his heaven and all was right with the world, and we knew we were going to have a paycheck."[11] In the 1980s, the Atlantic Richfield Corporation, a later owner of the Washoe works, announced the stack's closing and possible demolition. A community-wide effort to save the stack was launched because, in the poetic words of local union activist Tom Dickson:

ARCO save that stack, touch not a single brick
Signify the livelihood that made Anaconda tick.

Still let it stand there stark against the sky,
Like a somewhat obscene gesture catching every eye.[12]

Those who worked in the Pit sometimes reacted in horror to what their daily tasks meant for the historic landscape in being moved or even buried, intact and still alive. Pit truck driver Bill Long wrote: "When I dumped a load on the beautiful Holy Savior School in McQueen, I watched in my rearview mirror as tons of huge boulders and dirt slammed into the side of the multi-story building. It withstood the onslaught with only a barely discernable shudder. My heart was heavy as I pulled away. I felt like a murderer."[13]

What you encounter in today's Butte and Anaconda, as well as with the surrounding countryside and communities, is not unique to Montana. The degree is different here, but the story line is one found throughout the northern Rockies. As the region has been mined, farmed, and developed since the mid-nineteenth century, great disparity has existed between those who work the land and those who own and control it. The two worlds might be at odds, or they might strike an uneasy coexistence within the landscape. A good place to start in understanding and appreciating the region's architectural traditions is to accept how the machine embodied in modern corporate capital culture rearranged places and lives in the name of order, prosperity, destruction, and revitalization.

[1] Ruth Quinn, *Weaver of Dreams: The Life and Architecture of Robert C. Reamer* (Bozeman, MT: Leslie and Ruth Quinn, Publishers, 2004); David A. Naylor, "Old Faithful Inn and Its Legacy: The Vernacular Transformed" (master's thesis, Cornell University, 1990); Harvey Kaiser, *Landmarks in the Landscape: Historic Architecture in the National Parks of the West* (San Francisco: Chronicle, 1997); Linda McClelland, *Building the National Parks: Historic Landscape Design and Construction* (Baltimore: Johns Hopkins University Press, 1998).

[2] William Wyckoff, *On the Road Again: Montana's Changing Landscapes* (Seattle: University of Washington Press, 2006), xiv.

[3] As historian Timothy F. LeCain points out, these images of Butte the Bountiful continued well into the twentieth century. See his "'See America the Bountiful': Butte's Berkeley Pit and the American Culture of Consumption," *Montana The Magazine of Western History* 56 (Winter 2006): 5–17.

[4] Will Rogers to Betty Blake, June 17, 1909, in *The Papers of Will Rogers: Wild West and Vaudeville, Vol. Two: April 1904–September 1908*, ed. Arthur F. Wertheim and Barbara Bair (Norman: University of Oklahoma Press, 2000), 433n.

[5] Mary MacLane, *The Story of Mary MacLane by Herself* (Chicago: Herbert S. Stone, 1902), 10.

[6] Dashiell Hammett, *Red Harvest* (1929; reprint, New York: Vintage , 1992), 3–4.

[7] Michael P. Malone and Richard P. Roeder, *Montana: A History of Two Centuries* (Seattle: University of Washington Press, 1976), 177; Carroll V. West, *A Travelers' Companion to Montana History* (Helena: Montana Historical Society Press, 1986), 173.

[8] Steve Devitt, *Butte: The Town and the People* (Helena, MT: American Geographic Publishing, 1988), 55–56; West, *A Travelers' Companion to Montana History*, 173.

[9] Yi-Fu Tuan, "Thought and Landscape: The Eye and the Mind's Eye," in *The Interpretation of Ordinary Landscapes: Geographical Essays*, ed. D. W. Meinig (New York: Oxford University Press, 1979), 92.

[10] Two excellent studies of the mining culture in Butte and Anaconda are Mary Murphy, *Mining Cultures: Men, Women, and Leisure in Butte, 1914–41* (Urbana: University of Illinois Press, 1997); and Laurie Mercier, *Anaconda: Labor, Community, and Culture in Montana's Smelter City* (Urbana: University of Illinois Press, 2001).

[11] Mercier, *Anaconda*, 1.

[12] Dickson's poem is cited in Mercier, *Anaconda*, 217.

[13] Bill Long, "Driving Haul Trucks in the Berkeley Pit: Reminiscences of a Gritty Job," *Montana The Magazine of Western History* 56 (Winter 2006): 58.

The Industrial Undergirding to the Vernacular Architecture of Butte and Anaconda

Fredric L. Quivik

The rich built environments of Butte and Anaconda sprang almost entirely from the area's mining industry. The quest for gold first brought prospectors to Silver Bow Creek and the Butte hill. The discovery of placer gold and then ores rich in silver and copper, and later zinc and manganese, induced people to stay and to build permanent communities. But the two pursuits, mining and building community, are in many ways opposites: the former is inherently destructive, whereas the latter is constructive. Mining and community building therefore often operated at cross purposes. The built environments of Butte and Anaconda resulted from the struggles over which purpose would dominate. They exhibit the frequent victory of those who would let mining predominate, they exhibit the compromises people who wanted to build community were willing to make because mining gave Butte and Anaconda their reasons to exist, and they exhibit small victories that community builders were able to carve out of environments so dominated by mining.[1]

Two descriptions published in 1865 in the *Montana Post* demonstrate the potential conflict between those interested in building a community that could sustain human and other forms of life and those interested in extracting wealth from Butte's subterranean reaches.[2] Early that year, and shortly after gold was discovered at Butte, a correspondent fashioning himself "Joe Bowers" wrote to describe the community that had emerged in a sheltered portion of the Butte hill. Prominent images in his description include a stream and a sheltering grove of trees, components of an environment that might appear to welcome life: "Butte City is beautifully located on an eminence near the junction of the left and right branches of Silver Bow Creek, and close to a stately grove of pine trees, beneath whose shelter has suddenly come into existence a town, comparatively small as yet, but destined ere long to be one of the most flourishing and prosperous in the territory of Montana."[3]

Late in the year, another description appeared in the *Montana Post*, this time making no mention of living things or the environmental features that sustain life. Rather, the images invoke fire and molten rock, perhaps foreshadowing the processes—chemical and physical, and not biological—that would be employed to free metallic wealth from the environment:

> The scenery changed rapidly, and we were soon in the heart of that celebrated formation of quartz riven rock. Once upon a time, there must have been some hot work going on, for

the country looks as if it had been melted,
and set on end to cool.[4]

During the next few years, Butte followed the
pattern of most ephemeral western mining camps,
booming briefly and then waning.[5] Most prospectors
moved on to find greater riches, leaving a few persistent
Chinese miners to work the remaining placer claims
and a few other miners known as "quartz cranks," who
were determined to find a way to extract wealth from
the rock formations beneath the surface of the Butte
hill. Rock outcroppings showed signs of mineralization
to some trained eyes, but finding a way to work that
rock profitably would prove frustrating for a decade.
During the early 1870s, the population of Butte dropped
to only about a hundred year-round residents.[6]

Butte's initial boom was drawing to a close,
yet the ore deposits buried beneath the surface had
attracted notice outside the territory of Montana.
J. Ross Browne, an agent reporting to the federal
government in 1868 on mining and related activities
in the American West, had the following to say about
Butte:

> At Silver bar [*sic*] and Butte City the mines
> have done well. Placers only have been
> worked; but in every gulch where good placer
> mines are found, gold-bearing quartz veins
> are found also, many of which contain silver,
> copper, antimony, arsenic, and manganese,
> and are rich but very refractory. At Butte City
> some copper mines have been discovered, and
> a furnace erected for smelting. Owing to a
> defect in the blast it was not successful. The
> ore, which is quite abundant, is composed of
> oxides and carbonates in a concentrated form.
> It contains gold and silver, and with a well
> regulated furnace there would be no difficulty
> smelting it. These veins are found crossing
> a belt about one mile wide and four or five
> long, and show evidence of being deep and
> permanent.[7]

Butte Rises as a Smoky Mining and Smelting City

Interest in Butte's quartz lodes did not revive
significantly until 1875, when several quartz cranks
pulled together the financing to build small stamp
mills to crush silver ore and to recover silver and
small amounts of gold by amalgamation. Most widely
credited for spearheading the revival was William
Farlin, who had filed the Asteroid and other Butte
lode claims in the mid-1860s and had tried working
ores from them to extract gold. Farlin had taken some
samples of Butte quartz with him to Idaho, where he
worked in the mines while also learning more about
milling. From assays of those samples, he concluded

Alice mill, Walkerville: The Walker Brothers' Alice Gold & Silver Mining Company established the first successful large-scale silver-milling operation in the Butte district in 1877. From Harry C. Freeman, A Brief History of Butte, Montana, the World's Greatest Mining Camp (Butte above and below Ground) *(Chicago: Henry O. Shepard Co., 1900).*

the Dexter.[8] One of Butte's thirteen surviving headframes still stands at the Travonia, clearly visible from the interstate highway. It was built decades after Farlin's early efforts.

Farlin ordered a ten-stamp mill so that he could work the silver-bearing quartz from his Travona claim. He had the equipment freighted overland from the transcontinental railroad at Corinne, Utah, to a mill site located near the Travona mine on the east side of Missoula Gulch, about a half mile above the mouth of the gulch on Silver Bow Creek. By June 1876, the Dexter was crushing ore and recovering silver using the Washoe process, in which small amounts of salt and copper sulfide were added to

that Butte ores were more promising for their silver and copper. Returning to Butte in late 1874, he prepared to refile a dozen mining claims under a revision of the federal mining law that took effect on January 1, 1875. Those claims included the Asteroid, located on the southwest portion of the Butte hill. Farlin renamed it the Travona (alternately spelled Travonia) on January 1. He also secured financing from Deer Lodge banker W. A. Clark to build a stamp mill, which he named

the crushed ore in amalgamating pans to help make the silver amenable to amalgamation with mercury. The mill operated successfully on ore from Farlin's mine, but when the mill treated a lot of ore from a different mine, the presence of antimony and lead caused poor recovery of silver and yielded excessive lead in the bullion. Farlin was so deeply in debt to Clark that the banker actually controlled the mill, and Farlin could not afford to upgrade from the Washoe process to the Reese River process, which used a furnace to roast the ore with salt to release the silver for amalgamation. Later in June, Clark decided to finish constructing the reverberatory furnaces Farlin had started. By July, Clark had the mill and some of the furnaces operating.[9]

This episode exhibited the uncertainty involved in, as well as the need for adequate capital for, finding and developing practical processes for extracting value from ores in these early years. It also showed how important furnaces and their resultant smoke were to the eventual success of mining ventures in Butte.

The return of spring weather in 1876 brought a return of active mining and allowed several construction projects in addition to the Dexter to get under way. Despite Farlin's setbacks in getting his mill running, new enthusiasm greeted quartz mining in Butte. By April, more than one hundred miners were working for about thirty partnerships and small companies in as many small silver mines. There were still about sixty men working placers in the area. Copper was drawing considerable attention as well. Butte had fifteen small companies employing more than sixty miners and working veins in more than a dozen copper mines.[10]

The quartz miner given credit for initiating Butte's rise as an important copper producer was Bill Parks, who also achieved his long-awaited success in 1876. He had continued throughout the early 1870s to slowly sink his shaft on the Parrot lode, hoping to strike copper ore rich enough to ship or treat. In early 1876, by which time Parks's shaft was about 150 feet deep, he drove a crosscut 200 feet from the shaft and struck a vein of copper glance (chalcocite, or Cu_2S) four feet wide. Using a simple windlass, Parks and two men were able to hoist a ton or more of ore daily. He placed ore containing 40 to 60 percent copper in sacks and freighted it by wagon to Corinne, from where it was shipped by rail to Baltimore for smelting.[11]

As the Fourth of July in the United States' centennial year approached, the reemerging mining camp was convinced that it was truly embarking on a new era of prosperity. Butte citizens decided to stage an elaborate Independence Day celebration, complete with parade, fireworks, and speeches.[12] The main speaker was Charles S. Warren, who had worked in the county recorder's office during Butte's first boom. Now a prominent citizen, he was called upon to recite the camp's history. After crediting Farlin with bringing Butte back to life and recounting how Parks's persistence had paid off, Warren named the other mines who also showed promise. He concluded:

> The future is indeed promising, and within a short time will be heard the music of a hundred whistles of quartz mills—the horizon will be clouded with the smoke of scores of furnaces. . . . Take a view of the camp. For

four miles around Butte is but a net work [*sic*] of rich lodes; gold, silver, copper and lead abound and in such vast quantities that we cannot help but be the greatest mining center in the west, if not the world. Virginia City and the mines of Nevada, now producing millions of precious metals, will be eclipsed. All we need is transportation and works for the reduction of our ores. To you of faint heart and who feel discouraged, who for years have worked patiently and hard without a murmur, we would say, be of good cheer, hold your grip, for day is dawning. Butte will come out, and with flying banners. Here will be such a community in the near bye-and-bye as you do not dream of. The camp is now getting known throughout the world, and were it not for our isolation, a few weeks would see the capital of the world seeking investment here. [13]

Such boosterism was typical of many mining camps in the nineteenth-century American West, but in Butte's case Warren's boosterism proved prescient. Within a few years, Butte's horizon was indeed clouded with the smoke of scores of furnaces. Of even more interest to those promoting Butte was the arrival of the transcontinental railroads as well as ample capital from San Francisco and the East Coast. Some investors

Moulton mill, Walkerville: opened in 1881, this was W. A. Clark's contribution to the silver mining and milling industry in Walkerville. From Harry C. Freeman, A Brief History of Butte, Montana, the World's Greatest Mining Camp (Butte above and below Ground) *(Chicago: Henry O. Shepard Co., 1900).*

developed silver mills, the most successful of which employed roasting furnaces to enable better recovery of silver from the sulfide ores. The largest of the silver mills were located in Walkerville, just north of Butte and at the head of Missoula Gulch, which flows south through what is now Butte's West Side and joins Silver Bow Creek adjacent to Butte's sewage treatment plant.[14]

More importantly, Butte emerged as a major source of copper. By 1887, Butte surpassed Michigan's Keweenah Peninsula to become the world's greatest supplier of copper, a distinction it would hold until the end of World War I.[15] Butte attracted capital and rewarded many investments with fabulous profits; meanwhile, the investors tried to shine the most favorable light on the smoky atmosphere that accompanied Butte's rapid rise. Addressing the delegates at the Montana Constitutional Convention in 1889, local capitalist W. A. Clark extolled the virtues of the smoke emanating from Butte's furnaces:

> I must say that the ladies are very fond of this smoky city, as it is sometimes called, because there is just enough arsenic there to give them a beautiful complexion, and that is the reason the ladies of Butte are renowned wherever [sic] they go for their beautiful complexions. . . . I say it would be a great deal better for other cities in the territory if they had more smoke and less diphtheria and other diseases. It has been believed by all the physicians of Butte that the smoke that sometimes prevails there is a disinfectant, and destroys the microbes that constitute the germs of disease. . . . [I]t would be a great advantage for other cities, to have a little more smoke and business activity and less disease.[16]

Many in Butte shared Clark's rosy outlook on smoke, but by Montana's year of statehood, the emanations from Butte's furnaces were sparking controversy. In 1885, a group of Butte women had complained that the thick smoke from the smelters was damaging their flowers and other plants, a complaint that went largely ignored. At that time, most Butte residents still saw smoke as a sign of prosperity.[17] This view may have helped Thomas Couch, one of the Butte smelter managers, to more readily see benefits in the clouds of smoke. In an 1889 letter to a corporate official in Boston, Couch observed how helpful Butte's smoke had been in helping him view a solar eclipse the day before. The smoke was so thick that he could look directly at the eclipse without hurting his eyes.[18]

The mixed blessing of smoke in the air was described by one A. C. Snow in a letter to cousins in Moscow, Idaho, shortly after his arrival in Butte in October 1897. Snow had been a miner in the silver mines of Aspen, Colorado. Like so many silver camps in the West, Aspen had prospered until 1893 and the silver crisis, which eventually forced Snow to look for work elsewhere.[19] After visiting his cousins in Moscow, Snow took the train through Pullman to Spokane and then boarded the Northern Pacific eastbound for Butte. Arriving at 10:00 p.m., he immediately took stock of the place:

> I was much surprised for the city is much larger than I had expected. I fount [sic] the largest smokiest wickedest mining camp on

Looking south from the corner of Broadway and Main, Butte: Smoke from the Colorado smelter (A) and the Butte Reduction Works (B)
obscures Timber Butte (C). From Harry C. Freeman, A Brief History of Butte, Montana, the World's Greatest Mining Camp
(Butte above and below Ground) *(Chicago: Henry O. Shepard Co., 1900).*

the face of the earth, and if one is fond of Boom business hurry bustle noise excitement and crowds of people he can have it here to his heart's content. And I was much surprised to find the city building very rapidly and some of the largest buildings I ever saw. And the large amount of work going on in the city and mines and smelters is simply indescribable and wages are away up $3.50 a day 8 hours in the mines [illegible] out side.[20]

Although Butte was flooded with job seekers, Snow knew the manager of one of the mines and felt confident he could find work. After describing other aspects of the city, he returned to the theme of smoke: "Butte City is situated on the south slope of a low flat mountain. . . . [T]he mines are all in a bunch in the north part of the city, the smelters are located all around and smoke is no name for it. The country around looks desolate on the account of the copper smoke killing all vegetation."[21]

By January 1898, Snow was gainfully employed as a miner, but working conditions in winter were not healthful. He had such a bad cold he had missed two shifts. After working up a good sweat in the warm mine during the night shift, he was hoisted to the surface at 4 a.m., into the cold night air, where he had to walk to his rooming house.[22] Winter temperatures in Butte

often drop below zero. These were just some of the features of Butte: it offered good pay for anyone willing to work hard at dangerous tasks in a commonly brutal environment.

But the smoke caused the most hardship, especially for those not in the best of health. For example, in early February 1898, a man named Murdock McLeod was visiting his sister in Butte. McLeod suffered from asthma, which made him susceptible to Butte's smoke. When he was stricken with respiratory problems, his sister called a doctor, but McLeod died that same evening.[23]

In the twentieth century, Butte was often called the Mining City, while its companion in Montana's copper industry, Anaconda, was called the Smelter City. Those distinctions reflected the fact that the industry's dominant corporation, the Anaconda Copper Mining Company, known locally as the ACM, had by 1910 consolidated almost all of Butte's several prosperous mining companies into a single, giant industrial operation that featured an integrated network of mines in Butte, the world's largest nonferrous smelter at Anaconda, and a wholly owned railroad—the Butte, Anaconda & Pacific (BA&P)—linking the two. In fact, by 1912, the ACM was the world's fifth-largest industrial corporation.[24]

But before that consolidation was complete, and especially in the nineteenth century, Butte was an

Butte's mines were adjacent to and intermingled with its urban fabric of neighborhoods and business districts. This view, published in 1900, shows the Neversweat mine from the northeast edge of the central business district. From Harry C. Freeman, A Brief History of Butte, Montana, the World's Greatest Mining Camp (Butte above and below Ground) *(Chicago: Henry O. Shepard Co., 1900).*

important smelter city in addition to being the mining city known as the Richest Hill on Earth. Except for the Bell smelter along Blacktail Deer Creek, which was a failure and did not operate for long, Butte's nineteenth-century copper smelters were located along Silver Bow Creek, where they had access to water and could dispose of their tailings. The Colorado smelter—a joint venture between W. A. Clark and Colorado's N. P. Hill (who was well known for his copper smelter at Black Hawk)—was the first to succeed in Butte. Located along the south side of Silver Bow Creek near the mouth of Missoula Gulch, it went into operation in 1879.

The Montana Copper Company was the next to establish a smelter. Launched by the Lewisohn Brothers of New York City, who were prominent brokers in global metals markets, the Montana Copper Company owned the rich Colusa mines near Meaderville, once located where the east side of the Berkeley Pit is now. The smelter, which went into operation in 1881, was also located near Meaderville, along Silver Bow Creek. Later that year, the Parrot Silver & Copper Company began operating its new smelter, located near the north end of Texas Avenue, northeast of where the Civic

Center now stands. Late in 1881, the Utah & Northern, a branch line of the Union Pacific Railroad, reached Butte, linking the city to Utah and the nation's first transcontinental railroad. Two years later, the Northern Pacific was completed across Montana, giving Butte access to two transcontinental railroads. Improved transportation would further spur the development of smelters for Butte's copper mines.[25]

W. A. Clark built his own smelter near Meaderville in 1884. A year later, the Butte Smelting Company built its Butte Reduction Works along Silver Bow Creek at the foot of Montana Street, upstream of the Colorado smelter. In the late 1880s, Clark sold his Meaderville smelter to a group of New York and Boston capitalists and acquired the Butte Reduction Works, expanding it over the next two decades to be Butte's largest and longest-lived copper smelter. The eastern capitalists to whom Clark sold his Meaderville smelter were the Lewisohns and some Boston investors, including A. S. Bigelow, who owned several important copper mines on Michigan's Upper Peninsula. Combining the Montana Copper Company with Clark's Colusa and the Mountain View mine (a fabulously rich mine developed but not mined by Charles X. Larabie), Bigelow, the Lewisohns, and the others formed the Boston & Montana Consolidated Copper & Silver Mining Company (B&M), which would become one of the most profitable of Butte's giant copper companies. The B&M referred to its two Meaderville smelters as its upper and lower works. At about the same time, Bigelow and his associates bought another group of Butte mines, established the Butte & Boston Mining Company (B&B) as a separate company, and built yet another smelter along Silver Bow Creek just downstream from Meaderville. It began operating in the fall of 1889.

The last major nineteenth-century smelter to be built in Butte was the MOP smelter, built by the Montana Ore Purchasing Company. The MOP was a creature of F. Augustus Heinze, who would become notorious for using the law of the apex as a means for tapping veins of copper ore that other companies believed belonged to them. While rights to those veins were being contested in court, Heinze grew rich operating several mines in Butte that gave him access to the veins. Heinze first fired the furnaces of his MOP smelter in 1893.

Smelting was important for several reasons. First, it was crucial to Butte's ability to rise as a major mining center. Without smelting, only the richest of Butte's ores could have been shipped to smelters elsewhere and still generated a profit; the costs of transporting the 95 percent or more of the ore that consisted of valueless mineral would have been too great. A relatively high percentage of Butte's working population in the nineteenth century worked in smelters (or silver mills).

Of the people listed in the 1885 Butte City Directory (nearly all of them men), more than 11 percent had occupations in metallurgical facilities (smelters or mills), while 29 percent were miners and underground workers.[26] Thus, milling and smelting contributed significantly to the livelihoods of Butte families.

And then there are the environmental consequences of smelting. More than any other facet of the mining enterprise in Butte (before the advent

Butte & Boston smelter, Butte: Owned by many of the same investors who developed the Boston & Montana, the B&B opened its smelter along Silver Bow Creek in 1889. From Harry C. Freeman, A Brief History of Butte, Montana, the World's Greatest Mining Camp (Butte above and below Ground) *(Chicago: Henry O. Shepard Co., 1900).*

of open-pit mining at the Berkeley Pit in 1955, that is), smelting and the related metallurgical activities devastated Butte's environment.

Butte's environment may seem to be dominated today by the Berkeley Pit, the East Continental Pit, and the mine waste and tailings that are stored north of the Berkeley Pit in what was once a valley at the headwaters of Silver Bow Creek. Gone from view are remnants of

Montana Ore Purchasing Company smelter, Butte: Developed by F. Augustus Heinze 1893, the MOP was the last of the big nineteenth-century Butte smelters to operate. It continued smelting until 1910. From Harry C. Freeman, A Brief History of Butte, Montana, the World's Greatest Mining Camp (Butte above and below Ground) *(Chicago: Henry O. Shepard Co., 1900).*

Butte's first period, during which most mineral wealth was extracted by hydraulic means. The subsequent periods are depicted in Butte's built environment, but visual evidence linking the community to those periods continues to disappear.

The community of Walkerville, at the top of the Butte hill, grew up around some of Butte's most important silver mines and mills. The small houses of Walkerville accurately represent the typical dwellings of miners and their families. The headframe at the Lexington mine was built by the Anaconda Company in the twentieth century, but the mine itself was one of Butte's important nineteenth-century silver producers. Foundation remains of some of the silver mills, including the Lexington mill, survived into the 1980s, but they have since been obliterated by the Superfund remediation that started in the 1980s and continues today.

Butte itself grew from two centers. Uptown Butte, the historic commercial district, is located at the heart of the original townsite, platted in 1876. Residential neighborhoods grew in all directions from that core. The second center was located along Front Street, which parallels the tracks of the Burlington Northern, following the alignment of the tracks of the first railroad to reach Butte in 1881. Those tracks in turn roughly parallel Silver Bow Creek. After the railroads arrived, retail and warehousing businesses developed along Front Street and the streets extending up the Butte hill toward the original townsite. Eventually, the space between the two centers filled with a warehouse district along Utah and Arizona streets, with residential neighborhoods both east and west of those two streets, and with neighborhood retail developments along some of the other major north–south streets, including Montana and Main.[27]

Most of the mines were east and north of the original townsite, so working-class neighborhoods

Lexington mill, Walkerville: A. J. Davis' first Lexington mill (1877) was located near the present corner of Park and Arizona, but his mine was located in Walkerville. He sold his property in 1881 to a French syndicate, which built a new, larger mill next to the mine in 1882. From Harry C. Freeman, A Brief History of Butte, Montana, the World's Greatest Mining Camp (Butte above and below Ground) *(Chicago: Henry O. Shepard Co., 1900).*

W. A. Clark of Butte and N.P. Hill of Black Hawk, Colorado, capitalized the first successful copper smelter in 1879. This photo shows how it appeared at the turn of the twentieth century, by which time it had grown considerably. From Harry C. Freeman, A Brief History of Butte, Montana, the World's Greatest Mining Camp (Butte above and below Ground) *(Chicago: Henry O. Shepard Co., 1900).*

Perhaps the most well known of these neighborhoods was Meaderville, an unincorporated community along the creek due east of the original townsite. Meaderville thrived until the 1950s, when expansions of the Berkeley Pit completely subsumed it. East of the Front Street center, a neighborhood of working-class dwellings developed along Second Street, which was fairly close to the Parrot smelter. Second Street survives, but all of the blocks north and east of it have also succumbed to the Pit. Another little neighborhood developed on the little hill just south of the Colorado smelter (the westernmost of the Butte smelters). Called Williamsburg, it was named for the first manager of the Colorado smelter. Being a considerable distance from the Berkeley Pit, many of the houses in Williamsburg survive. The neighborhoods west of the original townsite were the greatest distance from the mines and smelters, and many people in Butte's professional and commercial classes built their houses there. Some houses on the west side are as

developed in those directions. Most of the working-class neighborhoods on Butte's east side have been destroyed by expansion of the Berkeley Pit toward Uptown Butte, but much of Centerville survives. Centerville is the unincorporated area of the hill between Butte and Walkerville. Mills and smelters developed along Silver Bow Creek, and neighborhoods developed near them as well.

modest as the miners' cottages of the east side and
Centerville, but many others are considerably larger
and more ornate. The west side is also where Butte's
successful mining capitalists built their impressive
mansions.

The commercial strip development of the
second half of the twentieth century occurred along
Harrison Avenue out on what Butte folks call the
Flats. Much of Harrison Avenue north of I-90,
however, dates from the early twentieth century,
when Butte's streetcar suburbs extended out onto
the Flats. Many retail buildings along the north
end of Harrison Avenue date from the 1910s and
1920s. One business, Fran Johnson's sporting goods
shop, is housed in the Socialist Hall, a building that
represents the political complexion of Butte during
the World War I era. The neighborhoods east and
west of Harrison feature some wonderful Craftsman
bungalows. Beyond those neighborhoods are other
older houses, which were moved there from near the
Berkeley Pit in the 1950s and 1960s as the surface
mine expanded. The Anaconda Company would
buy homeowners' property but would allow them to
move their houses to new locations. Many houses
in Meaderville, the east side, and the McQueen
addition (east of Meaderville) were thus moved and
still exist on the Flats, often concentrated together in
neighborhoods of such houses.

*Gagnon mine, Butte: Some mines were right in the midst of
Butte's urban fabric. The Gagnon, which supplied ore to the
Colorado smelter, was located just NE of the Butte-Silver Bow
Courthouse. From Harry C. Freeman,* A Brief History of Butte,
Montana, the World's Greatest Mining Camp (Butte above
and below Ground) *(Chicago: Henry O. Shepard Co., 1900).*

Metallurgical Wastes in Butte

Butte is located in a semiarid part of North
America, and Silver Bow Creek is quite a small stream.
Butte's smelters therefore suffered from chronic water
shortages. Moreover, after a decade of intense mining
and smelting, the hillsides near Butte were becoming
barren of trees, needed not only for mine timbers but
also for fuel. In 1888, the Boston & Montana decided to
build a new smelter elsewhere, eventually abandoning
its two Butte smelters. The company chose a location at

Great Falls, which afforded plenty of water plus ample water power that could be generated from power houses along the Missouri River adjacent to Black Eagle Falls. The B&M began operating its new Great Falls smelter in 1892 and soon after closed its two Butte smelters.

Despite the closure of the B&M's upper and lower works, Butte in the 1890s had five large copper smelters from the southwest part of Butte upstream to Meaderville—Colorado, Butte Reduction Works, Parrot, B&B, and MOP—which discharged vast volumes of what are now considered pollutants into the environment. These pollutants were discharged in two principal forms: smoke and tailings. The two tables here show the volumes of tailings (table 1) and sulfur (table 2) in the smoke that the Butte smelters discharged in the late 1890s.

Table 1: Copper Tailings Discharged Daily at Butte (Average)[28]				
1895–1898 (tons/day)				
Smelter	**1895**	**1896**	**1897**	**1898**
B&B	220	150	300	300
Butte Reduction Works	55	80	155	190
Colorado	165	190	205	175
MOP	170	195	170	190
Parrot	95	115	275	235
Total	**705**	**730**	**1,105**	**1,090**

Table 2: Sulfur Discharged Daily in the Air at Butte (Average)[29]				
1895–1898 (tons/day)				
Smelter	**1895**	**1896**	**1897**	**1898**
B&B	52	31	60	60
Butte Reduction Works	15	21	39	49
Colorado	26	31	34	30
MOP	56	65	55	63
Parrot	37	38	72	61
Total	**186**	**186**	**260**	**263**

Because processing ore by concentration was much less effective in the nineteenth century than in the twentieth, especially after smelters began using the process of flotation about 1915, the tailings discharged as a by-product from the Butte smelters around 1900 still contained much of the copper minerals originally present in the ore as well as other heavy metals, including arsenic, lead, and cadmium. Some smelters tried to impound their tailings, but such efforts (with the exception of the Butte Reduction Works after about 1905) were half-hearted at best. Thus, although large tailings piles accumulated adjacent to each of the smelters, large volumes of tailings also washed downstream, especially during spring runoff or heavy rain, leading to large deposits of tailings along Silver Bow Creek and the Clark Fork River from Butte downstream to the Milltown Dam near Missoula. (Many tailings deposits have been remediated as part of the Clark Fork Superfund Project, and the streamsides and streambeds have been restored, but tailings are still visible along some reaches of these streams.) The large tailings piles next to the Butte smelters were excavated during World War II to be reprocessed by flotation to recover the copper still present in the tailings. Only

Speculator mine, Butte: The Speculator and the adjacent Granite Mountain mine, both owned by the North Butte Mining Company, were the scene of the worst hard-rock mining disaster in U.S. history, when 165 miners died in 1917. The headframe of the Granite Mountain still stands, visible from the Memorial. From Harry C. Freeman, A Brief History of Butte, Montana, the World's Greatest Mining Camp (Butte above and below Ground) *(Chicago: Henry O. Shepard Co., 1900).*

was in the form of sulfur dioxide. As the Butte mines were extended deeper into the earth, the arsenic content of the ore increased, so smelter smoke also discharged increasing volumes of arsenic. Butte's thick smelter smoke was thick with sulfur dioxide, damaging vegetation on the Butte hill and threatening human health.

Smelter smoke had led to civil unrest in the early 1890s in an episode well chronicled by Don MacMillan in his aptly titled book *Smoke Wars*. Responding to the public outcry against the smoke, Butte's city council passed an ordinance in December 1890 intended to regulate the roasting of ores in open heaps, a low-cost method the smelters had

thin layers of tailings residue survived World War II, the most visible of which was the Colorado tailings. All of the Butte tailings have been remediated under Superfund, eliminating what for decades had been a prominent feature of the Butte landscape.

Most of the sulfur discharged with the smoke

used prior to the advent of roasting furnaces, which discharged the smoke into the atmosphere through stacks. Some smelters complied with the ordinance, but one, owned and operated by the B&M, lit some fresh piles of ore. Citizens demonstrated outside city hall, hoping to compel the government to enforce the

Parrot smelter, Butte: This smelter was the site in 1884 of the first successful use of the Bessemer process on copper. By 1900, when this photo was published, the Parrot smelter had closed and Parrot ores were being smelted at Anaconda. From Harry C. Freeman, A Brief History of Butte, Montana, the World's Greatest Mining Camp (Butte above and below Ground) *(Chicago: Henry O. Shepard Co., 1900).*

ordinance. The mayor hired a contractor to extinguish the B&M's piles.[30]

But as the volume of ore being treated in Butte increased through the 1890s, so did the volume of smoke, despite improvements in the technologies for roasting ore and dispersing smoke. The 1890 ordinance notwithstanding, these were conditions that led to A. C. Snow's vivid description of Butte and to Murdock

McLeod's death in the late 1890s. In mid-December 1898, a winter inversion caused another thick pall to settle over the city. The newspapers reported more people checking into the hospital with pneumonia and other respiratory ailments. Some died. Conditions became so dire that on December 12 a committee composed of the mayor, the chief of police, and the chairman of the county commissioners visited all of the smelters, asking each manager to close until the inversion lifted. The committee was met courteously at each smelter and shown the operations. What amazed the committee was the apparent absence of smoke at each of the works. Likewise, the smelter managers expressed their inability to explain the source of the smoke troubling the city, although R. D. Grant at the Parrot was certain it did come from the smelters. The managers all stated that they would be willing to temporarily close if the other Butte smelters did. A mass public meeting was called for the next night at city hall.[31] Meanwhile, the Centennial Brewery had its own solution to the problem:

> In these days of smoke and trouble when the undertaker gives you a pleasant greeting and mentally asks how much you will be worth to him dead, it is necessary that one should take the greatest precautions to overcome disease. The best beverage during the smoky season is Centennial beer. It will, in a measure, counteract the smoke and strengthen your lungs. Old time residents of Butte who have tried it say that beer gives better relief than any other stimulant.[32]

Other people who could afford it had a more certain solution to the problem: leave town. The well-to-do booked passage on the trains to neighboring cities and stayed in hotels until the smoke cleared.[33]

At the public meeting, a committee of five was appointed to study solutions to the problem. Representatives of the smelter companies generally agreed that they would be willing to close if that was the public will. As in the early 1890s, they also restated that making sulfuric acid from smelter fumes could never be profitable at a remote location like Butte. Thomas Updegraff, who lived in Meaderville and worked at the Montana Ore Purchasing Company smelter, said that "his wife and children had been buttering their bread with smelter smoke and he did not want to take this bread out of their mouths."[34] The *Daily Inter Mountain* editorialized that there were two possible solutions to the smoke problem: close the smelters (and eliminate many payrolls), or connect each of the smelters to a giant flue system and convey the smoke to stacks on the neighboring hills. The newspaper advocated the latter. The paper also

Butte Reduction Works, Butte: Located just west of Montana Street, W. A. Clark's smelter grew to be the largest in Butte and smelted copper until 1910. From Harry C. Freeman, A Brief History of Butte, Montana, the World's Greatest Mining Camp (Butte above and below Ground) *(Chicago: Henry O. Shepard Co., 1900).*

discharged. Like the other Butte smelters, the Butte Reduction Works discharged thousands of tons of tailings onto the banks of Silver Bow Creek throughout its active period of operation. During the early years, smelter managers did little to prevent tailings from washing downstream; in fact, smelter workers would encourage spring runoff in the creek to erode as much of the tailings as possible and make room for more tailings in the coming season. That practice ended late in the nineteenth century when the smelter began receiving complaints from downstream property owners, farmers who alleged that tailings in the creek were being deposited on their croplands and damaging production.[36]

suggested that Butte's citizens should be willing to put up with some unpleasantness, given its dominant industry: "Butte would be a pleasant place to live if it had no discomforts; so would be hades."[35]

Remains of buildings at the Butte Reduction Works are now gone, but the site best represents the complex relationships the Butte smelters had with their environment in trying to manage the by-products

The first response of the Butte Reduction Works was to build a plank flume to convey the creek through the tailings pile so that tailings would not flow into the creek. Soon, however, smelter workers turned to another material, slag, to impound the tailings and prevent them from flowing into the creek. Crews erected movable forms and then ran molten slag in cars out on trestles

Smelter workers building slag walls at the Butte Reduction Works, ca. 1905. Ladles of molten slag are being poured into forms atop the wall. The ladles were carried on cars run out on a trestle. From Harry C. Freeman, A Brief History of Butte, Montana, the World's Greatest Mining Camp (Butte above and below Ground) *(Chicago: Henry O. Shepard Co., 1900).*

Smelter workers arranging the forms for use in building slag walls at the Butte Reduction Works, ca. 1905. From Harry C. Freeman, A Brief History of Butte, Montana, the World's Greatest Mining Camp (Butte above and below Ground) *(Chicago: Henry O. Shepard Co., 1900).*

so that the slag could be poured into the forms. By this means, the crews were able to build a slag wall more than ten feet high that completely encircled the area where tailings were deposited. Rather than maintaining an open flume to convey the creek through the tailings deposit, smelter workers built a culvert. The upstream (eastern) segment was built of cast-in-place concrete, while the downstream segment was also built of cast smelter slag, a free and abundant material at the facility.

Missoula Gulch flowed only seasonally, but when it did it discharged into Silver Bow Creek at the Butte Reduction Works tailings pile. Because large volumes of tailings from the Walkerville silver mills washed down Missoula Gulch, and because the Butte Reduction Works did not wish to sacrifice valuable space in its tailings impoundment to those silver mill tailings, it built a double slag wall along the northwest side of the impoundment. This double wall would convey any flow from Missoula to the west, where it could discharge into Silver Bow Creek downstream of the Butte Reduction Works tailings impoundment.[37]

As mentioned earlier, all of the tailings deposits at the Butte smelters—including those at the Butte Reduction Works—were reprocessed during World War II to recover copper. Nevertheless, much of the slag-wall tailings impoundment survives and is visible just west of Montana Street.

Other Metals Mined at Butte

Copper was by far the major metal produced at Butte, but it was certainly not the only metal. As already described, miners vigorously mined and milled silver until the silver crash of 1893. Thereafter, Butte continued to produce large volumes of silver, but mainly as a by-product of copper mining and smelting. Early in the twentieth century, the market for zinc expanded and the processes for treating zinc ores developed such that Butte emerged as an important zinc producer as well. The ACM grew into a major zinc producer, as did W. A. Clark and the independent Black Rock mine. After Clark sold his copper properties to Anaconda in 1910, he continued to mine and mill zinc until he died. In 1928, shortly after his death, his estate sold his zinc properties, including the Timber Butte mill, to the ACM. Remains of the Timber Butte mill are still visible on the north slope of Timber Butte, south of Butte. The large concrete ore bin structure of the Timber Butte mill survives as the OXO Foundation, home of the late Bob Corbett, a much beloved conceptual artist and architect who developed plans for superinsulated houses for low-income families.

One other metal from Butte's rich mining history deserves mention: manganese. Ores from some Butte mines had long been known to be relatively rich in manganese, but the manganese was not exploited on a large scale until World War II, when the strategic

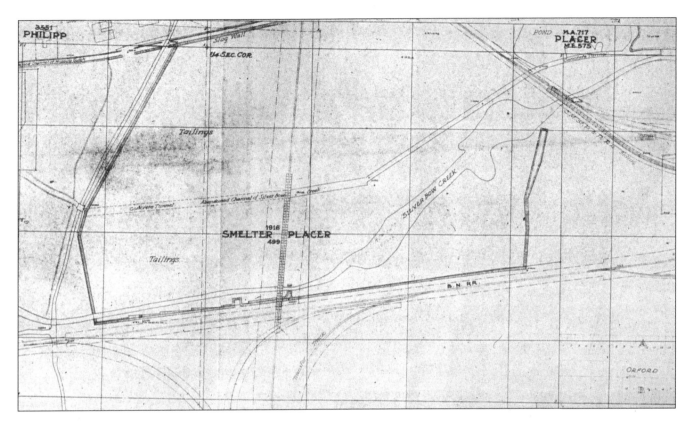

importance of the metal led the United States to work closely with the Domestic Manganese Development Company to purchase and process manganese ores at the former Butte Reduction Works, now owned by the ACM. Some of the richest manganese ores were located relatively near the surface in an area extending from around the Emma mine, just below the Central Business District on the Butte hill, south to Second Street and southwest to near the Travona mine. Mining

Slag-wall tailings impoundment at the Butte Reduction Works: The slag walls used to impound tailings (A & B) are clearly visible in this plat map. Note the double slag wall (B) intended to convey Missoula Gulch west of the tailings impoundment. The map also shows the original bed of Silver Bow Creek and the culvert that conveyed the creek under the tailings pile. Courtesy Clerk and Recorder's office, Butte–Silverbow.

of these ores through the Emma and Travona shafts led to subsidence, which in turn caused considerable damage to residences and other buildings that stood above the mine workings. Most of the structural damage occurred during the 1940s and 1950s. When property owners noticed that subsidence had damaged their property, they would typically file a claim with the ACM, which would pay for repairs in exchange for a clause in the deed to the property that absolved the ACM of responsibility for any damage caused by subsidence thereafter. Widespread encumbrances on deeds in the area, which came to be known as the Subsidence Zone, caused the neighborhood to be redlined by banks and insurance companies and to fall into disrepair. Much of Butte's surviving historic working-class housing stock may be found in the Subsidence Zone, but it is in very poor condition, and the neighborhood is pocked with numerous vacant lots where damaged houses once stood.[38]

Smoky Developments at Anaconda

Battles over Butte's smoky environment likely would have continued well into the twentieth century had it not been for the consolidation of those several large nineteenth-century mining companies into the Anaconda Copper Mining Company. The ACM grew up alongside the other above-named Butte mining companies, but almost from the beginning it was a

Significant ruins of the nineteenth-century smelters survive at Anaconda and are visible from the golf course. This view shows an opening to one of the reverberatory furnaces at the Upper Works. Note flue on hillside in background. Photograph by Fredric L. Quivik.

much larger operation than the others. The ACM had more mines, and its smelters were much larger.[39]

The Anaconda Copper Mining Company's story is well known. Marcus Daly bought the Anaconda mine from Michael Hickey and Charles Larabie in 1880 and enticed three San Francisco mining entrepreneurs—George Hearst, James Ben Ali Haggin, and Lloyd Tevis—to invest in his new property. The mine yielded silver that repaid their investments almost immediately. When the shaft at the Anaconda mine reached the water table, Daly saw that its greatest potential was as a copper mine.[40]

To treat the copper ore, Daly again turned to his San Francisco partners, asking them to build him a smelter. What followed is one of the most unfathomable episodes in early Butte history. Daly, Haggin, Hearst, and Tevis were all experienced in various aspects of financing, operating, and profiting from mines and mills for precious metals, but none had experience in base metals. Looking at the copper market, they would have seen that it had been rapidly expanding for years, but they also had to have known that the market was dominated by Michigan's producers of native copper and that the price of copper had been dropping in recent years, despite growing demand. Dropping prices should have made investing in the complex works needed to reduce Butte's sulfide ores seem risky. The syndicate could have known about electricity, but they could not possibly have foreseen what electrification would mean to the copper market.

In early 1883, as the syndicate considered how to proceed, Daly could have looked around Butte and seen that the Colorado smelter had a daily capacity to treat about sixty tons of ore, the Montana and Parrot smelters each could treat about one hundred tons daily, and the Bell smelter was struggling to reopen with a capacity of thirty tons per day. The concentrators at these smelters needed considerable supplies of water

to operate their jigs and tables and to carry tailings away. Water in Butte was in short supply, so it was not surprising that Daly chose to build his new smelter somewhere with more abundant water. What did amaze all onlookers was the scale of the reduction works he and the syndicate decided to build twenty-six miles west of Butte on the north side of Warm Springs Creek. When the new works opened, it had a capacity of about five hundred tons per day, and construction continued with a goal to increase that capacity immediately to one thousand tons. At a stroke, the largest concentrator in the United States was located in the territory of Montana.[41]

Within a few years, production from Daly's Butte mines exceeded the capacity of the Anaconda smelter and Daly began constructing a new reduction works a couple miles downstream. When it went into operation in 1898, it became known as the Lower Works, and the original Anaconda smelter became the Upper Works. Combined capacity of the two works was nearly three thousand tons per day. Yet this capacity still could not match the output from the Butte mines, and the works' technologies were growing obsolete. At the turn of the twentieth century, rather than remodeling the Upper and Lower Works, the ACM decided to build an entirely new reduction works on the south side of Warm Springs Creek. The new works would be designed to accommodate expanding or remodeling

The Washoe Stack is the only structure surviving from the Washoe Reduction Works. When the smelter was being demolished in the early 1980s, citizens of Anaconda asked ARCO to let the stack remain standing as a monument to smelter workers who had toiled there for decades. The stack is also a monument to the industry's efforts to find a technological solution to the environmental damage caused by smelter smoke. Photograph by Fredric L. Quivik.

each department without impinging on the activities of other departments. Known as the Washoe smelter, the new works went into operation in 1902.[42]

The first big step in the corporate consolidation was the Amalgamated Copper Company, a giant holding company formed by Daly in association with capitalists associated with the Standard Oil Trust.[43] Amalgamated had acquired the ACM and most of the other large companies in Butte by 1901. Within a few years, the Parrot, Colorado, and B&B smelters were all closed and the ores from their mines were being sent to Anaconda for smelting. In 1906, Amalgamated reached an agreement with Heinze whereby Heinze would sell his Butte copper properties, including the MOP smelter, to the Red Metal Mining Company, a new entity closely allied with Amalgamated. Shortly thereafter, Red Metal closed the MOP smelter and started sending ores from Heinze's former mines to Anaconda for smelting. In 1910, Red Metal and all of the Amalgamated companies transferred their properties to Anaconda, which then became Amalgamated's sole operating company. At about the same time, Amalgamated negotiated a deal with W. A. Clark in which he would sell all of his copper-producing properties to the ACM. Shortly after that transaction was completed, Clark's Butte Reduction Works closed as a copper smelter and the ACM began shipping copper ore from Clark's mines to Anaconda for smelting.

By the end of 1910, nearly all of the major copper mines in Butte were owned and operated by the ACM and most of the copper smelters had closed. The lone exception was the Pittsmont smelter, the remains of which are still barely visible (behind piles of mine waste) east of the Clyde E. Weed concentrator along the south edge of the Berkeley Pit. The Pittsmont smelter remained independent of Anaconda until it closed in the 1920s.

Environmental Consequences of Smelting at Anaconda

The transfer of nearly all copper smelting to Anaconda had several consequences for the built environment of the upper Clark Fork basin. Most obviously, it led to the creation of a smelter city, where workers who once would have lived near the Butte smelters now resided. It led to the construction of three giant smelters, the remains of which are still visible on the landscape. The sole structure surviving from the third of those smelters, the Washoe smelter, is the 585-foot stack. The rest of the Washoe smelter was entirely demolished during the 1980s after ARCO (which bought the Anaconda Company in 1976) closed the smelter. The Upper Works and Lower Works were demolished at the beginning of the twentieth century, leaving extensive foundation ruins in place. Perhaps the most visible of those ruins are the large flues that conveyed smoke from the smelter furnaces up the hillsides to hilltop stacks. Thus the most prominent surviving evidence of each of the three Anaconda smelters are structures used to manage smelter smoke, a substance that early promoters of Butte thought would symbolize its success but that in later years caused great discomfort, if not ill health, for many. The Anaconda Company built the flues and stacks for its first two smelters to get the smoke out of the work environment, where, under certain atmospheric conditions, it could become intolerable for the smelter workers.

When Anaconda built the Washoe smelter, each smelting department (for roasting furnaces, reverberatory furnaces, blast furnaces, and converters) had its own two-hundred-foot stall, which was sufficient to carry smoke aloft. Almost as soon as the Washoe smelter went into operation in early 1902, however, farmers in the Deer Lodge Valley began to notice more of their livestock dying. The Deer Lodge Valley is five to ten miles wide and extends from the confluence of Silver Bow and Warm Springs creeks on the south to the Clark Fork River's confluence with the Little Blackfoot River, about twenty-five miles to the north. The valley was one of the early agricultural settlements in Montana as stock growers established livestock operations to supply mining camps with beef and as smaller farmers raised grain and dairy products for the camps. One of the earliest of those livestock

Tailings deposit at Grant-Kohrs Ranch, Deer Lodge: This deposit of tailings and others like it on the Grant-Kohrs historic site are a fitting component of this unit of the National Park Service. The owner of the ranch testified at the smoke and tailings trial in the early twentieth century. Photograph by Fredric L. Quivik.

operations was the Grant Ranch, located on the north side of the town of Deer Lodge. Conrad Kohrs bought the ranch in the 1860s, and it became the basis of one of Montana's largest livestock enterprises.[44] The Grant-Kohrs Ranch is a unit of the National Park Service's national historical parks; it interprets the nation's nineteenth-century livestock industry. By the early twentieth century, though, farmers in the Deer Lodge Valley were raising sheep, hogs, chickens, and horses as well as cattle, and they were growing potatoes and other vegetables for residents of Butte and Anaconda in addition to hay and grains.

When the Deer Lodge Valley farmers found more of their livestock dying after the Washoe smelter went into operation in 1902, they summoned veterinarians, who concluded that arsenical poisoning was the cause of death. Farmers and veterinarians alike believed that the source of arsenic killing the livestock was the smoke from the Washoe smelter. The farmers filed complaints with the ACM, which readily acknowledged its culpability. The company paid farmers more than $300,000 in damages and closed the smelter until it could reconfigure how it discharged smoke.

The solution, ACM engineers believed, was to connect each of the four smelting departments by a system of flues to a single giant flue running up the hill south of the smelter to a three-hundred-foot stack atop the hill, intended to carry the smoke to the upper atmosphere, where it would be diluted to harmless levels. The main trunk of the flue had a very large cross section that was intended to slow the velocity of the gases and allow fine solids (such as arsenic trioxide dust) to settle out. The company boldly announced it had conscientiously responded to the harm done to livestock and had implemented a state-of-the-art solution to prevent future damage. The ACM also boasted of the commercial advantages of capturing the flue dust so it could be resmelted. [45]

Many farmers did not believe that the new flue-and-stack system had solved the problem, and they continued to complain of ailing and dying livestock. In 1905, Fred Bliss, an Idaho resident who owned a farm in the Deer Lodge Valley, filed suit in federal court on behalf of his neighbors, who had organized as the Deer Lodge Valley Farmers Association. Bliss asked for an injunction to close the Washoe smelter if the ACM did not cease spewing smoke across the Deer Lodge Valley. The ensuing trial entailed fourteen months of proceedings, a total of 237 witnesses, and some twenty-five thousand pages of testimony. It was said to have been the longest and costliest injunction suit ever brought before an equity court in the United States. [46]

In addition to Bliss's own testimony, his lawyers were able to marshal a broad assortment of farmers and ranchers from the area to describe for the court the extent of damages the Washoe's smoke had caused. The farmers' central complaint was that their animals were being poisoned by smelter smoke, but witnesses also described extensive damage to crops, timber, and other vegetation. One common symptom attributed to the smoke was sores or ulcers that appeared in the nostrils of horses. Cattle would scour (suffer from diarrhea), not shed their winter hair, develop watery eyes, and often deliver dead calves or slink their calves (deliver them prematurely). Calves born alive were unusually weak. Dairy cows quit giving milk. Animals' breath gave off what their owners described as the odor of garlic.[47]

Both sides in the litigation presented expert witnesses, including academic scientists. Two chemistry professors working under contract to the federal government—Robert Swain of Stanford University and W. D. Harkins of the University of Montana—completed some of the first field research in the case during the summer of 1905. By installing testing devices at the smelter, they tried to determine the quantity of arsenic leaving the smelter's stack. Swain and Harkins testified for the farmers that the Washoe stack discharged forty-four thousand pounds of arsenic across the environment daily. Daniel E. Salmon, a noted veterinarian and founding chief of the U.S. Department of Agriculture's Bureau of Animal Industry, testified on the symptoms of arsenical poisoning exhibited by the Deer Lodge Valley livestock.

The farmers also successfully entreated the federal government to supply experts from the U.S. Department of Agriculture to assess the damage being caused by the smelter. W. G. Weigle, of the U.S. Forest Service, examined the effects of smelter smoke on forestlands around the smelter. J. K. Haywood, of the USDA's Bureau of Chemistry, assessed the chemical effects of emissions from the smelter, including those of sulfur dioxide on plant life and those of arsenic on animal life. He also examined the effects tailings had on crops when applied to fields by irrigating from streams impregnated with tailings. The USDA's Bureau of Animal Industry also sent Robert J. Formad to the Anaconda area to investigate the impacts of smelter emissions on animal life.[48]

Smelter manager E. P. Mathewson enlisted his own impressive team of experts. He asked Duncan McEachran, a prominent Canadian veterinarian from Montreal, to visit the Deer Lodge Valley during the summer of 1905 to inspect livestock conditions and then help the ACM prepare its technical case. McEachran assembled a team of nationally regarded veterinary experts, including Leonard Pearson, a Pennsylvania State veterinarian and member of the faculty at the University of Pennsylvania; Theobald Smith, of Harvard University; and Veranus A. Moore, of Cornell University. Interestingly, all three were graduates of Cornell, and Smith and Moore had earlier worked for Salmon at the USDA's Bureau of Animal Industry. McEachran and the ACM had asked Salmon to be a part of the company's veterinary team, but Salmon declined. The ACM also presented such experts as F. W. Traphagen, of the Colorado School of Mines, and Harry Snyder, of the University of Minnesota, to offer soil analyses suggesting that agricultural problems in the Deer Lodge Valley stemmed from causes other than smelter smoke.[49] Seeking a plant pathologist to determine the effects of smelter smoke on vegetation, Mathewson secured the services of Ralph W. Smith, of the University of California at Berkeley.[50]

The Anaconda Company won the case in 1909. After the lengthy proceedings and a long period of deliberation, Judge Hunt ruled that there did appear to be arsenical poisoning but his legal ruling was based on what he considered the more important argument concerning the economic damage that would be done to the Butte-Anaconda area if the smelter were closed. Using the "balancing doctrine" prevalent during the late nineteenth and early twentieth centuries, he reasoned that farmers in the Deer Lodge Valley would suffer more harm from closure of the smelter, and consequent closure of the Butte mines, due to loss of markets for their produce than the harm smelter smoke might be causing.[51] The farmers appealed, but the Ninth Circuit upheld Judge Hunt's ruling. The farmers took their appeal to the U.S. Supreme Court, which refused to hear their appeal on a technicality.[52]

The Bliss case would not be the end of legal challenges to the ACM and the smoke its Washoe smelter spewed into the air, and the company's next opponent had much greater legal resources. In 1907, even before Judge Hunt had ruled in the Bliss case, President Theodore Roosevelt's administration began preparing cases against Anaconda and other western mining companies over damage caused by smoke from their smelters to surrounding national forest resources. Roosevelt left office after the 1908 election,

and it took some time before President Howard Taft and his administration decided to proceed with legal action against the ACM. During the first year of the Taft administration, the Department of Justice (DOJ) continued working on the Anaconda and other smelter smoke cases. Government experts also continued to study the impacts of smelter smoke on the environment surrounding Anaconda.

Finally, on March 16, 1910, James W. Freeman, U.S. Attorney for the District of Montana, filed suit against Anaconda in the Montana District Court of the Ninth Circuit Court of the United States. The suit sought to enjoin the ACM from operating the smelter in such a way that it discharged harmful smoke and gases over the property of the United States.[53] Unlike the Bliss case, in which the main concern of the complainant was arsenic in the smelter smoke killing livestock, the main concern in the U.S. case was sulfur dioxide in the smelter smoke causing damage to vegetation, especially on national forest lands.

As the United States began preparing its case against the Anaconda Company, residents near the Washoe smelter observed that damage to their environment was continuing. Henry Eccleston, who farmed about ten miles southeast of the smelter, noticed that the timber on the hills south of the smelter was sickly and dying. For example, an area known as the McCune Cutting, where contractors had cut timber for the ACM on the public domain during the nineteenth century, had been regenerating itself until the Washoe smelter went into operation in 1902. Eccleston believed that smelter smoke was killing the young trees. Margret Quinlan, who lived about fifteen miles northeast of the smelter, said that sometimes the smoke from the smelter dropped down into the Deer Lodge Valley and was so thick she could smell it and hardly see through it. She occasionally had to send her daughter out of the valley to get her away from the smoke. Mrs. Quinlan claimed that doctors believed her daughter's poor heath was caused by "smelter poisoning." Lizz Newsome had a small farm less than two miles southwest of the smelter and along the boundary of the U.S. Forest Reserve. She had noticed from her place that fir trees were the first to be affected by smelter smoke. She had once raised chickens, but she claimed smelter smoke turned their combs black and yellow and made their feathers curl, preventing the birds from molting. Because these symptoms led to the death of her chickens, she could no longer make a living from her farm and she had left it.[54]

In collecting scientific evidence to support its case, the government enlisted the services of chemist R. E. Swain, who had testified for the farmers in the Bliss case, and his Stanford colleagues G. J. Peirce, a professor of botany, and J. P. Mitchell, an assistant professor of chemistry. Among other findings, the Stanford scientists concluded that "the barrenness and desolation surrounding a smelter handling sulphurous ore are not mere coincidence but are the inevitable effects of which sulphur dioxide is the specific cause."[55] The U.S. Forest Service also had several consultants and its own experts in the field around Anaconda collecting evidence. For example, forest supervisor P. S. Lovejoy found in 1910 that damage had increased in many areas around Anaconda compared to what he had observed when first surveying the areas in 1907 and 1908. He estimated that the cost of damage to trees from smelter smoke was greater than $1.75 million.[56]

As the government and the ACM prepared for trial, their attorneys continued trying to negotiate an agreement that would avert a trial. The government's position was that it was entitled to collect payment for damages to federal property but that it would be best to wait to determine what those damages had been until after the ACM ceased causing the damage. It was therefore in the interests of all concerned for the U.S. government to work with the ACM to find technological means for eliminating the causes of injury. A joint effort would be possible under the auspices of a "board of experts," convened to examine various technical methods for abating the pollution problems at the smelter and to recommend their adoption to the ACM. During the course of negotiations, the two parties had reached agreement on a variety of issues, such as the composition of the board and what kinds of technical remedies the ACM could be expected to adopt. The ACM wanted to be certain that it would be obligated to consider only processes that were "practicable" at their works.[57]

Negotiations proved fruitful, and on April 13, 1911, Benjamin B. Thayer, president of the ACM, and Attorney General George W. Wickersham, representing the United States, signed an agreement under which prosecution of the case would be suspended as long as the ACM complied with the terms of the agreement.[58] The first paragraph of the agreement stated:

> [D]efendant Anaconda Copper Mining Company agrees that it will at all times use its best efforts to prevent, minimize and ultimately to completely eliminate the emission and distribution from its smelting works at Anaconda, Mont., of all deleterious fumes, particularly those containing sulphur dioxide. But the said defendant, by entering into this stipulation does not concede that it has caused to be emitted from such works any fumes which are injurious to any of the interests of the complainant.[59]

The agreement also stipulated that (1) a three-man Board of Experts would be established to conduct its own research and to oversee ACM investigation of emissions from the smelter and of techniques and processes the ACM could implement to reduce its emissions in compliance with the agreement; (2) the ACM would implement methods and equipment that the Board of Experts recommended to move the smelter toward compliance with the agreement; (3) the ACM would pay for the costs of the Board of Experts and of experts the Board might retain; and (4) as long as the ACM complied with the terms of the agreement, the government would suspend its case against the ACM, but if the ACM ceased complying with the agreement the government could proceed with the suit. The agreement also named the first three members of the board and stipulated how each member would be replaced in case of resignation or death.[60] The Board of Experts soon came to be known as the Anaconda Smelter Smoke Commission.

Under the auspices of the Smoke Commission, scientists and engineers, most of whom were employed by the ACM, gained greater understanding of the contents of smelter smoke, of the effects of those contents on living things, and of methods that could be used to remove the harmful contents before the smoke was discharged into the atmosphere. Because both parties agreed that any method recommended to the ACM should be "practicable," the Smoke Commission looked for technologies that would provide a financial return to the company for its investment in implementing the method. This was not much of a problem with regard to recovering arsenic, because a lively market had developed for using arsenical pesticides in agriculture (for example, controlling boll weevils in the cotton fields of the South).

Finding a market for all the sulfur that could theoretically be recovered from the Washoe smelter's smoke, however, proved a more daunting task. During the 1910s, the ACM built an acid plant at the smelter to convert sulfur recovered from smoke into sulfuric acid, some of which could be used for ore treatment processes and some for manufacturing phosphate fertilizer, but the market for sulfur and products containing sulfur was relatively small in the region of the country readily accessible from Anaconda. Consequently, the new technologies implemented at the recommendation of the Smoke Commission ended up recovering less than 10 percent of the sulfur content of the smoke; the remainder continued to be discharged out the stack and spread across the environment, killing crops and timber.[61]

The Smoke Commission's recommendation for addressing the arsenic problem was more effective, largely because technology for recovering dust from smelter smoke yielded not only arsenic trioxide, which was a marketable by-product, but copper, lead, and other metals as well. Working closely with ACM

engineers, the Smoke Commission recommended in the mid-1910s that the company install Cottrell electrostatic precipitators at the base of the stack to recover more dust from the smoke stream. The commission also recommended that the company replace the existing 300-foot stack with a 585-foot stack, which would induce a stronger draft for drawing smoke through the precipitators and would discharge the smoke higher in the atmosphere. The new construction would cost more than $2 million. Because of materials shortages caused by U.S. involvement in World War I, however, the ACM was allowed to delay construction until 1918.

Once constructed, the Cottrell treaters at normal operating levels allowed the ACM to recover more than 85 percent of the total dust and fume in the smoke, including about 94 percent of the copper, 78 percent of the lead, and 80 percent of the arsenic. In 1923, the ACM recovered $1,130,000 worth of materials from flue dust collected by the electrostatic precipitators and related equipment. About $700,000 of that amount represented the gross value of the arsenic recovered. To recover those materials, it had cost the company about $700,000 for operating and maintaining the Cottrells, smelting the flue dust in the special reverberatory furnace, refining the arsenic, and so forth, yielding a net profit of more than $400,000. This figure represented 17 percent of the cost of installing the stack, treaters, and

Canyon of slag along Silver Bow Creek, Butte: This feature, built to keep Butte Reduction Works tailings out of Silver Bow Creek, is clearly visible from Montana Street. Photograph by Fredric L. Quivik.

related equipment.[62]

Entering the 1920s, then, the ACM had greatly reduced the amount of arsenic it was discharging into the atmosphere over the Deer Lodge Valley. The company had also acquired much of the farmland and ranchland north and east of the smelter; for property it had not acquired, the company had obtained easements stating that the ACM was no longer liable for any damage done by smoke. On the other hand, the ACM had done little to reduce the amount of sulfur dioxide being discharged into the atmosphere. This was not a problem on lands to the north and east that the company owned or on which the company held smoke easements, but it was still a big problem for national forest lands south and southwest of the smelter.

Frustrated that a decade of threatened litigation and of research and development by the Smoke Commission had not remedied the Forest Service's complaint that smelter smoke was damaging lands and timber on the Deerlodge National Forest, district forester Fred Morrell devised a new plan, one that would use terms of the 1922 Act to Consolidate National Forest Lands. Although the act had been passed to help consolidate national forest boundaries resulting from the irregular pattern of homestead entries, railroad land grants, and other mechanisms by which private parties had acquired lands from the public domain, Morrell saw that it could also be used to redress problems on the Deerlodge National Forest. He proposed that the Forest Service and the ACM negotiate land exchanges whereby the government would transfer title to damaged forest lands in the vicinity of the smelter to the ACM, and in return the ACM would deed to the government forestlands elsewhere in Montana that were adjacent to national forests and had not been damaged by smelter smoke. The exchanges would be approximately acre for acre and board foot of timber for board foot of timber.[63]

By early 1924, the U.S. Forest Service and the Anaconda Company had agreed in principle that a land exchange would be a good way for the company to avoid potential damage claims for the harm smelter smoke had caused to national forest resources, but there were still significant details that had to be addressed by other entities, such as the Department of the Interior, the Department of Justice, and the Smoke Commission, before any exchange actually took place. By 1926, those issues were resolved, and the Forest Service and the ACM negotiated the details of the first land exchange, featuring 22,000 acres of damaged lands. From then through 1936, the United States and Anaconda negotiated six land exchanges by which the government deeded more than 110,000 acres of damaged lands near the smelter to the company in return for a like area of healthy forestlands elsewhere in Montana.[64]

Meanwhile, in the mid-1920s, the ACM implemented selective flotation, a new method of concentrating ores at the smelter that resulted in less sulfur-bearing material being sent to the furnaces for smelting. Selective flotation made it possible to make the concentrates rich in copper sulfides, the minerals the company wanted to smelt, while the iron pyrite, which was also rich in sulfur, was sent to the tailings ponds. This greatly reduced the volume of sulfur being discharged in the smoke and began to lessen the damage to the forestland not already included in the land exchanges.[65]

Consequences for the Landscape Today

Visitors to Anaconda in 2009 will see many features on the landscape that resulted from early twentieth battles over damage to property, battles we would now think of as environmental battles (people in the early twentieth century did not yet conceive of an abstraction called the environment that merited protection; they did, however, recognize through a long tradition of common law that property merited protection). The 585-foot stack still stands atop smelter hill as a state monument. Driving into Anaconda from I-90, one can still see tailings along the banks of Silver Bow Creek. On the south side of Montana Highway 1 lies grazing land once owned by members of the Deer Lodge Farmers Association, farmers whose livestock had been killed by smelter smoke. North

Stream-side tailings just above Silver Bow Canyon: Until recently, the banks of Silver Bow Creek were almost entirely lined with broad beds of tailings from Butte to the Warm Springs Ponds. The stream-side tailings are being excavated and hauled to the Opportunity Tailings Ponds as part of the Superfund remediation. Photograph by Fredric L. Quivik.

own food. The company both believed that having workers tied to the land would create a more stable workforce and wanted to demonstrate that productive agriculture could take place under the plume of the stack. Northwest of Opportunity lies a vast expanse, nearly six square miles in area, that is the site of the Opportunity Ponds, a set of six impoundments that the ACM used to store tailings from the 1910s onward. This is the area where much of the contaminated materials from Butte, from the streamsides between Butte and Anaconda, and from behind the Milltown dam near Missoula are being disposed as part of the Superfund remediation.

Getting closer to Anaconda, just west of the road to Wisdom and the Big Hole River, one can see a large hill with rather straight slopes, evenly planted with grass. This is a giant tailings pile, known as the A & B ponds, built to store tailings in the 1950s before construction of the Clyde E. Weed concentrator in Butte obviated the need to

of the highway is the community of Opportunity, a model community developed by the ACM in the 1910s on land acquired from aggrieved farmers. The ACM subdivided the land into five- and ten-acre parcels, selling them to smelter workers who wished to live on land that would allow them to produce some of their store tailings at Anaconda. The Anaconda Company worked diligently in the 1970s to establish the vegetative cover on the A & B ponds. Just beyond the ponds rests a giant slag pile, which began to be built in 1902 when the Washoe smelter commenced operations. In former years, smelter workers would pour molten slag into big ladles and then transport the ladles to disposal sites, where the slag would be poured to cool into a solid mass. The ACM innovated the method of discharging molten slag from a furnace directly into a stream of rapidly flowing water, which would cool the slag suddenly, causing it to fracture into small particles the size and consistency of sand. The water would then convey the granulated slag through flumes to disposal areas, where the water would drain out through the pile, leaving the slag behind. Granulated slag is mostly silica and iron oxide and is environmentally inert.

Approaching the edge of Anaconda, one can look at the hills that form the north edge of the valley and see the remains of the Upper and Lower Works. Especially visible are the ruins of the flues on the hillsides. Between the highway and those hillsides is the Old Works Golf Course, designed by Jack Nicklaus and built as part of the Superfund remediation in the Anaconda area. The gold course is built over tailings and slag left from the Upper and Lower Works. Because their technologies were less advanced than those of the Washoe smelter, the tailings and slag they discharged were richer in heavy metals and other contaminants. Rather than excavating those materials, located in a sensitive area adjacent to Warm Springs Creek, the golf course was built as a means of managing the materials in situ so that they would not contaminate surface or ground waters. Large piles of black slag in the midst of the golf course are leftovers from the Old Works; the traps at the golf course consist of granulated slag hauled over from the slag pile at the Washoe smelter. After testing, the Environmental Protection Agency determined that granulated slag would be safe for use as trap material at a golf course; also after testing, Jack Nicklaus determined that granulated slag is equal or superior to beach sand as trap material.

Butte and Anaconda have rich architectural heritages, but to fully appreciate the kinds of built environments the builders and residents in those cities of the Montana copper industry were trying to achieve, it helps to understand the environments over and against which they were building their own surroundings. The environments of Butte and Anaconda were characterized both by majestic natural settings and, more immediately, by prevalent smoke. A few people may have thought that smoke was a symbol of prosperity, but for many it was much more than a symbol—it was a source of hardship, and of ill health, for people as well as for other living things. We cannot experience that smoke today, but we can see its many manifestations in the surviving features of the built environments of Butte and Anaconda.

[1] Several scholars have written about the struggles by residents of Butte and Anaconda to create communities in the midst of an environment dominated by a powerful industrial corporation; see Mary Murphy, *Mining Cultures: Men, Women, and Leisure in Butte, 1914–1941* (Urbana: University of Illinois Press, 1997); Laurie Mercier, *Anaconda's Labor, Community, and Culture in Montana's Smelter City* (Urbana: University of Illinois Press, 2001); John Mihelich, "The Richest Hill on Earth: An Ethnographic Account of Industrial Capitalism, Religion & Community in Butte, Montana" (PhD diss., Washington State University, 1999). While those excellent studies focus on the economic, political, and institutional environments established by a powerful industrial corporation, this essay also looks at the physical environment that corporation created.

[2] The author first developed this idea in Fredric L. Quivik, "Landscapes as Industrial Artifacts: Lessons from Environmental History," *IA: The Journal of the Society for Industrial Archeology* 26 (2000): 58–60.

[3] Letter to the editor from Butte City, *Montana Post*, January 7, 1865, copied in William J. Wilcox, "His Record of Anaconda," typescript, ca. 1934, folders 22 and 23, box 13, closet 2, Records of the Anaconda Copper Mining Company, Butte-Silver Bow Public Archives, Butte. In his lengthy "Record," Wilcox copied excerpts from many old newspapers, including the *Montana Post*, Montana's first newspaper, published in Virginia City. In cases where the citation is to Wilcox's copies of early newspapers rather than to the original, it will be so noted.

[4] *Montana Post*, December 9, 1865 (from Wilcox, "His Record of Anaconda").

[5] Although detailed citations are given throughout, much of this early history of Butte is drawn from the author's PhD dissertation: Fredric L. Quivik, "Smoke and Tailings: An Environmental History of Copper Smelting Technologies in Montana, 1880–1930" (University of Pennsylvania, 1998).

[6] Michael P. Malone, *The Battle for Butte: Mining and Politics on the Northern Frontier, 1864–1980* (Seattle: University of Washington Press, 1981), 8–10; Kate Hammond Fogarty, "A History of Butte, Montana," (undated, unpublished ms.), Butte Public Library Collection, Butte–Silver Bow Public Archives, Butte, p 4; *Montana Post,* February 18, 1865; February 25, 1865; March 4, 1865; March 11, 1865; May 20, 1865 (from

Wilcox, "His Record of Anaconda"); *New Northwest*, November 11, 1870; May 27, 1871; June 24, 1871 (from Wilcox, "His Record of Anaconda"). The prevalence of Chinese miners in worked-over areas is nicely analyzed in Randall Rohe, "Chinese River Mining in the West," *Montana The Magazine of Western History* 46 (Autumn 1996): 14–29.

7 J. Ross Browne, *Report on the Mineral Resources of the States and Territories West of the Rocky Mountains*, Executive Document No. 202, U.S. House of Representatives, Second Session, 40th Congress, 1867–68 (Washington, DC: Government Printing Office, 1868), 504.

8 Malone, *The Battle for Butte*, 15–16; *Butte Miner*, June 3, 1876, 3; Charles S. Warren, "The Romance of Butte," speech delivered July 4, 1876, reprinted in the *Butte Miner*, Semi-Centennial Issue, July 5, 1926, 4.

9 Malone, *The Battle for Butte*, 15–17; Ralph I. Smith, *History of the Early Reduction Plants of Butte, Montana*

(Butte: Montana School of Mines, 1953), 3; *Butte Miner*, June 13, 1876, 3; June 17, 1876, 3; July 1, 1876, 3; July 20, 1876, 3; August 25, 1876, 3; *New Northwest*, February 4, 1876, 3; March 10, 1876, 3; April 28, 1876, 3; June 16, 1876, 3; "Indenture between William L. Farlin and William A. Clark," document dated January 31, 1876, and "Indenture between William L. Farlin and William A. Clark," document dated February 23, 1876, Transcribed Deed Book 3, pp. 337–46, Clerk and Recorder's Office, Silver Bow County Courthouse, Butte.

10 *New Northwest*, April 18, 1876, 3.

11 Warren, "The Romance of Butte," 5; *Butte Miner*, June 8, 1876, 3; June 17, 1876, 3; June 27, 1876, 3; July 8, 1876, 3; *Engineering & Mining Journal* (hereafter cited as *E&MJ*) 22 (July 15, 1876): 45; Malone, *The Battle for Butte*, 16.

12 Malone, *The Battle for Butte*, 17.

13 Warren, "The Romance of Butte," 6.

14 For a detailed history of the development of Butte's silver mills,

see Quivik, "Smoke and Tailings," 89–111, 149–54.

15 Otis E. Young Jr., "The American Copper Frontier, 1640–1893," *The Speculator: A Journal of Butte and Southwest Montana History* 1 (Summer 1984): 7.

16 William Andrews Clark, address to the Montana Constitutional Convention, in *Proceedings and Debates of the Constitutional Convention 1889* (Helena: State Publishing Company, 1921), 754, quoted in Michael P. Malone and Richard B. Roeder, *Montana: A History of Two Centuries* (Seattle: University of Washington Press, 1976), 150.

17 *Butte Daily Miner*, July 14, 1885, cited in Donald MacMillan, *Smoke Wars: Anaconda Copper, Montana Air Pollution, and the Courts, 1890–1920* (Helena: Montana Historical Society Press, 2000), 26.

18 Thomas Couch's perspectives are documented in his letterpress books, containing copies of frequent and very detailed letters he sent to

Boston & Montana Consolidated Copper & Silver Mining Company officials in Boston and New York, especially to A. S. Bigelow. Couch's letterpress books are in the possession of Jim Combs, a collector of memorabilia who has been generous in granting me unrestricted access to the volumes. See Couch to A. S. Bigelow, letter dated January 1, 1889.

[19] Malcolm J. Rohrbough, *Aspen: The History of a Silver Mining Town, 1879–1893* (New York: Oxford University Press, 1986), 225–30.

[20] A. C. Snow to Mr. & Mrs. Major & Ella C. and Capt. Geo S., letter dated October 11, 1897, private collection of Lon Johnson, Columbia Falls, MT.

[21] A. C. Snow to Mr. & Mrs. Major & Ella C. and Capt. Geo S., letter, October 11, 1897.

[22] A. C. Snow to Ella Collins, letter dated January 19, 1898, private collection of Lon Johnson, Columbia Falls, MT.

[23] *Daily Inter Mountain*, February 3,

1898, 5.

[24] Christopher Schmitz, "The World's Largest Industrial Companies of 1912," *Business History* 37 (1995): 87.

[25] For a detailed history of the development of Butte's copper smelters, see Quivik, "Smoke and Tailings," 116–49, 164–77, 217–37.

[26] These figures are drawn from the author's analysis of *Crofutt's Butte City Directory* (Butte: Daily Intermountain, 1885). It may have been that the miners were slightly underrepresented in the city directory because some miners were transient and were not recorded by the directory's enumerators.

[27] The centers from which Butte expanded in response to various industrial developments are described in Dale Martin and Brian Shovers, "Butte, Montana: An Architectural and Historical Inventory of the National Landmark District," unpublished report prepared by the Butte Historical Society, 1986.

[28] Fredric L. Quivik, "Expert Report,"

unpublished report prepared for the U.S. Department of Justice in *United States v. ARCO*, the Clark Fork Superfund case, August 1997, pp. C-46, C-86, C-109, C-143, C-172. A copy of the "Expert Report" is available in the library of the Montana Historical Society, Helena.

[29] Quivik, "Expert Report." To generate conservative estimates, it is assumed that 30 percent of the weight of the materials smelted was sulfur, even though records from the period indicate that more than 34 percent of the materials smelted was sulfur.

[30] The best account of this early smoke controversy in Butte is MacMillan, *Smoke Wars*.

[31] *Daily Inter Mountain*, December 12, 1898, 3; *Butte Miner*, December 13, 1898, 6.

[32] *Daily Inter Mountain*, December 12, 1898, 3.

[33] *Daily Inter Mountain*, December 14, 1898, 6.

[34] *Daily Inter Mountain*, December 15, 1898, 5.

35 *Daily Inter Mountain*, December 13, 1898, 2; December 14, 1898, 2.

36 A. H. Wethey, testimony in *Magone v. Colorado Smelting & Mining Company, et al*, vol. 4, pp. 37–38, no. 222 in equity, 1903, Circuit Court of the United States, Ninth District, District of Montana, RG-21, National Archives, Seattle Branch.

37 Quivik, "Smoke & Tailings," 289–97.

38 The author and others at Renewable Technologies Inc. in Butte conducted a thorough survey of structures in the Subsidence Zone and reported on the results in a report prepared for the Butte Community Union and the Butte–Silver Bow Urban Revitalization Agency in 1985. Quivik, Bruce von Alten, and Jim E. Richard, "Preservation of a Neighborhood: A Neighborhood Preservation Plan for Central Butte," contract to Butte Community Union, November 1985.

39 The best overall history of the Anaconda Company is Malone's *The Battle for Butte*. Isaac F. Marcosson's company-commissioned *Anaconda* (New York: Dodd, Mead, 1957) is also insightful and reliable though limited in scope.

40 Malone, *The Battle for Butte*, 29–31; Marcosson, *Anaconda*, 46–52.

41 For an overview history of the Anaconda smelters, see Quivik, "Smoke and Tailings," 157–64.

42 Quivik, "Smoke and Tailings," 198–203.

43 Malone's *The Battle for Butte* provides a good overview of the Amalgamated consolidation, but for the most thorough description see R. Ernest Richter, "The Amalgamated Copper Company: A Closed Chapter in Corporate Finance," *Quarterly Journal of Economics* 30 (1916): 387–407.

44 Malone and Roeder, *Montana*, 113.

45 Gordon Morris Bakken, "Was There Arsenic in the Air? Anaconda versus the Farmers of Deer Lodge Valley," *Montana The Magazine of Western History* 41 (Summer 1991): 30–32; Quivik, "The Tragic Montana Career of Dr. D. E. Salmon," *Montana The Magazine of Western History* 57 (Spring 2007): 39–40.

46 MacMillan, *Smoke Wars*, 101–4; D. E. Salmon, "Arsenical Poisoning from Smelter Smoke in Deer Lodge Valley, Montana," in *American Veterinary Review* 39 (April 1911): 21; John Houston McIntosh, "A Million for a Smoke Eater," *Technical World Magazine* 13 (April 1910): 162.

47 Angus D. Smith, testimony at trial, U.S. Circuit Court for the District of Montana, *Fred J. Bliss v. the Washoe Copper Company and the Anaconda Copper Mining Company* (hereafter *Bliss v. Washoe*), 2:641–736, Records of the Anaconda Copper Mining Company, MC-169, Montana Historical Society, Helena; Kenneth D. Smith, testimony in *Bliss v. Washoe*, 2:760–809, 3:810–97; Bryon Howells, testimony in *Bliss v. Washoe*, 3:1007–67; Conrad Kohrs, testimony in *Bliss v. Washoe*, 7:2590–622; Ephraim Staffanson, testimony in *Bliss v. Washoe*, 8:2911–78; George Parrott, testimony in *Bliss v. Washoe*, 8:3152–84, 9:3185–215; William Evans,

testimony in *Bliss v. Washoe*, 9:3468–529; Morgan Evans, testimony in *Bliss v. Washoe*, 11:3980–4024; W. C. Staton, testimony in *Bliss v. Washoe*, 15:5956–68.

48   W. D. Harkins, testimony in *Bliss v. Washoe*, 13:4851–976; Robert E. Swain, testimony in *Bliss v. Washoe*, 4:1206–60; Daniel E. Salmon, testimony in *Bliss v. Washoe*, 50:19867–20024; Bakken, "Was There Arsenic in the Air?" 39–41; W. G. Weigle, "Report on Conditions of Plant and Animal Life in and around Deerlodge Valley, Montana" (unpublished report, October 6, 1906), 1, box 239, Research Compilation Files, 1897–1935, Entry 115, Records of the U.S. Forest Service, RG-95, National Archives, Washington, DC; J. K. Haywood, "Injury to Vegetation and Animal Life by Smelter Wastes," USDA Bureau of Chemistry Bulletin no. 113 (Washington, DC: Government Printing Office, 1908); Robert J. Formad, "The Effect of Smelter Fumes upon the Livestock Industry

in the Northwest," reprinted from *The Twenty-Fifth Annual Report of the Bureau of Animal Industry, 1908* (Washington, DC: Government Printing Office, 1910).

49   Leonard Pearson, testimony in *Bliss v. Washoe*, 48:18891–19038; Theobald Smith, testimony in *Bliss v. Washoe*, 47:18428–575; V. A. Moore, testimony in *Bliss v. Washoe*, 44:17319–506; Duncan McEachran, testimony in *Bliss v. Washoe*, 45:17716–87; Bakken, "Was There Arsenic in the Air?" 39–41; D. Arthur Hughes, "Cornell Veterinarians," *Cornell Alumni News* 7 (February 15, 1905): 299–302; Ellis Pierson Leonard, *A Cornell Heritage: Veterinary Medicine, 1868–1908* (Ithaca: New York State College of Veterinary Medicine, 1979), 81–85, 91–96, 96–100; F. W. Traphagen, testimony in *Bliss v. Washoe*, 35:13731–813; Harry Snyder, testimony in *Bliss v. Washoe*, 60:23914–98. See also D. McEachran to Veranus A. Moore, letter dated January 2, 1906; E. P. Mathewson to Veranus A. Moore, letter dated

January 2, 1906; D. McEachran to D. E. Salmon, letter dated January 2, 1906; E. P. Mathewson to D. E. Salmon, letter dated January 2, 1906; Duncan McEachran to E. P. Mathewson, letter dated January 27, 1906; all in file 4, box 445, Records of the Anaconda Copper Mining Company (hereafter "ACM Records"), MC-169, Montana Historical Society, Helena.

50   Leonard, *Who's Who in Engineering* (1926), 719–720, 1402; E. P. Mathewson to Prof. S. Fortier, letters dated February 10 and February 24, 1906, file 4, box 445, ACM Records; E. P. Mathewson to Prof. R. W. Smith, letter dated February 24, 1906, file 4, box 445, ACM Records; E. P. Mathewson to Prof. Ralph E. Smith, letter dated March 6, 1906, file 4, box 445, ACM Records.

51   On the uses of the balancing doctrine by U.S. courts in the late nineteenth and early twentieth centuries, see Christine Rosen, "Differing Perceptions of the Value of Pollution Abatement across Time

[52] and Place: Balancing Doctrine in Pollution Nuisance Law, 1840–1906," *Law and History Review* 11 (Fall 1993): 307–81.

[52] Bakken, "Was There Arsenic in the Air?" 41; MacMillan, *Smoke Wars*, 123.

[53] For a general discussion of the Taft administration's actions leading up to the filing of the suit against the ACM, see MacMillan, "The Struggle to Abate Air Pollution," 258–82. See also Ligon Johnson to the Attorney General, letters dated November 10, 1909, and January 31, 1910, and Complaint filed by the U.S. in the Circuit Court of the United States, Ninth Circuit, District of Montana, *United States v. Anaconda Copper Mining Company and Washoe Copper Company*, no. 967 in equity, document dated March 10, 1910, both in box 514, Straight Numerical Files (Folded), entry 112, General Records of the U.S. Department of Justice (hereafter "DOJ"), RG-60, National Archives, College Park, MD.

[54] All of these observations are from affidavits by Deer Lodge Valley residents recorded in 1908 and filed in box 274, DOJ: Lizz Newsome (affidavit recorded October 29, 1908), 124–27; Margret Quinlan (affidavit recorded October 29, 1908), 121–23; Henry H. Eccleston (affidavit recorded October 31, 1908), 143–45.

[55] G. J. Peirce, R. E. Swain, and J. P. Mitchell, "Report on the Effects of Smelter Smoke on Vegetation and the Conditions of the National Forests in the Vicinity of Anaconda, Montana" (unpublished report prepared for the U.S. Department of Justice, February 5, 1913), 90, box 84b, General Files Prior to 1954, Records of the U.S. Bureau of Mines (hereafter "BOM"), RG-70, National Archives, Washington, DC. This report is in two sections, one on botanical investigations (pp. 1–90) and one on chemical investigations (pagination starting over again, pp. 1–80). The conclusion quoted here is from the last page of the section on botanical investigations. The section on chemical investigations ends with ten conclusions describing evidence of widespread levels of sulfur high enough to harm plant life and of arsenic high enough to harm animal life.

[56] P. S. Lovejoy, "Report on Damage to Deerlodge National Forest Caused by Fumes from Washoe Smelter" (unpublished U.S. Forest Service report, July 3, 1911), box 84b, General Files Prior to 1954, Records of the U.S. Bureau of Mines, RG-70.

[57] See, for example, the correspondence between Attorney General Wickersham and the ACM's Kelley during the closing days of negotiations: C. F. Kelley to the Attorney General, letter dated March 9, 1911, and Attorney General to C. F. Kelley, letter dated March 30, 1911, box 886, DOJ.

[58] For a general discussion of the negotiations between the government and the ACM following filing of the suit, culminating in the 1911 agreement, see MacMillan, *Smoke Wars*, 203–215.

[59] "Agreement between United States Department of Justice and Anaconda Copper Mining Company" (agreement dated April 13, 1911), box 84b, BOM.

[60] "Agreement between United States Department of Justice and Anaconda Copper Mining Company," April 13, 1911; *E&MJ* 91 (April 1, 1911): 683, *E&MJ* (May 6, 1911): 892.

[61] Quivik, "Smoke and Tailings," 440–41.

[62] Quivik, "Smoke and Tailings," 433–36.

[63] Quivik, "Smoke and Tailings," 457–67.

[64] Quivik, "Smoke and Tailings," 467–84, 487–90.

[65] Quivik, "Smoke and Tailings," 484–87

What's Your Heritage Worth? Gallus Frames, Community, and Experience in Butte, Montana

John Mihelich

On December 1, 2005, while living in Butte conducting research on the culture of the community during its underground mining era, I briefly experienced what it was like to work in the mining industry in Butte. Continuing a long-standing tradition of "lighting the frames," a small group of Atlantic Richfield Company (ARCO)/Anaconda Copper Mining Company (ACM) retirees worked each winter to place and maintain Christmas lights on several of the mining headframes still left in Butte. In the heyday of underground mining, electricians and ropemen decorated the gallus frames every Christmas for the company and "lit" them each Thanksgiving Eve.[1] I had helped this group with a variety of small projects during my time in Butte and had spent many hours listening to them talk about their lives and mining copper. As they prepared to work on the Christmas lights that year, my uncle John T. Shea volunteered my services. I don't remember the temperature that December morning, but it was one of those sunny, frigid, windy Butte winter days. I accompanied Joe Navarro, Tommy Holter, John Bailey, and John T. Shea to the Belmont, the Travona, the Kelly #2, and finally the Anselmo. I discovered that the wind

blows harder 120 feet off the ground.

After gathering materials and driving a short way to the mine yard, we prepared to ascend the Belmont gallus frame. Joe and I climbed the five or six flights of stairs (about six stairs each) that went straight up the vertical legs of the frame. The steps led to a deck used historically to attach the "cages" to the cables leading down the mine shaft. From the deck, a horizontal catwalk ran from the vertical west leg to the angled northwest leg, where it joined with the long line of steps and rail that tracked up the angled length of the northwest leg to the top deck of the frame. Once across the catwalk, Joe, leading the way, paused and said, "We'll just take it slow; we are not getting paid." He said not to tell him if I got scared.

As we began to climb, Joe explained how, when holding the rail carefully with both hands during the climb, they used to say "one hand for the company and one hand for you." We stopped about three times on the way up so Joe could catch his breath. Although I welcomed the rest, I preferred to continue without pause because the height and the cold frayed my nerves and stopping only gave me more time to think about what I was doing—and to look down. With my knees shaking, and barely holding my balance, I wondered if Joe had experienced a similar sensation on his first trip up one of the frames. I just wanted to get up to the deck and off those steps. It was a steep trip to the bottom on the steps and a straight shot to the bottom off them! The last stop was about five steps from the top deck. Joe stood on the step and untwisted a wire around an electrical insulator swaying with the wind just above the rail. I thought he might salvage the insulator for use at the top to protect one of the wires from weathering against the handrail of the deck. However, when he freed the insulator from the wire, still standing on the stairs, he turned back and handed it to me. He said, "Here, a souvenir. Someday when you have an office, put it on your desk and you'll always remember this day and climbing up the Belmont."

When we finally reached the top, Joe said, "Here we are. I told you you'd have a view from up here." We stood there a few moments, temporarily forgetting the cold wind as we surveyed the city. Joe then turned to a brief lesson on the workings of the frame, wheels, and cables before we checked and repaired all of the strings of lights and the star atop the frame. John Bailey, an electrician by trade, then turned on the power to the lights from the ground so we could check them again.

Having made the repairs, we started the journey down the stairs. Joe said he would go first to show me the safe way to get to the bottom intact. We descended facing away from the frame, with our backs to the stairs. Joe instructed me to lean back and hold onto the rails. "Remember," he said, "two hands for yourself." Apparently, the company was not involved in this

trip after all. He explained how some of the veteran ironworkers would drape their arms over the railings and kick their feet up in front of them on the railings and slide to the bottom. With a little care to loosen the grip of their hands as they slid over the rivets holding the side posts of the rail to the steps, they made a quick and easy descent. Later that day, coming down the Anselmo Mine headframe after visiting the Travona, I saw Tommy Holter, a former ropeman, make half of this move. He laid his shoulders across the rails, leaned back, and slid down the rails with his feet lightly skipping on each step. I was behind him, carefully placing one foot in front of the other on the descending steps. He reached the bottom well before I was halfway down. He had made the trip before many, many times when they maintained the frames, cables, and wheels, and he knew the ropes.

I spent much of my fieldwork listening to men talk about the process of mining, their work, and their lives in Butte. Nearly every week for eighteen months, I visited the ARCO retirees' club, where members spent much of their time recounting their experiences on the Hill in the mines, in the bars, and in their

Facing Page: *Figure 1. Anselmo gallus frame & mineyard, Butte, Montana early 20th century. Photographer unidentified. Courtesy World Museum of Mining, Butte (WMM 3413)*

neighborhoods. Shortly after my first visit to the club, I borrowed the *Mining Engineer's Handbook* from the Montana Tech library and voraciously read relevant chapters to get a sense of the mining terminology embedded as second nature in the stories floating around the coffee table at the club. While some of the men wanted little to do with me, a steady group of them gradually welcomed me into their conversations and openly shared their stories. They came to call me "the kid," often razzed me about why it was taking me so long to "write a book," and frequently reminded me that not all learning "comes from them books"—a reference to my graduate study.

One day early on in my visits, a short, gruff-looking man asked me how old I was after (Frank) Panisko had talked about a clown school and mentioned one had to be eighteen to twenty-five years old to attend. With a half-serious nod in my direction, the man said that somebody ought to send me there and then asked me how old I was. I told him I was thirty. After a short pause, he looked at me and said, "Thirty years old and still in school? Ya' must be a slow learner—I was done when I was thirteen." I also individually and more formally interviewed many men who worked in the mining industry, including miners, boilermakers, ropemen, bosses, station tenders, motormen, hoisting engineers, and people who worked in the offices in various capacities for the Anaconda Copper Mining Company. In the process of writing about mining in Butte, including the content that fills most of this article, I asked several of the men to review my writings, which they did and approved.

An understanding of life in Butte firmly rests on knowing a good deal about mining practice during the underground mining era. "The miners made this town, not the rich people" says my grandmother, Rose Mihelich, an assessment echoed in the minds of nearly everyone I spoke with during my research on the city. Although the actual miners were the heart and soul of the mining operations—John T. Shea, a ropeman on the Hill for thirty years, fondly characterizes them as the "best craftsmen on the Hill"—the term *miner* in my grandmother's usage extends from those who actually blasted the ore to the various craftsmen and laborers who collectively worked the mines. Based on the practice of underground industrial copper mining, the miners and, in turn, the rest of the folks working and living in the city carved a culture, a way of life, and a heritage on Butte Hill—represented then, as today, by the massive black structures called "gallus" frames.

The Copper

As the Butte mining camp, based first on gold placer and then silver mining, transformed into a copper mining community, it was destined to become a thriving, sustained metropolis isolated, with the copper ore, in the cradle of the Northern Rockies. Mining copper, even from rich veins, was a different beast than mining precious metals. In 1885, the *Engineering and Mining Journal* forecast the fate of Butte as the community embraced the nature of copper and became intertwined with world markets:

> Western miners who are in the habit of mining only for gold and silver have been accustomed to work out their mines in the quickest way possible (a policy for which much is to be said where the precious metals are concerned); but copper, they have found, can not be treated in this way. Copper, like iron and coal, is strictly a commercial metal, and the world will have no more of it than it can use.[2]

Copper was a commercial metal largely valued for its physical properties, including its malleability, ductility, and electrical conductivity—all important to industrialization. Copper wires and cable became increasingly important both to industry and to daily life of people all over the industrial world as they adopted electric lighting and machinery. Living on and with copper demanded extraction in massive amounts, over the long run, in capital-intensive operations. The backs (and lungs) of immigrants offered the labor for mining the copper, but the gallus frames that lifted the ore out of the earth were the backbone of the extraction process.

As Butte rapidly developed around the copper mines, the community reflected the nature and routine of the work in the underground mines. The mines ran around the clock, stopping only for temporary shutdowns caused by a decrease in the market price of copper, by strikes or accidents, or by the need to conduct maintenance. The vital parts of the city, including its bars and restaurants, remained open throughout the twenty-four-hour day. Stories claim that the process for christening a new drinking establishment in Butte entailed breaking the lock out of the front door—there was no need for the door ever to be locked if the bar never closed. In periods of peak production, three shifts a day of men "went down" the shafts into the mines and returned to the surface coming off shift. Coming off shift, day in and day out, or "round in, round out" as the miners used to say, the men often stopped by their neighborhood bar for a shot and a beer before returning to their homes or to a boardinghouse.

Every miner's life passed from the surface world to the underground world via the entrance guarded by and regulated through the gallus frame or "headframe" (see Figure 1). The insulator that Joe handed me on the Belmont rests on my desk as a reminder of my work with Joe, John, John T., and Tommy; of all the stories the people of Butte shared with me; and of the central practical and enduring symbolic importance of the gallus frames as they stood sentry over both the production of copper and the crafting of life on Butte Hill. Significantly, and silently, although with a compelling story to tell, many still stand. I hope to share something of what was passed to me about how gallus frames worked, about the experience of working with them, about the men who did the work, and about why they still punctuate the landscape of the Richest Hill on Earth, the Mining City, Butte, America. For all its faults, failures, and defeats, the community earned its monikers honestly.

The Frame

The sole practical purpose of the gallus frame was to provide leverage for pulling and lowering loads into and out of the underground mine. Concrete footings anchored the relatively simple machine on the surface directly over the "shaft," the rectangular, usually vertical, opening to the mine (see Figure 2). Four rigid legs bolted to the footings rose from the corners of the base to form the frame, with two legs standing vertical, each with another leg angled toward it. Numerous crossmembers joined and reinforced the four legs. Planking, called the "sheets," floored the ground under the frame. The size of the frames varied as did the material used in

their construction. Massive lengths of wood formed the earlier and smaller frames. Larger and stronger, steel "latticework" frames later replaced the wood frames, and, still later, stronger solid steel "I" beam frames replaced some of the latticework structures. The larger steel frames stood from 100 to 180 feet high.

The gallus frame was essentially a massive pulley consisting of the frame holding a set of wheels at the top, each strung with a cable, designed to transfer the force used to lower and raise men and material in and out of the mine. Two "main" hoist cables each passed over a wheel atop the frame. John T. Shea, who replaced many cables when they wore out, described the cables: "The hoist cables at the Kelly, the Con, the Anselmo, and the Belmont were all inch and seven-eighths. You could change a cable in any one of the mines. But the ones at the Con and the Kelly were the longest because the Con was so deep." One end of the cable wound around the massive drum of the hoist housed in the "engine room," which was built on the surface some distance from the headframe. The "engine," powered by either compressed air or electricity in Butte, turned the drum one direction or the other, winding and unwinding the cable, which in turn lowered or raised "cages" or "skips" (depending on the situation) that were attached to the other end of the cable. The cage, used to haul men and materials, was a box-shaped structure made with iron bars with a grated bottom. The skip was a tall, solid-walled, rectangular metal bucket that carried the ore out of the mine.

In multiple ways, the gallus frame depended on balance to function. Both the hoist and the gallus frame shouldered the load on each cable. The cables strung over the main wheels of the gallus frame each traveled through corresponding, side-by-side compartments of the shaft. They wound around separate but parallel drums on the main hoist in the engine room such that the two drums formed a large cylinder split in half. The halves of the cylinder could rotate independent of each other, but, in normal operating mode, the cylinder rotated as a unit in either direction. On one half of the cylinder, the cable was wound over the top; on the other, the cable wound from the bottom.

With the cables wrapped in opposite directions around the drums of the hoist, and when both drums were engaged, the load on one cable traveled down the shaft while the load on the other cable traveled up, counterbalancing to some degree the weight of each other. If the rotation of the hoist drum reversed, so did the direction of each cable. One engineer explained the counterbalance principle of the hoist: "When the rope on one drum would come off the top, see, and the rope on the other drum come off the bottom, so when one was coming up the other was

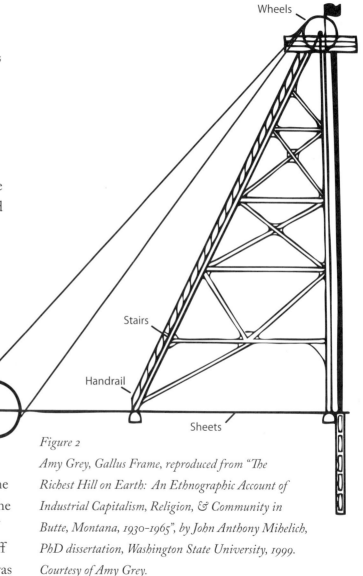

Figure 2

Amy Grey, Gallus Frame, reproduced from "The Richest Hill on Earth: An Ethnographic Account of Industrial Capitalism, Religion, & Community in Butte, Montana, 1930-1965", by John Anthony Mihelich, PhD dissertation, Washington State University, 1999. Courtesy of Amy Grey.

coming down, figure that out, they called them counter-balance." He continued:

> Both drums were turning in the same direction, but one rope was coming in at the top and one was coming in at the bottom, a lot of guys could never figure that out, how the hell do you do that, and that was the answer, one was an overshot rope and the other was an undershot rope. It was very interesting side of it, my father explained all that stuff to me when I was much younger, before I ever got around a hoist, it was beneficial to me, I broke in a lot of guys up there.

The weight of the empty skip, and the cable itself, traveling down the shaft aided the hoist with the weight of the loaded skip coming to the surface. During normal operations, the wheels atop the headframes continuously turned in one direction or the other. Any prolonged stoppage of the wheels caused concern.

A third, smaller wheel atop the frame supported a cable running through a third, smaller compartment in the shaft and connected to a second, smaller hoist.

Facing Page: *Figure 3. Leonard main hoist engine room, Butte, early twentieth century. Photographer unknown. Courtesy World Museum of Mining, Butte (WMM 1116)*

Called the "chippy" hoist, the smaller hoist raised and lowered men and materials, especially timber, needed in the mine during the shift. Finally, some of the deeper mines, such as the Mountain Consolidated Mine (the Con) and the Steward and the Leonard, had a hoist and engine room at a deep level. Ore was hoisted from lower levels by the underground hoist and transferred to the main shaft so that the main hoist could bring it to the surface. John T. explained:

> At the Con, the big ones only went right to the 4400. But then they had another on the 4000 of the Con, they had a hoist, an engine room and everything down there. And then they had their own skips, they were smaller. They'd bring the rock up, and they'd dump it in what they call a transfer chute. And the transfer chutes would come over to the big chutes in the big shaft, and then, the big ones would go down and get it from there and haul it to surface. The Steward had an underground hoist on the 4000, the Leonard had one . . . and then the rock from the bottom levels of the mine were hoisted up to that.

Steel "shoes" welded on the sides held the cages and skips in place as they traveled on "guides" running the length of the shaft. The shoes were short, three-sided square steel tubes with the two protruding sides hugging either side of the hardwood guides (about six by eight inches times the length of the shaft) standing vertically on the walls of the shaft compartments. The sides of the cages were also equipped with mechanisms called "dogs," which were held open by the tension on the cable from the weight of the cage or skip. In the event of a loss of tension, or "slack," in the cable—for example, if the cable broke—the dogs quickly closed and gripped the guides to stop and hold the cage in place, preventing it from plunging to the bottom of the shaft.

At the surface, men "changed over" the cages and skips depending on whether rock or men were to be hauled through the shaft. The skips traveled the shaft most of the day hauling rock. For lowering and raising men, the cages, stored hanging to the side on the gallus frame, replaced the skips. This replacement, or "changeover," took only about five minutes. At the start of a shift, the cages lowered the new workers to their appropriate places in the mine. Four cages hung from one cable, and six men, two rows of three front to back, squeezed in each cage when the shift was lowered. A seventh squeezed in the end, facing the middle to expedite the process when raising the shift at the end of the day. Lowering the shift, twenty-four men at a time, sometimes took over an hour, with the men taking their turn in the cage depending on what level, or how deep

into the mine, they were headed. The process began at the lowest level and worked its way up.

For the bulk of the day, the men underground loaded the skip with ore from a storage "pocket" at some level in the mine. The skip was then hoisted to the surface, where it automatically dumped into holding bins built adjacent to the gallus frames. Near the end of the shift, the skips again were swapped for the cages and the main hoist lifted the shift to the surface. At changeover, the cages were run to the bottom of both compartments to "sweep" the shaft. Sweeping cleared the shaft of any chunks of ore that may have lodged in the shaft after falling from the skips during the daylong process of hoisting ore.

The People

The primary task of underground mining was to extract ore from the ground using a cable pulled by an engine over a pulley supported by a gallus frame. Despite the often cited triumph of technology in industrial production, people were central in the process. In the case of the gallus frame, men at both ends of the machine controlled the cables through a challenging and complicated coordination of efforts. On the surface, the hoisting engineer ran the hoist in the engine room and moved the skips and cages through the shaft as directed. Engineers went through an extensive training and apprenticeship program, as

Frank, a retired hoisting engineer, explained: "I was 1st class engineer, you started out as an oilier, then you get a 3rd class license, then a 2nd class license and then a 1st class license, and then you were ready to go anywhere, it took four years for the apprenticeship."

On the other end of the cable, men underground, usually designated as "station tenders," communicated with the engineer through a "bell" system somewhat resembling a Morse code. They pulled the cords that rang the bells in the engine rooms in a particular pattern. Based on his interpretation of the bell code, the engineer moved the hoist, raising, lowering, or stopping. The code told the engineer what level to take the cage or skip, when the cage or skip was "clear," and when it needed to be raised or lowered only slightly. Ray, a retired engineer who remembered pulling ore from a number of mines, described the code for hoisting ore: "When it gets loaded, they give you two-one-and-two, it's in the clear. That means it's yours, do what you want, and you come up with it."

The process of moving men and ore tested patience, resolve, and wits day in and day out as workers depended on one another to meet production expectations and to ensure safety and survival. Underground mining in general entailed a significant amount of trust, but this was nowhere more apparent than in running the cable, because the men at either end could not see what was going on at the other. The engineer sitting in a building at the surface could not see the cages and skips as they traveled underground, and those underground could not see other levels in the mine, the surface, or inside the engine room. The cables were marked and the engineers had the aid of a depth gauge on the hoist, but for the most part engineers relied on the station tenders' bells and their own ear, developed through years of training and experience, to control the cages and skips. Shaking his head for emphasis, Ray told me in no uncertain terms that it was an unnerving job moving cages with "people's lives hanging from that cable." Hoisting copper ore also tested both men and machine day in and day out. Frank described the challenges of hoisting the particularly high-grade ore from the Leonard Mine: "I could tell there when I was running that damn deep level hoist . . . [we] were hoisting from the 38 and 3900. That's where they were finding that stuff there. Boy, when you get a skip of that on there, that damn hoist could barely take it. She'd barely take it. And that was the richest ore on the Butte Hill."

As in most industrial production, time and efficiency lorded over the cable operations. Thus, along with knowing where and when to move the skips and cages, the engineer also regulated the speed of the cable. The engineer moved the skips at a much higher speed than the cages, at about 1,500 feet per minute, called "rock speed." Frank remembered running the hoist at the Kelley, the newest and fastest shaft on the Hill, with the "biggest hoist motor made in the world. . . . It was some hoist, that son of a gun, 2800 feet a minute with a ten ton skip on the end of it."

The company kept a "tally" of how many skips came to the surface each day, which pressured the engineer somewhat to keep the skips moving rapidly. A good tally was more than 100 loads, but at the Kelley Mine, Frank explained, the company expected "130 on the graveyard shift, and if you didn't get that you have to answer why. That was 10 ton skips, that's 1,300 ton a shift, so a skip in a minute and a half, that was really rambling." A continuous paper tape, called a "stool pigeon," tracked every movement of the hoist through the day and counted the dumpings of the skip. The skip was lowered to the "pocket" underground where miners and motormen dumped and stored the ore. At the Kelley, the pocket was on the 4600 level and ran to the 4800. Frank explained: "There was a guy in the control room, at the 4800 as they called it, and another guy standing at the station. He would put a red mark on the cable, when it was right at his eye level, he would signal the other guy to open the door and he would load that skip that quick (snaps his fingers), ten tons of rock in that skip."

Because the engineer never saw the skips and cages reroute to the surface and they were in his hands once he heard two-one-and-two, he relied on his knowledge and feel to rapidly hoist the skips the appropriate distance to the surface. Once to the top of the mine, the skips dumped automatically into the holding bins, and then the engineer dropped them back down the shaft. Sometimes, however, the engineer, who continually kept in mind the depth and speed of his skips, made an error. It was not unheard of for the engineer, thinking his skips were lower than they actually were, to pull the skip, or even the cages, right over the top of the gallus frame. "They call that 'hitting the wheel,'" Frank remembered. "On the end of that rope, that's a lot of weight, the weight of the loaded skip and the cable itself. If that ever got away from you, you could never stop it. . . . A lot of guys hit the wheel. My dad used to say, 'Hell, you're not an engineer until you hit the wheel, because you only do it once.'"

Moving the cages was even more challenging because men's lives, rather than a load of ore, hung at the end of the cable. The cages were hung two, four, or sometimes five deep from the cable. The engineer lowered the cages to a specified level, "spotting" whichever cage the station tender "rang" for with the bells. Once the men got off or on a particular cage on a specified level, the station tender sent another bell signal to the engineer so that he could spot another cage or move to another level. Considering the fact that the cages might be three or four thousand feet down the shaft, spotting the cages for men was exacting work.

Ray described in detail a typical process of lowering the shift. The station tender got on the cages at the surface with the men and, once the men were loaded, rang the engineer to indicate the desired level. For instance, according to Ray: "You always, at the Con, started with the bottom level first. So when he starts out, he'll give you ten-and-two. Ten-and-two means 4200. He gets on the 42 and he wants to go to the 40, so he rings nine-and-five, that's the 40. You never stopped until you got a stop bell, unless you got lost, and then you stopped immediately." Once at the station, the maneuvering from one cage to another went something like this:

> When he leaves the men off, he gives you two-and-one. Two-and-one. Two-and-one means down. . . . He gives you two-and-one, so you pull that down and spot the next one. Then he does the same thing again, he gives you two-and-one, you spot the next one, one right after another. . . . Once all the men are on the station, he gets on the cage, and he'd go one-and-two. Then he goes to the next level. You spot the one he is on because you don't want to get lost, you want to make sure that station tender is there. . . . He takes the men he wants . . . then he'd give you two-and-one, two-and-one. When you're hoisting the shift, it's just the opposite. . . . He spots

the cage he is on . . . then he gives you one-and-two, one-and-two . . . then you spot the next one up here. Then he gives you one-and-two and you spot the next one.

Figure 4. Belmont Mine cages, Butte, early twentieth century. Photographer unknown. Courtesy World Museum of Mining, Butte (WMM1025)

The description is a bit confusing, and rightly so as it conveys a sense of the complexity of the bell system. Ray explained how quickly the bells rung: "It was not a slow ding, ding, ding; it was a very rapid ring of bells." As he demonstrated the sound by rapidly tapping his pen on the table in front of him, I asked, "So you have to count those that fast?" He replied, "You don't count them, you just listen, if you count them you'll never get them. Now some people may count them, but I never count them."

At times, particularly when pulling skips over and over, the job was routine. Frank put it like this: "There was two compartments, one [skip] was on one side and the other was dumping on surface, then when they rang the bell to take it to the 4800 you would go home, the top side is already dumping as the other one is loading, it's that quick too, it was a busy thing I tell you, but I like those, just sit back there and pull skips." More than busy, it was serious work with men in cages—their lives depended on the coordination between the station tender and the engineer, and something could go wrong at any time. Reflecting on his days running various hoists on Butte Hill, Ray remarked, "I don't know how we never killed guys."

The cages with men were hoisted at only about eight hundred feet per minute, called "man speed." Engineers could set the hoist to man speed, which both regulated the upper speed of the hoist and added safety precautions so the cages could not be pulled through the wheels—the breakers would kick out if the cages came up too high, stopping the electric hoist. However, practice did not always reflect policy. Both the main hoist and the chippy were used to lower the shift, and, as Ray explained, one time the safety officers, or the Safety First crew, "threw the man speed on at the Con chippy." He told this story:

> Now they threw the man speed on at the Con chippy one time. And it cut it to half the speed. Safety First came up and said, "now you always have to keep that at man speed when you are lowering the shift." I said "you bet" [laughs]. Well, [the men going on shift] were supposed to be down at 9:30, and it was 11:00, and they were still not down [laughs]. So they come and they says, "don't do that no more, never do that no more" [laughs].

As this story reflects, the pressures of time and efficiency expectations provided, or necessitated, some leeway in the speed at which engineers drew the cages through the shaft. However, time and efficiency were not the only ways in which engineers exercised their freedom to vary the speed of the cages. As one miner explained, some engineers would "really give you a ride." Ray, of course, said (chuckling) that he never did that because he knew someday he would have to ride the cage down the mine and he wanted that ride to be safe. At other times, engineers unknowingly moved men at an unsafe speed.

A story told more than once at the ARCO retirees' club coffee hour, to the great amusement of those within earshot, illustrates some of the antics that infused the mining day with some pleasure and pain and the propensity of people in Butte to confer nicknames. Apparently, one man wanted a ride out of the mine, so somebody told him to jump on top of the skip and hang onto the cable. They told him that once he got on to "ring two-one-and-two." As stated above, two-one-and-two signaled the engineer that the skip was "clear" and he could hoist it at full speed. The man went up at rock speed, and since the engineer could not see him on top of the skip, when the skip dumped back down he went. Once loaded again below, the skip was cleared by the station tender, and the engineer hoisted the skip up and down with the man riding on top. Finally, the station tender looked down the shaft at the skip to make sure the automatic dump was loading the skip properly and saw the man on top. Sticking one's head out into the shaft posed a severe danger as a skip could come flying by, taking one's head with it, so people rarely leaned out for a look. Once spotting the man, the station tender signaled the engineer, who pulled the skip to surface at a slower speed and paused

to let the man off. According to the account, the man had "that big cable squeezed to practically nothing!" From the adventure, he earned the nickname "Skip."

The Ride

While the engineer and station tender controlled the cable, other men had to ride it, and the experience could be harrowing. One longtime Catholic miner said that every time he went down in the cages he drew the cross on his chest, blessed himself, and asked that he arrive safely. When he got to the proper level, he would look up and say "thanks." Men vomited in the cages, showering those in the cages below; occasionally a limb slipped outside the cage as it traveled through the shaft; and often, once packed in the cage, the men began kicking the shins of those across from them and a foot battle ensued.

Each trip down the shaft also carried the possibility of "going into the woods," a phrase referring to a wreck in the shaft. In the case of a wreck, the cage became lodged or tangled in the wooden guides and timber lining the shaft, known as the "woods." On one occasion, a crew of craftsmen, traveling down the mines to fix a problem, went into the woods. When they got that wreck fixed, they headed down once again to address the original problem. They went into the woods again. The second time, they simply went home, declaring, "Twice in the woods in one day is enough!"

Although soothed by the rhythmic clicking as the shoes rode the guides, every person who went down in the cage knew it could be his last ride.

On one's first trip down the shaft, however, little could soothe the nerves of a "greenhorn." Although nearly every greenhorn feared his first journey into the darkness, few let on. Joe recalled the first time he "went down." He had already heard many tales of the dangers in the mine, and he would soon assemble a collection of his own, but stories of "going into the woods" offered plenty of reason for Joe to fear his initiatory ride in the cages. He had quit school at age seventeen and was "sitting around the house not doing much one afternoon." His father said, "Let's go for a walk. I have to pick up my paycheck." When they arrived at the ACM pay office, Joe's dad told the clerk to give his son a "card." The card was a "rustling card," issued by the ACM, which enabled the youngster to work in the mines. The clerk said they could not hire him because he was too young. The father firmly replied, "He's going down with me. Now give him a card." Joe's father was an experienced miner, and this was sufficient to convince the company to give him a job.

Joe recalled his experience of heading down the shaft at the Mountain Consolidated Mine as his father's new mining partner. He said: "I about shit my pants, but I wouldn't let anyone know that. I told everybody, 'this ain't so bad.'" He explained how his dad taught him the ins and outs of mining and described what happened when, after collecting his first paycheck, his dad took him to one of the numerous bars in Butte. As they "bellied up," his father said, "Bring us a beer." The bartender replied with the obligatory "I can't serve him; he's too young." Joe's father answered: "He's my partner; he's doing a man's work. Now give him a beer." Joe drank the beer, but, as a greenhorn, he knew he had a long way to go to equal his father as a miner.

Butte was beset with masculine bravado such as Joe displayed with his statement "This ain't so bad," when, in fact, he was very scared of his first ride in the cage. One of the least understood, if not one of the potentially most destructive, of these expressions of masculinity was the thorough integration of drinking into Butte life along with the central role bars played in neighborhoods. The workers on the Hill spent much of their life in dangerous manual labor making a living for themselves and their families. However, I was often told that the men "broke more rock in the bar" than they ever did underground. The workday did not end for many men until they gathered, on the way home, at one of the numerous neighborhood drinking establishments. There they would put their lunch "buckets" on the bar, buy a shot of whiskey and a beer for a dime, and rehash the day, previous days, and long-past days with their compatriots. Those who did not practice this routine every day at least stopped in the bar on payday. One man told a story about asking an old-timer why miners drank so much. The man replied: "Well son, they go down in the mines every morning, and they don't know if they will come up again. If they do come up, they are happy and want to enjoy a drink. They don't know when the end will come."

The Caring

When the underground mines were open, iron workers, called "ropemen" on the Hill, cared for the gallus frames to sustain their function in ore production. Ropemen performed any work that had to do with the cables or erecting and dismantling the gallus frames. They installed new cables and coated them with pine tar when needed, sometimes each week, to protect them from the copper water in the shafts. They lowered equipment down the shaft that would not fit in the cage, usually by "tying" it below the cage or to the bare cable. They also built, replaced, and maintained the numerous pumps and pipelines on the surface and in the mines.

One responsibility of the ropemen involved getting the wrecks out of "the woods." In each engine room, a visible sign reminded engineers that, in the case of "slack cable in the shaft, shut down and call the ropemen." Slack cable alerted the engineer to a wreck in the shaft. The ropemen were called, loaded into the free cage, and lowered to the wreck, where

they proceeded to do whatever it took to free the stuck cage and any men in it. Many ropemen spent as much time in the mines as on the surface, lowering, installing, or maintaining equipment. Often, following strict union proscriptions governing the type of work each craftsman could do, they worked in "composite crews" consisting of two ironworkers, two boilermakers, and a machinist. John T., a ropeman on the Hill for over thirty years, told the following story about the events and dangers in working on the "ropegang":

> We were taking down the Leonard headframe, and we had to take down the flagpole first. We had a derrick set up to lift it out and set it on the platform handrail so we could then lower it. It was all done with ropes. As we lifted the flagpole out, the rope broke, down went the flagpole, all the way down the gallus frame. Everybody on the ground was running in every direction. Luckily nobody got hurt. We came down that night, and [chuckles], the foreman of the mine come over to our boss and he said, "don't ever do that again!" The boss said, "I won't, there was only one flagpole."

John T. was also part of the crew mentioned above that went into the woods twice in one day and decided to go home because that was enough.

The ropemen, as well as the other craftsmen, often had to work odd hours or overtime to fix a problem. The company wanted as little loss of production as possible. John T. tells the following story about one of these overtime nights when he was called to repair a wheel atop the Leonard gallus frame:

> I got a call Thursday night after I got home from bowling. I used to grab a pork chop sandwich on the way home from bowling, but for some reason I didn't that particular night. We got the call and started to fix the wheel at about nine o'clock that evening. At about 2:30 a.m., the boss sent somebody down to get the crew something to eat. He brought back chicken salad sandwiches. It was Friday, Catholics could not eat meat on Friday, and the guy that went to pick up the food was not Catholic. The rest of us damn near killed him!

They worked all day that Friday until four o'clock in the afternoon without eating.

With the strength of their steel and a design to withstand decades of use, gallus frames carried a sense of permanence, and some have indeed endured decades of winters in Butte. However, ropemen knew well the capricious nature of mining and disassembled and moved many frames on the Hill. John T. talked often about moving, modifying, dismantling, and erecting the frames:

> In 1950 we put up the Kelly. We went down and took it down at the Leonard, after we took it down, and then we brought it back up to the Kelly and we remodeled it, widened it and raised it up. . . . We got the Kelly headframe up, and then we, there was another crew putting in the hoists and that, the big engines. . . . Then, that was just the one main hoist, the big headframe was all in, the idling towers were there, they had another crew putting up the idling towers. . . . And then in 1952, they started sinking the Kelly shaft. Well they had a wooden frame up and we put the big frame up over it. But then we started. We went to the Anaconda and took the headframe down. . . . The next stop was the St. Lawrence, and we took down the gallus frame, and then, those frames were lattice work, and they just took 'em up and stored them up behind the Diamond Mine. They never put them up no more. . . . From there we went up the hill to the Mountain View, and we took the Mountain View down. Then we took the High Ore down. Then we

come down and we took Tramway #4 down. And we took it back up to the Kelly and we put it up. That's the Kelly #2, is the Tramway #4. We put that back up, then, we went back down and we took down the Berkeley, we took down the East Colusa, we took the West Colusa, we took down the Alex Scott, that's the, we put that back up, that's the Lexington. Then was stopped doing all the destruction, and then we went down, went back up and helped a lot around the Kelly.

While underground mining still produced ore, the ropemen knew each time they took down a large gallus frame that they would reassemble it over another shaft on the Hill. As underground mining gave way to open pit methods, the large frames still held the sense of permanence but they grew increasingly quiet. However, for many in tune with the legacy of this city or who grew up while the whistles blew and the wheels turned or who worked on and under the headframes or who depended on the work conducted through them, the gallus frames permanently encode a memory in material form. The more I learned about Butte and its mining heart, the more the gallus frames dominated my perception of the Hill.

In the era when the community of Butte beat to the rhythm of the underground mines, the daily cadence set by the wheels and whistles and work of the gallus frames provided residents with a sense of comfort, routine, security, and meaning. The whistles in the engine room blew at regular intervals, marking the end of the shifts. The wheels turned around the clock, lowering and hoisting the shift and dumping the copper ore into the holding bins on surface. They churned out the material of the sometimes grueling work of mining and of labor's tenuous relationship with the company. The frames marked the worksite, the place where fathers toiled, and the neighborhoods where people lived. In the early days of Butte, before automobiles, people lived in the shadow of a gallus frame because they built their homes as close to the mines as possible to shorten the walk to work.

Each mine had a name, a history, a reputation, an identity based on underground happenings known only to surface dwellers through the frame. The Anaconda Mine, the claim where abundant copper was first encountered in Butte, was named, with a bit of irony, after the constricting snake. Some in Butte would say that the snake, at times, coiled more tightly around the body of a miner than around any prey in the Amazonian jungle. Such names as the Anselmo, the Belmont, the Tramway, the Granite Mountain, the Mountain Consolidated, the Travona, the Orphan Girl, the Kelly, the Diamond, the Original, the Steward, the Lexington, the Leonard, and others contributed to the

North Butte Mining Company
Granite Mountain Mine

Scene of Worst Metal Mine Disaster
in U.S. History—June 8, 1917

163 Miners Lost Their Lives

lexicon in Butte.

While the headframes provided only one of the images that dominated social life in Butte, Butte's life oriented around the gallus frames because of the centrality of copper mining. Lit with lights at night, they shone brilliantly, giving rise to the phrase "the glittering hill." Only through the gallus frames could one make passage from the world of the sun to access the vast underground labyrinth of danger, riches, camaraderie, and mystique. Underground was a man's world, an adult world, a world of labor. It was also, as nearly all who ever took that first ride down the shaft for a shift as a "greenhorn" will attest, a world of humility, albeit punctuated with a Butte-sized dose of bravado.

The gallus frames signaled both prosperity and the enduring struggle of life for the working community. If the wheels atop the gallus frames turned, life was in order—at least in terms of how order was established in Butte. Any time the wheels stopped for any duration, there was cause for alarm. The wheels stopped only for accidents, work stoppages, or the end of an era. Each case threw the rhythm and

Facing Page: *Figure 5. Granite Mountain mine, Butte, after 1917. Photographer unknown. Courtesy World Museum of Mining, Butte.*

balance of the community out of order and often led to human suffering. The wheels have been stopped, for the most part, since the late 1970s, when the ACM phased out underground mining and left only the open-pit operations, which themselves finally shut down in 1983. My uncle John T. Shea remembers that last day:

> And then when the shut the pit down, they shut the whole pumping operation down [which still used some of the mine shafts]. July the 30th, 1983, I was the last ropeman left on the Hill cause I was the oldest one in seniority. . . . I worked overtime on the last day, I had to go around and pick up all the propane tanks. We were the last ones that left, I always remember a good friend of mine went by in his truck and, he called me on the radio and he said, "hey harp," and I said, "ya," he says, "been nice working with ya, so long!" [laughs].

Life does go on in Butte, but it beats to a different drummer and has a different order. To be sure, life changes, and often in many ways for the better. Life was not necessarily "better" in the underground era of Butte, but many who remember the old order have a story to tell—and they are fond of telling stories. The stories are central to their individual and community identities, and many see gallus frames as an important part of such stories.

In 1986, Montana Resources took over the mining properties from ARCO and sold some of the underground mines, including the gallus frames, to New Butte Mining. Then New Butte Mining began cutting up the steel at the Mountain Consolidated Mine, across the street from my uncle's house on 7 West Pacific, to sell as scrap iron. My uncle, along with many others, never quite relinquished his responsibility and care for the gallus frames. He kept them working during the days of mining, and he is determined to keep them working, in another sense, for future generations of Butte residents as well as for those interested in what life was like in Butte, America. Sustaining the work of the gallus frames depends on both preserving the structures and telling the stories. John T. tells the stories any chance he gets—not just for the enjoyment of telling them but also because they represent a community, a generation, and a way of life. He thinks that we need to remember from whence we came and that, by extension, we can learn something from the past about living today. I will close with my Uncle John's explanation, as he can tell it like no other. One day at his house on Pacific Avenue, he offered this:

They were going to tear all the gallus frames down. Well, that's when I got on that committee and we got the people of Butte behind us. And we got the governor and the senator and everybody else. We raised enough hell in there. That guy from New Butte Mining told me, he said, "We're going to take the Lexington gallus frame down." I said, "Good luck." He said, "What do you mean?" I said, "You better have bullet-proof vests." "What for?" he said. I said, "Well, that's where mining started in Butte, Montana. I guarantee, they'll shoot you right off the gallus frame." A few months later they were in the Kelly Mine yard. I went up there and the same man told me, "We're going to take down the two gallus frames at the Kelly Mine." I said, "I'll guarantee you one thing. . . . You take the first one down, you'll hang off the second one."

Many shared my uncle's sentiments, and, as such, the frames continue to hold an important, if not profound, presence in Butte. The relics of the history of industrial copper production still have a sense of permanence, and they preserve something of the essence of the community. My uncle continued:

Figure 6. Leonard gallus frame "blow," Meaderville, Butte, 1973. Photo Copyright © Karl Volkman 04/05. This image is copyrighted. Unauthorized reproduction prohibited. Courtesy World Museum of Mining, Butte (WMM 1428).

They salvaged that whole shop out of there, but they didn't touch the gallus frames. Like I'll tell you and I tell those little kids on the mining tours, "Remember one thing, this is your heritage. This is something that was left to you by your grandparents and your great-grandparents. My father came from the old country to go to work in these mines. So did your grandfather and great-grandfather. They all came from the old country to work in these mines. This is what *made* Butte, the people that came from the old country. This is your heritage, this is Butte, there's only one place like it. Scrap iron sells for $70 a ton, but what's your heritage worth?"

Note: The Ray Calkins Memorial Research Fellowship from the Butte Historical Society (1996) assisted with the research from which this paper is drawn. Please also note that all quotations without source notes are drawn from the author's personal interviews (1995–2004) with the people mentioned in the text.

---

[1]   The term *gallus* is formally spelled "gallows," but I will use "gallus" throughout because it is nearer to the pronunciation of the word in Butte. The word is pronounced "gallus," with the "g" as in *game*, the "a" as in *bat*, and the "u" as in *us*.

[2]   Unnamed miner, "The Copper Mines of Butte, Montana—The Outlook for 1885," *Engineering and Mining Journal* 39 (May 23, 1885): 351.

Maintenance Base for the Copper Conveyor: The Butte, Anaconda & Pacific Railway and Its Roundhouse and Repair Shops, 1914

Dale Martin

In the fall of 1914, another day begins in Anaconda, Montana. The sun rises on the town, on the largest copper smelter in the world, which reduces ores extracted from the Butte hill to nearly pure copper, and on a variety of supporting activities, including a railway.

Great long-term change is occurring, both far away and close by. In Europe, the Great War, only months old, is already consuming the unprecedented quantities of metals, including copper and zinc from Montana, that will characterize twentieth-century industrial warfare. Pulling the trains working around Anaconda's smelter hill and drawing power from new overhead electric wires are boxy electric motors that look nothing like the familiar steam locomotives that were doing the same job just a year ago. This is the first high-voltage electric railway to be converted from steam power for economic reasons, and not—as in earlier instances—to remove smoke from long tunnels or cities. Less than a year since full implementation, it is working as intended.[1]

The Butte, Anaconda & Pacific Railway (BA&P) is based in Anaconda, the site of the roundhouse and repair shops, the switchyards and industrial spurs, and the general offices. A part of the Anaconda Copper Mining Company (ACM), the BA&P's primary functions—since its construction in 1893—have been to carry the ores from the Butte hill to the smelting works in Anaconda. It also hauls away the copper anodes and other products of the smelter. In smaller quantities, it also carries mine timbers, fuels for Anaconda operations, general merchandise, and passengers, express, and mail. More than five hundred employees are based in Anaconda and Butte as well as the railway junction community of Rocker, three miles west of Butte, and track maintenance bases along the line. In its main task, the railway collects ore from large bins on mine headframes on the Butte hill; assembles the nine or ten daily westbound ore trains at the Rocker switchyard; and disassembles the trains at East Anaconda, twenty miles farther west, for delivery up a steep, curving track to the smelter. Across town, on the northwest edge of Anaconda, are the railway's primary facilities for maintaining its locomotives and cars.[2]

The Shops

The functional layout of structures, equipment, and activities at the BA&P's West Anaconda shops resembles that of thousands of railway operating terminals around the world. By the mid-nineteenth century, railways were commonly repairing, maintaining, and, occasionally, constructing rolling stock (locomotives, freight and passenger cars, and company service equipment such

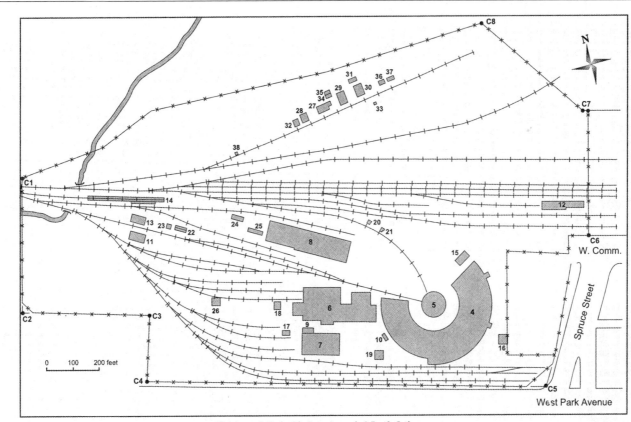

West Anaconda Yards of the Butte, Anaconda & Pacific Railway

Key to sketch map

Note: Numbers 1-3 are not shown on this map; they are the Montana Union Depot, a shed, and the B.A.&P. General Office

4. Roundhouse	12. Wrecking crane house	21. Gasoline house	29. Bridge & buildings lumber shed (w)
5. Turntable & pit	13. Sand house & dryer	22. Diesel tanks	30. Bridge & buildings lumber shed (e)
6. Machine shop & locomotive repair	14. Coal dock	23. Pump house at diesel tanks	31. Bridge & buildings truck garage
7. Blacksmith & boiler shop	15. Paint shop	24. Brass storage shed	32. Bridge & buildings pipe shop
8. Warehouse & office	16. Yard office	25. Parts storage	33. Bridge & buildings hose house
9. Acetylene welding machine	17. Acetylene generator building	26. Air brake shack	34. Bridge & buildings tool house
10. Shops toilet	18. Acetylene & oxygen storage	27. Bridge & buildings carpenter shop	35. Bridge & buildings carpentry tool house
11. Oil house	19. Tool/repair house	28. Bridge & buildings paint shop	36. Bridge & buildings cement shed
	20. Hose house		37. Bridge & buildings cement shed

Figure 30—Index map to features at West Anaconda railroad complex.

as snowplows) at industrial complexes, usually called "shops." Located in terminal cities and at regular intervals on long main lines, these shops typically formed the largest concentrations of railway workers, from more than one hundred workers at West Anaconda to thousands in railway shop towns like Altoona, Pennsylvania; Roanoke, Virginia; and Hillyard, next to Spokane, Washington.

The BA&P's shops consist of four large buildings, many smaller buildings and structures, a dense array of tracks, and many locomotives, cars, and track-maintenance machines awaiting repair or their next service.[3]

The center of visible activity is the brick and wood roundhouse, a semicircular (five eighths of a circle) building internally divided into twenty stalls, most for locomotives and two for painting rail cars. The stalls are reached over a turntable, a sixty-foot-long bridge that spins on a center bearing in the middle of a circular pit. In the roundhouse stalls, locomotives are inspected and maintained. Narrow inspection pits between the rails allow workers to get underneath the engines. For major repairs, locomotives can be moved on two tracks into the

Facing Page: *West Anaconda yards of the Butte, Anaconda & Pacific Railway. From Brian Shovers,* Butte & Anaconda Revisited: An Overview of Early-day Mining and Smelting in Montana *(Butte: Montana Bureau of Mines and Geology, 1991). Used by permission.*

north half of the brick machine shop building, with its distinctive roof monitors, just west of the roundhouse. In the south half, workers use various machine tools to cut, lathe, drill, mill, and otherwise shape metal. The wood-paved floor absorbs oil and offers a soft landing for dropped tools. In the brick boiler and blacksmith shop, just south of the machine shop, workers maintain the steam locomotives that have been retained to operate on the railway's tracks that lack overhead electric power. Boilermakers tend to the demands of the firebox and boiler, in which an inch or less of steel separates fire and exhaust from boiling water and high-pressure steam. Blacksmiths forge hot iron and steel to shape parts for locomotives and cars.

The people who repair the railcars do much of their work outdoors, tending to the brakes, wheels, and couplers. The other large building in the complex is the wooden storehouse, which contains most any parts, supplies, and other materials that might be needed for any operation within the complex.

The complex contains several dozen other smaller buildings and structures. Auxiliary to the roundhouse are facilities for coal, fuel for the steam locomotives, and sand, the latter sprayed under locomotive drive wheels to improve traction. Other small buildings and sheds house specific materials, including paint, flammable oil supplies, ice, and lumber. One small structure contains a fire-fighting hose cart, with five hundred feet of hose.

Based in this complex are the locomotives and cars that make up the regular daily traffic of eight passenger trains, up to two dozen freight trains, and even more transfer and switching operations.

After 1914

From 1914 to 1918, the BA&P and its parent ACM experienced tremendous changes. War-driven economics, labor tensions, and tumultuous politics both pushed and disrupted mining and smelting in Butte and Anaconda. The immediate postwar years saw the beginning of a decades-long decline for railroads in the United States. In the early 1920s, the BA&P passenger trains lost many riders to buses and automobiles on the first paved intercity road in Montana, between Butte and Anaconda. Rail freight not directly associated with mining and smelting, such as express, perishables, and general merchandise, also diminished. Continuing strongly, however, the westbound ore and concentrates to Anaconda and eastbound smelter products kept the BA&P busy.[4]

The motive power maintained at the roundhouse and shops changed over the subsequent decades. Use of steam locomotives ended in the early 1950s, and the electric motors stopped pulling trains in 1967, leaving the work to diesel-electric power. The railway itself survived the difficult decades of the 1970s and 1980s, during which ARCO took over The Anaconda Company and then just a few years later shut down and dismantled the smelter and ceased copper mining in Butte. In the mid-1980s, ARCO sold the BA&P to several managers, who renamed it the Rarus Railway. Montana Resources Inc. acquired and reopened the open-pit mine in Butte, with the Rarus carrying the copper concentrates on the beginning of their long journey to Asian smelters.[5]

Most recently, in May 2007, a Florida-based owner of railway short lines, Patriot Rail Corporation, purchased the Rarus Railway and two months later restored its historic name. According to Patriot Rail's website, the BA&P now carries "copper tailings, impacted soils, copper concentrates, beer and slag." It also runs the Copper King Express, a seasonal tourist train that offers views of, among other sights, miles of "impacted soils" along Silver Bow Creek. Through decades of changes, the roundhouse, repair shops, and many associated buildings and structures survived, and they now house Patriot Rail's maintenance of its twelve locomotives and other rolling stock.[6]

Most of the hundreds of railway shops that existed in the United States before the mid-twentieth century have been either demolished or radically diminished in structures and activities. This loss is due to decades of decline in the railway business, to diesel-electric power replacing maintenance-intensive steam locomotives, to the abandonment of some railroads, and to contemporary rail operating and labor practices.

Anaconda is the site of a rare example of a surviving, working, largely unaltered railway shops complex built in the late nineteenth and early twentieth centuries.

Beyond current operations and properties, a few historic BA&P features survive. For instance, an electric boxcab locomotive once maintained at the West Anaconda roundhouse is now displayed in the Anselmo mine yard on the west side of Butte. Repainted and paired with an auxiliary tractor-truck that distributed the pulling power over more wheels on the rails, this "cow-and-calf" combination is coupled to an ore hopper car and caboose. Another holdover from the early days, Rocker, the former railway switchyard town just west of Butte, remains active in the transportation economy as an oasis for truckers and motorists on interstate routes 15 and 90.

No longer surviving in Anaconda is a building just across the street, to the south of the BA&P roundhouse and shops. The large brick streetcar barn was the last major remnant of the Anaconda's street railway system. Until they ended service in 1951, the Anaconda streetcars were the last operating urban rail transit in Montana. The carbarn was demolished in 2008.[7]

Copper mining and milling continues in Butte. Locomotives and cars of the Butte, Anaconda & Pacific Railway, maintained in Anaconda, still carry copper (and molybdenum) concentrates westward across the lower Butte hill.

[1] William D. Middleton, *When the Steam Railroads Electrified* (Milwaukee, WI: Kalmbach, 1974), 206.

[2] Histories of the BA&P include Charles V. Mutschler, *Wired for Success: The Butte, Anaconda & Pacific Railway, 1982–1985* (Pullman: Washington State University Press, 2002); Brian Shovers, Mark Fiege, Dale Martin, and Fred Quivik, *Butte and Anaconda Revisited: An Overview of Early-day Mining and Smelting in Montana*, Special Publication 99 (Butte: Montana Bureau of Mines and Geology, 1991), 51–55; Middleton, *When the Steam Railroads Electrified*, 204–15; and Gordon W. Rogers, "Where Electrification First Made Good," *Trains* 23 (July 1963): 16–28.

[3] A map of the shops is in Shovers et al., *Butte and Anaconda Revisited*, 54. Also useful are the Sanborn fire insurance maps of Anaconda, available online, in black and white only, without the color coding of building materials.

[4] Mutschler, *Wired for Success*, 79–89.

[5] Mutschler, *Wired for Success*, 105–16.

[6] Patriot Rail Corporation, http://www.patriotrail.com, News section, 2007-05-01 and 2007-07-19; and Copper King Express, http://www.copperkingexpress.com.

[7] Erin Nicholes, "Out with the Old," *Montana Standard*, February 9, 2008.

"Report of Investigation of Sanitary Conditions in Mines, and of the Conditions Under Which the Miners Live in Silver Bow County": An Introduction

Patty Dean

Nearly forty years ago, long-time Montana Historical Society board member, E. E. MacGilvra, took receipt of a photograph album, described in the accompanying letter as: "a typical, turn of the century, common black photograph album (11" x 15" size). It contains 86 pages of text and 66 pages of photographs (one or two per page)." In early twentieth-century Pica type, its flimsy title page read: "Report of Investigation of Sanitary Conditions in Mines, and of the Conditions Under Which the Miners Live in Silver Bow County." The Anaconda Company's chief custodian, Wayne Worley, had discovered the album somewhere in the cavernous Hennessy Building where the Company had its headquarters. MacGilvra subsequently delivered the album to the Montana Historical Society where its photographs, in particular, have been utilized by a wide variety of researchers.

Sometimes the most precious treasure arrives in the most modest wrapping and circumstance. And such is the case with this extraordinarily rich historical resource. According to the report's first paragraph, it was "undertaken to determine, if possible, the source of the high death rate form Tuberculosis in Silver

Photo No. 3 A. View of yard at 347 East Mercury Street (Dago Village).

Bow County." The text of the typewritten report is now digitized and online at the Montana Memory Project site at http://cdm15018.contentdm.oclc.org/u?/p267301coll2,776. A case study of Progressive Era public health methodology, the report describes and quantifies a variety of factors believed to influence the high tuberculosis rate in a city estimated to have a population of 50,000 people. Examining a wide variety of the built environment, sections of the report and accompanying photographs documented mines (underground & above ground change houses, etc.), 438 residences that housed nearly 3,000 occupants (single-family, multi-family, hotels, and boarding houses), streets and alleys, the county poor farm, a few saloons and stores, and dairies within the city proper. The study concluded that conditions in the mines and conditions on the surface, i.e. built environment, combined with a lack of education, were responsible for concentrations of tuberculosis in specific sections of the city.

Although the report's intent was to identify and record public health issues, its usefulness extends well beyond. One remarkable aspect of the photographs is that their prospect is not the front of a residence but rather behind it. Such a vantage point is particularly important in Butte as living space in this metropolis was at such a premium that these "rear" residences could be viewed as secondary neighborhoods. Indeed, a quick scan of early twentieth-century Butte city directory addresses, Sanborn Fire Insurance maps, or entries in the 1910 U.S. Census confirms the high number of people whose homes had no direct access to a city street. And, although the city had opened a forty-acre dump and crematory by 1906 for the incineration of dead dogs and other animals, the facilities were apparently not adequate, given the piles of refuse and number of living (and dead) livestock and fowls that populate the report's photographs. The infrastructure necessary for the disposal of waste water, whether excrement or environmental, was also not satisfactorily dealt with.

As historian Mary Murphy inquires, "[I]f we look to photographs as we look to other sources of information about the past—letters, diaries, newspapers, court records—how then do we interpret them and what can they tell us?" Conversely, filmmaker Errol Morris, in his revelatory blog in *The New York Times*, has repeatedly raised the question: "What do we see—or *think* we see—in photographs?"

Such perspectives are worth pondering as you view the selected photographs that document Butte's circa 1910 built environment in this electronic reconstruction of the album. The captions under the photographs are the original ones written nearly 100 years ago and correspond to the digitized report's text.

All photographs from "Report of Investigation of Sanitary Conditions in Mines, and of the Conditions Under Which the Miners Live in Silver Bow County" [1908-1912]. Courtesy Montana Historical Society Research Center Photograph Archives, Helena (Lot 8, Box 1).

Photo No. 5 A. Rear of 312 East Park Street, under stairway.

Photo No. 7 A. 510 South Dakota Street, showing back yard.

Photo No. 85. Shows back yard and toilet of #337 East Park Street.

Photo No. 86. Shows back yard of 1100 Block on East Broadway. X shows the opening into the shallow sewer which has been provided for carrying off slops. General conditions around this place were very insanitary.

Photo No. 87. Is the rear of #480 East Broadway, showing the general junk pile and children at play.

Photo 88. Shows the back yard of 430 Lee Avenue. The general conditions are very insanitary.

Photo No. 89. Shows a manure pile at the rear of 435 East Mercury Street. This is an old manure pile.

Photo No. 90. Is the rear of 346 East Broadway. The conditions are very good here.

Photo No. 91. 712 No. Wyoming. X marks dead chicken. General conditions very insanitary, entire block is one general junk pile.

Photo No. 94. Rear of 145 East LaPlatte St. Great deal of filth around, this place is insanitary.

Photo No. 95. Chicken yard at 20 O'Neill St., Centerville. The arrow points to wheel barrow of manure, place wet and filthy and only 16 X 20 feet wide, with turkeys, chickens, geese, the goat and dog.

Photo No. 96. Same as
No. 94, very filthy and
insanitary.

Photo No. 99. Another view of
20 O'Neil Street, Centerville.

Photo No. 101. "A", back yard of 60 East LaPlatte Street, Centerville.

Photo No. 103. General catch-all in Centerville, natural drainage only sewer known.

Photo No. 122. No. 1600 Second Ave., out on the flats. The body of water remains the whole year around.

Photo No. 123. Rear of West LaPlatte Street, Centerville.

Photo No. 129. Rear of Main Street, in Meaderville.

Photo No. 125. Toilet at 320 West Daly Street, Walkerville. Very filthy and dirty, floor covered with feces. X marks a pile of manure.

Photo No. 126. Shows a hole in West Daly St., Walkerville. The water in here has no outlet and has green color.

Anaconda: A Short Story

Edward B. Reynolds (edited and with an afterword by Matthew Basso)

Editor's Note: Edward Reynolds wrote the short story "Anaconda" for *Men at Work*, a 1941 Federal Writers Project (FWP) anthology that, because of World War II, was never published. Harold Rosenberg, the editor of *Men at Work* and later in his life one of the nation's best-known art critics, asked FWP authors from around the country to submit stories about people doing their jobs. In the hope that this collective project might provide a unique window into American work ways and the lives of workers themselves, the FWP stipulated that the authors either had to have witnessed the labor they were writing about or had to have done it themselves. Reynolds, who had worked at the Anaconda Reduction Works several times, was an ideal candidate for the assignment. In the "Sketch Biography" that he submitted with his short story, Reynolds, who was born and raised in Anaconda, wrote that he first worked in the smelter on weekends as a high school student. The wages he earned at the plant helped him complete a journalism degree at Montana State University, but he always considered "the copper college" an equally important educational experience. He told Rosenberg that "it would take a book to tell of the Micks and Slavs and Swedes and Russians; the Cousin Jacks, the Polacks, the Italians, the Germans . . . of the varied occupations, as many in number

as the works is huge." Reynolds described the story below as depicting in detail only "a small part" of what went on at the plant, "with but a cursory glance at the remainder." Even with those caveats in mind, I believe "Anaconda" is one of the best—and most interesting—literary portraits of the built environment of a once mighty industrial site.[1]

He shoved the white card into the timekeeper's window and growled a greeting. While he waited for the clerk to go through the familiar routine of making out a time card, he continued grumbling to himself. He had been grumbling on the street car all the way up the Hill to the works. Grumbling ever since the clerk in the employment office downtown had given him a work card for the Stack.

The Stack! Rappin' treaters or dumping flue dust. That was a job for sodbusters and greenhorns. Not for a guy that had been born and raised right here on the ground, here in Anaconda, whose residents do not look at the morning sky to see how the weather is, but whose first glance is at the Big Stack to see how the smoke's coming out. They don't ask one another's health, they ask, "What shift you on?" "How's she going?" is hello; "Tap her light" is good-by. Why, his parents had been there when Old Marcus himself, the Copper King, had bellied up to the bar he'd had built as an exact reproduction of the Hoffman House in New York. The Stack! Jeez, you'd think there was

Coming to work at the Stack off the trolley, Anaconda, Montana, 1945. Photograph by R. I. Nesmith. Courtesy Montana Historical Society Research Center Photograph Archives, Helena (Lot 19 A210).

enough Okies and Arkies laying around to take those jobs. You wouldn't think they'd put a guy in a hell hole who'd worked every place from the high line, dumping ore, to the hot metal. If times hadn't been so tough with him, he'd have told that employment clerk where he could stick his card. But…Well…Hell!

The card hustler handed him the pink pasteboard and said, "Give this to McClelly at the Stack. You'll have to walk. You're the only rustler and there's no sense in sending a bus for just one man. Besides, you should worry; you're getting paid from now on. If walking's the hardest work you have to do, you'll be lucky."

"Okay, okay. Let's have her."

He took the card and started up the road to the Stack. It was a hot July day and the exertion of climbing soon made him remove his jacket. A couple of flies buzzed around his head with soothing sounds. They reminded him of fishing—of luxuriously stretching his legs on the bank of a stream and baking in the sunlight. Far up, on top of the mountain, the Big Stack reared upward to the height of 585 feet. A silvery-grey mass drifted from its top and lazily blended into the deep blue of the sky. Its soft cloud-like formations looked deceptively gentle against the background made hard by the glaring sun. He almost forgot his grumbling.

As he kept mounting upward the Big Stack began to grow and became formidable. It lost its beauty, and its size became overpowering. He began to think again of his job. He was certain he wouldn't get one of the better jobs. A rustler was always put to either rappin' treaters or dumping flue dust.

When you rapped treaters you took a bamboo pole and rapped the dust from plates inside chambers that are built right into the stack. These plates are sheets of corrugated roofing steel, twenty-one feet wide and twenty-four feet high. They are hung vertically, twelve inches apart, in box-like chambers that form the treaters. Between them are rows of small chains, suspended at five-inch intervals. The chains carry a static charge of electricity at a tension of 62,000 volts. When the smoke and gases rise between the plates, the electricity charges the fine particles of dust and repels them from the chains to the plates. The plates are grounded so that the dust particles lose their electrical charge and cling to the plates until they collect in masses large enough to fall through the rising gas to hoppers in the bottom of the chamber. . . . Dumping flue dust is when you get into the tunnel underneath the treaters and pull the lever that opens these hoppers so the dust runs into ore cars to be hauled away to the arsenic plant.

It all sounds fine when you explain it that way, but the new man wasn't thinking of technical processes. He wasn't concerned with the fact that arsenic recovered as a by-product from the smoke and gases that formerly passed off into the air as waste matter now form the basis of a huge industry in itself. He wasn't concerned with farmers who dusted their fields and fought insect plagues with that same arsenic. He was thinking of the 62,000 volts in the chains and the burning and poisonous qualities of arsenic.

It was true that precautions had been taken to eliminate the danger of electrocution and that men were rarely killed. But he remembered cases when something had gone wrong. He remembered stories of the smell of burning flesh, of the blue hole where the juice had passed through a man's feet on out of his body, of rigid forms toppling from the cat walk. He realized that these stories were told by men whose constant companionship with death causes them to exaggerate tragedy in order to relish it the more. He realized all this, but the stories were there in his mind. And, somehow, death by electrocution seemed tawdry after the violent, threatening spectacle of the hot metal.

It was the same with dumping flue dust. That didn't bring violent death, but there was always the chance of getting burned. Here, too, you took precautions, to keep the dust away from your skin. When you sweat and the dust touches your skin it turns to arsenious acid that eats into the body and

Joe Messer, lifter, at the new converter, Washoe Smelter, Anaconda, 1943. Photograph by R. I. Nesmith. Courtesy Montana Historical Society Research Center Photograph Archives, Helena (Lot 19 A371).

Lowering new machinery, Flotation, Washoe Smelter, Anaconda, 1942. Photograph by R. I. Nesmith. Courtesy Montana Historical Society Research Center Photograph Archives, Helena (Lot 19 A102).

leaves nasty sores. There is something unpleasant and humiliating about these sores—under the arms, between the legs, around the waist. You look at them and treat them in the privacy of your room. You're ashamed of them. No, it's not like the hot metal, where the leaping, roaring flames and the fiery glow of molten metal places danger on a high level.

As he reached the high line where they dump the great cars of copper ore from the Butte mines, he stopped on a landing of the stairway to "take five" and look back. Below him stretched the reduction works—immense and spreading, like the reptile the plant was named for. The great buildings seemed to flow down the mountainside, wrapping themselves around rocky ledges with snakelike purpose. They were built that way to take advantage of gravity. Raw ore was dumped in at the top and wandered down through the buildings, everywhere undergoing different processes, to the smelters at the bottom of the hill. Here the treated ore was fused and turned into molten copper.

Because he had worked in almost every department on the Hill, his eye, as it roved from building to building, visualized what was happening in each. He watched an automatic dumper grasp in its iron claws a big ore car, fresh from the mines of Butte. He saw it pick it up and turn it upside down, spilling the rock into a huge bin.

He imagined the scene inside the great building

The Washoe Stack, Anaconda, 1943.
Photograph by R. I. Nesmith. Courtesy
Montana Historical Society Research Center
Photograph Archives, Helena (Lot 19 A396).

Workers in locker room, Washoe Smelter, Anaconda, 1942. Photograph by R. I. Nesmith. Courtesy Montana Historical Society Research Center Photograph Archives, Helena (Lot 19 A142a).

built right onto the bin. He could see the doors open and the ore come tumbling down onto the iron bars called grizzlies. He could hear the crashing of rocks, too big to pass through the bars. He could see and hear them moving toward the crushers—in whose jaws they were crunched and chewed until they were at last spewed out, small enough to drop between the bars to conveyor belts below.

In another building farther down the Hill he could sense the ore being crushed still further until it was sand. He could hear the chattering and throbbing of the Hardinge mills with their iron balls pounding the sand. He could see the Anaconda and the Dorr classifiers letting the finely ground ore through and rejecting the coarser stuff. He could hear the bubbling and murmuring of muddy water rushing through little flumes called launders as it washed the finely ground ore toward the flotation machines.

The flotation machines in another building mixed the ore with pine oil and chemicals and blew air into it, until the mixture became a slimy foam. In this process the copper sticks to the oily bubbles and rises to the top; the waste material at the bottom is washed away. The slime goes to great Dorr thickening tanks where it is brought to the consistency of pancake batter. Then it is passed over Oliver filters, shaped like barrels and the water is drawn out. He could see these giant mud pies, rich in copper, zinc, lead, gold, silver,

and other metals, being scraped off and loaded in cars for a trip to the roasters.

As his eye moved toward the roaster building, he saw one of the little trains of cars dart out and puff its way up the track. Alongside the big railroad cars these trains looked like toys, but they were big enough if you had to work on them. Little sputtering engines, charged with compressed air, rushed the cars along like a crotchety old spinster herding a crowd of children. The train mounted to the top of the roasters and dumped its load of concentrates.

Inside the roasters the furnaces were built with several floors, and on each floor revolving arms shaped like wide garden rakes pushed and stirred the concentrated ore which dropped from one floor to another. The ore glows a deep orange-red as the sulphur commences to burn. Finally it comes out at the bottom red hot and is dumped into trains of iron cars that carry the smoking material called calcine to the smelting departments at the bottom of the mountain.

His eyes dwelt on the smelters with a mixture of respect and hatred. The blackened buildings with their giant stacks looked like the charred remains of a forest fire. Down there was the hot metal; with its menace that fascinated him. He could see the calcine being dumped into the reverberatory furnaces along with charges of dust and unroasted concentrates. He could hear the roar of the gas used for fuel. From the door of each furnace came a wild red glow like the blood-shot eye of a Cyclops.

He could see the converter furnaces, huge truncated cones, that spouted flames, changing from yellow through orange and red to blue. Then there were the fiery rivers of molten copper when they tapped the furnaces, and the darker slag or waste material that was discarded. There were anodes, 630-pound slabs of copper—the finished product as far as the smelters were concerned. These would be further refined and made into wire and cables, but that was some one else's concern.

The rustler on the stairway finished his mental tour as his eyes lit upon the main flue. Sixty feet wide and extending twenty feet above and seventeen feet below the ground, it ran from the smelters on up the Hill towards the Big Stack. Nearly a mile of smaller flues from the various furnaces were connected with it. As it neared the Stack it widened out to one hundred and twenty feet. This is the flue that carries the smoke and gases, rich in metals, that must be recovered by the treaters. The rustler swung his jacket over his shoulder and started climbing upward once again, his grumbling mood returning as he toiled up the steps.

When he reached the top the Stack no longer had form. It was too big—a huge mass of bricks that went up and up and up, overpoweringly. He found the office and gave his time card to the boss.

"Go over to that white stack. You'll find a man there who will tell you what to do."

He entered the door of the shack, a tiny one-room affair, and found a fellow stretched on a bench, reading a copy of *Western Story*. It was Mickey O'Brien, an old friend. He laughed.

"So they finally got you, too."

"Yeah. I guess it's better than nothin'!"

"Yeah, that's right. Is that all you got to do?"

"This is plenty," Mickey tossed the magazine to one side. "You know as well as I do, any time you get a chance to read there's a catch in it."

"That's a fact."

"Remember that guy we saw down town that looked as if the side of his face was eaten off by cancer?"

"Yeah?"

"He had this job before I did. He got some arsenic in his tear duct."

Mickey went to a cupboard from where he took a big roll of cheesecloth, clothes and other gear. "We're dumping flue dust," he said. "I'll show you how to wrap up."

He tore off a large hunk of cheesecloth and wrapped it around the rustler's head, tying two ends behind so that it fitted like a cap, with part hanging down over his neck and shoulders like the riggings

Arabs and members of the Foreign Legion wear on the desert. He took another piece of cloth and wrapped it around the rustler's face like a bandit's mask. Another cloth went around the neck and a smaller piece was placed over the bridge of the nose, connecting the mask and cap so that only the eyes peered out.

The rustler now pulled on a pair of rubber boots that reached his knees. Then he got into a pair of woolen coveralls that hung to his ankles, and buttoned them up around his neck and wrists. Fur trimmed goggles went over the cheesecloth on his face, fitting tightly around his eyes. A large dust mask covered his nose and mouth so that the air he breathed would be filtered. Over everything went a woolen hood with an opening for the eyes, nose and mouth.

Lastly, he drew on a pair of gauntlet gloves and over them a pair of canvas sleeves that reached from his wrists to a point above his elbows. When he had finished dressing no part of him was exposed. Mickey, while dressing likewise, told the rustler to follow him and to copy his actions.

The two men made their way to the tunnel under the treaters. As they walked

Arsenic worker, Washoe Smelter, Anaconda, ca. 1942. Photograph by R. I. Nesmith. Courtesy Montana Historical Society Research Center Photograph Archives, Helena (Lot 19 A34).

the hot July sun beating down on the rustler's heavy woolen clothes started him sweating. He remembered what would happen if the arsenic dust reached his skin with all that sweat, and he tried hard to stop, but the thought caused him to sweat even more. At the tunnel they found a couple of huge ore cars spotted on the tracks.

Mickey gathered some gunny sacks and started cutting them into small strips with a knife. With these they began to chink the cracks in the bottom of the cars, which could be opened like hoppers in order to dump their contents. It seemed to the rustler as if they'd never get those holes and cracks filled up. Every time he thought he was through he'd take a look and see daylight. At last Mickey tapped him on the shoulder and started toward the door.

When they got out into the sunlight again, Mickey led him to an air hose and started to blow the dust from his clothes. Carefully, he went over every section of cloth; satisfied at last, he removed his hood and muzzle.

"You want to be real careful to blow off good," Mickey told him. "Then wash good in cold water. If you don't you might get some dust on you and get burned. I've been here two weeks now, and I haven't gotten burned yet. Some guys'll get burned the first day."

They went inside and stripped down. It was

11:30 so they started to eat their lunches. After lunch Mickey returned to his western stories, while the rustler found himself an old newspaper. About one o'clock they dressed again to get ready for the actual dumping of the dust.

"When you pull the lever," Mickey said, "pull it slow. This flue dust is finer than water. It'll shoot down into the car if it's going too fast and boil up and splash all over the place. Take it easy."

The rustler nodded.

"I ain't given you no baloney," Mickey added. "I seen cars standing half full of water when it's been rainin'. And I seen that flue dust shoot right through that water and run out cracks that weren't big enough to let that water out. That's why we got to chink it careful."

They went back into the tunnel and Mickey showed him how to pull the lever. In no time at all a thick dust fog had settled like a pall over the place. Mickey became a ghostly shape flitting around cars that seemed like things from another world. The silence interspersed with the soft phut-phut of the dropping dust was frightening. He wished it would hurry. He wondered if his clothes and that dust mask could really keep the arsenic out. His thoughts caused him to sweat and his glasses began to steam. Unconsciously he reached up to wipe them off. When he touched them he remembered the man with his eye eaten out by arsenic. He became panicky and opened the lever a little wider to hurry it. There came a soft sound like the rustling of silk and a flood of dust slapped him in the face and trickled down over his clothes. The car was boiling over. He was almost ready to run when he felt Mickey's hand gently but firmly pushing the lever closed. When the dust once more resumed flowing in a slow steady stream, Mickey passed on, giving him a slap on the back. It seemed like ages before he saw Mickey signaling him from the top of the car that it was full and he could close the hopper tight.

When they got out in the sunlight again it was like coming into a new world. Blowing the dust off his clothes, he was even more careful than Mickey had been in the morning. At last they were finished, and removed their work togs. In the shower room, he blew off his town clothes, too, with an air hose.

Context, Subjectivity, and the Built Environment at the Anaconda Reduction Works: An Afterword

Matthew Basso

This afterword uses Edward Reynolds's wonderful 1941 short story "Anaconda" and some of my own research on three Montana copper towns—Butte, Anaconda, and Black Eagle—during the World War II era to consider aspects of the relationship between the built environment and the formation of individuals' sense of themselves and others' sense of them.[2] Reynolds's story tracks a local Anaconda man who seeks work at the Anaconda Reduction Works late in the Great Depression. The protagonist shares his observations about being hired and then traveling through the plant to his eventual work site at the Stack. Reynolds's rich portrait of the Reduction Works offers many ways to consider the place of landscape and the built environment in people's lives. I argue that it reveals a geography of masculine status, visible only to workers, that overlays the built environment of the plant.

It's fitting that Reynolds, in his effort to detail the workings of the Anaconda Reduction Works—more commonly called the Anaconda smelter—chose to have his protagonist moving toward and eventually working in the Stack. Whether you're a native of Anaconda or have only passed it driving down I-90, the Stack likely looms large in your memory of the town. Yet, while folks with widely divergent associations to Anaconda share this tie, what the Stack represents to them can vary dramatically, as Laurie Mercier noted in a 1988 article on the subject.[3]

For some, the 585-foot landmark, which is the single remaining piece of the once massive Anaconda Reduction Works, is the last vestige of an industrial past that saw thousands of locals employed in good jobs. The continuing presence of the Stack in Anaconda, after the rest of the Reduction Works was torn down following the plant's closure in the early 1980s, prompts, for this group, memories of better times, of America's industrial might, and of the vibrant immigrant culture that once characterized the town. For others, the Stack symbolizes the pollution that came from the Reduction Works, sudden job loss, and corporations' abandonment of small-town America.[4] A third cohort, made up of the men and the few women that worked at the Anaconda Reduction Works, experienced the Stack in a way that only they, and perhaps those with whom they shared that insider knowledge, understood.

In this article, I uncover those insider resonances in a historically attuned way. This can be challenging because the extant evidence does not always speak directly to such questions, but I believe such an approach can reveal another layer of how the built environment shapes our lives.[5] Although Anaconda and Butte are now "postindustrial" places, the general precepts the story "Anaconda" offers about how worker subjectivity interacts with the built environment may also apply to other cases.

As Reynolds's protagonist illustrates, for folks employed at the smelter, the Stack provided a key landmark by which to map the other work areas at the Reduction Works. For workers, thinking about the Stack also led inevitably to thinking about the jobs housed within and around the structure. Witness the narrator's characterization of the difficult and dangerous work involved in "[r]appin' treaters or dumping flue dust." Rather than positions that were sought after by all workers because they showed one's manliness, they were "job[s] for sodbusters and greenhorns"—that is, men who had never worked at the plant before and farmers who, during hard times and lulls in agricultural work, often sought jobs at the Reduction Works. In another story about life at the smelter, Reynolds characterized these "sodbusters and greenhorns" as comprising mainly the "Okies and Arkies," who, like John Steinbeck's Joad family, famously left the lower Midwest during the Dust Bowl to seek work in the West.[6] "Anaconda" shows that jobs in the smelter—as well as the men who occupied them, whether they were "sodbusters" or experienced locals—and the structures that housed them, such as the Stack, had discrete reputations about which outsiders, misled

by stereotypes about how status is formed among the working class, often had no clue. In short, the reputation of a job, especially in regard to masculine status, emerged from more than a job's inherent difficulty and danger.

Research by sociologists and historians who concentrate on workplace dynamics indicates that the perception of a job and the workers who occupy it is established early in the life of a work site by the actions of the employer and the initial cohort of employees. Although these scholars tend to focus on gender and race segregation, and not on the relationship between the built environment and subjectivity per se, their studies of meat packing, electrical goods, textile manufacturing, cigar making, and other industries clearly show that workers saw the distinctions among various jobs geographically. Once set, the reputation of a job was very difficult to change.[7] Nonetheless, a comparison of the reputation of certain site-specific jobs within the Anaconda Reduction Works in the pre–World War II period to how workers perceived those jobs and sites *during* World War II indicates that the narratives workers created about jobs were mutable to a certain extent. The importance of paying attention to context—meaning place, time, and the specific identities of the people engaging with the structures and spaces in question—as we assess the meanings insiders ascribe to built environments emerges immediately in Reynolds's story.

The protagonist begins his journey into the built environment of the Reduction Works in the same place as most other workers did: the Company's downtown employment office. In this brief scene, context operates in multiple ways. First, this is one of a handful of times that "Anaconda" takes the reader outside of the smelter, illuminating the difference between the worlds within and outside the plant gates. The other notable instance of this is when the protagonist's imagination takes us to his favorite fishing spot, where he imagines "luxuriously stretching his legs on the bank of a stream and baking in the sunlight." Occurring as it does when the protagonist is laboring to reach his prescribed work site, the Stack, this mention of leisure space joins the idea of leisure to the "natural" landscape/nonbuilt environment around the town. Thus, natural spaces of leisure are contrasted with the plant's built environment and the physical nature of smeltermen's work.[8]

The contrast between the built environment of the downtown employment office and that of the smelter is perhaps not as obvious as that between the worlds of labor and leisure. Yet, in regard to the human geography of the smelter both before and during World War II, the white-collar labor that characterized the employment office provided an important foil for the smelter's blue-collar employees as they sought to claim the financial and psychological wages that combined to help form workers' masculine status.[9] This is a second overlay of context in relation to the employment office. The desire to claim status over bosses emerged in part, as Reynolds's short story shows, as a response to the reality that the white-collar men who worked in the employment office and other supervisory sites had power to influence the material realities of smeltermen's daily lives. Recall the protagonist's anger at being assigned to work at the Stack: He had been "[g]rumbling ever since the clerk in the employment office downtown had given him a work card for the Stack. The Stack! Rappin' treaters or dumping flue dust. That was a job for sodbusters and greenhorns. Not for a guy that had been born and raised right here on the ground, here in Anaconda." The worker's displeasure reminds us that Anaconda's smeltermen—like their counterparts in Butte and Black Eagle and, indeed, throughout the U.S. labor movement in the last half of the 1800s and the first half of the 1900s—cherished a sense of themselves as "independent" working men who strove to maintain "equality" with their bosses.[10]

Historians and gender studies scholars have shown that, when working-class men perceived the exercise of power by white-collar men as unfair, they reacted not just by complaining but also by making an effort to seize back control and by their own superiority in the realm of masculinity. Steve Meyer's study of the auto factories, for example, shows that this effort could occasionally include fights and other physical violence. In Butte and Anaconda before and during the war, contests with specific foremen and other managers more often led to wildcat strikes by the workers of a particular area of the plant or mine. More subtle forms of assertion often found workers championing their "productive" masculinity with its physicality over the intellectual labor and uncertain productivity of their bosses. In Montana's copper facilities, foremen, clerks, and other lower-level managers consistently heard workers refer to them not as "company men" but as "company boys."[11] Sometimes workers used this term jokingly, to kid men who had left labor's ranks, but at other times it became a way to emasculate clerks and managers, particularly those who seemed either overly beholden to the company's upper echelon or unwilling to deal with workers fairly. A similar trace of derision accompanied other examples of local vernacular for white-collar workers, including "book miners" or "fifth floor guys"—mining technicians who worked on the fifth floor of the ACM headquarters in Butte—and "pencil pushers" or "ink slingers"—timekeepers who kept track of the workers' hours. On the other hand, local terms such as "Brains" for a smelter's assaying and chemical department appeared laudatory. "Big Boy," a name for the smelter manager, was more ambiguous.[12]

At least one of the nicknames used for managers had a clear spatial undertone, but even when the terms used to draw distinctions between employee and employer masculinity did not specifically reference the geography of the plant, insiders still saw the built environment of the plant as compartmentalized along these lines. For although a company "owned" the grounds, equipment, and structures that a plant comprised, workers and supervisors each were tied to certain spaces and places within and, as the references to Anaconda's bars (a worker space) and the employment office (a bosses' space) show, even outside the facility. Many of the battles between employees and employers were sparked by arguments about who controlled the space in which workers and bosses most often interacted. Labor historians use a geographic metaphor in describing these as fights over control of the "shopfloor." In a plant the size of the Anaconda Reduction Works, there were far more areas where employee and employer met than just the formal "shopfloors" where production occurred. Each of these places witnessed interactions that helped define the meaning of the surrounding built environment for insiders.

Among the places that witnessed a contest between employee and employer was the area between the plant gate and the timekeeper's window. Even though Reynolds's short story does not mention it, any smelter worker of the time would have encountered a management representative, the watchman, either at the gate or on the way to the timekeeper's window. The watchman was also the last person associated with the Company that workers encountered on their way out of the Reductions Works. The practice of employing watchmen to surveil workers as they entered and exited the plant marked this particular space as one that the Company owned and controlled, while also, like the gate itself, serving as a reminder that the entire facility was owned by the ACM and, thus, theoretically was controlled by management. However, as the above photograph illustrates, workers often responded to this projection of power by studiously ignoring the watchmen and thus, arguably, the ACM's claim of control.

When Reynolds submitted "Anaconda" to the editor of *Men at Work* in the middle of 1941, the timekeeper at his window and the watchman at the gate symbolized administrative oversight and a form of white-collar masculinity that drew status through its connection to the Company's power. That symbolism continued during World War II, but workers who had tended to either poke fun at or ignore the watchmen and timekeepers began to see these men as representing the inequities in the U.S. government and the ACM's policies regarding wartime labor. As early as the summer of 1942, production workers at all three of the ACM's major Montana copper facilities exhibited frustration with what they saw as the Company's effort

to protect white-collar workers like timekeepers and watchmen from more difficult production jobs or from military service.

Although workers were never keen about the lack of trust implied by the use of watchmen, prior to World War II, management had traditionally appointed "old employees of the plant" to these security positions as a reward for their service on production jobs. In the first year of the war, however, with government demands for greater security against both outside attacks and possible sabotage from within, the watchmen force grew and came to be constituted of a mix of younger and older workers.[14] Initially, it seemed possible that the watchman's position, buttressed by semi-military authority, accoutrements, and guns, might be akin to soldiering and thus hold a fairly high status among smeltermen. But, like most Americans, Montana's copper men perceived a difference between actual soldiers and homefront guards.[15] In addition, the presence of older men amid the watchmen diminished the apparent abilities and masculine status of these security forces. Furthermore, once early fears of a Japanese invasion subsided, the contribution of those forces to the war effort appeared questionable. Most importantly, the able-bodied men on the watch force were perceived as being protected from difficult production jobs and military service by the ACM and, therefore, as placing a burden on other men in the plant either to take more difficult production jobs or to join the military.[16] Thus, during World War II, the area between the timekeeper's window and the gate that was peopled by watchmen came to represent white-collar masculinity and Company power in heightened ways.

As the narrator moves away from the watchman at the gate and the timekeeper's window and enters the more densely industrial areas of the Reduction Works, in no way does he leave behind the contest over control of the built environment. In the section of "Anaconda" that sees the narrator arrive at the Stack, Reynolds alludes to the presence of bosses in these areas and to their power to direct workers. Scholars have written extensively about the shopfloor battles that take place between foremen and workers in these productive parts of plants. These engagements comprise the more classic examples of the struggle between management and labor; they produce their own insider's geography of the plant that links the built environment to perceptions of subjectivity in ways both similar and different to the watchmen example.[17] However, as my purpose is to allude to the multiple ways within the plant that the built environment intersects with subjectivity, I want to shift away from the employee-employer dynamic and toward two other facets of this issue that I mentioned at the beginning of this essay: workers' perceptions about tasks associated with certain machinery; and the tie between workers and certain jobs.

Industrial-era commentators—including workers themselves—frequently argued that the machine age dehumanized the workplace. In the mid- to late nineteenth century, the rhetoric around this development typically referenced the death of the "artisan" and the birth of the factory worker. The Great Depression, with its turn toward working-class culture, saw an upsurge of concern about the machine age and what it would mean for laborers. Charlie Chaplin's *Modern Times* is perhaps the best known meditation on the issue from the 1930s, but journalism and proletarian fiction of the era also focused on the question.[18]

Reynolds's "Anaconda" very much fits within the New Deal tradition of contemplating the industrial process, as indicated by the protagonist's meditations from "the highline," his next stop on his journey to the Stack. The protagonist "imagined the scene inside the great building built right onto the bin. He could see the doors open and the ore come tumbling down onto the iron bars called grizzlies. He could hear the crashing of rocks, too big to pass through the bars. He could see and hear them moving toward the crushers—in whose jaws they were crunched and chewed until they were at last spewed out, small enough to drop between the bars to conveyor belts below." The story "Anaconda," like *Modern Times*, sometimes seems to suggest that the machines dominate the man. However, like much of the proletarian fiction of the era, "Anaconda" also continues to center the human's role within the larger industrial structure.

Moreover, whereas *Modern Times* and many other texts from the era seem to treat all machines as similar, "Anaconda" depicts the varying emotional response workers can have to machinery in the plant. When, for example, the smelterman gazes upon the built environment of the actual smelter area within the plant, especially the hot metal section, readers glimpse an especially intense inner response. Reynolds writes:

> His eyes dwelt on the smelters with a mixture of respect and hatred. The blackened buildings with their giant stacks looked like the charred remains of a forest fire. Down there was the hot metal; with its menace that fascinated him. He could see the calcine being dumped into the reverberatory furnaces along with charges of dust and unroasted concentrates. He could hear the roar of the gas used for fuel. From the door of each furnace came a wild red glow like the blood-shot eye of a Cyclops.

For the author, the "mixture of respect and hatred" elicited by the hot metal's "menace" imbues the place with the ability to provide status that is seemingly not shared by any other location within the plant, as his other writings on the subject underscore.[19]

The two jobs the protagonist expects to be assigned upon reaching the Stack, rappin' treaters and dumping flue dust, reinforce the site-specific response of workers and also reinforce the lack of predictability regarding the jobs that smeltermen consider as deserving respect. Rappin' treaters and dumping flue dust share the traits of danger and dirt, as the last third of the story shows, with working the hot metal. For the protagonist, a lifelong Anacondan and veteran of several stints in the smelter, the treaters recall "stories of the smell of burning flesh, of the blue hole where the juice had passed through a man's feet on out of his body, of rigid forms toppling from the cat walk." Yet, the treaters did not have the same reputation as the hot metal section. As the narrator notes: "Somehow, death by electrocution seemed tawdry after the violent, threatening spectacle of the hot metal."

If the treaters come up wanting in comparison to the hot metal, the danger inherent in dumping flue dust was seemingly even less worthy of masculine status. It "didn't bring violent death, but there was always the chance of getting burned." Apparently worse than burns were the "nasty sores" which men who worked the flue dust could develop. In a language that clearly ties masculine status to the particulars of this job, the narrator remarks: "There is something unpleasant and humiliating about these sores—under the arms, between the legs, around the waist. You look at them and treat them in the privacy of your room. You're ashamed of them." These wounds he compares to "the hot metal, where the leaping, roaring flames and the fiery glow of molten metal places danger on a high level." Notably, even after he goes through the process of dumping flue dust, and feels the panic associated with the possibility that "the side of his face" would look like it "was eaten off by cancer," there is no sign the job has been elevated in the estimation of the protagonist.

The "tawdry" danger associated with the built environment of the treaters and the "humiliating" sores and potential facial disfigurement associated with the flue dust could well have been the reason that working the Stack became "a job for sodbusters and greenhorns." However, as I implied earlier, the profile of the workers first associated with the Stack could have also been the source of the place's low status. Since the ACM first began employing large numbers of workers at the end of the nineteenth century, Anglo and Irish workers in Butte and Anaconda had fought to distance themselves from other immigrant groups that were considered, by the pseudo-scientific race theories of the day, as not fully white. Thus, in Butte, Serbs, Slavs, Mexicans, Filipinos, and others considered lower than the Irish and Anglos were sent to work in mines that had the

reputation for having wetter, hotter, and generally more difficult working conditions.

In Anaconda, a similar process occurred. The most obvious example involved the small number of black workers at the smelter. African Americans, the group that found themselves placed on the lowest spot in the American racial hierarchy, were entirely barred from working in the Butte mines through the time when Reynolds wrote "Anaconda." At the smelter, they were allowed to work only in segregated crews and only at two jobs: the acid section and, when the acid section broke their bodies, on the janitorial crew. Some white smeltermen claimed the acid section was not the most difficult place to work in the smelter, but in so doing they reinforced how areas of the smelter gained the reputation, often through their ties with a particular group, for providing a specific status.

Surprisingly, the racial heritage of Edward Reynolds and his family provides one of the best windows onto the arbitrary operation of race in Anaconda. Both of Reynolds's parents held prominent places in the community. Born in Kentucky, his father Claude lived in the smelter city for thirty years and served for a period as the President of the Anaconda Smelterman's Union. Reynolds's mother, according to the *Anaconda Standard*, was born in New Orleans and "came to Anaconda as a young woman and during her 24 years' residence here gained by her noble character and charming personality the friendship of all with whom she came in contact." Marie Reynolds's maiden name was Roxborough, and although her Montana Certificate of Death listed her as "White," her family appeared in the Ohio and Louisiana census as black. Her sister Cornelia was a prominent member of the "Sisters of the Mysterious Ten . . . A Negro Order" based in Kentucky. Under the "one drop rule" that became codified into law in numerous states across the U.S. during the first decades of the twentieth century, this made Edward and his siblings either black or "mulatto." That classification would typically have barred them from the privileges, like better working conditions and higher pay, that came with whiteness. And, in fact, the 1910 Montana census listed not only both women, but also all the Reynolds children and Claude himself as "mulatto." A former Anaconda resident confirms locals knew about the family's racial background, yet by 1920, after having been effectively treated as white for over a decade, the family saw themselves legally shifted to that category in that year's census.[20] Why Anacondans received the Reynolds so warmly while they marginalized other families of color remains a mystery, but there is no question that, due to their unique place in the community, they influenced the spatial dimensions of identity formation in complex and even contradictory ways.

The Reynolds family story obviously underscores the power of local context, but to buttress my argument here let me note one other development at the smelter during World War II that profoundly affected how particular jobs were perceived. In early 1944, after fighting against their employment, Anaconda's smeltermen witnessed women joining their ranks in production jobs.[21] It takes little effort to imagine how the particular jobs women were allowed to take on the shopfloor had their reputations change dramatically. In this case, and in that of ethnic workers and black workers, context again helps us see how the built environment and subjectivity intersect.

I want to conclude by raising the question of the other, perhaps overlooked, ways that space, place, and time influence the meaning of built environments for particular audiences.[22] Using only Reynolds's short story as a prompt, we can sense, for instance, an awareness by Anacondans not just of their immediate surroundings and current context but also of an expansive geography and deeper history. The protagonist alludes to both aspects of this broader perspective when he notes that he was "born and raised right here on the ground, here in Anaconda" to parents who "had been there when Old Marcus himself, the Copper King, had bellied up to the bar he'd had built as an exact reproduction of the Hoffman House in New York." The historical consciousness reflected in this passage will not surprise those who know at least a little about Montana's industrial working class. That historical consciousness ran also to narratives about workers' organizations like the Western Federation of Miners and immigrant associations like the Clan Na Gael, as the historians who have told the story of these immigrant workers have noted.[23]

We should be equally unsurprised about the geographic side of the cosmopolitan nature, to paraphrase Mark Twain's evaluation, of these workers.[24] If we judge by the protagonist, smeltermen obviously felt connected to the Anaconda Copper Mining Company's empire, which had its headquarters in the aforementioned New York and owned plants in every region of the United States as well as overseas in places like Chile. The wide-ranging locals of the International Union of Mine, Mill, and Smelter Workers also connected Anaconda's smeltermen to their "brothers" around the United States, providing another geographic network influencing how Anacondans thought about their place in the world. Perhaps most importantly, the residents of these three towns felt a keen historical and spatial connection to their immigrant homeland as well as to those of their friends—whether it was Ireland, England, Wales, Scotland, Italy, Serbia, Croatia, Finland, Mexico, Lebanon, or any of the other nations that sent workers to Montana's copper towns.

There are no doubt many other approaches we could take to the nexus of issues raised by reading "Anaconda" with landscape and the built environment in mind. But, coupled with an effort to understand the complex topography of meaning that overlays the built environment of any work site, I believe that weighing the influence of historical and spatial affiliations like those noted above provides a productive framework for any evaluation of how people experience the landscape and built environment in which they live.

[1]   Harold Rosenberg, ed., *Men at Work: Stories of People at Their Jobs in America*, unpublished manuscript, "Writers' Program, Work Projects Administration," 1941, box A-852, folder 1 and 2, Records of U.S. Work Projects Administration, Library of Congress, Washington, D.C. Reynolds submitted the story with the title "A Day's Work." That story is available in the Library of Congress holdings. It, along with his "sketch biography," other Montana stories associated with the Men at Work project, and instructions to potential contributors, are also held in MC 77, box 9, folder 7, Work Projects' Administration Records, Montana Historical Society Archives (MHSA), Helena. Montana State University Special

Collections also holds "Men at Work" materials in Collection 2336, "WPA Records, 1935–1942," box 89.

On instructions to authors and the purpose of Men at Work, see also Harold Rosenberg, "Preface," in the *Men at Work* manuscript at the Library of Congress. For an overview of the Federal Writers Project see Jerry G. Mangione, *The Dream and the Deal: The Federal Writers' Project 1935–1943* (Boston: Little, Brown, 1972); and Jerrold Hirsch, *Portrait of America: A Cultural History of the Federal Writers' Project* (Chapel Hill: University of North Carolina Press, 2003).

2   An early version of my research on Butte, Anaconda, and Black Eagle during World War II appeared as "Metal of Honor: Montana's World War II Homefront, Movies, and the Social Politics of White Male Anxiety" (Ph.D. diss., University of Minnesota, 2001). The final version of this work is under contract with the University of Chicago Press.

3   Laurie Mercier, "The Stack Dominated Our Lives," *Montana The Magazine of Western History* (Spring 1988): 40–57. The Stack is famous enough to have its own Wikipedia entry, which notes that it remains "the tallest and possibly largest free standing masonry structure in the world," so large, in fact, that the Washington Monument "would easily fit inside." Available at http://en.wikipedia.org/wiki/Anaconda_Smelter_Stack (accessed October 4, 2008).

4   Mercier, "The Stack"; Laurie Mercier, *Anaconda: Labor, Community, and Culture in Montana's Smelter City* (Urbana: University of Illinois Press, 2001); Donald MacMillan, *Smoke Wars: Anaconda Copper, Montana Air Pollution, and the Courts, 1890–1920* (Helena: Montana Historical Society Press, 2001); Patrick Morris, *Anaconda Montana: Copper Smelting Boomtown on the Western Frontier* (Bethesda: Swann, 1997).

5   There were, and are, different levels of outsiderness, of course. While the smelter was still in operation, townspeople who did not work there, especially those with relatives laboring in the smelter, had a knowledge base akin, but not identical, to smelter workers. We can surmise that working-class people, even if they did not live in Anaconda, also had a different sense of the place, whereas white-collar tourists who saw the plant from a distance likely had little clue about this insider's world.

6   Sodbusters, greenhorns, Okies, and Arkies recur often in oral histories of Anaconda and Butte. See, for example, OH 484, Perle Watters, interviewed by Laurie Mercier, March 25, 1983, MHSA. John Steinbeck, *The Grapes of Wrath* (New York: Penguin, 2002).

7   Patricia Cooper, *Once a Cigar Maker: Men, Women, and Work Culture in American Cigar Factories, 1900–1919* (Urbana: University of Illinois Press, 1987); Ruth Milkman, *Gender at Work: The Dynamics of Job Segregation by Sex during World War II* (Urbana:

University of Illinois Press, 1987); Mary Blewett, "Manhood and the Market: The Politics of Gender and Class among the Textile Workers of Fall River, Massachusetts, 1870–1880," in *Labor Engendered: Toward a New History of American Labor*, ed. Ava Baron, 92–113 (Ithaca: Cornell University Press, 1991); Rick Halpern, *Down on the Killing Floor: Black and White Workers in Chicago's Packinghouses, 1904–54* (Urbana: University of Illinois Press, 1997). My interest in and understanding of space and place and its relationship to subjectivity, though substantially different in focus, are also influenced by such cultural geographers as Doreen Massey and Linda McDowell. See Doreen Massey, *Space, Place, and Gender* (Minneapolis: University of Minnesota Press, 1994); and Linda McDowell, *Gender, Identity and Place: Understanding Feminist Geographies* (Minneapolis: University of Minnesota Press, 1999).

8   On outdoor leisure for workers, see Lisa Fine, *The Story of Reo Joe: Work, Kin, and Community in Autotown, U.S.A.* (Philadelphia: Temple University Press, 2004). On leisure more broadly in Montana's copper communities, see Mary Murphy, *Mining Cultures: Men, Women, and Leisure in Butte, 1914–1941* (Urbana: University of Illinois Press, 1997).

9   On the material and psychological privileges of masculinity, see Simone de Beauvoir, *Second Sex* (New York: Bantam, 1961); and R. W. Connell, *Masculinities: Knowledge, Power, and Social Change* (Berkeley: University of California Press, 1995).

10   David Montgomery, *Workers' Control in America: Studies in the History of Work, Technology, and Labor Struggles* (New York: Cambridge University Press, 1979); Ava Baron, ed., *Labor Engendered: Toward a New History of American Labor* (Ithaca, NY: Cornell University Press, 1991); Peter Way, *Common Labor: Workers and the Digging of North American Canals, 1780–1860* (Baltimore: Johns Hopkins University Press, 1997); and, especially, Steve Meyer, "Rough Manhood: The Aggressive and Confrontational Shop Culture of U.S. Auto Workers during World War II," *Journal of Social History* 36, no. 1 (Fall 2002): 125–47.

11   Meyer, "Rough Manhood." One example of such a confrontation occurred on May 16, 1944, when thirty-five to forty miners at the St. Lawrence Mine walked out, unwilling to work any longer for a shift boss they despised. On this event, see: Munzenrider, "Long Distance Call to J.J. Carrigan [and E.S. McGlone]," May 17, 1944; S. M. Goettlich to Oscar Baarson, May 20, 1944; War Production Board Agreement between the Anaconda Copper Mining Company and Butte Miners Union No. 1, May 20, 1944; all in "War Production Board Records," Anaconda Copper Mining Company Collection, 239, 8/7, MHSA. See also "Company Action Causes Shutdown at Saint Lawrence," *Miner's Voice*, May 19, 1944, 1; "Miners Walk Out at St. Lawrence: Action

Is without Notice to Company," *Montana Standard*, May 19, 1944. For an example of the use of the term *company boys*, see OH 904 William Tonkovich, interviewed by Laurie Mercier, February 27, 1986, Black Eagle, MT, MHSA. Clark Davis, *Company Men: White-collar Life and Corporate Cultures in Los Angeles, 1892–1941* (Baltimore: Johns Hopkins University Press, 2001).

12   "Mining Jargon," in Box 18/12, MC 77, Works Progress Administration Records, MHSA. "Mill and Smelter Jargon," U.S. Work Projects Administration, Montana Writers Project Records for 1939–41 (originals at the Colorado Historical Society), MF 250, reel 5, MHSA.

13   The story of the tensions over Black Eagle's watchmen has survived in far more detail than that of Anaconda or Butte. Therefore, I use records from that smelter community to flesh out the changing perceptions of managerially related workers. As for the background on the wartime watch force, like the rest of the copper production facilities in the area, the Black Eagle smelter was encouraged by regional military command, early in the war, to closely examine its security. Initial military plans issued in January 1942 called for 150 soldiers to guard the Black Eagle plant, but with every soldier theoretically earmarked for frontline duty, this proved impractical. Instead, the plant hired more guards and watchmen, whom the military deputized as part of its Civilian Auxiliary Military Police force. Later in the war, the status of the special watchmen became even further eroded, perhaps partly because the Company often guided returning older men to those positions. In March 1944, the ACM decided to substantially trim the watch force "in view of the present acute labor shortage," indicating that their work was now clearly less valued than that of the men on the production lines.

Just a few months later, in June, the Ninth Security District commander decided that the remaining special watch force was no longer needed and discharged the last special watchmen from the Civilian Military Auxiliary Police. Certain measures had been taken in an attempt to ensure that younger men thus dismissed could return to their earlier positions with their masculine pride intact. All of the watchmen had maintained their seniority in the departments from which they transferred and, upon their dismissal from the watch force, each of the men received a letter of commendation. But it is difficult to tell whether these factors mitigated the doubts directed at younger watchmen with regard to their masculine wartime duty, particularly as they were forced to give up such trappings of masculinity as "riot guns," military designations, and "the wearing of arm bands denoting that they are members of the Auxiliary Military Police." Memorandum from R. B. Caples re: plant defense, January 19, 1942; Floyd S. Weimer, monthly luncheon agenda, April 21, 1942; Memo re: watchmen as Civilian Auxiliary Military Police force, October 16 1942; COL C. K. Wing to Caples, correspondence re: Ninth Service Command surveillance program, October 26, 1942; R. B. Caples to H. C. Riddle, correspondence re: watchmen, May 6, 1940; Notes on Potential Watchmen, December 17–19, 1941; H. N. Doran, Memo re: Men added to watching department, December 16, 1941; all in 169/176/5, MHSA—see other documents in this folder as well; Floyd Weimer to R. B. Caples, correspondence re: watchmen drawdown, March 17, 1944; R. B. Caples Memorandum re: Disbanding Special Watching, June 22, 1944; both in 169/176/6, MHSA.

14   Of the fifteen men appointed in mid-December 1941 to the special watch force, five were under forty, with the youngest being thirty years old. Six others were fifty-five or older, with the oldest man being sixty-seven. H. N. Doran, Memo re: Men added to watching department,

December 16, 1941, in 169/176/5, MHSA.

15   On the question of home front versus frontline soldiering, see chapter 7 of my forthcoming study (under contract with University of Chicago Press) of Montana's copper communities during World War II.

16   Besides earlier citations regarding this issue, see also *Meeting Transcripts*, October 15, 1942, 14–18, Victory Committee Records, Anaconda Copper Mining Company Collection, MHSA.

17   Montgomery, *Workers' Control*; Meyer, "Rough Manhood."

18   *Modern Times*, Charles Chaplin Productions, 1936. Leo Wolman, Machinery and Unemployment" *Nation*, February 22, 1933, 202. On 1930s proletariat fiction, see Daniel Aaron, *Writers on the Left* (New York: Avon, 1961); and Michael Denning, *The Cultural Front: The Laboring of American Culture in the Twentieth Century* (New York: Verso, 1997).

19   Edward Reynolds, "Blood and

Bread," in MC 77, box 9, folder 7, Work Projects Administration Records, MHSA.

20   "Mrs. Marie R. Reynolds," Certificate of Death, State of Montana Bureau of Vital Statistics, June 29, 1929; "Anaconda Woman Passes in Butte," *Montana Standard*, June 28, 1929; "Claude Reynolds Called by Death," *Montana Standard*, August 13, 1933; *Ninth, Twelfth, Thirteenth, and Fourteenth Census of the United States, Jefferson County, Kentucky, Orleans County, Louisiana, and Deer Lodge County, Montana*; *History of the United Brothers of Friendship and Sisters of the Mysterious Ten* (Louisville, KY: Bradley and Gilbert Company, 1897).

21   On hierarchies among immigrants in Butte and Anaconda, see David Emmons, *The Butte Irish: Class and Ethnicity in an American Mining Town, 1875–1925* (Urbana: University of Illinois Press, 1989); ch. 1 and ch. 5 of my book in progress; Pat Kearney, *Butte Voices:*

Mining, Neighborhoods, People (Butte: Skyhigh Communications and Artcraft Printers, 1998); and Mercier, *Anaconda*. See also Basso, ch. 9; Robert Vine, *The Women of the Washoe* (Butte: Butte Historical Society, 1989), on women in the Anaconda smelter.

[22] There are, of course, other ways this story highlights the built environment and landscape. For instance, the protagonist's journey from the timekeeper's window to the Stack reminds us of how intimately landscape shapes built environment and workers' relationship to that environment. Reynolds indicates that the walk between the timekeeper's window and the stack is long enough that a worker would normally take a bus. The protagonist's experience of the site shifts as he climbs up the road: "The Big Stack began to grow and became formidable. It lost its beauty, and its size became overpowering." When he gets to the "highline," he stops to appraise the plant below him: "The great buildings seemed to flow down the mountainside, wrapping themselves around rocky ledges with snakelike purpose. They were built that way to take advantage of gravity." This description suggests that something as mundane as the pitch of the ground shapes the plant's defining features and its reptilian representation in the eyes of its workers.

[23] Emmons, *Butte Irish*; Murphy, *Mining Cultures*; Mercier, *Anaconda*; and Michael Malone, *Battle for Butte: Mining and Politics on the Northern Frontier* (Seattle: University of Washington Press, 1981).

[24] George Everett (with a grateful nod to Rufus A. Coleman), "Mark Twain's Trip to Butte," available at http://www.butteamerica.com/twain.htm (accessed October 12, 2008).

Housing on the Rocky Mountain Urban Frontier: Multifamily Building Forms in Butte, Montana, 1890–1916

Brian Shovers

Flats and rooming houses are in great demand throughout the city, especially in the business district. . . . [T]ransients find it almost impossible to secure accommodations. The Turkish baths have been crowded nightly, and many Butte visitors have been forced to stay up all night, or sleep in chairs.

—*Butte Miner,* September 23, 1906

Between 1890 and 1916, mining for copper precipitated an unprecedented explosion in Butte's population and—as the above excerpt from a Butte newspaper describes—an accompanying shortage of housing. Within a brief period of thirty years, the young upstart gold mining camp blossomed into a thriving industrial metropolis, the largest population center between Minneapolis and Spokane. From 1865 to 1895, the wooden false fronts of the Butte commercial district gave way to a more substantial, permanent architecture of stone and brick. The sense of permanence reflected in the masonry banks, retail stores, and theaters that lined Park and Main streets was echoed in the new multifamily residences along the perimeter of the Central Business District. The two-story, brick-veneered duplexes and fourplexes,

clustered around the main arterials crisscrossing the Butte hill, represented a solution to a serious housing shortage at the turn of the century and expressed a building form translated to Butte from the East.

To better understand the architectural forms that appear in Butte beginning in 1890, it is important to examine multifamily housing as it developed in other industrial cities during the last decades of the nineteenth century. During the 1870s and 1880s, European immigrants crowded into the eastern seaboard cities of New York and Boston, where they found work in factories and mills. Commonly, the only available housing for these millions of new Americans was the tenement, a dwelling divided into separate spaces for different families. Tenement dwellers faced cramped, unsanitary rooms without adequate light or air. A major housing reform movement inspired by the poor working and living conditions in large American cities and the development of an interurban transportation system spawned the creation of suburban residential areas just outside the congested inner city, as well as new housing styles adapted to suburbia.[1]

The electric streetcar opened up new housing opportunities for middle-class workers' families seeking refuge outside the city center. By 1890, 51 cities boasted electric streetcar systems. By 1895, the number had exploded to 850 and Butte counted itself among these modern cities.[2] Upon arrival in the suburbs, former

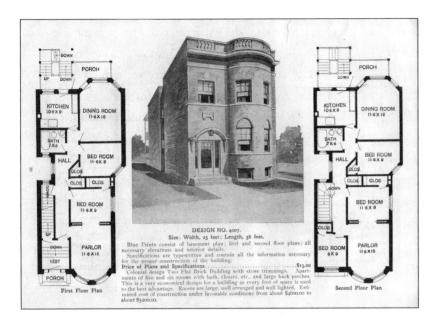

DESIGN NO. 4007.

First Floor Plan

Second Floor Plan

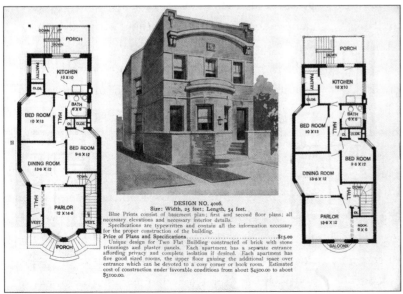

DESIGN NO. 4006.

Top: *Figure 1. A brick duplex from William Radford's* Portfolio of Plans: A Standard Collection of New and Original Designs for Houses, Bungalows, Store and Flat Buildings *(Chicago: Radford Architectural Co., 1909).*

Bottom: *Figure 2. Another example of a brick duplex plan promoted by William Radford.*

tenement dwellers sought affordable, homelike environments, which ultimately were provided by housing speculators in the form of three-decker wooden flats and two-story brick flats. Both forms borrowed stylistic elements from the more elaborate Victorian homes of the period, and they provided the tenant with an aura of upward mobility as well as the amenities of more space, light, air, and a reprieve from the claustrophobic atmosphere of the inner city.

Ironically, the industrialization that bred deplorable living conditions within the city also contributed to the accouterments of suburban life: modern plumbing features, such as porcelain sinks and zinc-lined bathtubs, were now available, as were manufactured woodwork detailing for porches and interiors and higher quality, less expensive bricks to embellish building exteriors.[3] The building forms adapted to these new materials emerged not solely from the drawing boards of professional architects but also from stock plans in building manuals and from contractors' careful analyses of completed buildings.[4] Builders in the East and Midwest used several forms that ultimately reappeared, somewhat altered, some two thousand miles away in Butte during the first two decades of the twentieth century (see figures 1 and 2).

According to Sam Bass Warner in *Streetcar Suburbs*, the multifamily building forms that appeared in the new residential areas surrounding Boston were shaped by several factors, including the size of lots, the high price of land close to the factories and streetcar lines, the popular architectural styles of the day, and the ideas of conservative entrepreneurs reluctant to make risky investments (see figures 3 and 4).[5] These speculative builders, including contractors, real estate agents, small business owners, and skilled artisans, tended to repeat a couple of successful styles. In 1916, John Ihler, field secretary of the National Housing Association, studied housing in Providence, Rhode Island, and reported that floorplans were repeated and erected house by house rather than in groups. The deep, narrow floorplan matched the shape of the lots, and the parlor and kitchen were located along one side of the duplex, with the two bedrooms along the other side. He also noted that the simple designs were embellished with bay windows, stained- and leaded-glass windows, and hardwood floors. Similar factors would eventually influence the style and form of multifamily dwellings in Butte.[6]

Butte's Transformation from Mining Camp to Urban Metropolis

> Butte grew up around the mines which gave it its reason for being. Today, to the south and west, it has grown far away from them; houses there are newer, more comfortable and attractive; many, particularly on the west side are graceful; few are a delight to see. But the city as a whole remains functional, like those functional black triangles above the mines— built for one engrossing purpose: to unearth the wealth in the depths of the hill.[7]

Although this description of Butte was written in 1949, it also accurately describes Butte from 1890 to 1916. The city's rural, pristine surroundings could not mask Butte's industrial character. The trappings of industrialism appeared in Butte with the advent of silver mining in the 1870s and the arrival of the railroad in 1881. With the railroad came the necessary

Top: *Figure 3. Multifamily housing found in the streetcar suburbs of Boston in the 1890s from Sam Bass Warner,* Streetcar Suburbs: The Process of Growth in Boston, 1870–1900 *(Cambridge: Harvard University Press, 1978).*

Bottom: *Figure 4. A brick duplex built in the Boston suburbs and a form replicated across the nation by the 1910s. From Warner,* Streetcar Suburbs.

building materials, the promise of capital investment, and the cultural baggage containing the memory of an eastern urban landscape—all of which when combined would create a modern metropolis at the foot of the Continental Divide.

By 1883, the expansion of the copper mining industry caused a great demand for skilled and unskilled wage laborers. Large numbers of newly arrived immigrants from Ireland and Cornwall responded to the call for workers. These early itinerant miners secured housing in wood-frame rooming houses and boardinghouses on the north and east side of the Central Business District, within walking distance of the mines. The largest boardinghouse, the Mullin House, located in Centerville (an unincorporated neighborhood north of the Central Business District along Main Street), accommodated two hundred single miners, with several miners sharing the same

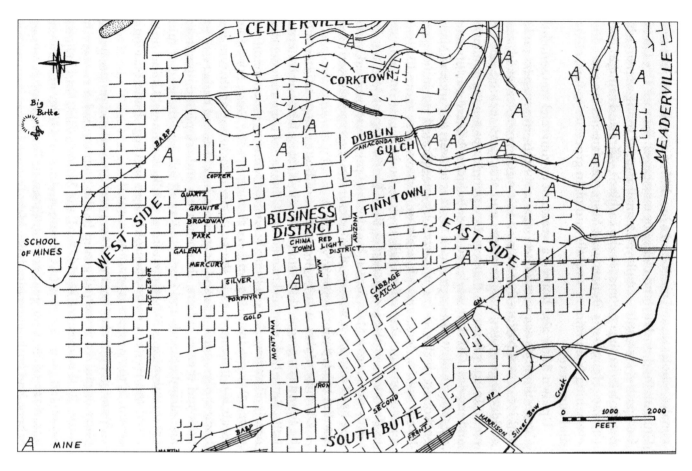

Figure 5. Map of Butte neighborhoods, 1910. From Mary Murphy, Mining Cultures: Men, Women, and Leisure in Butte, 1914–41 *(Chicago: University of Illinois Press, 1997).*

bed sleeping in shifts. When miners' families arrived, this form of housing proved inadequate. Inexpensive single-family shotgun houses and four-square worker's cottages ultimately replaced the boarding houses in Centerville and East Butte, an area punctuated by mines shafts and headframes (see figure 5).[8]

The rapid expansion of copper mining and ore

Figure 6. A bay-fronted Butte duplex found at 319 South Washington. Brian Shovers, photographer.

processing in Butte transformed Butte from a camp to a city in short order. In 1898, 2,500 men worked underground in Butte's 260 underground mines; by 1910, that number had grown to almost 7,000 men in 344 mines. At the same time, more than 5,100 men and 2,600 women supported the industrial workforce in trade, domestic, and personal service, professional

jobs, public service, and a large clerical contingent. Coincident with the exponential growth of the mining in Butte came a tremendous demand for goods and services, and those employed in this facet of the economy also needed housing. This growing middle-class group of small business owners, retail clerks, secretaries, railroad workers, and skilled craftspeople sought housing within walking distance of work, especially dwellings that offered the modern amenities of electric lights, running water, and central heat.[9] Real estate agents, building contractors, and other perceptive entrepreneurs responded to this demand by constructing functional yet tasteful duplexes and fourplexes close to the service centers of the local economy (an area bounded on the west by Excelsior, on the east by Main Street, on the south by Aluminum Street, and on the north by Copper Street).

Between 1890 and 1920, more than 396 one- and two-story multifamily dwellings sprang up in Butte. These structures can be divided into five basic forms or types, each with innumerable variations on a basic theme. The earliest form, which was especially popular in the area north of Park Street between 1890 and 1910, was the single bay–fronted brick flat (see figure 6). The most distinguishing feature of this form remained the bay, projecting the full height of the building on either side of the entry, and its flat roof with Victorian Gothic style corbelling along the top. Builders embellished the

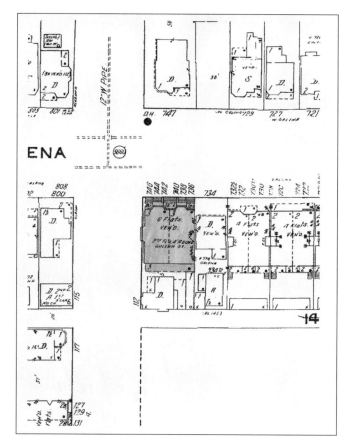

Figure 7. A Butte fourplex found at 738–744 West Galena. Brian Shovers, photographer.

Figure 8. A Sanborn Fire insurance map depicting the 700 block of West Galena.

Gothic form with leaded- or stained-glass windows in the transom and with decorative scroll and frieze work on the porches. The long, narrow lots in Butte facilitated this building form. The functional floorplan repeated itself within this form, with the front door opening into the living/dining room, which was connected to the kitchen at the rear through a series of arched openings, with two bedrooms off the living room and the kitchen.[10]

A slight variation of that form comes with a double bay–fronted flat, which features two opposing polygonal or rounded bays reaching from the ground to the flat roof. Typically, the single or double entry appeared between the two opposing bays, with an interior stairway leading to the upper flat(s). Occasionally, a porch, extending the full height of the building, framed the entry. The floorplan typically imitated the single bay–fronted flat (see figures 7 and 8).[11]

Above: *Figure 9. The porch-fronted Butte walkup at 608–612 West Galena. Brian Shovers, photographer.*

Right: *Figure 10. A typical floorplan for a Butte fourplex, located within walking distance of the Central Business District, ca. 1910.*

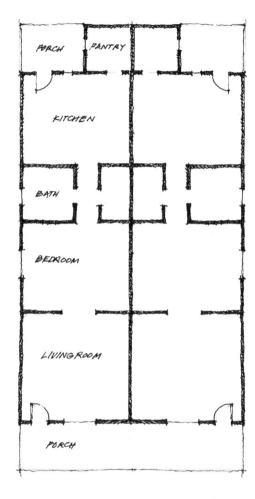

PLAN DIAGRAM
612 WEST GALENA

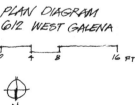

The next most important form—which we will call the porch-fronted walk-up flat—emerged south and west of the Central Business District between 1906 and 1916. This period, characterized by consolidation of the local mining industry under Amalgamated Copper (eventually the Anaconda Copper Mining Company) and the growth of the city's population from fifty thousand to more than eight-five thousand, saw construction of many multifamily housing units. The wooden, two-story porch represented the primary design feature of these brick-veneered fourplexes. The bilateral symmetry of the door and window configuration, a central stairway splitting the porch in half, and the use of a pediment over the porch entry pointed back to Neoclassical styles. The porches, framed by a flat, hipped roof supported by plain wooden posts and balustrade, created a transition space between the interior and the street, an important element of the Gothic Revival cottage. The floorplan constituted a series of arched openings separating the front parlor in the front from the kitchen in back (see figures 9–12).[12]

The porch-fronted walk-up blended the financial considerations of the owner/builder with amenities desired by a growing commercial middle class of men and women seeking housing within walking distance of a burgeoning business district. In a 1984 interview, Mary Weldon, the owner and

Above: *Figure 11. A Butte fourplex with porches at 219–221 South Washington. Brian Shovers, photographer.*

Right: *Figure 12. A Sanborn Fire insurance map of the 200 block of South Washington.*

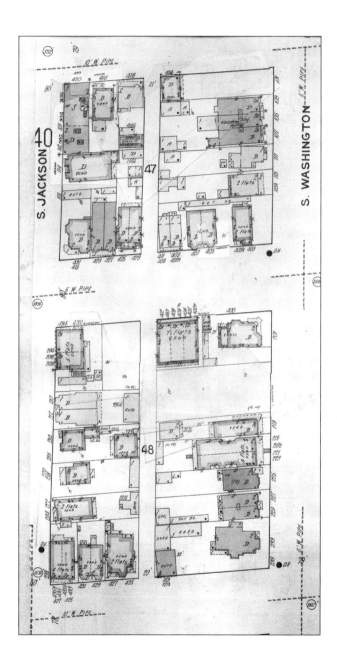

resident of a porch-fronted walk-up at 647 South Idaho, reflected on the historical importance of providing the modern conveniences of an indoor bathroom, electric lights, a gas cooking range, and hardwood floors to salaried workers while posing little economic risk to the property owner. A front porch provided an exterior space for socializing during the brief Butte summer, while an enclosed back porch provided additional storage. During the first decade of the twentieth century, these multifamily dwellings remained within walking distance of the neighborhood grocery, churches, schools, and theaters as well as the streetcar line. The monthly rent of $20 remained within the means of a clerk earning $70 per month, and Hennessy's Department Store offered furniture and floor and window coverings for small monthly payments.[13]

Two other basic multifamily forms appeared in Butte during the early part of the twentieth century: the two-story flat facade with two central entries and the one-story brick duplex with two central entries. The distinguishing feature of the two-story fourplex is an arched entryway leading to an interior stairway and the street-level apartment. The one-story brick duplex usually had a wooden porch with turned posts and a spindled frieze and a leaded/stained-glass transom. The interior resembled a shotgun house with a long, narrow hallway leading from the front to the back,

Above: *Figure 13. A Butte fourplex at 910–916 West Galena in the form of a double-bay fronted fourplex built in 1906. Brian Shovers, photographer.*

Right: *Figure 14. A Sanborn Fire insurance map of the 900 block of West Galena.*

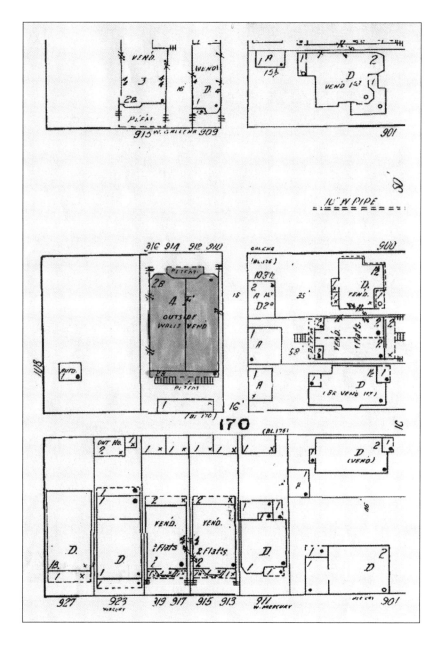

adjacent to a series of connected rooms. This form appears most predominantly south of the Central Business District, an area occupied by railroaders, warehouse workers, and some miners[14] (see figures 13-15).

A Profile of Owners, Builders, and Tenants

An examination of the Butte city directories and U.S. census records from 1900 to 1920 provides insight into who built, owned, and lived in the growing numbers of duplexes and fourplexes built during Butte's transformation into a regional metropolis in a three-block area of West Galena Street (600–900) within walking distance of the business district. Between 1906 and 1913, nine two-story brick fourplexes appeared on this one residential street. The owners ranged from the inspector at the Butte Water Company, Met Alexander (611–615 West Galena), to Thomas C. Bowden, a mine engineer at the Mountain View Mine (638–646 West Galena), to Charles Plumley, a contractor (736–746 West Galena). Only one of these men, Plumley,

Above: *Figure 15. A brick duplex found at 800–802 S. Maryland built to house Butte railroad men and warehouse workers in south Butte. Brian Shovers, photographer.*

Right: *Figure 16. A Sanborn Fire insurance map of the 800 block of South Maryland.*

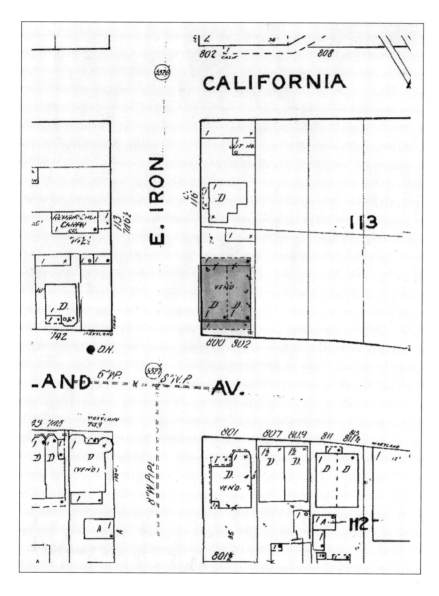

represented both the owner and builder and a resident in the dwelling for a short period.

The list of residents over time included car salesmen, miners, a reporter, a clerk of the district court, a bank cashier, and Butte's only Socialist mayor, Lewis Duncan. Between 1911 and 1914, Duncan, a Unitarian Minister and political activist, lived in a handsome duplex at 704 West Galena during a period of unusual labor unrest in Butte (see figure 17). Another apartment in this complex was rented by Frank Bigelow, editor of the labor newspaper, the *Free Lance*. The largest of the buildings at 910–916 West Galena (forty-four by sixty-four feet) cost its owner, an attorney named Lewis Forestell, $7,000 to hire contractor William Robertson to build in 1906. A slightly smaller fourplex at 628–630 ½ West Galena (forty-seven by forty-three feet) cost H. M. Mullin $4,000 to build in 1912 (see figure 18).

The huge demand for middle-class housing during this period of booming copper production made construction of these multifamily

Figure 18. A brick, porch-fronted fourplex at 628–634 W. Galena. Brian Shovers, photographer.

Figure 17. In the 1910s, Butte's Socialist mayor, Lewis Duncan, lived in this duplex at 704–706 W. Galena. Brian Shovers, photographer.

residences a sound investment. Classified ads in the *Anaconda Standard* in 1910 revealed that a three-room flat in Butte brought the owner $15 per month, while a six-room flat rented for $30 per month. As late as 1954, a four-room flat still rented for $25 per month. The amenities offered by these modern apartments represented a step above the much smaller worker's cottages or shotgun houses found closer to the mines in Centerville, Walkerville, and Dublin Gulch, which sold for about $750. Renting constituted a less risky financial proposition in a mining town jolted by periodic strikes, fluctuating world prices for copper, and a variety of other fiscal crises.[15]

Carpenters and building contractors—not architects—designed and constructed the Butte brick duplexes and fourplexes. For example, Charles

Passmore, who built several of the bay-fronted flats on West Quartz Street, advertised his services in the Butte Polk Directory under "Real estate, Loans, Mortgages, Civil engineering, and Architecture." Passmore arrived in Butte in 1889, on the cusp of the city's emergence as a copper mining center, and established an office with Thomas Jeffries and Fred Gutelius at 25 West Granite. Passmore lived in a Queen Anne cottage he built at 717 West Granite in 1898, where he resided until his death in 1946. In 1898, Passmore hired architect George De Snell, who designed for the firm until 1915, when he set up his own practice. Thomas J. Angell Jr. began working in Butte as a carpenter in 1899 and during the next twenty years built a number of brick walkup fourplexes south of Park Street on West Silver Street (642–644 West Silver) while residing in the neighborhood. Another carpenter/contractor, Charles Elderkin, who lived at 621 South Idaho, constructed a number of porch-fronted flats in an effort to "provide alternative living arrangements to houses and apartments."

The question remains, however, of where these familiar Butte building forms came from. Some are reminiscent of brick duplexes and fourplexes found in published plan books from the first several decades of the twentieth century. William A. Radford, a Chicago architect and co-owner of the Radford Millworks in Oshkosh, Wisconsin, published a collection of more than three hundred designs for houses, bungalows, apartments, and commercial buildings in the 1909 volume *Radford's Portfolio of Plans*. Radford offered a set of working blueprints for $10, guiding the builder through every detail of these wooden and brick designs. In the introduction, Radford provides the rationale for investing in a flat: "The trend of modern investments is toward income property. It has been found by experience that there is no safer investment than in well rented real estate. . . . Flats are now equipped with every modern convenience that tends to make life easier and housekeeping a joy and not drudgery."

The exterior design elements and interior floorplans of these two Radford brick flats can be seen in several of the Butte duplexes. Both the Butte flats and the Radford plans feature a parlor, two bedrooms, a dining room, and a kitchen, measuring approximately one thousand square feet at a constructed cost of between $4,000 and $5,000 (see figure 19). *The Housing Book*—a book of floorplans for apartments for one, two, four, six, and nine families, published by William P. Comstock of New York in 1919—depicts a fourplex from Bridgeport, Connecticut, that resembles some forms seen in Butte (see figures 20–21). While the exact origin of the fourplex design in Butte remains a mystery, there are distinctive elements that remain quintessentially Butte, such as the split wooden stairway and porches.[16]

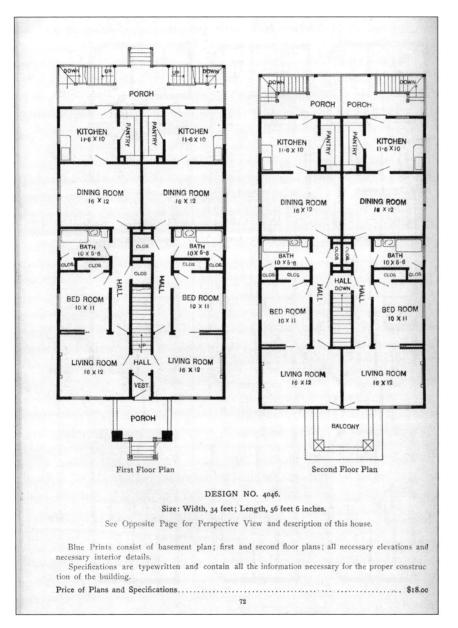

First Floor Plan   Second Floor Plan

DESIGN NO. 4046.

Size: Width, 34 feet; Length, 56 feet 6 inches.

See Opposite Page for Perspective View and description of this house.

Blue Prints consist of basement plan; first and second floor plans; all necessary elevations and necessary interior details.

Specifications are typewritten and contain all the information necessary for the proper construction of the building.

Price of Plans and Specifications.. $18.00

72

Figure 19. A plan published by William Radford in 1909 and distributed to builders throughout the U.S. was built at an estimated cost of $15,000.

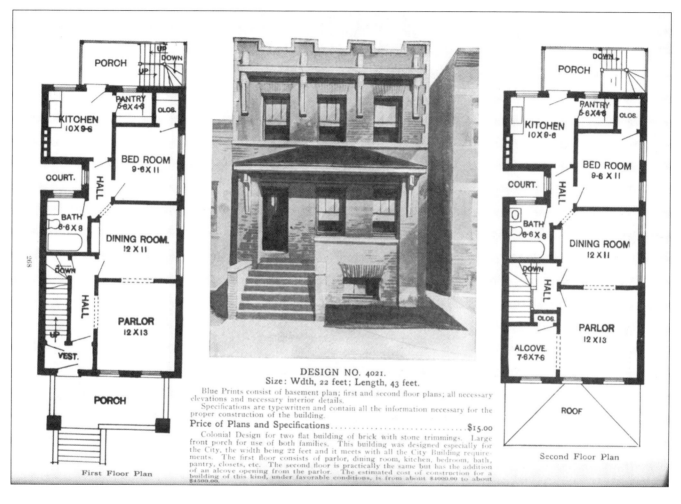

DESIGN NO. 4021.
Size: Wdth, 22 feet; Length, 43 feet.

Blue Prints consist of basement plan; first and second floor plans; all necessary elevations and necessary interior details.

Specifications are typewritten and contain all the information necessary for the proper construction of the building.

Price of Plans and Specifications..............................$15.00

Colonial Design for two flat building of brick with stone trimmings. Large front porch for use of both families. This building was designed especially for the City, the width being 22 feet and it meets with all the City Building requirements. The first floor consists of parlor, dining room, kitchen, bedroom, bath, pantry, closets, etc. The second floor is practically the same but has the addition of an alcove opening from the parlor. The estimated cost of construction for a building of this kind, under favorable conditions, is from about $4000.00 to about $4500.00.

First Floor Plan

Second Floor Plan

Figure 20. A fourplex built in Bridgeport, Conn. and disseminated by architect William Comstock in a plan book published in 1919. From William Phillips Comstock, The Housing Book *(New York: William T. Comstock Co. Publishers, 1919).*

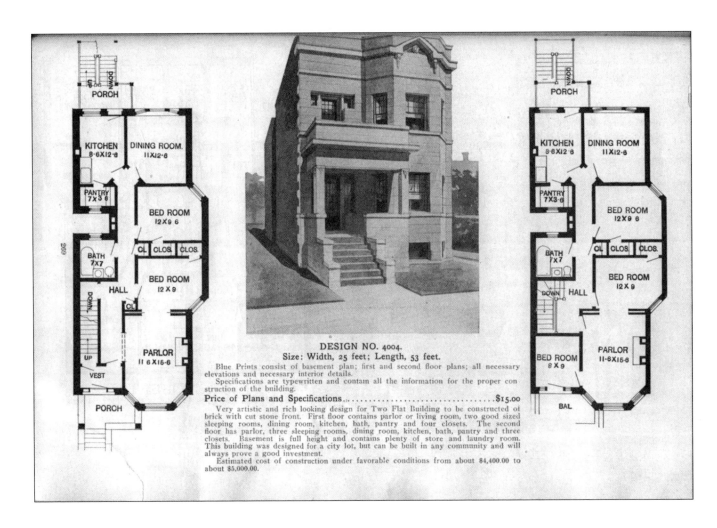

DESIGN NO. 4004.

Size: Width, 25 feet; Length, 53 feet.

Blue Prints consist of basement plan; first and second floor plans; all necessary elevations and necessary interior details.

Specifications are typewritten and contain all the information for the proper construction of the building.

Price of Plans and Specifications..................................$15.00

Very artistic and rich looking design for Two Flat Building to be constructed of brick with cut stone front. First floor contains parlor or living room, two good sized sleeping rooms, dining room, kitchen, bath, pantry and four closets. The second floor has parlor, three sleeping rooms, dining room, kitchen, bath, pantry and three closets. Basement is full height and contains plenty of store and laundry room. This building was designed for a city lot, but can be built in any community and will always prove a good investment.

Estimated cost of construction under favorable conditions from about $4,400.00 to about $5,000.00.

Figure 21. A detailed floorplan of Comstock's fourplex pictured in Fig. 20.

The Sociology of the Butte Fourplex

What economic, environmental, and cultural factors played into the phenomenon of the multifamily brick veneered flat emerging in Butte between 1890 and 1916? Most important were the availability and affordability of mass-produced building materials and household appliances. By 1910, common brick was available at both the Butte Sewer Pipe & Tile Company and Western Clay Company in Helena at a cost comparable to wooden-sided structures. Manufactured moldings and hardwood for flooring could be purchased locally at the Big Blackfoot Lumber Company, J. W. Haggerty Lumber, Largey Lumber, and Western Lumber Company. Porcelain sinks and bathtubs were sold at five firms in Butte, and nine businesses—including Hennessy's, Lander Furniture, and South Butte Hardware—offered electric and gas ranges for kitchens. Butte also had the tradespeople to do the work of building and finishing these fourplexes. At the time, Butte advertised 72 brick and stone masons, 93 building contractors, 144 electricians, 17 plasterers, and 90 plumbers.[17]

An equally important economic factor playing into the development of the fourplex design was the rapid expansion of the Butte middle class as the city transformed into an industrial mining metropolis. The thousands of underground miners and their families needed goods and services, which were provided by thousands of clerks, managers, and professionals. At the same time, thousands of women expanded their occupational choices beyond teaching, nursing, and domestic work into the commercial world of sales and secretarial work. These battalions of middle-class men and women demanded more modern housing for their families, and the brick duplex and fourplex met their needs. The high value of land within the original Butte townsite helped promote the development of multifamily housing on the narrow city lots. The proximity of these lots to the Central Business District and the Butte streetcar system (electrified in 1890) made them attractive to men and women working within walking or riding distance.[18]

In the mill towns of Massachusetts and Rhode Island, ethnicity and occupation played a significant role in who occupied the multifamily dwellings there, but in Butte, a person's nationality or line of work rarely mattered. The neighborhoods where we find the brick duplexes and fourplexes are not Dublin Gulch, Corktown, or Little Italy. A person's middle-class status played a central role in defining the tenants of these fourplexes on West Galena Street in 1910 and 1930. For example, the fourplex at 738–746 West Galena in 1910 housed a cashier at the newspaper, a clothing merchant, the assistant manager of the electric light company, a lawyer, and a department store clerk. The same dwelling in 1930 was home to a mine engineer, a School of Mines

Figure 22. The Leonard Apartments on West Granite built in 1906 to house a growing middle class population in Butte. Brian Shovers, photographer.

Figure 23. The Mueller Apartments on West Granite in Butte built along with a half dozen other multifamily dwellings during the early twentieth century. Brian Shovers, photographer.

instructor, a dressmaker, and an assistant manager of the local furniture store. None of these residents shared a country of origin, but all shared a place in Butte's growing middle class and most had families. These tenants were also influenced like never before by the mass media of newspapers and magazines, providing an ever more important glimpse into the world of consumer goods and lifestyles found from Philadelphia to Minneapolis to Denver to Butte.[19]

Although the popularity of the duplex and fourplex continued through the second decade of the twentieth century, after 1906 apartment living made inroads in Butte. Between 1906 and 1917, more than a dozen apartment buildings, some as tall as six stories, dotted the skyline of Butte. With World War I came a tremendous demand for copper, spawning a workforce of fifteen thousand miners underground in Butte. A dire shortage of affordable, modern housing emerged. Butte builders responded by erecting large apartment buildings, such as the Leonard and Mueller on West Granite and the Napton on East Granite across from Hennessy's (see figures 22 and 23).

With Butte's dominance of the world copper market in the 1890s, the newly formed city took on the urban industrial character of eastern cities like Providence and Pittsburgh. A convergence of mass-produced building materials, appliances, mass media, and a growing middle class familiar with the amenities of life found east of the Mississippi River created a cityscape unique to Montana. Architecturally and culturally, Butte looked nothing like its neighboring cities of Missoula, Bozeman, and Helena, and the

Figure 24. A representative example of the classic porch-fronted duplex, a form that appears to be unique to Butte (624–630 West Galena). Brian Shovers, photographer.

two-story brick walk-up flats played an essential role in Butte's architectural, cultural, and economic transformation from an upstart silver camp into an industrial city[20] (see figure 24).

[1] Leland M. Roth, *A Concise History of American Architecture* (New York, 1980), 138-141.

[2] Gwendolyn Wright, *Building the Dream: A Social History of Housing in America* (New York, 1981), 104.

[3] Wright, *Building the Dream*, 130.

[4] Wright, *Building the Dream*, 76.

[5] John Stahlberg, "Butte, the Copper Camp," in *Rocky Mountain Cities*, ed. Ray B. West Jr., 243–44 (New York, 1949); Patricia Raub, "Another Pattern of Urban Living: Multifamily Housing in Providence, 1890–1930," *Rhode Island History* 48, no. 1 (February 1990): 7–12.

[6] Mary Murphy, "Report on a Survey of Historic Architecture on Butte's

West Side" (Butte, 1981), appendix B, 2.

7   Murphy, "Report on a Survey of Historic Architecture," Appendix B, 1.

8   Dale Martin and Brian Shovers, *Butte, Montana: An Architectural and Historical Inventory of the National Landmark District* (Butte: GCM Services for the Montana State Historic Preservation Office, 1986), 42, 23.

9   *Sixth Annual Report of Montana Bureau of Agriculture, Labor & Industry* (Helena, 1898), 186; *Thirteenth Census of the United States, Vol. IV, Population, 1910* (Washington, DC, 1914), 216–18.

10 Martin and Shovers, *Butte, Montana*, 130–32.

11 Martin and Shovers, *Butte, Montana*, 82–84.

12 Brian Shovers, "Housing on the Rocky Mountain Urban Frontier" (unpublished manuscript, 1984), 1–2.

13 Shovers, "Housing on the Rocky Mountain Frontier," 9; Patty Dean, "Furnishing Butte: Consumerism and Homemaking in the Copper Capital, 1909–1912," *Pacific Northwest Quarterly* 97, no. 2 (2006): 79–80. There was a monthly payment of $15 on furniture bought on the installment payment plan, which was affordable to middle-class salaried workers.

14 Shovers, "Housing on the Rocky Mountain Frontier," 9–12.

15 Montana Historical and Architectural Inventory Forms, *Butte Landmark District Architectural Inventory*, 1984; *Anaconda Standard*, May 2, 1915, 14.

16 William Radford, *Radford's Portfolio of Plans* (Chicago, 1909), 268–69; William Radford, *Radford's Stores and Flat Buildings* (Chicago, 1909), 3; William Phillips Comstock, *The Housing Book* (New York: Comstock, 1919), 93–94.

17 *R. L. Polk's Butte City Directory*, 1910, vol. 24 (Helena: Polk), 825–913; *Thirteenth Census of the United States, Vol. IV, Population, 1910* (Washington, DC, 1914), 216–18.

18 Mary Murphy, *Mining Cultures: Men, Women, and Leisure in Butte, 1914–41* (Chicago: University of Illinois Press, 1997), 4–15.

19 1910 U.S. Manuscript Census, Microfilm 34, Roll 836 (National Archives, Washington, DC); 1930 U.S. Manuscript Census, Microfilm 34, Roll T626-1262 (National Archives, Washington, DC).

20 Jude Kinney, "Report on South Central Butte, Butte Architectural Inventory" (1984), 11; Shovers, "Housing on the Rocky Mountain Frontier," 12, 16.

Home Furnishings in the Mining City of Butte

Patty Dean

Note: A version of this article first appeared in *Pacific Northwest Quarterly*, Spring 2005. Reprinted by permission.

In the very early twentieth century, scores of Butte, Montana, residents remade their old homes or created new ones through the purchase of furniture and household goods on credit from their local Hennessy department store. The buying habits and decisions of some of the residents of this copper mining city—designated a National Historic Landmark in 1962—provide a window into what their lives were like away from the mines, the shops, and the saloons.[1] Attracting large numbers of Irish, English, and Canadian immigrants, Butte's population exploded 184 percent in the 1890s, reaching 39,165 by 1910, with nearly 33 percent of its population foreign-born whites. Close to 97 percent of the mile-high city's working population was male, with 34 percent employed in copper mining operations.

Few studies have peered into the domestic lives of workers, but home was one of the very few contexts where they could exert autonomy and fulfill aspirations.[2] To analyze with any certainty what the interiors of Butte workers' homes were like, however, is to immediately encounter a problem of evidence or,

Butte's rapid population growth at the turn of the nineteenth century led to residences sited adjacent to active mining operations as on Anaconda Road. Courtesy Montana Historical Society Research Center Photograph Archives, Helena (PAc 98-57).

to be more precise, a lack of conventional historical evidence. City directories and census schedules may be used to locate the street addresses of workers' houses. However, only some of these homes can be found intact, or even extant, because of eminent domain and the mid-twentieth-century open pit mining in Butte that gobbled up entire ethnic neighborhoods.

But stored within the archives of the Montana Historical Society, in the records of the Hennessy Company, which operated for nearly one hundred years, reside five volumes with handwritten entries recording credit purchases and credit agreements.[3] These seemingly ephemeral listings of credit purchases—when entered into a relational database that includes descriptive text from the store's newspaper advertisements, city directories, and 1910 U.S. census data—emerge as a rich record of taste making and consumerism as undertaken by a variety of Butte residents: immigrant miners from Ireland, England, and Eastern Europe, widows, newlyweds setting up housekeeping, dentists, boss carpenters, bank clerks, window dressers, and other workers. Such information provides a better understanding of how some homes looked in the Copper Capital of the Northwest, and how inhabitants ordered their domestic worlds within an industry-dominated city.

At the turn of the nineteenth century, Hennessy's was like other major department stories then multiplying across America's urban landscape. Self-described as "Montana's leading store," Hennessy's sold "clothing, shoes and furnishings . . . notions, millinery, carpets, furniture, draperies, china and house furnishings, stoves and ranges, groceries, meats, wines, liquors and cigars" wholesale and retail.[4] Public events at Hennessy's resembled industrial expositions, with, for example, demonstrations of lace making by visiting young Irish women and an exhibit of Navajo rugs from the Crystal Rock Reservation [sic] in New Mexico.

Hennessy's flagship store designed by Minneapolis architect Frederick Kees advertised itself as "Montana's leading store." From Harry C. Freeman, A Brief History of Butte, Montana, the World's Greatest Mining Camp (Butte above and below Ground) (Chicago: Henry O. Shepard Co., 1900).

The store also marketed "souvenirs of the Butte Mines," which included copper inkwells, drinking cups, napkin rings, buttonhooks, and shoehorns.[5]

Butte residents were in the mainstream of American commerce as a result of the city's extensive freight train service: two transcontinental railways—the Northern Pacific and the Chicago, Milwaukee and St. Paul—plus links to two other transcontinental

Hennessy's heavily promoted its successful furniture department, placing numerous ads in local newspapers and city directories such as the 1909 Butte City Directory. From R. L. Polk & Co.'s Butte City Directory, Helena, 1909.

Public events at Hennessy's resembled industrial expositions with demonstrations of lace-making by "young women from Ireland" and an exhibit of rugs from a Navajo reservation in New Mexico. From Anaconda Standard, June 27, 1911.

railways— the Great Northern and the Union Pacific. Hennessy's representatives frequently negotiated directly with manufacturers and advertised that their savings were passed on to the customer. After the carloads of merchandise arrived in Butte, customers could purchase the goods by mail or telephone or by visiting the main store in the heart of the city's commercial district or branch stores in the Centerville neighborhood's Hibernia Hall or the nearby smelter town of Anaconda.[6]

Like other department stores of the era, Hennessy's ensured that customers knew of its stock through aggressive newspaper marketing, taking particular advantage of new printing technology that expanded column-width advertisements to full-size pages. Clear illustrations of products and eye-catching graphics and typefaces in the Butte and Anaconda newspapers conveyed and cultivated the "vision of the good life and paradise" to all potential consumers—native born and immigrant, literate and illiterate, adult and child.[7] Newspaper advertisements listed Hennessy's as the sole distributor in Butte and Anaconda for furniture from such companies as Berkey and Gay (for dining and bedroom furniture), the Oriel Cabinet Company (for fancy furniture), and the Sligh Furniture Company—all from the national furniture manufacturing center of Grand Rapids, Michigan. The store also distributed the fashionable mission-style furniture of the L. and J. G. Stickley Furniture Company of Fayetteville, New York as well as dining room and office furniture from the Johnson Chair Company of Chicago.

The company found quick success in its home furnishings department. In 1907–1908, an addition to the rear of its main building extended the third floor furniture and carpets salesrooms "from Main Street through to the further end of the new annex . . . a depth of nearly 400 feet."[8] Two years later, the store—hoping to broaden its base by reaching out to those customers with minimum cash resources—introduced an installment payment plan. The tone of its "Easy-Payment Plan" advertisements was straightforward and unprejudiced, targeting "the man or woman with limited means . . . to the realization of a pleasant home without paying [the] exorbitant charges the installment houses charge."[9] Over the next three years, hundreds of Butte residents took advantage of the plan and improved their home environments.

Who were these "men and women with limited means" who accepted Hennessy's invitation? To gather a representation of the customers, the author selected eighty-eight credit customers through a systematic random sampling of credit purchases made from December 1909 through May 1912.[10] The 1910 U.S. census yielded information on the nativity, marital status, occupation, home ownership status, age, household composition, and other information on seventy-two of these credit customers. Additional information on all eighty-eight of the customers was gleaned from various editions of the *Butte City Directory*.

This combination of evidence from the Hennessy ledgers, census data, and the city directories yielded expected, and unexpected, information. As might be anticipated, about 60 percent—fifty-three of the sampled eighty-eight credit customers—held some type of position in the city's dominant copper mining industry. Of these fifty-three, thirty-six were miners

This Hennessy's advertisement noted the popularity of its "Easy-Payment Plan." From Anaconda Standard, *November 7, 1909.*

while the remainder were employed as shift boss, timberman, station tenders, blacksmith, fireman, and other industry positions. The balance of the eighty-eight credit customers—40 percent—worked in nonmining positions and included two dentists, two police officers, five store clerks, a bookbinder, a carpenter, a clergyman, a barber, a saloon keeper, and a teamster.

Of the seventy-one customers traceable in census rolls, fifty-two married men comprised an overwhelming 73 percent of the selected credit

customers, followed by eight single men (11 percent), five widows (7 percent), four single women (5.6 percent), and one divorced male and one widower (each 1.4 percent). The high percentage of accounts bearing the names of married men is undoubtedly because men were the primary wage earners for many Butte households. Furthermore, the conventions and credit practices of the time did not extend to married women, who usually were financially dependent on their husbands.[11]

This sampling of Hennessy's credit clientele indicated a fifty-fifty split between those who were native born and those who were immigrants. In general, Hennessy's credit customers were slightly more prosperous than most Butte residents. For example, 43 percent of the "Easy Payment Plan" customers owned their homes, a rate 10 percent higher than for other Butte residents. Some of the credit customers boarded with family or friends, but their furniture purchases sometimes anticipated the end of such communal living arrangements.

The ledgers' significance lies in the detailed picture they provide of the homes of Hennessy's customers. What were the external technological and social tensions shaping and transforming the American home at this particular time? What consumer preferences and cultural values can be gleaned from the furnishing and decoration of the home, this "most private and independent world"?[12] What life circumstances motivated these Butte residents to transform their domestic surroundings?

The nineteenth-century concept of the home as a physical and spiritual refuge from an unpredictable and impersonal world persisted well into the twentieth century. Within the four walls of home, a woman or man could yield to the very human impulse of self-expression and exert some semblance of control. Social critics and reformers linked the morally minded home to the continuance and vitality of an American democracy.[13]

Writing for the national arts and crafts ideals monthly the *Craftsman* in 1907, Montanan Helen Fitzgerald Sanders labeled Butte as the "ugliest town on earth," indicating its lack of suitable homes, a consequence of its mining camp development and mentality.[14] Three years later, however, an article in the *Anaconda Standard* heralded "A Million Dollars in New Homes [in Butte]" and declared 1910 "the transition year, marking the departure from the old 'mining camp' status of the community with its large lodging and boarding houses, its tenements and hastily constructed

cabins, its renters and boarders, to that permanent city condition where men and women buy their own houses and plan to make their permanent homes here. . . . Today Butte is rapidly becoming a city of homes."[15]

What were the first household items purchased when lodgers left the hazards of the boardinghouse and set up their own homes? Nearly 43 percent of all of the credit customers' initial acquisitions were bedroom furniture and linens (such goods were also the most frequently purchased). Some cultural groups—Jews, Italians, and Slavs in particular—viewed the bed "unveiled at marriage as an emotional symbol of future family happiness."[16] It was a common practice for working-class Butte residents to lay out their family dead at home for wakes and funerals, transforming the bed into a setting for the cycle of life: conception, birth, illness, and death. Appropriately, the bedroom was also viewed as the place in the home where an individual's self-expression and sense of gender identity could be best realized.

The purchases by one young man and one young woman documented in the Hennessy ledgers underscore the primacy of the bedroom in the working-class home. In early 1910, James Knox, a twenty-eight-year-old miner, lodged at a boardinghouse operated by Emma Wapler, a thirty-one-year-old divorcée from Wisconsin. Knox shared living quarters with twenty-three other men, more than half of them copper

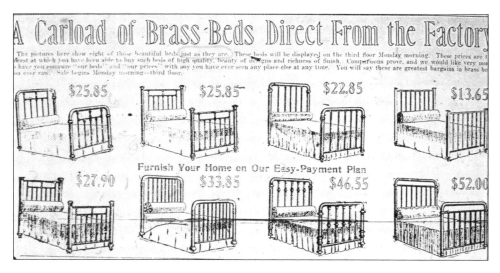

A Carload of Brass Beds Direct From the Factory

The pictures here show eight of those beautiful beds just as they are. These beds will be displayed on the third floor Monday morning. These prices are the lowest at which you have been able to buy such beds of high quality, beauty of designs and richness of finish. Comparisons prove, and we would like very much to have you compare "our beds" and "our prices" with any you have ever seen any place else at any time. You will say these are greatest bargains in brass beds you ever saw. Sale begins Monday morning—third floor.

$25.85 $25.85 $22.85 $13.65

Furnish Your Home on Our Easy-Payment Plan

$27.90 $33.85 $46.55 $52.00

Miner James Knox and other credit customers had a wide variety of brass bed price ranges and finishes available to them. From Anaconda Standard, *February 13, 1910.*

miners. By May 1910, Knox had moved to rooms in a large, three-story brick building adjacent to the Butte Brewing Company's malt storage

On May 7, Knox purchased forty-two items (some in quantity) of bedroom and living room furniture, a range and cookware, and a dining table and tableware for a total of $223.42. Perhaps because he was preparing for marriage, Knox's acquisitions for the bedroom included a $20 solid brass bed with a headboard and footboard composed of heavy two-inch posts and ten spindles. Other items included a box spring and full-sized mattress with cotton top and bottom, two feather pillows, four bedsheets, two quilts, one comforter, a pair of heavy cotton blankets with a wool-like fleecy nap, and a solid oak dresser with golden oak finish and a large plate mirror. About $15 was deducted from Knox's pay once a month at the Amalgamated Companies' Badger State and Boston and Montana mines and credited to his Easy Payment Plan account. He made fifteen payments to Hennessy's over a fourteen-month period for his many purchases.[17]

Young women also turned to bedroom furniture to start their homes. As a *Canadian Magazine* columnist observed in 1902, the "modern girl" who lived with her parents regarded "her room less as a sleeping place than as a sort of combination boudoir, library, reception and sitting-room. Here she sews, reads, studies, writes her letters . . . receives her feminine friends, and frequently brews herself a private pot of tea."[18]

Perhaps such autonomy within the family home is what twenty-one-year-old Dena Auerbach was seeking in her own bedroom purchases. A Minnesota-born manicurist, Auerbach and her four younger siblings lived with their Romanian Jewish parents in a rental apartment on West Park just off Montana Avenue. Her six-dollar bed was probably constructed of white-enameled iron shaped into "artistic" curves trimmed with brass rails and knobs. The box springs and mattress were also $6 apiece. A comforter, "both sides covered with heavy quality sateen in the choicest patterns and colorings," accompanied her new acquisitions.[19] Within a year, she had left her parents' flat and settled with some of her siblings nearby, where her attractive bedroom probably remained her private world within a shared residence.

Hennessy's credit customers had definite preferences for their bedroom furniture. Priced from $4 to more than $50, metal beds accounted for 73 percent of beds purchased by these credit customers. These metal beds came in a variety of materials and finishes: bright or satin for brass beds, the most popular bed of a wide range of Hennessy's customers; green, pink, and black enamel with brass trim for "fancy" iron beds; or Vernis Martin, a multicoated bronze pigment and varnish finish that simulated brass on iron beds. Why were metal beds selected over wood ones? Cost was probably one factor, but many Americans at the time also were apprehensive about sleeping in wooden beds, which they believed to be naturally dusty and likely to

Credit customer Dena Auerbach, a manicurist, and her younger siblings lived with their parents in this apartment building. Photograph by Patty Dean.

harbor poisonous bedbugs and germs. Additionally, the metal bed was easier to knock down and transport than a wood bed.

The more well-to-do Hennessy's customer, however, did purchase wooden beds. In December 1909, for example, James Barclay, owner of a substantial home on Butte's West Side, purchased a walnut bed for $85, a matching dresser at the same price, and a full-size mahogany bed for $65, also with a matching dresser for $95.

After their beds, Hennessy's credit customers turned to acquiring "case furniture" for their bedrooms, wardrobes, dressers, and specialized pieces such as chiffoniers. Workers prized wardrobes, dowry chests, and the like because they were large and relatively inexpensive.[20]

The oak wardrobe purchases of two miners, one who emigrated from Ireland in 1902 and another who arrived from Serbia in spring 1910, provide two examples of the special status case furniture held for working-class customers. The Serbian's wardrobe cost $25, and the Irishman paid $45 for his. The Irishman was a thirty-two-year-old married homeowner with two young children; perhaps this acquisition, his sole credit purchase, was to celebrate or commemorate an important event or family anniversary. The twenty-five-year-old Serbian was single, and his wardrobe was only one of dozens of furniture and household items he

purchased within a span of a few days at Hennessy's to create his home.

Although there are some similarities in their ages, immigrant status, and occupations, other factors besides the traditional ethnic preference for large case furniture may have influenced the consumer choices for these customers. For example, their residences may not have had closets. Nor is it possible to know if the families placed their new case furniture in the bedroom. If the wardrobe were to be used to store clothing rather than outerwear, for example, it may have been placed in the bedroom, provided there was adequate space. The Serbian's $25 wardrobe was described as "one of the largest, roomy kind with hat shelf above" and its placement might have been inside the home's entry, where it would have been easily admired and used by visitors.[21]

Dressers—ranging in price from $16.50 to $95 at Hennessy's—accounted for nearly 75 percent of case furniture purchases. Commonly composed of two small drawers on top and two full-width ones on the bottom, they were available in birdseye maple, mahogany, or oak with a golden finish or a more costly wax finish.

Miners selected nine of the ten golden oak dressers in this analysis, but both working-class and middle-class patrons could afford Hennessy's four models of mahogany dressers, given the generous price range of $31 to $95. Miners purchased three of the less expensive mahogany models, as did Grace Sower, who used her 15 percent discount as a Hennessy drapery department clerk. Sower, a forty-year-old Illinois native, lived with her widowed mother and two sisters—a forty-six-year-old dressmaker and a twenty-nine-year-old real estate loan cashier. Sower's massive dresser had a square front, mahogany pulls, and a plate mirror. She also bought three mahogany chairs and a mahogany table at the same time.

But Sower's purchase of mahogany furniture was the exception, not the rule, because the golden oak finish was the typical choice of the masses for its modest cost. (In fact, it appears to have been the only finish available in Sears, Roebuck and Company's 1908 retail catalogue.)[22] The majority of the furniture products acquired by Hennessy's credit customers were described as "golden oak" and included dining tables and chairs, rockers, china and kitchen cabinets, couches, even refrigerators. The wood's dramatic graining could be heightened by wax or a glossy golden shellac—and it was not always oak. Enterprising furniture manufacturers in Grand Rapids, Michigan, developed stains and graining machines to make softwoods emulate the more costly quarter-sawn oak or hardwoods.

Although Hennessy's offered a greater range of furniture woods and finishes than Sears, Roebuck and Company, the Early English (probably an antiqued oak finish), weathered oak, mahogany, and fumed oak options were distant seconds to golden oak for most of the credit customers. Some of the fumed oak furniture retailed at Hennessy's was manufactured by L. and J. G. Stickley of Fayetteville, New York, the famed Arts and Crafts furniture designers and manufacturers. While not the most costly furniture retailed at Hennessy's, fumed oak appears to have lacked a widespread acceptance among Butte customers. Its appeal seems to have been restricted to the store's U.S.-born professional and managerial customers, whose tastes were more current—for example, a Montana-born dentist, an Anaconda Copper Mining Company boss carpenter from Pennsylvania, and a New Yorker who served as secretary-treasurer for a shoe retailer.

Whereas wardrobes and dressers were for use by the whole family, other pieces of case furniture were more gender specific. A now-obsolete furniture form, the chiffonier—designed for storing men's shirts, underwear, collars, cuffs, handkerchiefs, and neckwear—was a common piece in the early twentieth century. Resembling a narrow chest of drawers, the chiffonier stood about five feet high and had at least five drawers. Some had small, cupboard-like compartments for oversized items and headwear. The mirror, typically measuring about twelve inches by twenty inches at head's height, assisted a man attaching a collar to his shirt or tying his neckwear. Two miners and a mine station tender, whose work attire would not have required collars or cuffs, acquired three of the four oak chiffoniers (ranging in price from $12 to $18.50), indicating more formal personal dressing and toiletry habits outside of the change house.

After their initial purchases of bedroom and case furniture, many Hennessy's customers turned their attention to other rooms in the home. Ideas about specific rooms of the home, particularly the role of the parlor, were changing. In the mid-nineteenth century, the parlor was viewed as the primary setting for social intercourse and rituals and was deemed adequately furnished when it contained a sofa, a few side chairs, a gentleman's armchair, a lady's chair, a center table, a fireplace, and floor and window coverings.[23] Interior plans of the early twentieth century—especially those similar to Butte's bungalows, workers' cottages, apartment buildings, and walk-ups—lacked the square footage to hold infrequently used pieces of furniture. There was no room for a parlor as such; multipurpose furniture in a dining room or bedroom could provide the appropriate seating and ambiance. Indeed, a 1910 newspaper advertisement offering "Three Rooms Furnished for $227.50 . . . as only Hennessy's can furnish a three-room apartment" omitted the parlor entirely, listing furniture, floor coverings, tableware, and so forth for the bedroom (which quite possibly doubled as a living room), dining room, and kitchen.[24]

Men working in the mines, such as these shift bosses (shown on their lunch break), occasionally purchased chiffoniers, though their jobs did not require them to wear the collars, cuffs, and neckwear that a chiffonier was designed to store. Courtesy Montana Historical Society Research Center Photograph Archives, Helena (Lot 8, box 1/11.05).

From Anaconda Standard, *November 6, 1910.*

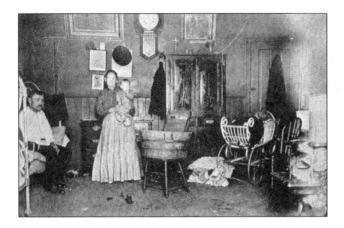

Margaret Byington's 1910 study of households in Homestead, Pennsylvania, documented the multiple purposes of a working class family's "front parlor" and would resemble those found in Butte homes. From Margaret Byington, Homestead: The Households of a Mill Town *(New York: Charities Publication Committee, 1910).*

As social worker Margaret Byington's 1910 study of households in the Carnegie mill town of Homestead, Pennsylvania, noted: "In one three-room house, where there were seven children, a room which had in it a folding bed, a wardrobe, the carriage where the baby slept in the daytime, and the sewing machine was referred to with pride as the 'front room', a phrase with a significance quite beyond its suggestion of locality."[25]

The concept of the suite itself —whether for parlor, dining room, or bedroom—did not appear to be sufficient enticement for Hennessy's promotions;

matching pieces were infrequently noted in its advertisements. A nine-piece dining room set in weathered oak, an expensive finish that appealed to few of the credit customers, was the only multipart suite Hennessy's spotlighted in its advertisements of this period. This suggests that only those who could pay cash for the more costly pieces in the first place would find matching pieces attractive. The store must have known its credit customers' preferences well, for few appear to have considered the "en suite" concept in their buying decisions—a direct contrast to the Sears, Roebuck and Company, which as late as 1908 still offered an assortment of its modestly priced three- and five-piece "parlor suites" to its mail-order customers.[26]

What furniture did these Butte residents use to portray the ambiance and opulence often sought in a living room? Rockers, center tables, and couches (some of which converted to beds) were used to render comfort and luxury in whatever room was designated for social calls and conversation. One of the least expensive but largest pieces of upholstered furniture, the couch, had been a popular form for nineteenth-century homemakers aspiring to convey their cultural acumen and refinement. Given the space limitations of many Butte homes of this period and the fact that no other large upholstered pieces were purchased in numbers by the credit customers, the couch was more likely used in a dining room or bedroom that did double duty as a

English immigrant miner John T. W. Williams purchased bedroom furniture, rockers, and tableware for the home he shared with his bride, Pollie. Photograph by Patty Dean.

living room.

The couches at Hennessy's ranged in price from $6 to at least $40, with the upholstery fabric accounting for the price differences. For example, the couch's silhouette, upholstery, and optional couch cover woven in faux Oriental rug patterns were considered "Turkish." The purchase of such "Turkish"-style upholstery and textiles by the middle class (or those aspiring to it) transformed their rooms into a cosmopolitan and languorous sanctuary, a respite from an often harsh and hurried workaday world.[27]

But the couch was not simply a middle-class piece of furniture; its imposing presence and ability to transform any room—regardless of scale or function—into a suitably furnished living room no doubt appealed also to customers of limited resources. Six of the eight couches acquired by credit customers furnished the homes of miners. Most of these customers were in their twenties and had been married for four years or less. Once again, miner James Knox is a representative example. He spent $22.50 for his couch, which probably had a golden oak frame and heavy, untufted tapestry upholstery (the least expensive upholstery alternative, which evolved from carpeting). Velour and leather were other upholstery options, with the different grades of leather available on both a $40 couch and a $20 one. Twenty-two-year-old English immigrant miner John T. W. Williams bought the $20 leather couch nearly a year after he had purchased a brass bed, a mahogany dresser and washstand, two rockers, and tableware for six. Williams and his eighteen-year-old English wife, Pollie, had been married only two years and were probably still accumulating household items.

Some miners purchased convertible steel couches or "sanitary" couches, associated with the health benefits of brass and iron beds. By day, the steel couch resembled an upholstered couch. At night, or after the miner's shift was over, the couch's steel frame unfolded to become a double bed with steel springs, transforming a room into a bedroom. Miner Albert A. LaDuke, a married forty-nine-year-old French Canadian,

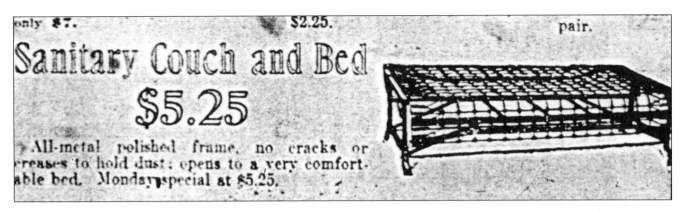

"Sanitary" beds were favored by workers for their moderate cost, hygenic attributes, and convertibility into a couch. From Anaconda Standard, *April 16, 1911.*

acquired a steel couch for $6. The convertibility and dual functions of the steel couch probably eased the space limitations imposed by the family's two-story walk-up flat and by the size of LaDuke's household, which included Stella, his Pennsylvania-born wife; their twenty-year-old building laborer son; their second son, an eighteen-year-old baker; and their two teenage daughters.

When not in use as a bed, the steel couch required a temporary covering to mask its mattress and frame. Upholstered couches were also frequently covered with an oversize spread to protect their upholstery. One typical cover, on sale for $1.89, was described as "warm, rich colors; fringed all round, 60 feet wide, 9 feet long, [and] very heavy." Such textiles

reinforced the couch's primacy in the living room while evoking opulence and a cosmopolitan taste.[28]

Hennessy's credit customers also purchased the daveno, a convertible sofa bed much more substantial and expensive than those of steel. The daveno was more popular with older, established consumers. From the representative sample of the company ledgers, credit customers purchased six davenos, ranging in price from $68 to $90. Although the company offered some davenos at the higher price of $175, davenos came in a sophisticated array of fumed oak, mahogany, or "Early English" styles.

A Butte bookkeeper bought one of the higher-end davenos for $90, while newlyweds Ben and Rose Isaac, who rented one of four flats in a walk-up, selected

Although the daveno converted from sofa to bed like a sanitary bed, it was more costly and popular with older credit customers. From Anaconda Standard, *April 6, 1911.*

a mid-range daveno with a fumed oak frame, rounded back, and wide arms for $70. Advertised as the "ideal bed for the crowded home or apartments," their daveno was upholstered in a brown faux leather. It contained "separate springs and mattress for sleeping, a wardrobe for the bed coverings, [and] when not in use [it folded] up with one motion into a handsome davenport."[29] Ben Isaac, thirty-eight years old and twice married, worked as a secretary-treasurer for the Chicago Shoe Company, a Butte store. This New York native was one of the few sampled credit customers to intentionally coordinate his purchases to suggest a suite, albeit only two pieces, with the purchase of a fumed oak rocker for $9.50 to accompany the daveno.

According to the sampling, miners purchased four davenos on credit. Daniel J. Cronin was a thirty-eight-year-old from Michigan who had been married for nine years to Charlotte Cronin, also a Michigan native; their six-year-old son had been born in Minnesota. Cronin's sole credit purchase, a "famous Owen daveno," was probably made by the D. T. Owen Company of Cleveland. An impressive presence in a living room with its "wide rounded arms, tufted back, plain seat and claw feet," this couch imitated expensive materials. Its "mahogany finish" would have been either veneer or a mahogany-colored stain on a less expensive wood.[30] The daveno's upholstery was "made by coating a cotton fabric with a nitro-cellulose preparation and

Annie Klick, the wife of out-of-work miner Fred Klick, brought a $55 graphophone home to this house in December 1909. Photograph by Patty Dean.

The graphophone (or phonograph) was a popular "Christmas Club" selection. From Anaconda Standard, *December 5, 1909.*

embossing the surface to imitate leather."[31]

The Victorian parlor often featured a piano, which served as an entertainment center for the family. But fewer early-twentieth-century Americans were making their own music; most relied instead on mass-produced phonograph recordings.[32] The phonograph was a popular piece of modern technology in Butte living rooms. Invented by Thomas Edison in the 1870s for office use, the phonograph eventually became an indispensable home appliance. According to one history of the time: "By 1915, Americans were spending $60 million annually on phonographs and records."[33]

When a December 1909 Hennessy's advertisement headlined "Something New" inquired, "Can you think of anything that would be more appreciated than a handsome Columbia graphophone?" the families of miners Fred Klick and Joe Wynne apparently answered "No!"[34] Even though the thirty-seven-year-old, German-born Klick had been out of work for twenty-four weeks in 1909 and his immigrant stepson, who shared the residence, had not worked at all that year, Klick's forty-eight-year-old wife, Annie, signed up for the Christmas Club phonograph promotion and brought home a $55 graphophone on the fifteenth of December.

Similarly, neither the unemployment of Louisiana-born Joe Wynne nor that of his adult stepson roommate impeded their purchase of a $25 phonograph and twelve records on Christmas Eve 1909. Shortly after the first of the year in 1910, he returned this phonograph to Hennessy's and upgraded to the $35 model. The phonograph was advertised as "a means of entertaining your friends and neighbors" and of providing amusement for young children.[35] Wynne's neighbors apparently did not mind the mechanized music. When the fifty-two-year-old miner was unable to make his $5 monthly payments in September and October 1910, his twenty-eight-year-old tenant Simon Daly, husband and father to three young children, authorized that Wynne's balance be deducted from his miner's paycheck.

Not only do the Hennessy's ledgers present an insightful overview of the types of furniture Butte workers preferred for their homes and apartments between late 1909 and 1912, but they are also useful in comparing the home furnishings of a range of Butte residents. For example, they illuminate the similarities and differences between the credit purchases of the following Hennessy's customers: an unmarried miner, Spiro Rafalovich, who immigrated from Serbia; Coloradoan Seligmann Herz, a husband and father who also worked in the mines; bank clerk Joseph Howard Andrews, who lived with his parents; and Hennessy's salesman and retail manager John H. Golden, who was married and had a son.

Once again, sleeping furniture—brass beds and folding beds—were among the very first purchases each of these four customers made. The newly arrived Serbian miner, Spiro Rafalovich, acquired one bed for $37.50 (nearly as much as bank clerk Andrews spent for his brass bed) and a second one, a mantel bed, for $40.50. A variation on the convertible bed, this mantel bed was probably constructed of quartersawn oak and measured six feet high and four feet wide when shut. Presumably manufactured by the Welch Folding Bed Company of Grand Rapids, an eighteen-by forty-eight-inch beveled mirror was mounted to the underside of the bed's folding wooden frame and configured to resemble a fireplace mantel.[36] Besides conserving valuable space in the flat Rafalovich shared with his male relatives, the illusion of a mantel lent validity to the room's dual purposes of living room and bedroom. The mantel also compensated for the probable absence of "the hearthstone…the foundation

Colorado miner Seligman Herz's 1910 duplex home. Photograph by Patty Dean.

Immigrant miner Spiro Rafalovich's first Butte residence was at the rear of an adjacent residence to this backyard. Courtesy Montana Historical Society Research Center Photograph Archives, Helena (Lot 8, box 4.01)

Seligman Herz's 1912 home. Photograph by Patty Dean.

Hennessy's clerk John H. Golden's home. Photograph by Patty Dean.

Credit customers frequently bought rockers in quantity and used them throughout the house. From Anaconda Standard, *July 3, 1910.*

stone of democracy."[37]

The rocker was a ubiquitous feature in living rooms, bedrooms, dining rooms, kitchens—nearly any room during this period—and the four customers discussed here purchased a total of nine rockers

ranging in price from $4.75 to $32.50. The rocking chair, in a platform rocker form, encouraged a less formal way of sitting and had slowly made its way into moderately priced parlor suites of the 1880s and 1890s. Miners Herz and Rafalovich purchased a total of five rockers: the first made of unidentified materials, one in wicker (a material "suitable for any room in the house or for the porch"[38]), one of quarter-sawn oak with reversible velour cushions and simulated leather, and two in mahogany. Bank clerk Andrews opted for a $32.50 leather rocker and two rockers of golden oak finish for $8.50 and $12.50, while Hennessy's employee Golden, who was enhancing an existing household, satisfied himself with a single golden oak rocker for $9.50. The words used to describe these rockers in Hennessy's advertisements aptly convey their allure and wide appeal: massive, artistic, easy and comfortable, roomy, strong, and well made. In short, such a rocker was just the chair a weary miner—or store clerk—would wish to rest in at the workday's end.

Rafalovich, Herz, Andrews, and Golden also purchased quantities of floor coverings, including

The wicker rocker and covered center table in this Butte home demonstrates the owner's knowledge of decorating trends. Courtesy Montana Historical Society Research Center Photograph Archives, Helena (943-136).

linoleum, rugs, and carpets. At first glance, the purchase of linoleum by all four customers is surprising because Golden was the only one who was currently a mortgage holder—the others were still renters. However, the working class often viewed linoleum as a rugtype floor covering and did not glue it to the floor; instead, it was weighted down with furniture or tacked down.[39] Linoleum attracted a wide range of buyers given its relative economy and easy-to-wash sanitary properties. Hennessy's advertisements emphasized its imitative

nature, noting that it was available in "handsome tile effects, beautiful mosaics, rich inlays," and heavily promoted the arrival of up to three railroad carloads of Philadelphia-made "Potter's Linoleum" at a time.[40]

Linoleum was usually associated with kitchens, pantries, bathrooms, and sunporches. But the large amounts of square yardage of linoleum purchased by Andrews (48.5 square yards) and Rafalovich (21.5 square yards) and the material's ability to portray various wood grains suggest that the material was installed in their smallish homes' living rooms, dining rooms, or bedrooms. To immigrants from European rural societies, floor coverings—whether carpets, rugs, or linoleum—conveyed upward mobility because in the "Old Country" floor coverings were found only in the homes of the upper class.[41]

In addition to linoleum, Hennessy's sold both carpets (long strips in rolls) and rugs ("a complete design for a single floor").[42] By the early 1900s, rugs had generally superseded carpets; carpets were tacked down, whereas rugs could be cleaned more easily by being simply rolled up, taken outside, and beaten. All four customers acquired rugs, ranging in price from 50 cents for a rag rug to an expensive nine- by twelve-foot French Wilton rug in "beautiful Persian soft-toned effects."[43] Tapestry- and Axminster-weave rugs were among the other rug types selected. Some of Hennessy's tapestry rugs, such as the $22.50 "Tapestry Brussels" purchased

The ubiquity and variety of linoleum are evident in this Hennessy's advertisement. From Anaconda Standard, *February 4, 1912.*

by Rafalovich, had a colored yarn pile looped into place by wires. The number of wires used per inch in the weaving indicated a quality product; the description of Rafalovich's rug noted it was "the finest 10 wire."[44] Both the Serbian miner and the bank clerk Andrews purchased room-sized Axminster-weave rugs, for $27.50 and $35, respectively. Axminster-weave rugs of this era were more similar to the moquette carpet, "a coarse back fabric with a deep tufted pile surface . . . [and were] a distinctly American product"—a characteristic the immigrant Rafalovich might have intuitively sought and embraced.[45]

If homemaking is a quest for stability and permanence, the lives of these four customers following their furniture purchases remained as fluid and unpredictable as before.[46] In 1914, John H. Golden was replaced as dry goods manager at the Centerville store. Probably building on his earlier "gent's furnishings" experience from Hennessy's main store, Golden clerked at Fashion Tailoring for two years before opening his own Golden Tailoring Company, which prospered at least until 1925.[47] Spiro Rafalovich continued to work at the High Ore mine before leaving Butte in 1917; eight years later, he returned to work in the Orphan Girl mine.[48] A penciled note on the ledger page documenting Seligmann Herz's charges and payments reads: "05-14-1912 Stored furniture at Sullivan's/429 North Washington. His address now Norwood Blk [Block]."[49] Mining pipeman Alex M. Sullivan was Herz's neighbor, and Herz's new Norwood Block address may have been a boardinghouse. Neither Herz nor his wife appear in subsequent city directories, and there are no indications of where they went or why they left—whether together or separately—or what the final disposition of their furniture might have been.

Bank clerk J. Howard Andrews began work for the Youlden Grocery Company in 1913.[50] On February 24, 1917, his wife, Ada May Andrews, shot him dead during lunch at the Butte Grill. Andrews's lavish spending habits (as evidenced by the money he spent at

Hennessy's) were detailed in the articles following his death: "It was not uncommon for him to give a dollar to a messenger boy, who did some service for him as a tip. A bill for $113 worth of wearing apparel, which Mrs. Andrews found on her husband's person, was the cause of a quarrel between the pair some days ago. These clothes the wife alleges were given to Ida Simmons."[51]

Both Simmons and Mrs. Andrews had been prostitutes—residents of Butte's "restricted district"—with Ada (known as Evelyn Smith in that context) continuing to ply her trade for fifteen months following their marriage. The newspaper also reported:

> She had purchased a lot in Floral Park [a Butte streetcar suburb] and had deposited $3500, her savings of four years, in her husband's name with a view of building a home. Mrs. Andrews claims that Andrews drew her money from the bank and spent it on other women, among them Ida Simmons. . . . The [elder] Mrs. Andrews, it is said, urged her son to do the right thing, to stand by his wife and make a home for her. Andrews, it is said, maintained an attitude of indifference.[52]

As bizarre as this episode may seem, it nonetheless illustrates the pervasive expectation early-twentieth-century Americans had of the home's ability to redeem and elevate.

No single formula can adequately render the complexities of the home, its furnishings, and the larger worlds in which the occupants discussed here lived. Bedrooms, living rooms, dining rooms, and kitchens were the prized spaces in their small residences, and as they added the latest layers in home furnishings to whatever they had brought with them, these consumers created their own special places weaving identity, family, and stability in the midst of a grimy industrial city high in the Northern Rockies.

1   Dale Martin and Brian Shovers, *Butte, Montana: An Architectural and Historical Inventory of the National Landmark District* (Butte; GCM Services for the Montana State Historic Preservation Office, 1986), 33–34.

2   Lizabeth A. Cohen, "Embellishing a Life of Labor: An Interpretation of the Material Culture of American Working-class Homes, 1885–1915," *Journal of American Culture* 3 (Winter 1980): 752–75. See also Mary Murphy, *Mining Cultures: Men, Women and Leisure in Butte, 1914–1941* (Urbana: University of Illinois Press, 1997), and Roy Rosenzweig, *Eight Hours for What We Will: Workers and Leisure in an Industrial City, 1870–1920* (Cambridge: Cambridge University Press, 1983).

3   Hennessy Co. Records, vols. 17–18 and 47–49, MC 228, Montana Historical Society, Helena.

4   *Butte City Directory* (Helena, 1911), 329.

5   *Anaconda Standard*, June 27, 1911. The *Anaconda Standard*, a daily newspaper published in nearby Anaconda, was founded by copper baron Marcus Daly in September 1889; he hired Syracuse, New York, native John Hurst Durston as editor. The European-educated Durston returned briefly to the East to recruit his staff and to purchase up-to-date printing equipment. From the beginning, the *Standard* prided itself on its advertisements' appearance and taste, realizing such excellence would ensure steady revenue.

6   Hennessy's has often been labeled as a "company store" because of its founder Daniel J. Hennessy's relationship with Marcus Daly and the fact that Daly's Anaconda Company offices were on the store's sixth floor. Four years after Daly's death, however, in 1904, the Standard Oil–controlled Amalgamated Copper Company sold its interest in the Hennessy Company to Hennessy himself. See Michael P. Malone, *The Battle for Butte: Mining and Politics on the Northern Frontier 1864–1906* (Helena: Montana Historical Society Press, 1995), 59, 150, 167.

7   William Leach, *Land of Desire: Merchants, Power and the Rise of a New American Culture* (New York: Vintage, 1994), 9.

8   *Butte City Directory* (Helena, 1908), 371.

9   *Anaconda Standard*, October 10, 1909.

10 I focused on a ledger documenting credit accounts and furnishing purchases from October 1909 through December 1910. To ensure a systematic random sampling of the 388 accounts initiated in this period, I planned originally to record the purchases for every third account in the ledger for this period. However, a number of these accounts were for commercial enterprises and some were for non-Butte residents, so I bypassed these entries to proceed to the next account.

11 Lendol Calder, *Financing the American Dream: A Cultural History of Consumer Credit* (Princeton, NJ: Princeton University Press, 1999);

[12] see ch. 4, "Hard Payments: The Rise of Installment Selling."

[12] Cohen, "Embellishing a Life of Labor," 752.

[13] See Clifford Edward Clark Jr., *The American Family Home, 1860–1890* (Chapel Hill: University of North Carolina Press, 1986), and Helen Fitzgerald Sanders, "Redeeming the Ugliest Town on Earth," *Craftsman* (June 1907).

[14] Sanders, "Redeeming the Ugliest Town on Earth," 316.

[15] *Anaconda Standard*, December 18, 1910.

[16] Cohen, "Embellishing a Life of Labor," 767.

[17] A survey of day wages in Butte, conducted by an assistant professor of mining at the School of Mines at Columbia University in 1913, demonstrated that Butte miners, muckers, trammers, and machinists were better paid, at between $4 and $5 a day, than were similar workers in the anthracite mines of Pennsylvania or on Minnesota's Iron Range. See Robert Peele, ed., *Mining Engineers' Handbook* (New York: John Wiley and Sons, 1918), 1357.

[18] Elizabeth Collins Cromley, "A History of American Beds and Bedrooms, 1890–1930," in *American Home Life, 1880–1930: A Social History of Spaces and Services*, ed. Jessica H. Foy and Thomas J. Schlereth, 130–31 (Knoxville: University of Tennessee Press, 1992).

[19] *Anaconda Standard*, October 5, 1909.

[20] Cohen, "Embellishing a Life of Labor," 765.

[21] *Anaconda Standard*, November 13, 1910.

[22] *Sears, Roebuck and Company, 1908, Catalogue No. 117: The Great Price Maker*, ed. Joseph J. Schroeder (1908; rpt, Chicago, 1969).

[23] Katherine C. Grier, *Culture and Comfort: People, Parlors and Upholstery, 1850–1930* (Amherst: University of Massachusetts Press, 1988), 203–8.

[24] *Anaconda Standard*, April 22, 1910.

[25] Margaret F. Byington, *Homestead: The Households of a Milltown* (1910; reprint, New York: Arno, 1969), 55.

[26] Sears, Roebuck and Company, 451–55.

[27] Grier, *Culture and Comfort*, 193.

[28] *Anaconda Standard*, April 30, 1911.

[29] *Anaconda Standard*, April 7, 1912.

[30] *Anaconda Standard*, April 30, 1911.

[31] Grier, *Culture and Comfort*, 303.

[32] Donna R. Braden, "'The Family That Plays Together Stays Together': Family Pastimes and Indoor Amusements, 1890–1930,", Foy and Schlereth, ed., *American Home Life, 1880–1930*, 156.

[33] Jessica H. Foy, "The Home Set to Music," in *The Arts and The American Home, 1890–1930*, ed. Jessica H. Foy and Karal Ann Marling (Knoxville, University of Tennessee Press, 1994), 73.

[34] *Anaconda Standard*, December 5, 1909.

[35] Foy, "The Home Set to Music," 74.

[36] *Anaconda Standard*, April 16, 1911.

[37] Sanders, "Redeeming the Ugliest Town on Earth," 316.

[38] *Anaconda Standard*, July 3, 1910.

[39] E-mail from Pamela H. Simpson to the author, July 15, 2005. See also

Pamela H. Simpson, *Cheap, Quick and Easy: Imitative Architectural Materials, 1870–1930* (Knoxville: University of Tennessee Press, 1999).

40   *Anaconda Standard*, May 7, 1911.

41   Cohen, "Embellishing a Life of Labor," 765.

42   F. M. Adams, ed., *The Drygoodsman's Handy Dictionary* (St. Louis: The Drygoodsman, 1912), 11.

43   *Anaconda Standard*, March 10, 1912.

44   *Anaconda Standard*, March 31, 1910.

45   Adams, *The Drygoodsman's Handy Dictionary*, 12–13.

46   David Emmons emphasizes this search for stability by merchant and miner, the former seeking "respectability and prosperity" and the latter pursuing "steady paychecks and safer working conditions." See David Emmons, *The Butte Irish: Class and Ethnicity in an American Mining Town, 1875–1925* (Urbana: University of Illinois Press, 1990), 156.

47   *Butte City Directory*, 1914–1925 editions.

48   *Butte City Directory*, 1917 and 1925 editions.

49   "Lease Ledger/3/Hennessy Merc. Co.", Vol. 17 (1909-1914),Hennessy Co. Records, 1889-1941, acc. MC 228, Montana Historical Society Research Center, Helena.

50   *Butte City Directory* (Helena, 1913), 100.

51   *Butte Daily Post*, February 24, 1917.

52   *Butte Daily Post*, February 24, 1917.

The author would like to acknowledge the Montana Historical Society's Bradley Fellowship that underwrote this research project, as well as Brian Shovers and Carroll Van West for their perceptive suggestions throughout the paper's various stages. Liz Dean's fieldwork assistance was also most appreciated.

"Redeeming the Ugliest Town on Earth"
Helen Fitzgerald Sanders on the Arts and Crafts Movement in Butte

Mary S. Hoffschwelle

Butte's historic identity as "the richest hill on earth" and the battleground of the "War of the Copper Kings" is well-known. And perhaps its fame as "the ugliest town on earth" is not surprising for a city ravaged by mines and smelters. Less well-known is Butte's place on the reform agenda of the American Arts and Crafts movement. This design reform movement drew its moral and design inspiration from British Aesthetic artists and critics, most notably William Morris and John Ruskin, and sought to adapt their principles to American design traditions and manufacturing techniques. The natural and built environments shaped human values and behavior, Arts and Crafts advocates believed. The modern industrial United States, they argued, required homes and domestic furnishings that would promote personal integrity and civic engagement through sensory experiences of structural integrity, utility, and harmonious combinations of color, form, and pattern.[1]

In the article "Redeeming the Ugliest Town on Earth," first published in the June 1907 issue of the *Craftsman*, Helen Fitzgerald Sanders argued that the Arts and Crafts movement could save Butte's soul. Sanders undertook this mission not only as a prominent member of Butte society and the daughter-in-law of prominent Montana attorney (and former vigilante) Wilbur Fisk Sanders but as a prolific writer of poetry and prose on Montana and the West. Her interests extended from the region's history to its natural resources and conservation efforts. Like many of her peers among western writers and artists, she was especially fascinated by Native American cultures.[2] Other American followers of the Arts and Crafts movement also shared these interests, providing Sanders with a receptive audience for her work in the pages of the *Craftsman*, Gustav Stickley's journal of the arts, culture, and political economy.

Thanks to articles about the city and its "copper kings" in mass-circulation magazines, Sanders knew that many Americans envisioned Butte as a place worthy of its own circle in Dante's *Inferno*. *Life* magazine had even nominated Butte for the title of "meanest city in the United States."[3] Subscribers to the *Craftsman* may have already read of Butte in another prominent American Arts and Crafts journal, the *Philistine*, published by Roycroft Shop founder Elbert Hubbard. Indeed, Sanders's title recalls Hubbard's 1903 characterization of Butte as "the ugliest city on earth."[4] "Fra Elbertus" had painted Butte in lurid tones as "a city built on a hill and run wide open," where "not a tree, nor flower-bed, nor spring, nor a grass-plot even a yard square" could be found.[5] Perhaps Sanders wrote to defend her adopted hometown against Hubbard, especially after he followed up his 1905 lecture tour in Montana by quoting a Miles City newspaper's claim that "Butte is like one of those female denizens of the Chicago Bad Lands, very touchy on the subject of virtue."[6]

"Redeeming the Ugliest Town on Earth" concluded a series of four essays Sanders published on Butte and the Craftsman movement in 1906 and 1907. The first three appeared in the *Overland Monthly and Out West Magazine*, a San Francisco publication founded in 1868 by writer Bret Harte and publisher Anton Roman. *Overland Monthly* listed among its "many famous contributors" Mark Twain, John Muir, Charlotte Perkins Gilman, Frank Norris, Jack London, Ella Wentworth Higginson, and Joaquin Miller, as well as Helen Fitzgerald Sanders.[7] Between 1905 and 1917, Sanders was a frequent contributor of poetry, fiction, and essays on Montana and the West; she also managed the *Monthly*'s northwest office in Butte. Sanders began writing about Butte for *Overland Monthly* with the August 1906 article, "Work of the Woman's Relief Committee of Butte for San Francisco," an account of the fund-raising campaign she organized for earthquake victims.[8]

Having asserted Butte women's claim to the virtues of empathy and generosity, Sanders addressed the campaign to redeem Butte's landscape. In "Butte—The Heart of the Copper Industry," which appeared in the *Overland Monthly*'s November 1906 issue, Sanders first retold the familiar story of Butte's early days and the struggle for control of its rich copper deposits; she then turned to a favorable account of the Butte Mine Workers Union and "the down-trodden of other lands" who flocked to Butte despite "the dark stories of the unfair town, and its reputed resemblance to the Inferno itself." Sanders claimed that, since the removal of smelting operations to Anaconda in 1903, the smoke had cleared to reveal a city where "home-spirit" and "pretty houses and gardens" promised to challenge "the Copper God."[9]

Her subsequent article, "The Craftsman Movement and What It Means," published in March 1907, introduced Gustav Stickley to the *Monthly*'s readers and suggests why Sanders thought the Arts and Crafts philosophy both aesthetically pleasing and relevant for the built environment of Butte. She found it "assuredly refreshing to turn from the sensational periodicals, setting forth the infamy and debauchery of strike and mob and voicing the doctrine of discontent," to Stickley's assertion of the dignity of work and the worker, which resonated with her own appreciation of Butte's organized miners and patchwork of ethnic groups. She lauded Stickley for envisioning a "democratic art" that would "fill the needs of the American people sanely and with honesty of purpose" through its simplicity, utility, and comfort.[10]

These design principles could guide Butte's "redemption," Sanders explained in the *Craftsman*. Writing for Arts and Crafts enthusiasts across the country rather than for westerners, Sanders located Butte within the *Craftsman*'s ongoing discussions of ugliness and redemption. Many other writers in the *Craftsman* claimed the Arts and Crafts philosophy would not only reshape urban environments but bring about a democratic culture grounded on mutual respect for all forms of labor. But beginning with Ernest Crosby's series on nineteenth-century architecture, "ugliness" became the magazine's code word for all that was wrong about American design. Stickley himself demonstrated how to move "[f]rom Ugliness to Beauty" by stripping down the ornate Victorian interior; and, just a few months before Sanders's essay appeared, Giles Edgerton showed the *Craftsman*'s readers "How New York Has Redeemed Herself from Ugliness."[11]

Sanders moved the *Craftsman*'s battle against ugliness to its reputed capital city. Butte had once deserved its reputation, Sanders admitted, but now residents were, literally, building a better future. Like Stickley, Sanders argued that reform begins at home, pointing to the Craftsman-style houses that were among the first to rise along new streets on hillsides above Butte's city center. Neither of the homes shown in her essay followed specific designs from the *Craftsman*, yet their facades and interiors would have seemed familiar to the magazine's readers.[12] Arts and Crafts architects had quickly absorbed the bungalow, such as Samuel Barker's, into their repertoire. The bungalow's strong horizontal lines corresponded with the Arts and Crafts movement's emphasis on structure, and American Arts and Crafts designers added regional vernacular traditions to the bungalow's antecedents from British colonial India.[13] Alfred Longley's boxy foursquare house boasted the back porches advocated by Stickley to capture mountain views for those who hungered for natural beauty.[14]

Both interiors exemplified Stickley's preferences for built-in cabinetry, strong structural furniture, and planes of subdued color. These elements, Craftsman advocates believed, fused into an atmosphere of warmth and restfulness that would promote harmony within and outside the domestic sphere. The Longley living room and hall, for example, captured what Stickley later described as the "typical Craftsman division between the two rooms by means of heavy square posts and panels open at top." Along with the dining room, these rooms constituted the heart of a Craftsman home, nourished the soul of the family, and welcomed visitors into their tranquil life.[15]

For those lacking the salutary influence of a Craftsman home, Sanders reported, manual training classes in Butte public schools gave working-class youth access to an education and a classless future. Sanders described high school students being "instructed… after Craftsman models," presumably not only making Craftsman-style items, whose plain designs and emphasis on structure lent themselves to student projects, but also imbibing the intellectual and moral attributes Stickley believed would follow when students associated "the work of the hand with the work of the head." Sanders echoed many of the points Stickley himself made in the *Craftsman*: manual training provided a more natural way of learning than studying books, instilled self-discipline as well as a healthy respect for both physical and intellectual labor, and obviated class division.[16]

By themselves, however, Craftsmen homes and manual training could not redeem Butte, for, as can be glimpsed in Sanders's essay, the Arts and Crafts advocates who claimed to speak for all laborers really addressed themselves only to progressive members of the urban middle class, depended on rather than subverted mass production, and constructed domestic environments that felt stark and uncomfortable to other Americans.[17] Consequently, over the past century, the reputations of Gustav Stickley and the American Arts and Crafts movement, along with such regional writers as Helen Fitzgerald Sanders, have ebbed and flowed as scholars have exposed the blinders of class, race, and ethnicity that limited their vision and doomed them to failure.[18] Nevertheless, Sanders reminds us why Stickley and the Craftsman movement could be so compelling. For readers of the *Craftsman*, the possibility of Butte's redemption gave hope that their own cities might transcend the degradations of industrial capitalism. For its Butte adherents, the Craftsman movement arrived at the right time to reshape a corrupt mining camp into a city of moral homes and honest citizens striving for the common good.

---

[1] Gustav Stickley, "Style and Its Requisites," *Craftsman* 1, no. 1 (October 1901): v–viii; Gustav Stickley, "The Influence of Material Things," *Craftsman* 1, no. 3 (January 1902): v–vi; Gustav Stickley, "The Craftsman Idea of the Kind of Home Environment That Would Result from More Natural Standards of Life and Work," *Craftsman Homes* (New York: Craftsman, 1909; reprint, New York: Dover, 1979), 194–205. See also Richard Guy Wilson, "American Arts and Crafts Architecture: Radical though Dedicated to the Cause Conservative," in *The Art That Is Life: The Arts and Crafts Movement in America, 1875–1920*, ed. Wendy Kaplan (New York: New York Graphic Society/Little

Brown, for the Boston Museum of Fine Arts, 1987), 114–17; Leslie Greene Bowman, *American Arts and Crafts: Virtue in Design* (Boston: Bulfinch Press/Little, Brown, for the Los Angeles County Museum of Art, 1990), 33–42; Barry Sanders, *A Complex Fate: Gustav Stickley and the Craftsman Movement* (New York: Preservation Press/Wiley, 1996).

2 Sanders's book-length works include *Trails through Western Woods* (New York: Alice Harriman, 1910); *Petalesharoo and the Star Brave* (Butte, MT: McKee, 1910); *A History of Montana* (Chicago: Lewis, 1913); *The White Quiver* (New York: Duffield, 1913); *The Dream Maker* (Boston: Cornhill, 1918); and *Little Mother America* (Boston: Cornhill, 1919). Her last published work was the memoir *X. Beidler: Vigilante*, ed. Helen Fitzgerald Sanders in collaboration with William H. Bertsche (Norman: University of Oklahoma Press, 1957). Many thanks go to Patty Dean for sharing her research on Sanders with me.

3 Harry Majors, "The Meanest City in the United States," *Life* 35 (April 12, 1900): 326; see also Ray Stannard Baker, "Butte City: Greatest of the Camps," *Century Illustrated Magazine* 45, no. 6 (April 1903): 870–79; William MacLeod Raine, "The Fight for Copper," *Frank Leslie's Popular Monthly* 42, no. 4 (February 1904): 37–46; C. P. Connolly, "The Story of Montana," I, *McClure's Magazine* 27, no. 4 (August 1906): 346–61; II, *McClure's Magazine* 27, no. 5 (September 1906): 451–65. Butte received even more attention as the home of sensational author Mary MacLane; see J. P. Mowbray, "The Higher Hysterics," *Critic* 41, no. 3 (September 1902), 213–17. These and all other citations to contemporary periodicals, except the *Craftsman*, are derived from *American Periodicals Series Online 1740–1900*, http://proquest.umi.com/pqdweb?RQT=302&COPT=SU5UPTAmVkVSPTlmREJTPTEoNEQ@&clientId=15756&cfc=1.

4 Hubbard also observed that "most folks think that only two people live in Butte—W.A. Clark and Mary McLane [*sic*]." [Elbert Hubbard], untitled article, *Philistine: A Periodical of Protest* 17, no. 2 (July 1903): 50–59.

5 In his essay "Down a Butte Copper Mine," Hubbard described his experiences as a descent into hell; this essay was reprinted in Elbert Hubbard, *Elbert Hubbard's Selected Writings*, vol. 7, *On My Way* (New York: William H. Wise, 1922; reprint, [Kila, MT]: Kessinger, 1998), 146–51, http://site.ebrary.com/lib/uscisd/Doc?id=5003571.

6 Hubbard lectured in Miles City, Helena, and Butte. [Elbert Hubbard], untitled article, *Philistine: A Periodical of Protest* 22, no. 2 (January 1906): 58. Hubbard attributed the "subject of virtue" quotation to an article by Sam Gordon for the Miles City newspaper describing the *Butte Miner*'s negative reaction to Hubbard's lecture.

7 Harold Just, "The Story of the

Overland Monthly," *Overland Monthly and Out West Magazine* 48, no. 6 (December 1916): 551–52.

8   Helen Fitzgerald Sanders, "Work of the Woman's Relief Committee of Butte for San Francisco," *Overland Monthly and Out West Magazine* 48, no. 2 (August 1906): 48–51.

9   Helen Fitzgerald Sanders, "Butte— The Heart of the Copper Industry," *Overland Monthly and Out West Magazine* 48, no. 3 (November 1906): 1–27. Sanders made pointed reference to eastern writers who had "drifted in from the East, stopped a few days at the club, drank good wine, smoked cigars, and gone down a mine; then they have promptly written articles noticeable on account of their conspicuous lack of knowledge." However, several of the themes in her essay echo Ray Stannard Baker's 1903 balanced portrayal of Butte in "Butte City: Greatest of the Camps."

10   Helen Fitzgerald Sanders, "The Craftsman Movement and What It Means," *Overland Monthly and*

Out West Magazine 49, no. 3 (March 1907): 226–29. Emulating his British Arts and Crafts hero William Morris, Stickley made these the basis of his design aesthetic; see "An Argument for Simplicity in Household Furnishings" and "Style and Its Requisites," *Craftsman* 1, no. 1 (October 1901): iii–iv, v–viii; "Utility—Simplicity—Beauty," *Craftsman* 1, no. 2 (November 1901): v–vi. These and all other citations to the *Craftsman* are derived from "Digital Library for the Decorative Arts and Material Culture," *University of Wisconsin Digital Collections*, http://digicoll.library. wisc.edu/DLDecArts/.

11   Frederick S. Lamb, "The Beautifying of Our Cities," *Craftsman* (July 1902): 172–88; Susan F. Stone, "The Town Beautiful," *Craftsman* 6, no. 2 (May 1904): 125–29; Ernest Crosby, "The Century of Ugliness," *Craftsman* 6, no. 4 (July 1904): 409–10; Ernest Crosby, "The Beauty of Ugliness," *Craftsman* 7, no. 1 (October 1904): 65–66; [Gustav

Stickley,] "From Ugliness to Beauty," *Craftsman* 7, no. 3 (December 1904): 31–20; Giles Edgerton, "How New York Has Redeemed Herself from Ugliness—An Artist's Revelation of the Beauty of the Skyscraper," *Craftsman* 11, no. 4 (January 1907): 458–71.

12   Another Butte house was constructed on one of Stickley's Craftsman designs. See [Ray Stubblebine,] "No. 65—Butte, Montana," *Stickley's Craftsman Homes, 1904–1916*, http://www. craftsmanhomes.org/No._65_ Found_in_Butte.html. The Barker bungalow has some affinity with the "Craftsman Clapboard House: Series of 1906" design, which Stickley published in *Craftsman* 5 (June 1906): 386–95, but the two have very different rooflines, porch treatments, and materials.

13   Ellis, "How to Build a Bungalow," *Craftsman* 5, no. 3 (December 1903): 253–60; Clay Lancaster, "The American Bungalow," in *Common Places: Readings in American*

Vernacular Architecture, ed. Dell Upton and John Michael Vlach (Athens: University of Georgia Press, 1986), 79–106. The U.S. Census listed Samuel Barker variously as a civil and a mining engineer. *Twelfth Census of the United States: 1900—Population*, Butte City, district 98; *Thirteenth Census of the United States: 1910—Population*, Butte City, district 110.

14   "Porches, Pergolas and Balconies, and the Charm of Privacy Out of Doors," *Craftsman* 9, no. 6 (March 1906): 840–45. Longley, a geologist, was a draftsman for the Anaconda Copper Mining Company. *Bulletin of the American Institute of Mining and Metallurgical Engineers* 151 (July 1919), lii.

15   Stickley, *Craftsman Homes*, 35. The design Stickley described was originally published as "Craftsman House, Series of 1907: Number V," *Craftsman* (May 1907): 216–23. "The Living Room, Its Many Uses and Its Possibilities for Comfort and Beauty," *Craftsman* 9, no. 1 (October 1905): 57–70; "The Dining Room as a Center of Hospitality and Good Cheer," *Craftsman* 9, no. 2 (November 1905): 229–40; "The Hall and Its Importance in the Modern House," *Craftsman* 9, no. 4 (January 1906): 530–38.

16   "Manual Training and Citizenship," *Craftsman* 5, no. 4 (January 1904): 406–12; "Manual Training and the Development of Taste," *Craftsman* 5, no. 5 (February 1904): 513–17; "Learning to Be Citizens: A School Where Boys and Girls of All Creeds, Races and Classes of Society Work Together," *Craftsman* 9, no. 6 (March 1906): 774–88.

17   For more on Butte's environmental history and reform, see Janet L. Finn, "Seeing the Forest through the Trees: The Green Legacy of Alma Higgins," in *Motherlode: Legacies of Women's Lives and Labors in Butte, Montana*, ed. Janet L. Finn and Ellen Crain, 204–23 (Livingston, MT: Clark City Press, 2005); Donald MacMillan, *Smoke Wars: Anaconda Copper, Montana Air Pollution, and the Courts, 1890–1924* (Helena: Montana Historical Society Press, 2000)..

18   Negative assessments of Stickley's Craftsman movement, and of the American Arts and Crafts movement in general, include Gwendolyn Wright, *Moralism and the Model Home: Domestic Architecture and Cultural Conflict in Chicago, 1873–1913* (Chicago: University of Chicago Press, 1980); and T. J. Jackson Lears, *No Place of Grace: Antimodernism and the Transformation of American Culture, 1880–1920* (New York: Pantheon, 1981), 59–96. More positive portrayals can be found in Wilson, "American Arts and Crafts Architecture," Bowman, *American Arts and Crafts*; Barry Sanders, *A Complex Fate*; and Ray Stubblebine, *Stickley's Craftsman Homes: Plans, Drawings, Photographs* (Salt Lake City: Gibbs Smith, 2006).

Redeeming The Ugliest Town On Earth
Helen Fitzgerald Sanders

Six years ago Butte, Montana, bore the undisputed title of the ugliest town on earth. Following the logic of the excellent Vicar of Wakefield, whose philosophy saw hope in the very fact that he had reached the ultimate limit of misfortune, Butte, having attained the maximum of ugliness, had at least gained a point from which to start. Towns, and more especially western towns, do not stand still, and since Butte could not move downward, it must of necessity climb up.

The ugliness of Butte was the direct result of artificial conditions. Nature had clad the mountains upon which the city rests with pine grove and thicket of fern; she had erected about it noble peaks, robed royally in purple haze and shining with the perennial benediction of the snow. Within the memory of living men the site of Butte had borne the columned canopy of the forest, the rush of clear streams, the gay patchwork of grass, bitter-root and the myriad mountain flowers. But the hand of man had turned vandal here, and in ruthless quest of copper, shafts were sunk, smelters arose, clouds of sulphur smoke killed the last bud and sprig, and the hills stood naked, lean and stripped. The approach to the city from the East bore a startling likeness to Dante s description of the out-lying regions of Purgatory. The huge boulders thrown from

Craftsman house in Butte, owned by Alfred Longley.

their native pedestals by pre-historic convulsions lay scattered in grotesque heaps, and on the desolate cairns and wastes was the ever-present stain of the smoke. If, perchance, a traveller entered the town in the shades of evening over the Continental Divide, the similarity to the scenes of Dante need not end with the approach to Purgatory, for beneath, swimming in a palpitating sea of smoke which filled the bowl of the valley with opal waves, lay the likeness of the Inferno itself. There tall chimneys were capped with points of flame; long, lurid, crawling streams of molten slag burned the heavy darkness into a crimson glow, and, occasionally, a bright flare of red light, when the slag was dumped, completed

Another view of Alfred Longley's Craftsman house in Butte.

a scene of picturesque horror.

The town itself, in the impartial light of day, presented a less diabolical but more monotonous appearance. Row upon row of ugly little houses and a few even uglier large ones told eloquently of the status of the place. Had a stranger, ignorant of his environment, been set down in Butte, he would have known at a glance toward the long, low hill bristling with shaft-houses and smokestacks, and the multitude of cheap, unlovely houses that crouched beneath, just the character of the town in which he stood; he would have seen in the shaft-houses the reason for its being and the mastering idea of its people; in the rows of cottages and tenements indifference to comfort

and beauty. These were not homes; they were the capital of the landlord. If architecture, or the lack of architecture, ever spoke, it was here, and its language was unmistakable.

In this prevailing ugliness the story of Butte was told. The fame of the copper mines spread across the seas, around the world, and poor and adventurous fortune-seekers of all lands flocked here as had the earlier Argonauts to the golden shores of California. They came, lured hither by the hope of wealth, to stay a little while, then pass on to pleasanter pastures. No one cared to make this temporary abiding-place more lovely; anything would do for the few months or years and then,—there was the cherished vision of a far-away Elysium called Home. First the log cabin sheltered the prospector from the cold, then, as the camp grew, this crude form was supplanted by the tenements and cottages built to rent, and in a few cases, by gaudily expensive mansions of mushroom millionaires. There was a certain rugged picturesqueness in the log cabin which these later dwellings lacked, for in their unsymmetrical and unreasonable forms were seen the worst of many styles and the best of none. Every square foot within the walls of a house was crowded with people. The custom of renting rooms was general and the town supported a surprising number of small boardinghouses. A homely sage has said, with keen wisdom, that no man ever died fighting for his boarding-house; one might go farther and say that where rented houses prevail over homes, civic improvement will decline if it has ever existed, for the hearthstone of the home is the foundation stone of democracy. At this time, Butte was virtually a city of rented dwellings, and these poor places, where people wasted the greatest hour of their lives,— the Present, for the will-o'-the-wisp of the Future—were unredeemed by a glimpse of green, a single flower or the shielding charity of a vine.

The moral effect was self-evident. What wonder that the children of Butte, especially the boys, were notoriously bad? What wonder that their starved little hearts, with never a flower nor a spear of grass to look upon, should be turned from the beautiful and good, blighted and stained as the place in which they lived? God pity the little children whose playground is the barren street: who do not know the joy of growing things and the ever wonderful growing of the seed into the plant! Not only the children felt the contamination of perverted environment. The treasure was too vast to be undisputed, and from greed, the mastering evil,— greed of the same type that would rob us of Niagara Falls and our greatest natural possessions,—corruption, bribery and political debauchery soiled the name of the state. It was as if the hungry throats of the dark shafts were never satisfied; that they were usurers of the most relentless sort, demanding compound interest for the

The living room in the Longley house.

wealth they yielded. The forests were stripped to be consumed by their tunnels and drifts; the honor of men sank in their depths and not infrequently a human life was offered up under crashing rocks, an awful sacrifice on the altar of Mammon. And over all, the cloud of smoke hung heavily, hiding the blue sky, the mountain heights and the sun, until men forgot to turn their eyes above. While the pall drifted thick and dark overhead, the bell of the cathedral tolled with appalling frequency and victim after victim of pneumonia was taken down the winding way to the barren graveyard in the "flat." It is of record that one of these grim processions of death

The dining room in the Longley house.

was lost in the smoke which seemed maliciously to deny the dead a couch of earth on which to rest.

In spite of such disadvantages the camp grew into a city, and as thousands of people flocked to its mines, these conditions became unbearable. First, the old practice of roasting ore in heaps upon the ground was prohibited, then one by one the smelters were shut down and the output of the mines sent to the great Washoe Smelter at Anaconda, a town twenty-five miles distant. Thus the smoke drifted away forever and left the air pure to breathe, the sun clear to warm the blood and made possible the existence of a city worthy of the name. Little by little, people came to understand that

vegetation could be a concrete reality and not a tradition. The discovery of enormous ore bodies extending for miles across the "flat" up the scarred sides of the Rocky Mountains assured the future of Butte's resources past the life of the present generation, and somehow those poor toilers, who had come to stay a while and then pass on, found themselves at the end of years, still toiling with the dream of home farther away, and a yearning instead for something better here and now. They had forgotten to live during that period of oblivion, and they were waking, as after a long, long sleep. The impulse was general. Money was plentiful enough and people began to build homes,—homes with tentative little gardens which flourished and grew. The earth was ready for seeds; men's minds were ready for new ideas.

And as the seeds were dropped into the soil which gave them forth again in diverse forms of plant life, so the germ of a new idea planted in the public mind took root and grew, and the fruit of it was the craftsman movement. It could not have come to Butte at a more opportune time. People were reaching out for some tangible way to redeem the barren ugliness and the wasted years. Men and women long exiled from the beautiful took it up with the vigor of enthusiasm and it was not long before its results were seen in material form. The first definite move was up out of the gulches to the slopes commanding a sweeping view of the undulating hills that rise into the lofty heights of the

Highlands to the south, the huge, beetling and bearded Main Range of the Rocky Mountains to the east, and the abrupt cone of the Big Butte to westward, with a glimpse of the noble peak of Mount Flieser [sic] in the distance. It would be hard to find a more beautiful or varied panorama of mountain scenery than this, and the sparkling clearness of the rarefied air takes the vision through miles of atmosphere and reveals the minutest detail on the silvered steeps. Here numbers of pleasant homes have been built, and grass, flowers and young trees deck the yards. Conspicuous among these places are the craftsman houses, which are well suited to the austere landscape. The warm shades of russet brown and soft green on the shingles of the houses, shown in the accompanying pictures, are a restful and harmonious contrast to the wide vistas of dull earth color. These homes are very new and the yards are not yet planted, but when the spring is farther advanced and a carpet of green is spread around them; when they are hung with the deep green garlands of Virginia creeper and woodbine, mellowing in the autumn into yellow, brown and red: when the tulips put forth their ringed cups of gold and scarlet geraniums flame in the flower beds, then they will be complete and not until then. On one block three craftsman houses stand side by side, looking northward, so that the view of the mountains is from their back windows. Never could the idea of the craftsman rear porch be more happily illustrated

Another Butte Craftsman house, owned by Samuel Barker

than here. In the long summer twilight when the sunset lingers in the west and the mountains draw about themselves such mysteries of purple and rose, it is a never-ceasing joy to sit and watch the peaks grow dim in the sanctuary of the night.

The interiors of these houses carry out the craftsman scheme and those who enjoy the broad hearths, the easy chairs and pleasant rooms forget that they are in Butte and remember only that they are in a home. This goes to show that wherever we are, in the most favored or unfavored regions, it still remains for us to create our environment and to make it what we will.

Thus far the betterment of Butte has been a matter of individual rather than organized effort; the private garden rather than the public square has

The living room in the Barker house.

reclaimed the wastes. One park, Columbia Gardens, is the public's sole recreation ground. It is situated at the base of the main range and extends up a canyon or cleft in the mountains. Groves of trees give shelter and shade, and beds of pansies, tulips and other garden flowers grow to perfection of size and color. These gardens are good so far as they go, but eighty thousand people who work need plenty of room to play. At an altitude of six thousand feet above sea level, the blood flows fast, men live at a high pressure of nervous tension, and for these reasons it is necessary that they rest and seek the peace that is of the open. One has only to watch the overladen cars going to and from the Gardens on a holiday or

Sunday during summer, and to see the congestion of that pleasure ground itself, to realize how the toilers in the mines long for the healthy recreation of the great out-of-doors. There is space enough around Butte to give all enough room and air. The mountains seem to be forever calling men forth to receive the gift of repose and joy that lies within their sheltering fastnesses.

While the craftsman movement has wrought this material change, it has also been a factor in moral and educational advancement. It came as a blessing to the idle hands of children who, hitherto, had used their energy mischievously, knowing no better vent for their native endowment of animal spirits. These were the children of the streets whom we saw awhile ago the objects of the truant officer's vigilance, who commonly landed in jail, there to learn by association the final lesson of crime. As a rule these children were bright and there was a way to their better natures, if only that way could be found. So manual training was introduced in the schools with success that its fondest advocates had scarcely dared to hope for. To make a good student the first essential is to create in the child a desire to study. A direct appeal to his interest will do more to keep him in school than a regiment of truant officers. Manual training furnished this impetus of interest to children who did not care for books. In the high school there is a room fitted with benches and tools, where large classes are instructed in manual training after craftsman models. The good which has been accomplished through this instruction cannot be too strongly emphasized, nor can it be fully reckoned until these young workers go out into the world. It has taught them the dignity of honest labor; the value of thrift; and it has equalized and balanced theory and fact, book and tool. It has showed them that the keynote of useful citizenship is individual striving toward a chosen end, and the reward of a task, in the doing it well. Work and pleasure should never be separated; in the doing of one we should achieve the other. Only in this way can we hope for the best results. The teachers who know the boys have been surprised to find that through some constructive process the worst truants and delinquents have been controlled by manual training; that the law of development extends from the hands to the head; that as the boy builds things of wood he builds the subtler structure of character. It is much the same with the young body politic as with the individual youth; there is always a way to healthy growth, and in Butte that way has been largely through the craftsman movement.

Butte is just beginning its better existence; it is just coming to realize that it has a heart as well as a purse, an aesthetic as well as a commercial existence. Looking into the future the work of improvement seems an enormous undertaking, but we have only to look back six years at what has been done in the immediate past to be sanguine of the fruit of the days to come. We

The Barker house's dining room.

must earn the beautiful by the toil of our hands and the love of our hearts, but if we must labor for that which is freely given as earth's offering in fairer lands, we appreciate the hard-earned reward even more. Nature, once cast out and spurned, does not easily return, still, as time passes, over the dun sweep of the hills a faint, yellow-green may be seen, the footfall of the spring, elusive and fleeting, born of the shower and blighted by the wind. It is scarcely more than a promise that in the days to come if we keep striving there may be greater heritage for us than the little patch of garden at our door. Even now, the seeker, who strikes out on the long road past the Big Butte where the distant peaks loom up silver-white to meet the brooding clouds, may find the ever-changing pageant of the wild flowers, threads of crystal streams fringed with tall, purple iris and willows, and, as the summer warms into maturity, the royal robes of haze will deck the hills even as the snow shall be their ermine.

In the redemption of the ugliest town on earth the philosophy of the whole CRAFTSMAN idea, material and spiritual, is embodied. Having passed through different stages from the crude camp of log cabins to the cheaply built city of rented houses and showy mansions, it has awakened to the desire for something better, and, through that desire, is becoming simplified, which is its salvation. Simplicity is selection; it is the rejection of useless and encumbering fallacies in order that we may retain only the best. One by one these fallacies have fallen away like autumn leaves, bringing us nearer to first principles and leading us, through the sufficient doctrine of "better work, better art and a better and more reasonable way of living," out of the smoke into the sunshine, out of the gulches to the hills, out of earth's depths upward toward Heaven. . . .

Yesterday there came a bluebird perching on the window sill, twig in beak, calling loudly to his mate. Strange little feathered householder seeking a place for his nest! The omen was a happy one, for

Blessed is the city when the birds come back to build!

Helen Fitzgerald Sanders, from the frontispiece to her History of Montana *(1913). Courtesy Montana Historical Society Research Center.*

Montana's Smallest National Historic Landmark: The Burton K. Wheeler House

Chere Jiusto

Burton Kendall Wheeler was one of Montana's most independent minded and nationally prominent Democratic senators. Raised in Massachusetts, he was drawn westward as a young law school graduate to "go anywhere that was wide open with opportunity."[1] Wheeler settled on Butte in 1905, where he built a general law practice and launched a political career, his philosophies shaped by the teachings from his Quaker upbringing and by his career as a progressive Butte lawyer living in a neighborhood of industrial laborers and railroad workers.

Wheeler rose through the political ranks in Montana to national stature and was elected to the U.S. Senate in 1922. His tenure was marked by his vigorous campaign for peace in the 1930s and 1940s and for the need to limit corporate and federal powers. According to historian Arthur M. Schlesinger Jr, Wheeler became "the most formidable of the Senate radicals."[2] During the buildup to World War II, he was central in framing isolationist arguments against entering the war. His antiwar fervor led him to contest President Roosevelt's plans for American intervention in the war to the point that he circulated to the press Roosevelt's secret 1941 Victory Plan for entry into the war and supported the America First antiwar committee.

Wheeler's legal cases included damage suits against mining and railroad companies, and his hard-shelled criminal defendants included a train robber, a safe blower, Butte madams, and the union men of the Butte mines. Wheeler felt at home in the bustling, cacophonous landscape of the mining city and identified with Butte's working citizens. He penned in his 1962 memoirs, *Yankee from the West*:

> Butte is not a pretty town. It is a honeycombed hill throwing up a network of trestles, railroad tracks, bunkers, transmission lines, etc. . .
> . The fiery smelters which shoot glowing abstractions into the big Montana sky also sometimes cover the entire city in winter with a soot that prevents you from seeing across the street. The arsenic smoke long ago killed all grass and trees in Butte.
>
> Yet there was something inspiring to me in the sight of the miners' neat one-story houses. Many of them did their own painting and plumbing and I was amazed at how clean and well furnished the houses were and how well dressed the wives and children were.
>
> Above all, it was a generous, democratic community. It didn't make any

difference who you were, where you came from, or how much money you had.[3]

Butte's ethnic neighborhoods were inviting to thousands of enterprising workers, and Burton K. Wheeler became part of their growing population. In 1908, he purchased a house at 1232 East Second Street and put down roots in the working enclave of South Butte at the base of the Uptown. Wheeler embraced the character and way of life in the working-class neighborhoods. For the next fourteen years, he and his wife, Lulu, lived on East Second Street and raised their young family there. Wheeler later recalled in his memoirs:

> In my second year on my own, my practice improved to the point where I could make a down payment on a $4000 four-room brick house on Second Street near the heart of the town. It was one of the more substantially built houses in that area and, with additions made as our family grew, it was to prove large enough for the Wheeler family all the years we lived in Butte.[4]

Wheeler was elected to the Montana House of Representatives in 1910. In Helena, he stood up to the influence of the Anaconda Copper Mining Company, allying himself with rising Montana Democratic Party leader Thomas Walsh and pushing for a stronger workers' compensation law. Following Walsh's election to the U.S. Senate in 1912, Wheeler was appointed U.S. attorney for Montana and held that office from 1913 to 1918. His tenure spanned the era of Butte's greatest political upheaval as unionists and socialists gained influence and challenged the dominion of the copper companies. Wheeler's steadfast refusal to charge Industrial Workers of the World organizer Frank Little with espionage during the politically charged summer of 1917 was controversial and courageous. It was a time of "mass hysteria" that ultimately led to Little's lynching from a Butte railroad trestle. Wheeler also refused to prosecute for sedition those who disagreed with the government's war policy, efforts that he felt overreached. These experiences fueled his campaign against the concentration and abuse of government power.

By the 1920s, Wheeler was a prominent figure in Montana. Although he lost election to the governor's office in 1920, he was elected in 1922 to represent Montana in the U.S. Senate. The Wheelers moved to Washington, D.C., where he served in the Senate until 1947. Always independent, as Montana's junior senator in 1923 Wheeler teamed up with Senator Walsh in the Teapot Dome probe, which exposed the corruption and influence of big oil in President Warren G. Harding's administration. The following year, Wheeler briefly broke ranks with the Democrats to run as a third-party

The Burton K. Wheeler House, 2009. Courtesy Dori Skrukrud, Butte Community Development Office.

candidate for vice president with the Progressive Party.

Wheeler held staunchly to an antiwar platform across the years. And although he was an early supporter of President Franklin D. Roosevelt, he opposed FDR over the issue of "packing" the Supreme Court with extra justices to ensure that New Deal programs could withstand legal challenges.

Wheeler is best known for his opposition to an American role in World War II. In 1941, he denounced Roosevelt's Lend-Lease Act, which authorized the president to sell, trade, or lend war materials to the Allies, saying it would draw the United States into war. It was during this debate that he made the famous declaration that the Lend-Lease act would "plow under every fourth American boy."[5] He held his staunch antiwar position until the Japanese bombed Pearl Harbor. After America's entry into World War II, Wheeler's camp lost support and his career drew to a close.

Wheeler's long career as a Butte politician and his life in South Butte appear to have galvanized his independent nature and his willingness to fight a good fight. The Wheeler family home placed him on equal footing with his South Butte neighbors, whom he regarded with friendship and respect, as he remembered in later years:

> The neighborhood was made up of railroad men, small merchants, and workers with modest incomes; I was the only professional among them. My choice of living there after I could afford an expensive residential section undoubtedly was worth extra votes every time I ran for office. But in truth this was not my motive in refusing to move. I simply enjoyed associating with these hard-working, fun-loving Irish, Welsh, and Cornish families. There was no pretension and there was plenty of merriment.[6]

Built in 1897 for $975, in many ways the Wheeler house was typical of the thousands of dwellings built in Butte's heyday. Its original owner was a Canadian warehouse worker, and the house at the time of Wheeler's purchase was a simple Victorian worker's cottage—one story, brick walls, four rooms, tiny yard. The arched brick openings and sixteen-over-one sash windows were typical late-nineteenth-century embellishments that enriched the design beyond mere utility.[7]

The Burton K. Wheeler House bears the imprint of the growing Wheeler family. By 1916, the four-room brick house had sprouted an upstairs with large dormer windows and a roomier floorplan. The Craftsman period makeover resulted in broad roof gables, bracketed eaves, exposed rafters, and the battered, shingled post on the front porch, giving the house an overall appearance of an early-twentieth-century middle-class dwelling.

Throughout Butte, since first settled, there was much intermingling of working and professional classes, and the trappings of heavy industry were mixed freely into the city's urban fabric. With the underground mines dug deep beneath the Butte hill, the city was perched atop an industrial beehive. As a result, mine yards, headframes, rail spurs, trolley lines, smelters, warehouses, tailings piles, and heavy manufacturers were common to most every neighborhood, and housing for workers was arranged in the spaces between and near these job sites. The Burton K. Wheeler property is typical of such homes, standing within a small six-block enclave that was hemmed in between the Northern Pacific Railway and the Great Northern Railroad lines and engulfed by industry.

The Wheelers' neighborhood was a gritty, noisy place. Across the tracks to the north were the old mine yards of the Butte, Curtis and Major Mining Company and the Alliance Mine as well as a set of stockyard corrals. The Western Iron Works bordered the neighborhood to the east. Down Second Street to the west, the Butte Gas, Light and Fuel Company refined coal into gas and coke, while across the tracks to the south loomed the Parrot Smelter.

This was Butte in its glory days. Embedded in the Butte-Anaconda National Historic Landmark, the Burton K. Wheeler House is an integral part of the working-class South Butte neighborhood. The home and its setting are a window into America's industrial past.

In 1976, a year after he died, Wheeler's modest Butte home became a National Historic Landmark for its association with a man who shaped the national discourse over war.[8] Its location offers insights into Wheeler's affinity with working people and how their attitudes and values helped shape his thinking during his time in Butte, a way of thinking that accompanied him onto the national stage. Occupying just a city building lot, the Burton K. Wheeler House is Montana's smallest National Historic Landmark, reflecting the humble background of Montana's controversial senator.

[1] Burton K. Wheeler with Paul F. Healy, *Yankee from the West: The Candid Story of the Freewheeling U.S. Senator from Montana* (Garden City, NY: Doubleday, 1962), 57.

[2] Arthur M. Schlesinger Jr., *The Politics of Upheaval, 1935–1936* (Boston: Houghton Mifflin, 1960), 142.

[3] Wheeler, *Yankee from the West*, 65.

[4] Wheeler, *Yankee from the West*, 67–68.

[5] Michael P. Malone, Richard B. Roeder, and William L. Lang, *Montana: A History of Two Centuries*, rev. ed. (Seattle: University of Washington Press, 1991), 312.

[6] Wheeler, *Yankee from the West*, 68.

[7] Michael Koop, "Montana Historical and Architectural Inventory Form for 1232 East Second Street, Butte-Anaconda National Historic Landmark," 1984, on file at Montana State Historic Preservation Office, Helena.

[8] American Association for State and Local History, "Burton K. Wheeler House, National Historic Landmark Nomination," 1976, on file at the Montana State Historic Preservation Office, Helena.

IMAGES & TALES: A PORTFOLIO OF BUTTE & ANACONDA ARTS

Mountain View Cemetery, Butte, *2008, photographic print, 8 x 10". © 2008 Roger Whitacre.*

Butte & Anaconda Cemeteries
Roger Whitacre

Mountain View Cemetery, Butte, *2008, photographic print, 8 x 10". © 2008 Roger Whitacre.*

Deer Lodge County Cemetery, Anaconda, *2008, photographic print, 8 x 10". © 2008 Roger Whitacre.*

Deer Lodge County Cemetery, Anaconda, *2008,*

photographic print, 8 x 10". © 2008 Roger Whitacre.

Deer Lodge County Cemetery, Anaconda, *2008,*

photographic print, 8 x 10". © 2008 Roger Whitacre.

Deer Lodge County Cemetery, Anaconda, *2008, photographic print, 8 x 10". © 2008 Roger Whitacre.*

B'nai Israel Cemetery, Butte, *2008, photographic print, 8 x 10".* © *2008 Roger Whitacre.*

B'nai Israel Cemetery, Butte, *2008, photographic print, 8 x 10".* © *2008 Roger Whitacre.*

Mount Moriah Cemetery, Butte, *2008, photographic print, 8 x 10".* © *2008 Roger Whitacre.*

Mount Moriah Cemetery, Butte, *2008, photographic print, 8 x 10".* © *2008 Roger Whitacre.*

Mount Moriah Cemetery, Butte, *2008, photographic print, 8 x 10". © 2008 Roger Whitacre.*

Holy Cross Cemetery, Butte, *2008, photographic print, 8 x 10". © 2008 Roger Whitacre.*

Mount Moriah Cemetery, Butte, *2008, photographic print, 8 x 10". © 2008 Roger Whitacre.*

A Tribute to Anaconda: Etchings & Collages
Joeann Daley

Machine Triptych, *1970, 3-plate copper etching, 11 7/8 x 21". From the* **Anaconda Series.** © *1970 Joeann Daley.*

Above: Washoe Theater, *1985, collage and etching (watercolor wash), 12 x 9". From* **Anaconda Reclaimed.** *© 1985 Joeann Daley.*

Left: Coming Home, *1985, etching, 3 5/8 x 11 5/8". From* **Anaconda Reclaimed.** *© 1985 Joeann Daley.*

The Nickel Coin Print, *1970, etching, 11 ¾ x 17 ½″. From the* **Anaconda Series.** © *1970 Joeann Daley.*

The Smeltermen, *1970, etching, aquatint, soft ground etching, 12 x 16 ½". From the* **Anaconda Series.** © *1970 Joeann Daley.*

Houses, *1972, etching (brown/black edition), 3 ¾ x 11½". From the* **Anaconda Series.** *© 1972 Joeann Daley.*

Bars, *1972, etching (sepia edition), 3 ½ x 12". From the* **Anaconda Series.** *© 1972 Joeann Daley.*

Churches (Steeples Over Anaconda), *1972, etching (sepia edition), 3 ½ x 12". From the* **Anaconda Series.** *© 1972 Joeann Daley.*

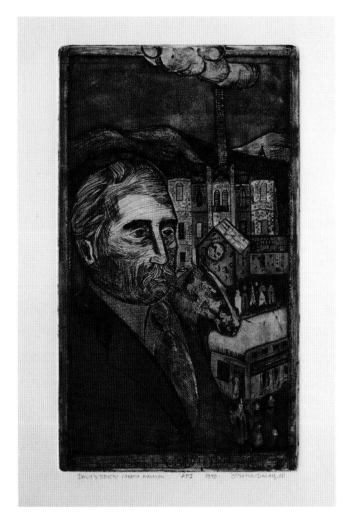

Daly's Town, *1970, etching, 12 ½ x 7". From the* **Anaconda Series.** *© 1970 Joeann Daley.*

Andiamo all futura (Let's go into the future), *1985, etching collage, 13 x 7". From* **Anaconda Reclaimed.** *© 1985 Joeann Daley.*

While the Giant Sleeps, *1985, etching collage, 12 x 18". From* **Anaconda Reclaimed.** © *1985 Joeann Daley.*

Above: The Bus No Longer Stops Here, *1985, etching collage, 16 ½ x 12 ½". From* **Anaconda Reclaimed.** *© 1985 Joeann Daley.*

Left: Everybody Out, This is the End of the Line, *1985, etching collage, 15 x 20". From* **Anaconda Reclaimed.** *© 1985 Joeann Daley.*

Visionary Butte: Photographs
Lisa Wareham

Alley Reflection, *March 13, 2007, digital photograph.* © *2007 Lisa Wareham.*

Cruel Beauty (Mountain Con Mine), *November 21, 2005, digital photograph.* © *2005 Lisa Wareham.*

Nightshift, *August 31, 2007, digital photograph.* © *2007 Lisa Wareham.*

Upstairs, *February 1, 2009, digital photograph.* © *2009 Lisa Wareham.*

Exit Only, *June 25, 2008, digital photograph.* © *2008 Lisa Wareham.*

Fenced In (Mountain Con Mine), *November 21, 2005, digital photograph. © 2005 Lisa Wareham.*

Footprints, *December 24, 2005, digital photograph. © 2005 Lisa Wareham.*

Framed, *July 16, 2008, digital photograph. © 2008 Lisa Wareham.*

Overhang, *May 13, 2008, digital photograph. © 2008 Lisa Wareham.*

Gates to the City, *March 13, 2007, digital photograph. © 2007 Lisa Wareham.*

Above: Through the Tunnel, *November 24, 2006, digital photograph.* © *2006 Lisa Wareham.*

Left: Layers of Texture, *December 24, 2005, digital photograph.* © *2005 Lisa Wareham.*

Facing Page: Sundown, *January 15, 2009, digital photograph.* © *2009 Lisa Wareham.*

Raindrops at the Belmont, *May 27, 2007, digital photograph.* © *2007 Lisa Wareham.*

Dirty Old Town: Addiction and Betrayal in the Mining City
Edwin Dobb

(This essay is a slightly modified version of a talk given at the Montana Historical Society on January 18, 2007.)

Shortly after I moved back to Butte, I found myself in the Silver Dollar Bar, sipping bourbon with an old-timer named Dan Price. Dan liked to drink. Even more, he liked to talk. And unlike many of the strangers I meet in bars, he actually had something to say. I bought another round, and yet another, doing all I could to encourage him.

Dan had worked in the mines, at least a dozen of them, but he didn't consider himself a miner. He had wanted most to go to college and study language. But his father had fallen ill, and Dan, the oldest son, was needed at home. So he did the next best thing: he became a lifelong self-taught student. He devoured books, guided only by his obsessions, which were many and various and never flagged. Equally fervent was his desire to share his literary enthusiasms. Nothing pleased Dan more than to recite for friends his favorite passages of prose and poetry. And nothing surprised me more than to be sitting on a barstool in Butte listening to a seventy-eight-year-old miner reciting word for word the prologue to *Look Homeward, Angel*: ". . . a stone, a leaf, an unfound door; of a stone, a leaf, a door. And of all the forgotten faces . . . Naked and alone we came into exile."

Naked and alone, that is, until we discovered the comfort and company of the well-honed, well-timed word.

Dan lived in a rundown shotgun shack next to another equally rundown shack, home to his older sister, who in her eighties still subscribed to the *Daily Worker*, as well as the *New Yorker*, and smoked marijuana with young poets who attended her occasional literary gatherings. I visited Dan often, and throughout the year, but in my memory it's always winter. Always about midnight. We've already shared a few drinks, and the room glows. Dan sits in his ratty, overstuffed chair next to the gas furnace, while at his feet and entirely surrounding the chair are piles of books and magazines. I'm reading to him: Heaney, Milosz, Yeats, Joyce. Dan, of course, doesn't rely on a text, delivering Baudelaire from memory. Or his beloved Thomas Wolfe. My favorite occasions were when he recited one of his own poems, all of which were attempts to give voice to something essential about his hometown. My hometown, too. Which is why I listened closely.

Dan died a couple years ago. One of the last times I saw him was a few months after the attacks of September 11th. "What're ya reading these days, Dan?" He showed me a worn edition of the Koran he'd found at the Goodwill Store, where he purchased most of his books, also the artwork that adorned his walls. This was not the first time he'd tackled the Koran, he explained, before reciting his favorite passage: "The measure of a man is the good that he does in this world." After a pause to let the line sink in, he added, "That's religion enough for me." As so often happened, the conversation eventually turned to Butte. What is it about the place? Why are we still puzzling over it, even now, in its decline? Dan looked at me and uttered what for him was as near to truth as utterance can get: "Butte's an addiction."

In the mid-sixties, when I was in my teens, Butte was no addiction. It was instead the source and locus of my alienation, my rebellion. I bridled against the Catholic Church, especially the arbitrary authority, small-mindedness, and petty vices of the priests and nuns, the full repugnancy of which was amply evident by the time I turned twelve. I also found oppressive the much-touted clannishness of my Irish relatives. Victims and perpetrators alike conspired in hypocritical tales about the importance of family loyalty and tradition, tales that masked generations of cruelty, alcoholism, sexual abuse and vindictiveness, ignorance and greed, a soul-deadening form of social conservatism.

Then there's the relentless self-mythologizing of Butte. The place that billed itself as wide open, tolerant, welcoming has also been hopelessly corrupt, prejudiced, and deeply suspicious of outsiders. And I can't overlook the nondomestic violence, which was as much a part of life aboveground as was danger underground. Here's another form of homegrown ugliness (like prostitution, cronyism, and institutionalized extortion) that's been sanitized in what might be called the Romance of Butte. But there was nothing romantic—nor unusual, for that matter—about the Saturday night my older cousin was brought to my house after yet another drunken fight. Two brothers had jumped Danny, in revenge for Danny having beaten one of them the previous weekend. Their weapons were broken beer bottles. They wore steel-toed boots just for the occasion. And they were merciless. Covering most of the top of Danny's head, which had been shaved in the emergency room, was a T-shaped pattern of stitches. Maybe a hundred of them, probably more. His upper front teeth had been kicked out. His face and arms were badly bruised. And that was only the visible damage, which was more than enough for my young eyes.

Why was Danny sprawled out on my parents' bed, asleep but still bleeding through his bandages, instead of at home? To protect his mother, who went to her grave believing—well, more likely, pretending—that her son never touched a drop of whiskey, never raised his hand in anger.

By the way, Danny later died of gangrene, after

suffering frostbite but refusing treatment, and that after passing out in the alley behind the M&M on a frigid Christmas day, which had followed a long morning of drinking, and years and years of such mornings, the fearless young bar brawler having become in middle age a dull-witted, useless-to-anyone drunk. "Danny had one job," quipped another cousin at Danny's wake, "and he did it well." Which, of course, got a big laugh, while helping keep alive the Romance of Butte.

Admittedly, what I've just said represents half a lifetime of surveying the past, distilling and recombining and reinterpreting what I could scarcely articulate while it was happening. Back then all I could say for sure was that I found Butte suffocating. So, at fourteen and fed up, I ran away from home. That much, at least, is indisputable. On Halloween night, a friend and I hopped a freight train bound for exotic, faraway Phoenix and the home of a former girlfriend, whom I'd neglected to tell about our plan. No matter. We were caught just as the train was about to leave the station in Dillon, one stop from the border. But the failed escape didn't lessen my desire to put Butte as far behind me as possible, both emotionally and geographically, an experiment that bcgan in earnest the day after I graduated high school, when I left town for good, and with the blessing—if not the full understanding—of my parents.

"Which of us is not forever a stranger and alone?" wrote Thomas Wolfe in the *Look Homeward* passage that Dan Price adopted as his personal prayer. My estrangement didn't last forever but a paltry twenty-five years, almost to the day. To be sure, I'd gone back now and again, but never stayed long. In time the trips became less frequent, and during my stays I took less notice, especially after I moved back East. Also being something of a self-mythologizer, I used to say that the urge to return to Butte didn't show itself until my last years in New York, when I retired for good from magazine editing and started writing full-time, and that when the urge did appear, it was sudden, irresistible—that I was seized by a desire to go home. But that's malarkey. I wasn't so much seized as gradually seduced, teased. More than that, I now see, I conspired in the seduction. All the time I was traveling ever farther away, I was looking over my shoulder, gazing homeward even as I renounced home, denying both my debt to Butte and its claim on me but never quite letting Butte out of sight, out of mind.

The last thing I wanted to admit, of course, was that by virtue of circumstance and character defect I'd been cast as yet another prodigal son who wakes up amidst his sorrowful wanderings only to realize that what he wants or needs most is what he left behind. Nothing so stereotypical or pedestrian would suit me. After all, since my teens I had been hard about the task of composing the Romance of Eddie, which in fact owed much to the Romantic tradition itself, especially the primacy of the imagination and the glorification of the individual. I would be the center of my own universe. I would be the inventor of my own identity. Instead of finding meaning, I would make meaning—unbounded by social or religious convention, untamed by the strictures of family, neighborhood, community. If I had any forebears of note, they were forebears I chose—not my mother and father, surely, or their parents, an absurd notion, but instead Camus, Beckett, and Nietzsche, Rimbaud, Nikos Kazantzakis, William Blake, Wallace Stevens, Borges and Rilke, Godard, Fellini, Bergman. There I was, then, in Buffalo, New York, followed by Long Island, Brooklyn, Little Italy, Greenwich Village, living out the defining myth of the West. The very picture of unconscious irony and contradiction. A self-made caricature navigating the urban wilderness of Manhattan with the aid of a rearview mirror.

Head East, young man, that you may know the singular pleasure of discovering the West . . . on your own terms. And those are indeed the magic words: on my own terms.

Although in retrospect I realize that the accidental re-enchantment of the West in general, and Butte in particular, had been building almost imperceptibly from the moment I crossed the Mississippi River, there were clearly delineated moments when I was forced to remember and, more

important, reconsider what I was trying in vain to forget. One of them took place in Buffalo. At that time, the late seventies and early eighties, I was still striving to write for the theater. To support my doomed habit, I took jobs anywhere I could find them—factories, assembly lines, manufacturing plants. All blue collar, though unskilled. And all reminiscent of Butte. In the multiethnic, working-class soul of one of America's landmark industrial cities, I detected a familiar reflection. And maybe because it was only a reflection of the place, instead of the place itself, I was for the first time not repulsed. Quite the opposite. In Buffalo, twenty times larger than Butte and located two thousand miles away, but also struggling to survive the decline of its major industry, I felt very much at home—and precisely because it possessed so much of what was best about home.

Another moment—rather, series of moments—that's worth mentioning took place in what at the time was my favorite bar in the West Village, the Corner Bistro. The Bistro was one of those ideal New York bars that functioned as both neighborhood joint and word-of-mouth retreat for writers, musicians, artists, and intellectuals. A sublime, harmonious, and often entertaining confluence of low and high culture. In short, bohemia, the place that will always be for me The Old Country. Among the other charms of the Bistro was its jukebox, which featured everything from Robert

Johnson to Willie Nelson, Duke Ellington to Jimi Hendrix, Patsy Cline and Patti Smith, Frank Zappa and Frank Sinatra. In that eclectic collection, I also found several tunes by the Pogues, the drunken louts who invented Irish punk. One song in particular I played every time I visited the Bistro—"Dirty Old Town." It wasn't written by the Pogues, but they turned it into one of their signature numbers. (And if you've ever been to a Pogues concert, you know what I mean. Believe it or not, they're still doing reunion tours.) In "Dirty Old Town," Shane McGowan sings, "Kissed my girl by the factory wall." Hinting not at industry romanticized but at the possibility of romance in an industrial setting, which is a crucial distinction. No sentimentality. No pretensions. No excuses.

I listened to the Pogues' "Dirty Old Town" again and again because I increasingly enjoyed being taken back, if only in reverie, to my dirty old town. And that much at least I was sure I liked about Butte. The brute fact of dirt—allied with the equally brute fact that no one saw a need to cover up the dirt. For many Montanans in exile, the odor that usually conjures up images of home is sage, with pine a close second. And I'm as susceptible as the next person. But for me there's another odor that's equally evocative—sulfur. The sharp smell of mine dumps, where I played as a kid. That the dirty old town in the song was an unpretty place dominated by factories also struck a personal chord. I

hadn't grown up on a farm or ranch. Rural culture was foreign to me. Indeed, much of Montana as a whole was foreign to me. If at long last I was going to own up to the influence of the past, it had been a largely urban past, on an island, as someone once observed, completely surrounded by land. The West I was starting to long for was a West that had much in common with the East I had escaped to. At heart, I realized, I was a city kid. No wonder Manhattan felt like home the instant I arrived there. No wonder it still does.

Here's the last and most consequential moment: back before SoHo was transformed from an artist's colony into an outdoor shopping mall for the rich and beautiful, I often stopped to browse at a second-hand photography store on Mercer Street. One day I found myself thumbing through the pages of *The Americans*, Robert Frank's somber black-and-white portrait of the U.S. during the 1950s. Page 61 in particular caught my eye. The photograph depicts two diaphanous lace curtains draped before a concrete ledge beyond which rows of stark frame houses and brick duplexes recede into the distance—an unassuming town seen from a fourth-story window, seen a long time ago, all drab gray and dull black and presented in Frank's usual raw manner. I continued studying the melancholy picture, puzzled and slightly unsettled, trying to fathom its attraction.

Perhaps, I thought, it's the theatricality of the

image that claims my attention. The curtains are parted halfway, but while the right one hangs straight down, the left curves from top to bottom, as if someone had only recently pulled it aside to permit a wider view. A drama seems imminent, and that expectation is further reinforced by the ledge, which, running along the bottom of the frame, recalls the floorboards of a stage. If so, the action most likely will begin where, in the distance, the houses yield to a hill stripped of vegetation. Located just this side of that slope is the only hint of motion in the entire photograph. A meandering wood fence surrounds a similarly barren patch of land, at one end of which huddle several wood buildings and the towering headframe of an underground mine. From the shaft, or very near the shaft, steam rises in a column forty, maybe fifty, feet high, its shape vaguely human, vaguely sinister, an ascending apparition that engulfs the skeletal headframe and looms over the neighborhoods spread before it.

Loosely organized and seemingly uncontrived, Frank's photographs often contain details that can be easily overlooked or underappreciated but which once fully grasped are unforgettable. This was one of them, and more—for me, much more. This particular detail triggered a detonation whose aftereffects continue to this day. Headframe? Mine yard? I turned to the facing page and read the caption for the first time: "View from hotel window—Butte, Montana." Incredibly, I had been staring at a picture of my hometown, the place where I passed the first eighteen years of my life, but without realizing it, not consciously, at any rate. Frank had stopped in Butte toward the end of his groundbreaking cross-country trip, and in that out-of-the-way place he found plenty of the postwar desolation he had encountered elsewhere—isolated billboards addressing nothing but night air; uneasy, distracted families in stalled cars; a vacant luncheonette; an idle post office; and this, the eastern, increasingly industrialized part of Butte as it once looked from a room in the Finlen Hotel.

Once looked. With that realization came a second, very different shock: the scene Frank's photograph depicted no longer existed. Streets and sidewalks, frame houses and brick buildings—most of the Eastside neighborhoods had been torn down or relocated to make room for the cavity known as the Berkeley Pit, the mammoth excavation that inaugurated the last stage of large-scale mineral extraction in Summit Valley.

That twofold sense of loss became the framework for my return: I was on a quest to reclaim the place that made me, a place that in some measure—the extent of which I was intent on finding out—no longer existed. And whatever I discovered would somehow find its way into my writing—articles and essays for periodicals, a book, a documentary film, notes for plays, scraps of novels. For the first time, my life and my life's work would merge; what I'd made of myself would be reconciled with what made me. And since I was by then an independent writer, free to go anywhere I wish, why not live on the edge of the largest Superfund site in the country? Why not the rural Romanian village known as Walkerville, where now I've resided for fifteen years?

Albert Camus, a favorite among my many appropriated ancestors, wrote this: "A man's work is nothing but the slow trek to rediscover, through the detours of art, those two or three great and simple images in whose presence his heart first opened." I agree. But there's more to it than that. The slow trek almost always transforms the traveler. He returns from exile to find that his long-lost Great and Simple Images may yet be great but perhaps not so simple. The trek that began with an open heart inevitably leads to heartbreak. He discovers that his home is both familiar and strange, that it's just as much elsewhere as any other elsewhere he's visited. And if he's an artist, he allows these tensions and contradictions to seep into his work, to shape its direction, making them a source of both delight and dismay. From my shanty on the Hill, I see a place that in many ways still repulses me. Suffocating, small-minded clannishness; a reputation for friendliness that masks hostility toward outsiders; a certain religious and social conservatism; ignorance and prejudice; mind-numbing self-mythologizing. It's all here. And I see nothing to be gained by pretending that the Dirty Old Town isn't dirty, including a history full of ruthless gangsters, bloodthirsty murderers, rapacious thieves—and that's not counting the Anaconda Company.

What I'm calling the Romance of Butte is of a piece with a larger effort under way in the West, a sentimental exercise in collective grief and regret that goes by several names but always privileges the word *place*. I attended a literary conference in Missoula called "Sense of Place" thirty-five years ago. Since then, that same conference has been duplicated throughout the West too many times to keep track. I wouldn't be surprised if at this very moment someone were organizing yet another one. Here's one thing you can be sure of: so much impassioned talk by so many bright people about something everyone agrees is so valuable probably means that that something is already lost. Gone. Never to be recovered, at least not in the form it's been assigned in this new secular religion. What's more, to the extent that local history and culture are celebrated in the absence of a critical perspective, such endeavors, however well-intentioned, are sterile. Let's drug ourselves with nostalgia instead of facing the messy, provisional, ever-problematic reality at hand, the reality that refuses to fit neatly within the confines of conventional narrative.

One of the characteristics that distinguishes my dirty old town, and which I've come to appreciate almost above all others, is that the dirt is on display. In the brute actuality of the mining landscape, the industrial ruins, I see a kind of beauty—the beauty of unashamed candor. No sentimentality. No pretensions. No excuses. Yes, many of my neighbors, godblessem, do a remarkably effective job of blinding themselves to aspects of the town that don't accord with the stories they tell themselves and others, the stories that, paradoxically, have contributed much to the Mining City's vitality and longevity. This is a place, we must remember, that's gone to hell and back. And more than once.

It's also true that, in the attempt to repair the ravaged land, the poisoned water—a noble and necessary task, certainly—we run the risk of burying or erasing and, therefore, systematically forgetting what we most need to remember. Reclamation as a kind of amnesia. As an inside-outsider, one foot in, one foot out, I intend to do everything in my power—in my roles as both writer and citizen—to make sure that doesn't happen. I view this as an act of love, the best way I know to pay respect to the place and people I long renounced, even, at times, ridiculed. But I'm keenly aware that some of my neighbors may see my twofold stance as an act of betrayal. And I take no comfort from the fact that after *Look Homeward, Angel* Wolfe wrote *You Can't Go Home Again*, the story of a writer whose novel about his hometown so angers his family and friends that he is forced to leave.

Going home, I've found, is easy. The hard part is staying home, writing and making a documentary film about my neighbors while living among them—and with every intention of being here afterward. How much easier it was when I could parachute into someone else's reality for a short time, then make pronouncements from a distance, waxing wise and arrogant with my drinking buddies at the Corner Bistro. Now, what I write matters. There are consequences. Consequences I cannot escape or ignore. Which, come to think of it, is a pretty good definition of community, the community I joined—voluntarily, for the first time—when I moved back home. I write with particular people in mind—including people who've died, like Dan Price, my parents and brother, characters who appear in my nonfiction work—not because I want to please them, although that's certainly part of it, but because I've grown so fond of them, so impressed by who they are and what they've made of their lives in this hard, often unforgiving place that I feel obliged to be straight with them.

My loyalty, in other words, sometimes takes a different form than theirs. Danny had one job. And he did it well. When my cousin said that, I not only laughed, I felt liberated. My load lightened a little. How could a mining town, where men, families, whole neighborhoods were routinely sacrificed, survive without black humor, without the extravagant and rebellious urge to laugh in the face of death? But let's not forget that Danny was a monster, a man of violence, a selfish, ignorant drunkard who abandoned his children, along with everyone else who cared about him. Hold these two views in mind at the same time, and maybe you get a little closer to the truth of Butte.

What I've just described is, of course, the Mining City version of the modernist dilemma. Though it's been around for a long time, that dilemma still has profound implications for writers, filmmakers, and other artists, as well as historians, sociologists, anthropologists, industrial archaeologists—implications that have been explored by others but by none so provocatively as the efforts of Leslie Fiedler, the brilliant literary critic who taught at The University of Montana for a brief, scandalous spell. In an essay titled "Waiting for the End," Fiedler addressed the limitations of regional literature. His case study was Jewish American stories and poems, but his analysis applies to all localized forms of writing that are self-congratulatory, defensive, apologetic, its excesses and omissions pandering to the author's local audience.

Such literature becomes universal only when, as Fiedler wrote,

> regional writers stop being apologists and become critics, abandon falsification and sentimentality in favor of treating not the

special virtues, be they real or fancied, but the weaknesses it shares with all men. Such writers seem often to their fellows, their very friends and parents, traitors—not only for the harsh things which they are led to say about those fellows, friends and parents in the pursuit of truth, but also because their desire for universality of theme and appeal leads them to begin tearing down from within the walls of a cultural ghetto, which, it turns out, has meant security as well as exclusion to the community that nurtured them.

So, to my fellow writers in Montana, I say: instead of composing odes to our cultural ghettos or, more likely, to the restoration of those ghettos, let's tear down what remains of the walls. Being seen by some as traitors is a small price to pay for such good and necessary work.

During the first few years after my return, I was often asked to explain the move. Lower Manhattan for East Walkerville? How come? Now the more likely question is whether I intend to stay.

Frankly, I don't believe I have a choice in the matter. It turns out that Dan Price was right about the magnetism of Butte. And in more ways than one. For starters, the sulfurous soil of home is laced with arsenic,

which is addictive. And I'm hooked again. Worse still, I
like it. This too: I had naively assumed that the literary
dimension of the quest would end with the completion
of the film—a dramatic exclamation point. Then I'd
be done with Butte, at least as a subject. But what I've
realized of late is that the place will be with me, and me
with it, for a long time to come.

Addict, traitor, native son.

This doesn't mean I won't run away from home
again. I will. And often, if I have my way. Just as I'll
return again and again. Because it is here, in Butte, that
my heart first opened.

Six Poems
Dennice Scanlon

My Grandfather's Hands

When I think of hands, my grandfather rocks
on the back porch with a wonderful
pipe and cane. Wine cellar summers ripen
three decades into memory—black
grapes in the vat, fat bottles and new
corks. I rush to his knee believing
time spills over.

Everything reeks in the space between
beams—brine from the cabbage
crock, pork slabs hooked
through the ribs, wisps of cinnamon
stick and watermelon rind, mash
beneath the still. It is in my grandfather's house
on Park, its number hard
multiples of four, where I recognize need
compounds the past, the vintage he renders like
    some
withered Merlin, wise old oak
leg and peg teeth.

What he brings to my life is a kitchen
feast steeped and salted. It gels

on the rim like a catch
in the throat. Sauerkraut steams. A big fork
pulls the sausage from a cast
iron pot. It's a harvest night
when pepper moths brush the creamy bowl
of his pipe and he rocks to the flapping
of the screen door. I'm too full to know
all brew is memory, the small fist
buried in a great dark palm.

Migration

How we used to find grosbeaks, sometimes
a purple finch on fall mornings
outside our school. The mountain ash
brought them in hoards and sent them south
spinning with the taste of long
full days. I watched them all
through catechism, stories of saints
brushed clean by the wings of grace.
When they reached the town's edge
birds grew common, stale

brown as tenement shacks, mud sparrows
huddled between the logs, old men

who lived alone. Sister Alicia taught us:
"Blessed are the poor. They shall rise
to the kingdom of light." At night
their tin cups clattered beneath the roof
slats, their rag and stick rhythms
broke my sleep. I could always sense
their coming—a peg leg slapping
on the pavement or rapping at my door
with mason jars to peddle, the honey man,
his beard white as sugar crystals

forming on a glass rim. Unlike the birds
who left each branch worn
chamois smooth, old men stayed the winter.
They walked the tracks behind coal
trains or dragged the rotting ties back
to camp. I'm wake in the cold to press
against the pane, watch the smoke
from their cabins catch the streetlight
glow and play with it, swirl
it like rare wine, bright birds

rising. Because I stayed on too, pausing
now and then at windows, waiting for trees
to darken with another flock. I remained

that fall the housing project cleared away
their shacks and the hobos packed up—
a late sun bouncing off their gypsy
clutter, jars and cans and stove pipes
swaying in flight.

The Difference in Effects of Temperature Depending on Geographical Location East or West of the Continental Divide: A Letter

I had a mind to begin by scraping April
from the ridge. When in doubt, the saying
goes, dwell on weather. Haven't we been blessed
with dusk, a thousand ways to grieve the sun
receding? You must find spring a welcome
change where little changes. It's easy
to spot along valley fencelines—the new
calves, Hawn's mended coop, snake-edged
alfalfa oddly whipped against the wind.
Rain doesn't mean as much here. Pigeons
clutter the eaves, softball's late
starting but words wear thin for clouds
in season, the sting of long drives home.

At fifty-two hundred feet, torn buildings
soar. You left before mines with names
dull as Alice closed Butte. The big strike
settled like copper rings on branches.

Cottonwoods wrapped around sewerlines to pop
them at the joints and dusted days took
root. I only mention it because land to us
is personal as choice, whether it swells
in bluffs, plateaus or Indian Corn,
we both know what's enough. Yours gives back
what you put in—grain, slim tops
of asparagus, early beets. Mine demands
something hard to thrive, a red metal core.
When it's gone, dying's less complicated,
slow, as one house at a time boards up,
another promise of work falls through, ground
that's left overlaps its people and keeps
them from the boundary of their dreams.

It weighs my mind to write this way
with sky in doubt, bringing April when gray birds
sulk in the eaves. There was more to say
but news is smaller on the page, neighbors
nice to lunch with, the friends we knew
still close. I wanted to tell you nights
are filmy and alive with bugs, invite you
for Shakespeare in the Park beneath a peeling
signboard, find a part for your eyes to play
out in stages or fold you like a paper star.
But I know what mountains divide, some
common ground unsettled. The best country
is one we can sow and leave with fewer words.

And the best letter brief, seasonal as wheat
or old town affairs. One that closes before
weather wilts ridges between with love.

The Golden Years

What a pink smell my mother's dress leaves
along the cupboard this June
morning, 1952. I watch her sprinkle
flour on the dough she's kneaded
since dawn and tire
waiting for odors to sweeten
the kitchen, of tales I know
by heart—one princess turned to stone
by a kiss, another locked
away in a tower, all those years of gold

let down. Outside legends flounder
in the heat, mineyards overrun
with buttercups, gravel
strewn beneath a battered sluicebox.
Yet glitter keeps me burning
to wrench it from the earth, hold it
hard in my hands and have nothing
else matter. My shovel
is only a twig that scrapes
the surface, while below me in a mine

tunnel, my father drills the damp
timbered walls, praying for stone to turn

his life toward the sun. Between summer
and November, my pockets fill with yellow
rocks. I linger on the front porch
steps to be swept up in a moment
of soil and stubble to his cheek, the hard
set lips, lunch pail
banging at my heels. My mother smiles
when she sees us, her eyes dark
as old stories. We sit at the table
for years, a single bulb shining
on a plate of golden hot rolls.

Ballad For A Butte Miner

4000 feet down the Leonard shaft, my father forked
drifts from a slab of bark and the beam shot
by a rusted headlamp. When cables popped
or caps exposed a copper vein, he mucked out
the dream every miner stakes on deep tunnel mud
caked red on his knees.

> Load up. We'll buck the Company contract.
> Suck the guts from this bastard drift.
> The scab we string in effigy will swing
> till the Irish curse their green.

The war raged for air in '22 from the stench
of Black Rock silt. Turned despair by '34 when
> stopes closed
with a blast. Some dug the ruins for silver chunks,
others a leg or son. Mercy had a name that year:
Union scale, first shift down, round in. Round out
the last one up.

> Settle my ass. Buck the Company contract.
> Suck the guts from this bastard drift.
> The scab we string in effigy will swing
> till the Irish curse their green.

Remember the Kelly cave-in, timber rot at the Lex,
> sulfur
burn and shattered words that raise day's pay
by the book. Lungs get hard after nerve goes limp
or sinks into a bar mirror. Overtime, wage cut,
time and a half, cut back, part time, lay off,
draw your time.

> Strike. Buck the Company contract.
> Suck the guts from this bastard drift.
> The scab we string in effigy will swing
> till the Irish curse their green.

Miners choose poison like levels onshift: Silicosis,
bootleg, gamble or bum. The mineyard thief who strips
his fire from Belmont fence, dark corn bottled
in pool rooms. Break out the best before cages drop
the midnight crew, slush buckets block the crosscut.
Pour the house three fingers and shoot for more.

    Keg up. We'll buck the Company contract.
    Suck the guts from this bastard drift.
    Cut down the scab who swings in effigy
    for the Irish burn our graves green.

the winter slope. Love dies. You learn to flood
the shaft that fails, dig for veins
you have no stake in.

Aren't all claims ancient where we settle our remains?
Do words come after flowers dry or white stoops sag
in the rain? And life we drain from timbered drifts—
will it still burn like the peacock rock it bubbles?
There's little shelter in mines that work
their own shift. No memory survives
the short way home.

Homestead

Dog days in high country offer no relief. I hunker
where trails climb to claims that turned the century
rich, ore Cape-bound for Scotland like a dream
of easy ways back. It must have paid panning
the creek with stillwater eyes, snapdragons to flutter
in spring. What words came after dredges tunneled
through for greed? Did old ones linger for a nugget
or sunday lighting up the ridge?

Roots and stone. Reason for returning autumn nights.
Pictures yellowed under glass, faces torn or buried
by the gray waste heaped behind, nothing grows
when you find the road to town. Cold sky deepens

Two Stories

Manus Dugan
        Ron Fischer

When a sudden gust of hot air blasted him, Manus Dugan sensed that something wrong had happened in the mine. The wet timbers receding into the dark of the crosscut seemed thin and fragile. Old worries tormented him. His child refused to be born. Madge was ten days overdue. Every night, he went to work with regret and now this. Dry air doesn't sweep down a mine stope twenty-six hundred feet underground, particularly from the direction of the elevator shaft. In the dark silence, Manus could hear the mine timbers creak and felt a shrinking in his bones. He left his ore car on the skid rail and walked toward the shaft to find out what it meant.

He pictured Madge at home lying across the bed. He could hear how the bedsprings would strain and see Madge's fist wad the purple blanket lying on their bed, her other hand clutching her swollen belly, her face grimacing because of a cramp. Desperation made him walk faster. Day after day, she was pregnant. It made him helpless. In the mornings, he came and lay beside her, listening to the ore trains rumbling over the sunlit hillsides of Butte, the day bright against the skein of green window shade. Sometimes she cried softly and he held her, feeling awake, feeling her heavy, auburn hair against his face until he drifted into dreams of the mine and its black tunnels.

"Let the other fools blast themselves to bits," she had said loudly when he had asked her to marry him a year and a half ago. Straight time for the Company, that's what she wanted him to work if she was going to get married.

"But there's money in contracting."

"Two hundred dollars is widow's pay when the mine caves. I don't want a man with dirt so deep on him he's got to let it wear off and who'll live past thirty-five only if he's lucky."

What could he say? She had red cheeks on winter days that put you in mind of the petals on a moss rose. Her bright eyes could glance on him and suddenly numb him all over, like having a hammer smack his thumb.

So he gave up mining, went straight time, and took the nipper's job. Maybe he still worked underground carting steel drills and dynamite to the contractors, but he didn't have to stand under loose rock or breathe the gray dust kicked from a miner's buzzie as it hammered hole after hole. After six months of straight time, she married him. It was the closest thing to gold yet.

Manus stopped cold. A black cloud rolled slowly down the crosscut toward him. Smoke hung about two feet off the floor and billowed around him. There was a fire burning somewhere. The shaft? He took a breath. The air tasted bitter as green willows burning and its ash nudged deep into his lungs where it twitched a cord that made him cough and hack. He backed ten feet away.

He could hear the faraway cracks of explosion and the dull thunder of fire. His neck muscles tightened. He looked at the shell of smoke and imagined bright gold flames bursting the dry timbers of the shaft into ribbons of black ash. The whole shaft, a tower of dry beams and planks half a mile long, was exploding into a volcanic hole. He could picture the glowing cinders and dark smoke rippling from the blazes, blood-red fire balls leaping higher and higher, the long well of liquid blackness roaring with its immolation, and the flames finally erupting on the surface into a blazing geyser, torching the headframe and the elevator cages, spraying the mineyard with white-hot embers, spewing a black cloud of soot into the sky.

In the distance, he heard someone inside the fumes wheeze for air and cough. "Faron!" He called the names of the miners he had just left. "Faron! Ansely! Faron!"

Manus sucked in a breath and charged into the curling cloud. When he needed to breathe again, he stooped over and kept his face in that margin of clear air left between the smoke and the ground. When the smoke filled the whole crosscut, he wrapped his arm around his head and breathed through the crook of his denim jacket. His carbide light was so dim it was useless. He smacked into a stull and knocked himself down. His cheek lay against the warm steel of the tram rail. His eye caught the sequin of his carbide flame reflecting off the worn steel. The mine rock looked gray against the feeble glow of carbide. No one coughed anymore. The air was hot as a furnace. Although he took his breath through his sleeve and held it as he crawled, his lungs flared as if scraped by a rasp. It was all he could do to hold a cough back.

He touched the man's shoulder, then grabbed a whole arm and felt the body flop. He felt for the man's nose to see whether he was still breathing. His fingertips touched something sticky and warm, blood. Had the man torn his own throat to get a gulp of good air? Manus bolted for clear air. He tripped over the tram rail, got up, and ran on, feeling dizzy and blind. The few minutes it took to stumble into clear air seemed unending. Had the entire crosscut filled up with smoke? Suddenly his carbide lamp opened like a small hand of light against the rock and receding timbers.

When he stopped and turned to look at the cloud swirling toward him, he felt like he had stood for years on this same spot. Life suddenly seemed to repeat itself. A drop of water fell from the rough ceiling above him and landed on his neck. His fingertips were stained with small rusty spots. Looking at them, he felt the bones of his spine bristle. He coughed and the phlegm in his throat tasted syrupy.

Trapped. There was no way up. Madge and the baby left without him. He had to calm himself. Staying out of the wood gas meant everything now. Somewhere ahead the other miners of the twenty-six hundred were still working. He had to warn them. He began running down the crosscut, his boots thudding against the rail ties, crunching the gravel of the railbed.

He met a crowd of miners who had also felt the rush of hot air and were making for the shaft. Bill Lucas smiled at him. Bill was seventeen, gangly legged and cocky. Bill's eyes darted from Manus to Leonard McClure, the miner who was breaking Bill in. Leonard saw to it that Bill was paying the price: blisters and backache. Manus liked Bill because he didn't peter out. He stuck to his job. Right now he was sorry Bill had.

"The shaft's on fire," Manus said.

Leonard shoved his hat back and rubbed his hairline. With his hat tilted back like a skull cap and with that leather apron over his trousers, Leonard looked like the barrel-chested Jewish butcher who had a shop on Main Street. Whenever he saw Leonard, Manus saw another version of himself, the man Manus was afraid he would become if he hadn't married Madge. Alone and angry, his best feelings blasted and mucked out years ago. The rich veins of compassion

traded for whiskey and the empty pockets the girls on Venus Alley leave a man with.

But what did it matter now? As certainly as he knew the smoke was drifting toward them, he knew that he faced the deepest stope he had ever come upon. This would test all the timber and lagging he had inside him. He couldn't panic. He couldn't let the whole mountain of his being collapse. There had to be a way out. "We got to hole up somewhere and keep the smoke from choking us."

"No," Murphy Shea said. Shea was a Wobblie. He shoved between Leonard and Bill. "The manways. We'll climb out of here."

"What the hell?" Leonard shouted. "We can't climb a half mile out of here." Bill Lucas didn't smile anymore. Spiro Bezersich, Al Cobb, Gozdenica, and the others stared at him.

"We can try," Manus said, knowing the Speculator Mine had a tunnel into the Rainbow Mine on the twenty-two hundred level. "The twenty-two. Just far as the twenty-two. We can walk into the Rainbow and ride the cage up from there."

"Twenty-two," Gozdenica said, "we make." Gozdenica started shoving through the miners, taking the lead toward the raise that had ladders coming down from the twenty-four hundred. As they walked, Manus made out the smudged faces of John McGarry, Spiro Bezersich, Krist Popovich, Joe McAdams, and Al Cobb.

Gozdenica, usually smiling-faced, turned to look at them. He seemed expectant and uncertain. The lime dry smell of dynamite lingered near the last drift they passed. Manus' shirt, wet with sweat, clung to him.

Leonard had a way of sprawling his elbows and legs to make himself the biggest man in a room. Bill Lucas butted around Leonard and Manus. Bill had quit school a year ago. Since then, Manus had watched him load ore cars, muck, and even drive mules on the tram. He was a fast learner who worked hard. As Bill walked in front of them, Manus could see Bill had even picked up Leonard's way of walking, high-headed, like he was some kind of wonder man who knew how to break a dollar's more worth of ore than any other miner, how to wash all the dust out of his blood with a couple of beers and hang on a little harder to those ringlet-haired chippies down in Venus Alley. Leonard, who knew stopes where the rock broke easy, bars where the silver dollars squeezed out of your hand like mercury, and girls who slid under you just as easy, was responsible.

In the manway, men bunched up as everyone waited for the fellow ahead of him to climb high enough so the miner's heels wouldn't boot against his head. Manways and stopes, tunnels and shafts, the mine was a honeycomb without honey. At least they weren't on the thirty-two hundred, Manus thought. The manways didn't go that deep. No one there had any chance of getting out. All he had to do now was open his palm and an iron rung suddenly filled it. He was climbing out.

At the twenty-four hundred, Manus followed the miners ahead of him down the crosscut and toward the next manway up. No one spoke. They panted and their clothes rustled, their heels crackled the ground. Manus' carbide and the miners' candles etched the bark-stripped posts into gray bones and fragmented their shadows into dark starlings that flitted and weaved across the rock wall.

Before they reached the manway on the twenty-four hundred, some miners ran into them from behind. Negretto and Worta, Evcovich and Jennis, Jovick, Ned Heston and Godre Galia, and some others—men from the twenty-four hundred. There were many now, maybe twenty or more.

"Gas cut us off," Ned Heston said. His hands looked like fat potatoes.

"How far back?"

"Coming fast."

Herb Carlson behind them stumbled into Manus and apologized. "They're shoving."

"Smoke's coming on 'em," Ned said.

At the manway, Manus heard Leonard shouting, "Keep climbing."

"He won't," Al Cobb said.

"Who's up there?" Leonard demanded.

"Gozdenica."

"That bastard better move his ass!"

Men were strung along the ladder, but no one climbed. "Let them down," Manus said, seeing that the highest men on the ladder were stepping down instead of climbing up. "Give them room."

"Come down," Leonard bellowed. "Get your ass off and let me up."

Steve came into view. "We're cut off. It's all smoke up there."

Manus shined his carbide upward and squinted into the heights. He saw billows of gas. Behind him men in the stope coughed. Leonard shoved to the iron ladder, clutched its rusty railing, and grabbed Popovich's shoulders as if he wanted to fling him against the wall. McAdams, Murphy Shea, and a few others pushed through the crush of men to get beside Leonard and get at the ladder.

"No one goes up," Manus said. The whites of Leonard's eyes bulged and Shea set his jaw firm.

"Stay here and die then," Leonard took the unlit cigar that he chewed on from his mouth and tossed it against the rock wall.

"Stay together." Manus looked at the wild eyes that showed like hens' eggs in his light. "No one can make that climb. Not in gas."

"We go 'til we drop," Leonard said.

"No!" Manus made a fist. "We hole up. All of us, in a blind drift."

"The twenty-four seventeen." Steve waved from the ladder. Cobb and Ned Heston repeated his words and headed out of the manway. Motes of dust rained through the dim light. Everyone else held their ground to see what Leonard did.

"All right, all right." Leonard waved them to follow Cobb and Heston. "The twenty-four seventeen."

Manus believed in his chances of living when he could keep moving. Al Cobb, a short man who wore a woodsman's cap cocked to his right side so that his oversized left ear stuck out like the handle of a coffee cup, led them toward the twenty-four seventeen. When everyone stopped, they were facing forty feet of a dead drift.

"What we do?" Jovick asked.

"For Chrissake. Bulkheads. Two of them. Here and there. Them posts and laggings. Pull that canvas off the vent. Pile up rocks. Dirt. We gotta build us two goddamn walls. One here. One away, about two yards away."

Manus pulled out a pocket knife and cut into the canvas of a vent. "We can use this to line it." La Montague started ripping more of it down. Cobb took a hammer left in the drift and knocked a stull out of a drift set.

They understood. Jovick uncoupled a hydraulic line. "Is there air?" Manus asked.

"Naw, dead."

"Take a couple pieces of pipe."

With the two walls shaping up, Bill Lucas suddenly disappeared down the drift. Manus wondered if he was following Leonard back to the manway. But Leonard was there, shoveling rock and dirt out of the drift and packing it into a mound against the bulkheads. Bill suddenly came back with a small waterkeg left in the crosscut. It was about a quarter full.

"We're gonna need this."

"Get behind the bulkhead."

McAdams and Gozdenica brought boards from the drift set walls. Manus saved a piece of canvas to make a flap for a crawl space between the inner wall and the bulkhead. He had trouble pulling enough saliva together to spit the pasty, sweet dust out of his mouth.

When the walls were finished, he and Cobb waited in the six feet of space between the makeshift bulkheads, plugging holes when they saw wisps of gray smoke seeping through. Where the wall met the ceiling was weakest. One candle burned in the blind drift where the miners sat, backs against the bare rock, and another flickered where Manus and Cobb sat. There were twenty-nine of them. They ripped their shirts, handed up trousers and socks to Cobb and Manus to seal out the smoke.

"That's enough." They settled back, like two rows of bats, their backs against the rock wall. Their naked flesh seemed white as talc in the pale glow of candlelight.

"Take this, for later." Manus gave Cobb a second length of pipe afterward. Cobb cocked his head, his protruding ear a question mark.

"What for?"

"When they come at us." Manus said it dryly. He gripped the pipe, thinking that no matter how hard it would be to swing on a man he had worked with, he'd rather see the miner hurt than dead. "Are you with me? If you can't, I'll understand."

Al hefted the pipe against his palm, then slowly nodded. His calloused palm was black with dirt.

Manus felt the weight of his watch and his nipper's pad touching his chest through his shirt pocket. He wondered whether Madge had had the baby. He took out his watch and checked the time, thirteen minutes after midnight. It would come at a time like this, he thought. They were only into the shift an hour.

It pained every time he took his watch out. Hours became the ballooning of men's shadows on the rock wall, the dank smell of wet earth mingling with burnt wax, the jab of a sharp rock against his back until the nerve twitched, the burning down of a candle until it sputtered and got replaced before dying out, the shuffle of men who took turns at watching the first bulkhead for seepage.

"We hit the motherlode this time," said Leonard.

Manus fingered his nipper's pad where it rested

in his shirt pocket and mapped out all the things he wanted to write on it. La Montague reached a cigarette to the short candle flame. His tobacco glowed ember red as he sucked on the scraggly rolled twig, creating the only color in the dullness.

"Put it out," Leonard said, but La Montague inhaled and turned the red glow gold. "You're burning good air." His arm stretched out and he snatched the cigarette from La Montague's face. La Montague cursed at him in French.

"Leonard's right," Manus said. "No one smokes. Give me the rest of it, La Montague. All you pass it up."

He dug a hole away from the wall and buried their tobacco. McGarry mumbled a tune to himself. Henry Fowler had a pack of cards and started a game with Mike Spihr and Atha Stewart. Negretto had his head lowered and mumbled over and over something quiet and Catholic. Murphy Shea leaned back on his elbows and kicked Negretto's feet. "God's a bum bastard." Negretto swallowed and looked away from Shea. Shea grinned, repeated himself and laughed.

Hours later, Manus took another turn between the bulkheads. The air smelled worse in this small space than in the big chamber. Smoke had seeped through. He couldn't see where, no fumes showed, but the air had fouled. The candle burned dimmer, and his breath came heavy as syrup. He didn't know which to fear more, the gas or the slow poisoning of the big chamber by every man whose breathing stole another fresh gulp of oxygen and who exhaled poison.

Away from the others, Manus took his nipper's pad from his trouser pocket. His partner, Steve Gozdenica, looked at the smudge of white paper Manus held in the dark chamber and looked away as if he didn't want to see it. Manus regretted that Gozdenica saw it. He wanted to write Madge, but he felt that saying anything somehow admitted defeat, betrayed the hope. He didn't write what he wanted to say or what Gozdenica, whose eyes kept shifting away from him, believed he was writing. He wrote just the facts:

> *Been here since 12 o'clock Friday*
> *night. No gas coming through bulkheads.*
> *Have water. All in good spirits.*

He squinted to see the dark pencil marks and held the white paper close to his eyes. He hadn't betrayed their hope.

"What time is it?" Leonard asked Mannus when he crawled back into the blind drift.

"Nine o'clock."

"Morning?"

"Naw, night."

"Saturday?"

"That's right." Twenty-one hours of waiting had passed. Leonard lay on his side without saying anything. Men had shit in the diggings, pissed. Sweat loaded with the sharp adrenalin of their fears had made their bodies smell sour as apple vinegar, and exhaled carbon dioxide soured the chamber even more. They took a turn at the water keg. Leonard passed his up.

The water was warm. Manus dozed for the first time until the rumble of sliding rock shook the blind drift.

"Someone's coming," Bill Lucas said.

Manus felt the ground tremble again, then heard rocks and timbers clunk as they fell against each other.

"It's a cave-in somewhere," Leonard said, "below us. Probably water they've poured on the fire's flooding the thirty-two hundred."

"Won't be long now."

"Won't they be surprised to find us?" Gozdenica said.

"We got to let them know we're here." Nick Jovick began tapping the compressed air line with a rock. Jovick made heavy thuds with a dirge-like slowness. A metallic clang knocked the walls, traveled down the crosscut and, as Jovick and Manus hoped, as far as the shaft, even up the shaft to some listening ear that could pick out his muted throb from all the noise and know it had bubbled up from half-a-mile underground, that someone was still alive and wanting rescue.

Then time became turns at hammering.

McAdams took a turn, Ned, even Murphy Shea. Shea's pace settled into the same slow thuds that Jovick had made. Manus could hear the hollow metallic ping travel up the compressed air line. Looking intently serious, Shea hammered with the earnestness of one in true prayer. Maybe that's what all prayer is, Manus thought, the monotonous hammering out of hope.

The pings wore into them. Far off in the mine, rock continued to slide. No one noticed it anymore. Spihr and Fowler no longer shuffled cards but stayed prone, close to the ground to get the good air that had settled there. The candle made only a faint glow now. In his trouser pocket, Manus had just two remaining stubs of the candles he had collected. He decided that when this candle was burned out he would let the darkness settle around them. It would make things worse, but there was no sense burning good air and using up their last hope for light. He wondered whether news of the fire had shocked Madge into giving birth.

"Is anybody gonna spell me?" came Krist Popovich's voice. "I've been at it longest."

Leonard took his place. After a long row of clinks, he hurled the rock against the pipe. It struck a sharp clang and opened every eye.

"It's no use. No one's coming. Not now. Not ever. I say we break the bulkhead and take our chances. The fire's gotta be out. The smoke's cleared enough for us to make a climb. What do you say, Manus?"

"We'll test it. Nobody'll get far in that gas. Me and Cobb'll check it first."

They pulled some canvas from the wall and ceiling. Smoke streamed through the dirt and chinks. Although Al raised a candle, the flow of black smoke wasn't hard to see.

"Close it up." Manus said. "We'll try lower. Maybe it's hanging above the floor." They shoved a pipe beneath the wall. Fumes flowed out of the pipe, even though its end was on the ground. Leonard didn't say anything after Manus told them about the gas.

"Me and you'll timber fifty-feet," Manus said to Bill. The boy had a vacant look on his face ever since Leonard threw the rock down. His open hands lay in his lap, palms up. The white of them showed in the dimness. His face seemed sunk, too hollow for sadness.

"That boy's already learned to tell a ping from a thud. Ain't no loose rock gonna take him out," Krist Popovich threw in.

"He's learned to bar down real good." Manus smiled at him.

"It's dangerous," Bill said.

"She ain't over yet." Manus looked from face to face when he said it.

"I mined. Least I can say I did."

"Damn rights," said Popovich. "We gonna get you home yet so you take the next shift out."

"Ain't no next shift in this mine."

"Be somebody got to put it back together."

Manus closed his eyes. Memory could beat this monotonous waiting, turn the darkness into blue sky with clouds unfurling like sails and driving across the vast open space of a valley—no walls, not even the rank smell of his own breath flowing back to him. After a while, Popovich got the hand-sized rock Leonard had thrown away and began rapping the pipe.

Manus passed the water keg around for everyone to dip a finger in so they could wet their lips. The keg had gone almost dry. After lying in the dirt so long, wheezing for a breath, roasting in the heat of the crosscut, a man became so thirsty his lips stuck together. Manus allowed them just a finger's worth and trusted them with the keg. As the keg passed from man to man, the wooden thumps of hands touching its barrel sounded.

When the keg came back, Manus took out his nipper's pad. He had seen their faces as each man pressed a glistening finger to his lips and he felt a need to explain. They blamed him for being trapped here. He sensed that in the way they looked at him. His pencil whispered across the scratchpad:

We were caught
in a trap. Gas
everywhere. Built bulkheads.
Could hear rock fall.

Rapped the pipe continuously
since 4 o'clock Sunday morning.
No answer.
Must be some fire. Hard
work ahead of the rescuers.
Have not
confided my fears to anyone.

The whittle of his pencil sounded on the coarse paper. No one slept, not if he could help it. They would be opening the sky left inside them or just vacant, listening, hearing his pencil whisper its soft words.

"Write my Beth," Murphy Shea said. Everyone had heard him write. "Tell her we did the best we could."

They called out names then. Sarah, Anna, Carolyn, Mary, Rachel. Manus heard only the thin sound of resignation roll through their throats. He thought of stockyard cattle. Leonard stood up. His dark shadow looked like an old grizzly sow's. His leather apron was gone. With his shirt gone, his skin burnished ghostly in the candlelight.

"Goodbyes is it?" He stepped forward as he said it. "I'm not gonna die waitin'."

"Don't make this ugly." Manus rose up and slapped the pipe against his palm, but he understood Leonard. He couldn't blame Leonard for wanting to fight out.

"You'd use a pipe on me, huh? How many are goin' with me? Stand up. Don't let Dugan stop us."

"You're choosin' for all of us if you break that wall, Leonard."

"And just who are you choosin' for?"

"I won't let you do it. It ain't time for that yet." Manus had the pipe poking up in front of him, ready to use it on any man who made for the bulkhead.

"I say it is. Get up." Leonard yanked Yrja Johnson up. James, Shea, Bezersich, and McGarry stood up too. Cobb stood and came beside Manus, flashing his pipe for them to see. Steve Gozdenica made a hard fist and joined Manus. So did Jovick.

"All right, it's us and them," Leonard said. "And the rest of ya? You gonna wait and die in here when the air goes poison?"

Bill Lucas stood up with Leonard this time, getting right beside him. Manus didn't swing on Bill when they charged. He went for Leonard, swung the pipe, and broke Leonard's head open. The big miner fell hard, the side of his face sticky with blood. Manus didn't whack him again but waited to see what Leonard would do next. Cobb shoved Bill to the side and used the pipe across his back. Jovick and Shea pushed and wrestled with the others.

Murphy Shea pulled Leonard away from the bulkhead. The fight was gone out of Leonard.

"I don't want them to hear about it up top,"

Manus said. "Don't you be saying what happened down here. It don't look good for miners fighting themselves. We got to keep our heads. If we wait things out, they won't have to carry us out of here on slats." He threw the pipe against the bulkhead. It rattled and bounced into the dirt.

Murphy Shea nodded agreement. "Manus is right."

Stretching and flickering to stay alive, the candle flame thinned into a faint wisp. The carbon dioxide from all their breathing had filled the chamber with dead air. The candle sputtered in a last try to draw more oxygen, then went out. The darkness plunged so absolute, Manus felt how near they had come to the abyss. It was like slipping out of his body and pulling the blackness into himself. How can there be anything solid again, he wondered. At first he felt lost. To get his bearing, his ears picked up every saw of breath, even the gurgle of air inside Al Cobb's throat, its gritty rasp against his teeth, tongue, and nostrils.

Without the light, the bulkhead at his back became the only real thing. The darkness settled the weight of inevitability on him. He sensed the others feeling it too. Someone groaned. A hush would pass and then someone else would moan or choke back a cry. Sometimes an outright cry sounded, like a muffled howl that ended in huffs of breath. When men called the names of women, the blurt of their voices stabbed the blackness like sudden lightning. Some prayed out loud and others burst out crying, making no effort to hold it in anymore.

Men pawed the ground to stir oxygen out of the dirt. Manus could hear the scrapes of their clawing. He did it too, scraped a trench to hold his face into, hoping the hollow spot might catch him one gulp of breath to relieve the tightness. It was slow suffocation. But he could breathe easier; scraping freed enough oxygen in the loose dirt to make a difference.

No one rapped the pipe any more or waited between the bulkheads where the gas had grown too strong. They lay weak, almost lifeless, and groaned for air. He didn't want to hear them breathe those last dying gasps. He pictured his own death coming to him as he slumped against the bulkhead—Madge left alone, except for his child. Maybe she had his child by now.

He called Madge's name into the darkness. Then he wrote his last note, using both hands to place each word:

If death comes it will be by all
oxygen being used from the air.
My Darling Madge,
It hurts my heart
to be taken from you.
Think not of me,

if death comes it will be
sleep without suffering.
I ask forgiveness
for any pain I ever caused you.
The place is for
you and the child.

He tucked the note into his trouser pocket. Dying together served no purpose. He didn't want their lives on his hands, not anymore. He didn't want to hold them back. They had waited long enough and now they were waiting for the inevitable.

"Leonard," he said. "Get up. It's time we make a try." Pulling planks away from the interior wall, he made a hole large enough to get easily through. He went to the outer bulkhead. "There's good air in the Rainbow. Head for the twenty-four raise." He forced himself to stand straight. Ned Heston joined him; so did McAdams. Bill Lucas got up but hesitated.

"Go on. Go!" Leonard sunk his head back down on the ground.

"Leonard?" Manus said, "You coming?"

"Go get 'em, Manus. I'll be resting right here, waiting for you to come get me. Tell Katie I want to see her dance naked to the Whiskey Bottle Honkytonk when they bring me up." The others lay prone, passed out, maybe dead or feeling too hopeless to try.

Manus and Ned tore a hole in the bulkhead. Gas swarmed lazily in. They headed down the drift, Manus, Ned, and McAdams with Bill Lucas following.

Manus went to the manway and began climbing the ladder. Only Ned and McAdams were behind him. He could not see Bill Lucas on the ladder. The smoke was pretty thick.

It made me hold my breath to hear that bell. First nine bells rang, then six, then two. The danger signal. Felt like a thunderbolt had cracked heaven open. Nine-six-two, just like that, from out of nowhere. Over and over. Then twenty-four bells. I had my mask off and could smell the sweet odor of burnt flesh that hung over the mineyard ever since the fire. You just don't get used to a thing like that. It seems to be in the air even when it isn't. The sky was grayer than before. It felt like it took an hour just to count off those bells.

A few women were wandering through the rows of bloated corpses. You couldn't stop them from doing that. They had to come and look. They'd hold handkerchiefs soaked in camphor over their faces so they could stand the smell. I could tell them it was useless. But that was useless too. It was a sorry sight, not something a woman should have to see. One hundred sixty-two by last count, corpses with black and swollen faces, fat cheeks like melons, noses buried, lips split and fingers big as butcher sausage. I'd carried over twenty of them up myself, but just thinking about what some poor woman had to carry the rest of her life left me cold.

I headed for the cage right away. You see, I was on the crew that checked the twenty-four hundred yesterday. There was nothing in that crosscut. I mean nothing, not one body anywhere.

Me and Tom O'Brien climbed in the cage together and went down to have a look. We found some boy. He kept telling us there were others. I believed him, but Tom said, "We got to get you out of here." Which we did because the boy got sight of a water keg by the station and a powerful urge was on him to have a drink. I had to hold him back. Ain't nothing more poisoned than water that's been through a fire.

There was a wind blowing. I didn't notice it myself, before that is, but when we got the boy up top, he started shivering and the bumps on his naked skin rose up. We got him to the dry fast as we could. Tom told the big boss that there were others down there. We must have walked right up to their bulkhead and turned around. Shit I thought and my stomach went tight, though I knew the best thing was not to think about it.

I had seen some awful things in the last three days, like the two station tenders who rode the cage down to find out what the smoke meant. That was the beginning of trouble. By the time the hoistman finally got scared, it was too late. He hoisted the cage and brought the fire right up the shaft. I was in the mineyard at the time. All we could do was stand there and watch. The fire just leaped up and surrounded the cage. Roasted those two fellows. When we took their bodies out, their shoes were even burned off them. It had cooked their arms and legs so they loosened and dropped off when we tried to lift them out.

So when I volunteered to go down in the mine and bring up the rest I knew I couldn't let myself get worked up by thinking about anything. If you do, you get emotional and first thing you know you're not any help at all.

We went for the others and brought them up two by two. Twenty-six of them! For the first time, the numbers seemed to count. I wanted one of them women to run over and throw her arms around her husband because he was alive. I wanted the clouds to lift and the sun to show itself. I wanted somebody, anybody, to come over and tell me the rest of my life was going to be all right and that I was going places.

Then this miner named Leonard started calling for Manus Dugan. It had got dark. There was no moon. Me and Tom went back down and started climbing the manways. We found three men. Two were lying on the ground. One was hung up on a ladder, caught from falling by the rungs. He had short curly hair. He looked clean and trim somehow. Tom helped me lift him down. They were dead. Smoke had got them. I checked the pockets of the one we found on the ladder and found his name on a piece of paper. Manus Dugan. A couple of notes were folded behind it. He had a wife and a child somewhere. I kept telling myself I had work to do and that I didn't feel a thing, not a thing—nothing.

The Tuna Fish Sandwich
Ron Fischer

I'm from Montaa-aaa-na. Sorry, I didn't mean to baa. It just happens sometimes. Slips right out. You know the state, the one that burns itself up every summer. If the forest fires haven't made the news already, they soon will, huge ponderosa pines exploding into golden geysers of flame, plumes of smoke rolling off ridges of green pine.

Or maybe it's the sheepherders you've read about, the ones who shoot replanted wolves or the new age women who run with wolves, on accident, of course. Or maybe it's the stockmen shooting at brucellosis-infected buffalo.

Of course, the story isn't always about men with rifles riding in pickups and shooting at wildlife. Sometimes it's about the wildlife. Mostly, the wildlife leaves the Montanans alone and picks on the tourists, most often California tourists, on accident, I'm sure. You know the story I mean, the grizzly bear that attacks sleeping campers, bites a man's face off, and chews a man's legs down to stumps. I wonder what makes a Californian so tasty to a grizzly?

There are some things you don't have to wonder about: menstruating women. Take a look. Go to Glacier Park or Yellowstone or the Bob Marshall Wilderness. You'll find the brochures: Having Cramps? Your Period? Don't Go Camping. You can bet that after one of these attacks, local newspapers will run an article trying to warn women campers about the dangers. The headline goes something like *Tampons: Bait for Bears* or *Have Your Monthly, but Save Your Lifetime*.

Now that's the Montana you read about in the papers, even if you don't read the local papers, which, I suspect, most Californians don't. Maybe you've even been to Glacier Park yourself, or maybe you've got a calendar with a picture of Yellowstone Falls on it, tumbling white water cascading over gray rocks and between luscious pines. You got to know this: that's not the part of Montana I'm from. I'm from a place called Anaconda. I grew up there and then moved twenty-four miles away to Butte. Butte's a mining town, and Anaconda's where all the ore dug up in Butte was sent, ground up, and melted down. It's the smelter town. *Smelter*. Listen to the word. You can hear the word *melted* in it and the word *smoke*. Smoke and melted. *Smelter*. That one word says it all. That's Anaconda, furnaces and smokestacks.

The first Californians who came to Montana were hydraulic miners looking for gold. When they found Anaconda, they hooked their hoses up to pumps down by Warm Springs creek, and they hosed all the dirt off the hillsides, flushed every bit of ground down their sluices that settled all the gold and silver out of it. Imagine it, the hills of Anaconda, piles of boulders, dry as bone, empty as the moon. There's no dirt in Anaconda. No trees. They chopped all the trees down to hold the mines in Butte up.

There is a mountain of black slag. If you think *smelter* sounds bad, say the word *slag* while you're looking at it. You'll want to gag. It's the stuff left over when the gold and silver and copper is scrubbed out of the rock. A mountain of mica waste. There's no fish in the streams around Anaconda, not in Warms Springs creek or the river it flows into, the Clark Fork. From Anaconda clear to Missoula, not a single fish, not even a water spider. To get the copper out of the rock, they soaked the ore in water. The copper dissolves. Places where they soak copper are called leach ponds. It has nothing to do with leeches, but I didn't know that when I was a kid. I kept trying to find me a leech—a big old, gnarly-looking thing, just to see what it would look like close up.

Now you can't keep leach water from soaking into the groundwater, or running off into a stream, so all the water around Anaconda and Butte is bad water, lethal. One time a flock of 262 Canadian snow geese landed in the big lake that was once the Berkeley Pit. All of them died. The *Silence of the Lambs* ain't nothing compared to 262 dead snow geese floating in bad water.

My dad was a smelterman. He used to bring arsenic home and spread it on our lawn. "Makes the grass green," he'd say and smile. It did too, real green, African green, rainforest green. It made my little brother sterile. I haven't had any children either, but since I'm a teacher, I hate to use a word like *sterile* on myself. *Sterile*. It feels like 262 dead snow geese.

One day my dad was making sandwiches in the kitchen.

"Why are you making sandwiches?" my mom asked him. It was a good question, a very good question. You see, my dad was old school. I never once saw him wash a dish, run a vacuum cleaner, mop a floor, wipe a counter, or make a sandwich. Besides, it was 1:30. We had just eaten tuna fish sandwiches, potato salad, and watermelon. That's what we ate in June when the sky was blue. I had to sit at table with Dad and listen to the smacking of his lips and the chewing sounds he made with his dentures. Why, indeed, was he making a tuna fish sandwich when we had just eaten?

"Leave me alone, Lily," Dad said. "I know what I'm doing."

He said it like the words had "open-at-your-own-risk" stamped on them. "All right," Mom said, "you know what you are doing."

That week, every day we finished lunch at one o'clock, and every day my father would go out to the backyard, get down on his hands and knees, and dig dandelions out of the lawn, and everyday at one-thirty, he came in and made two tuna fish sandwiches, wrapped them in wax paper, and put them in his shirt pockets. Then he would go back to digging dandelions.

"Guess he's hungry," my mom finally decided.

She said this to me as she looked out the back door and watched Dad dig up dandelions. She had a fallen look on her face, as if she had failed him in some way, the inadequacy, I guess, of her own tuna fish sandwiches.

During the depression, my dad was a single man. He and Mom didn't marry until 1945. All those years of the depression, he was a hobo, a man who rode the rails and looked for work. That's, in fact, how he came to Anaconda, riding on an ore train. He had even met Woody Guthrie once. He told me he had been all over this country, from the woods of Portland, Maine, to the grapevines of Monterey, California. Just like the song that Woody sang—"This land is your land. This land is my land, from California, to the New York island"— which was my dad's favorite song, the one he would hum to himself when he dug dandelions.

"Never had a hard time finding work," he said. "They always thought I was a Mexican."

My dad was an Ashkenazi man from Russia, but he did have dark skin and looked more like a Sephardic man, as if he ought to have come from Morocco.

"Mexicans always got the work, you see. They knew how to work. Never hurt the trees in an orchard. Never broke branches. Never ripped a vine. Worked for cheap and hard, and so did I."

I wanted him to tell me about the places he had been to and the hobo jungles and the railroad goons.

"Bad times," he'd say. "Lonely places. Roads so deserted, you'd think you'd never see your soul again. Makes me too lonely talkin' 'bout those times."

I think it had something to do with my dad being a hobo that made him make tuna fish sandwiches every day at one-thirty.

Now the state prison in Deer Lodge is 28.3 miles away from Anaconda. My dad and I marked it once on our 1962 red Falcon's odometer. You wouldn't think a place with no trees, no dirt, no fish, you wouldn't think a place like that would be a good place to hide out, but you see, the hills around Anaconda was full of these miners' shacks that those Californians built in the old days. Just an iron stove in them and a cot nailed to the wall, some old-time California newspapers for wallpaper.

About ten years before, a man driving to Yellowstone Park, a man going there to see the falls up close instead of on his wall calendar, well, this fella stopped and picked up two hitchhikers. The highway patrol found the man's corpse. His heart was cut out of him, and all his fingers and thumbs were missing. They found the two hitchhikers, who were from California, driving the man's car. Both of them had the man's fingers in their pockets. The police wondered what happened to the fella's heart, and these hitchhikers said they ate his heart.

I read the news about an escaped convict, one of the guys who were serving life sentences for eating that man's heart. I got this sudden idea for why Dad was making tuna fish sandwiches at one-thirty in the afternoon.

"Dad," I asked him, "why are you making tuna fish sandwiches at one-thirty in the afternoon?"

"That guy," he said.

"What guy?" I asked.

"Ha, you know, that guy in the alley."

"Oh," I said. Both my parents expected me to read their minds. If it was a thought in their heads, it was supposed to be something I knew too. I'd like to tell you I told my mom about the guy in the alley. I'd like to tell you that the police showed up and caught an escaped convict and that they found a tuna fish sandwich in his pocket. I can only tell you this: I thought about them dead snow geese. I thought about an old miner named Isaac who used to live in a miner's shack up on cemetery hill, probably the very place where that escaped convict was hiding out. I thought about my dad walking down a treeless road somewhere in Nevada and looking at the moon. I thought about a mountain of black slag, a century of black slag sitting on the edge of town, and no fish out there in Warm Springs creek, not even a tree growing alongside its banks. I went into the front room and folded up the newspaper that had two stories on the front page, one about an escaped convict and the other about a grizzly attack, and I carried it out to the backyard. This is true

what I am telling you, all of it. I put that newspaper in the garbage can that stood in our alley beside the garage. My dad was digging dandelions, big yellow dandelions, big as sunflowers, and was humming "This land is your land" to himself.

He looked up at me and said, "They make good salad."

It was a blue-skied day in June. That's what I remember. I put the garbage can lid back on the barrel. It made the sound of rusted metal clapping against rusted metal, and I caught sight of someone walking up the alley, just a blur of a green pant leg.

The End of the Line: Butte, Anaconda, and the Landscape of Prostitution
Ellen Baumler

First Came the Miners

At the bottom of the dingy basement stairway, rooms open to either side of a tunnel-like corridor. At the far end, a door once gave access to a flight of stairs up to the street level. These are no ordinary rooms, but rooms simply partitioned. The cold stone foundation forms the back wall of each room, and they all share one peculiarity that reveals their purpose: each cubicle has its own door with a numbered transom and a tall, double-hung window. This door-window-door-window pattern, once common in towns across the West, is the architectural signature of prostitution. Cribs, or "offices," like these in the basement of the Dumas Hotel were common in the red-light districts of Butte and Anaconda, Montana. Such areas, limited either by practice or by city ordinance to prostitution, are also commonly referred to as "restricted" districts. Today, there are no surviving remnants of this important business in Anaconda, but on the streets of Butte, surprising elements remain if you know where to look.

Like all western boomtowns, both Butte and Anaconda drew the ladies of the line at the first signs of settlement. A bawdy gold rush ballad recounts this phenomenon: "First came the miners to work in the

The Dumas Hotel is Butte's last standing parlor house, operated from 1890 to 1981. Photograph by Ellen Baumler.

mine, then came the ladies who lived on the line." It applied to the silver mining camp of Butte in the 1870s and to the smeltertown of Anaconda in the early 1880s, both of which had significant populations of single men. The first "ladies of the line" who drifted into Butte in the 1870s worked along Park Street, then the heart of the camp. Miners were not particular about the company they kept, and these women were simply part of the community. But when solid business blocks began to replace the unsightly temporary tents and shanties along Park Street, the city's geographic center and logical place for legitimate businesses, the women moved one street south to Galena Street. In the mid-1880s, former "Park Street girls" relocated

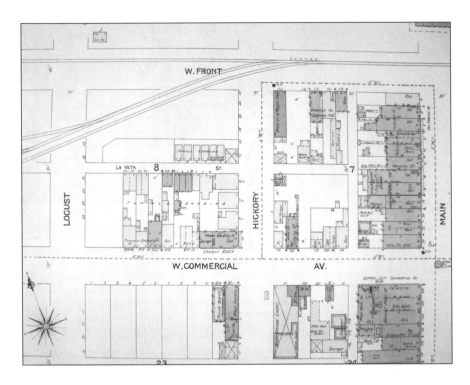

Sanborn map of Anaconda, Montana.

around First and Hickory streets in flimsy wooden shacks and cribs, centered around one parlor house known as the "Globe." The city jail, across the alley to the north, shared the block, a common juxtaposition in Montana towns. By 1891, a substantial, two-story brick brothel at 203 West First Street (later Commercial Street) catered to a slightly higher-class clientele than did the other, less permanent prostitution-related buildings. The house shared a party wall with a wholesale liquor store. A porch spanned the front, and windows—convenient for soliciting—lined the open side and back; a skylight in the roof lit the upper story. This and one other large, brick, single-story establishment at 222 West First Street bear the label "female boarding," the historic Sanborn-Perris Map Company's euphemism for prostitution. Another, more permanent establishment, the Landry Block, built between 1891 and 1896, featured a saloon on the ground floor and brothel rooms on the second floor accessed by an interior stairway at the back of the saloon. Other suspect buildings spread out across the north side of

there in one-room wooden cribs that lined both sides of the street. Dance halls, saloons, and gambling joints spilled over onto neighboring streets. By the late 1890s, Butte's restricted district had half a dozen luxurious parlor houses, numerous brothels, and hundreds of cribs, thereby earning its comparison with the much larger red-light districts of San Francisco and New Orleans.[1]

In Anaconda, prostitution in the 1880s clustered

West First Street between Hickory and Locust streets and the alley behind to the north, named La Vita (Veta) Street. The district included less than a square block. Size, however, was not the only difference between Anaconda's district and that of Butte.[2]

In most western towns, Chinese settlements and red-light districts adjoined. There were good reasons for this. Both prostitutes and the Chinese were outcast populations, in many places even confined by city ordinance to specific neighborhoods. In Butte, public women permanently located in an area roughly bounded by East Galena and East Mercury on the north and south and South Wyoming and Main streets on the east and west. Butte's Chinatown, eventually the largest in Montana, spread out on the opposite side of Main Street to the west along West Mercury. Prostitutes frequented the Chinese noodle parlors, where meals were cheap and hearty. They also relied on Chinese herbalists and physicians to supply them with birth control methods and cures for venereal diseases, neither of which were readily available from the mainstream medical community. Chinese physicians and pharmacists had opium at their disposal. Opium administered under supervision, to the point of overdose, induced spontaneous abortion. For these reasons, red-light districts typically adjoined Chinese neighborhoods.[3]

Anaconda's Chinatown, however, was an exception. The Chinese were a vibrant element in Anaconda's early community, although they endured the same discrimination as they did in most Montana towns. Anti-Chinese legislation brought much suffering to this ethnic group in the nineteenth-century West.[4] In Anaconda, the Chinese settled six blocks away from the red-light activity, to the east along Birch Street between First (Commercial) and Second (Park) streets. They set up laundries, opened enterprising businesses, and worked in private households as domestics and cooks. The Chinese commonly took the blame whenever there was no clear fault. On November 30, 1889, for example, the *Anaconda Standard* reported that madam Belle Riley's parlor house, between Front and First streets, caught fire and burned to the ground. Expensive parlor furniture and two trunks of belongings were all that survived. Because Belle employed a Chinese servant, officials assumed that the fire was his fault.

By 1902, Anaconda's Chinese population, which had once swelled to four hundred, had dwindled to a handful; most had moved on or settled in Butte's much larger district.[5] This is partly because the Chinese competed with Anaconda's women in domestic and laundry services. Women in mining towns and elsewhere had few business opportunities. This was especially true of Anaconda, where women were even more limited to operating boardinghouses and providing laundry services. Because Anaconda was a

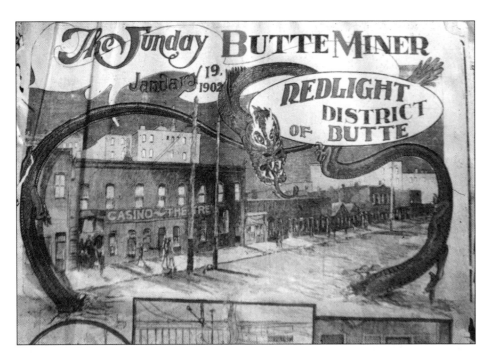

The Butte Miner *featured the red-light district in the Sunday edition of January 19, 1902.*

Street, half a dozen high-class establishments were evenly spaced along the north side of the street. The fancier the house was, the less it resembled a house of prostitution. The Windsor and the Dumas, for example, had no telltale rows of doors and windows, since the women who worked there had no need to solicit; the madam did that kind of work for them. These high-class houses resembled the upscale rooming houses found all over Butte. From the architecture alone, the building's function was indiscernible—only its location gave it away.[6]

company town, other private enterprises, for women and particularly for the Chinese, were not easy to establish and maintain.

The appearance of Anaconda's brick brothels parallels the pattern in Butte, but Butte, with its larger population, offered more establishments from which to choose. Cribs and brothels appeared along Galena Street, while one block to the south on East Mercury

From Brothels to Parlor Houses

Apartment living and lodging houses in urban areas during the second half of the nineteenth century were common, particularly in crowded areas like Butte. But many viewed communal living as detrimental to the family unit, and lodging houses in particular, whether respectable or not, were often viewed as places of prostitution.[7] Lodging house architecture of the Victorian era dictated the separation of common and private spaces. Fancy houses like the Windsor and the Dumas followed this model. Parlors and dining rooms where patrons could socialize were located downstairs, while private spaces—rooms and suites—were upstairs. This arrangement exactly mimicked the usual floorplans of lodging houses and the comfortable domestic spaces they provided.

The women in Butte's expensive parlor houses had gaudy tastes. By the end of the 1890s, at least three very high-class houses of prostitution in Butte could be found in the first block of East Mercury Street. High-rolling copper kings William A. Clark and F. Augustus Heinze and their wealthy business associates spent money lavishly in Butte. A "gentleman" could easily spend several thousand dollars for a night of partying in a luxurious parlor house. Lou Harpell's exclusive suites at 11 East Mercury, later known as the Hotel Victoria, had only a few select employees (four in 1900), but they were said to be among the most beautiful women in the world. Ruth Clifford ran the Windsor Hotel at 9 East Mercury. At the turn of the twentieth century, tastefully engraved RSVP cards announced the Windsor's grand opening and uniformed butlers greeted guests at the door. Parlor houses and their orchestrated domesticity suggest further comparison to elegant men's clubs of the period, which offered a similar private environment without pressures, responsibilities, or family distractions.[8] Parlor houses offered like comfort with, of course, a further commodity.

The fashionable three-story Windsor featured rounded, two-story oriel bay windows at the front corners, a central Palladian window, elegant stone trim, and twenty-four beautifully appointed rooms. Its two parlors featured expensive, satin-covered sofas and chairs, gilt-framed mirrors, tapestries, red draperies, and plants in brass jardinières. The elaborate dining room could accommodate a substantial number of dinner guests. The Chinese cook in charge of the kitchen and the two domestic servants occupied rooms at the back of the first floor. Oak and mahogany graced the bedrooms on the two upper floors. Madam Ruth was the epitome of the "purchased" high society Butte's instant millionaires had at their disposal. Newspaperman Warren Davenport recorded one observer's description in his scandalous book *Butte beneath the X-Ray*. Miss Ruth received her guests "in the ivory and gold room," he wrote, "which has a rich carpet of bottle green moquet with yellow flowers and Japanese silk portieres in parti-colors producing an effect which on clear nights can be heard as far as Anaconda."[9]

Anaconda's several higher-end brothels and houses never equaled the prestige or luxury of Butte's parlor houses, but that of Florence Clark, one longtime madam, came close. The Monogram, at 101 North Hickory, appeared when the district relocated to

Mainville around 1900. Florence operated the house for more than a decade. She owned an expensive, rubber-tired buggy and several blooded horses. One of these horses, Silk Stocking, held a record and raced the circuits in Salt Lake City, Oakland, and Spokane. Florence survived a near-fatal, self-inflicted overdose of laudanum in 1905.

Although Florence Clark generously patronized the local merchants, she was not benevolent toward her employees. She operated her house in a kind of partnership with saloon keeper William L. McLaughlin, who owned the Monogram's bar. McLaughlin occasionally helped Florence handle her legal issues, of which she had a few. In 1908, a police officer heard that one of the Monogram's women inmates wished to leave but was being held against her will. The officer found a seventeen-year-old at the house and attempted to escort her out. Florence grabbed the girl to prevent her leaving, whereupon the officer punched the irate madam and knocked her unconscious.[10]

While merchants may have appreciated Florence Clark's patronage, the way she ran her business underscores the lack of economic opportunity women often experienced working for a madam. Two women who escaped from the Monogram in 1911 told authorities that Florence kept them captive in the establishment, took their street clothes, charged exorbitant prices for their needs, and quickly made the women indebted to management. The two had worked for two years, their debts mounting every month. When the officer went to the Monogram to retrieve the women's trunks, he found the windows barred with steel like a jail. As reported in a news story at the time: "It was nothing more than a life of bondage."[11]

A Shift in Clientele

Times changed with the onset of the twentieth century. Butte's most glamorous houses began to change in character and clientele. William A. Clark, elected to the U.S. Senate through political machinations, moved to Washington, D.C.; Marcus Daly died; and the days of the copper kings were over. Outside investors and absentee landlords controlled mining interests. Friends and associates of the copper kings no longer came to Butte or Anaconda, and the parlor houses had few wealthy patrons. Cribs began to infill the spaces between Butte's grand houses. Prominent Helena businessman Anton Holter erected a series of brick cribs on Mercury Street, opposite the parlor houses. U.S. senator Lee Mantle was a later owner of this building, emphasizing the point that red-light real estate was a sound business investment. Owners protected their identities, hiring managers to collect the rents—usually between $2 and $5 per shift. The architecture of the Blue Range—as it is known today for the company that owns it—displays its original door-window-door-window arrangement. This well-preserved example of brick cribs recalls the era when scantily clad women, cloaked in cold-weather wrappers called "shady-go-nakeds," sat in the low windows, displaying their assets. They tapped provocatively on the glass at passersby with thimbles, rings, and chopsticks. The women showed no trace of modesty, leaning out of their windows and calling out "the vilest kind of language imaginable to people passing on the street."[12]

Behind Butte's Mercury Street houses, Pleasant Alley ran from South Wyoming to Main Street through the center of the block, where the least-favored women of the tenderloin lived and worked in ramshackle cabins and cribs. Butte's few African American and Japanese prostitutes, aging castoffs, and drug addicts frequented Pleasant Alley in 1900. Thieves and pickpockets lurked in darkened doorways a few steps from the back door of every parlor house. Butte's public women called this neighborhood the "burnt district" because they knew it as a dangerous place unfit for other purposes. The *Butte Miner* relished the shootings and stabbings that played out there, covering these events in minute detail. Such press bolstered the unsavory elements of the Mining City's reputation and served as a calculated invitation, challenging the toughest men to come to Butte and work in the mines.[13]

The districts in both Butte and Anaconda underwent dramatic physical changes as citizens

The Blue Range cribs are a rare surviving example of the door-window-door-window arrangement that is the architectural signature of prostitution. Paul Anderson, photographer. Courtesy Montana Historical Society Research Center Photograph Archives, Helena (PAC 97-63A).

clamored to tone down the blatant soliciting and clean up unsightly slums. The Butte, Anaconda and Pacific Railroad (BA&P) began service in 1893, linking the two industrial centers; the tracks cut through the undeveloped north portion of Anaconda's tenderloin. The jail moved to city hall, and cribs quickly sprang up next to the vacant building, facing the tracks. This caused the city fathers embarrassment, and a high board fence in front of the cribs quickly cut off the passengers' views of the seedy area. By 1900, however, a city alderman had successfully lobbied to move Anaconda's district north across the railroad tracks to the Northern Addition, created specifically for this purpose. Locals knew the area as Mainville, after saloon keeper Bruno Mainville, who owned a bar and maintained red-light properties there.[14]

Not all red-light businesses moved across the tracks. Sam Landry continued to operate his saloon and upstairs brothel at the corner of Hickory and Commercial (formerly West First Street). In 1902, grafting among police officers and city officials came to the forefront when a city alderman accused the police chief of allowing Landry to operate his business.[15] Landry, however, continued to run his enterprise until his death in 1911.

Prostitution in Anaconda, Butte, and elsewhere in Montana was never legal, but loopholes in the system allowed the women to work. Cities, including Butte and Anaconda, collected $5 or $10 monthly fines that allowed prostitutes to "legally" conduct business. Graft was common among elected officials and police officers. The red-light districts were thus sometimes called "the twilight zone," because they were places of twilight legality. Monthly fines collected in Butte were especially lucrative for city hall because of the numbers of women working there. Many estimate that between 1910 and 1916, there were as many as a thousand women working in the district at any given time.[16]

Although Anaconda's restricted district had moved its location, officials realized that this was not possible in Butte. In 1902, the *Butte Miner* issued a special Sunday section on its red-light district, addressing the problems of solicitation, unhealthy conditions, urban blight, alcoholism, and the graft city officials openly accepted from public women. Much debate had centered on this question in the early 1900s, but officials also realized that the district could never serve any other purpose; rather, it would have to be razed and rebuilt. No one favored such a huge undertaking, so city ordinances attempted to control the most blatant problem—that of open solicitation on public thoroughfares. To quell the women's enthusiastic, brazen advertising on Galena and Mercury streets, the city ordered them to wear high-necked blouses, lengthen their skirts, and draw their blinds.[17]

The women defied the ordinance first by drawing their blinds and cutting holes in them. Finally, however, they adapted by cutting doors and windows into the backs of their cribs, thus reversing the orientation from the public streets to the back alleys. Pleasant Alley, once home to the castoffs of the business, now became the heart of the district. Two- and three-story frame and brick cribs created a labyrinth of narrow walkways. On any Saturday night, as many as four thousand miners strolled the alley, looking to spend their paychecks. This concentrated activity helped the mining industry because it kept the men too busy to organize against management. Butte businesses depended on the women's patronage, and as long as they had customers, public women adapted to the changes imposed and their lives remained thus intertwined with the Butte community.[18]

In January 1916, copper rose to a high of twenty cents a pound and more than fourteen thousand miners received a raise of twenty-five cents per day. Butte's district exploded with building activity, and cribs appeared in every possible location. The activity was short-lived, however. The nation embarked on World War I in 1917, and federal law closed red-light districts across the nation to prevent the spread of venereal disease among the troops. Prostitution—like alcohol during this same period of Prohibition—did not go away; it simply went undercover, operating in many Montana towns in hotels and furnished rooms.[19]

Last Madams

Ann Harding ran the New York Rooms, Anaconda's last brothel, from 1944 to the mid-1950s. Located first at 15 ½ Main and then in 1944 at 313 ½ East Park, near city hall, the business closed in the mid-1950s after a patron fell or was pushed out of a second-story window and later died, causing publicity and legal problems for the madam.[20] The house opened again briefly in the mid-1960s and then closed for good,

ending prostitution's run in Anaconda. All vestiges of the business in Anaconda have been obliterated. Mt. Haggin Homes, a housing project, now covers the older red-light area where the Landry Block once stood, and nothing remains of the cribs and buildings across the tracks, where the establishments of Mainville entertained the men of Anaconda. Even Ann Harding's furnished rooms eventually met the wrecking ball.

By the end of the 1930s, Butte's red-light district had survived reforms, crusading evangelists, World War I, and Prohibition. As the decade of the Great Depression neared an end, young Ray Wainwright came to Butte as an electrical engineer for the Montana Power Company's Gas Division. Wainwright became familiar with the district through his work on the gas lines that ran through it. He and his colleague often walked home through Pleasant Alley, known by this time as Venus Alley or Mercury Alley. Wainwright recalled:

This block off Mercury . . . was lined with "cribs" on either side, and the women lived in old houses which faced the street itself. I would judge that there were several hundred women in Mercury Alley in those years. There was even a mezzanine balcony at that time. . . .

We would walk through and kid the girls. But, you know, we never did go in. A good friend who was the lab technician at the hospital convinced us that there was too much disease. Stay away, and we did! But that did not stop us from walking through. . . . The Dumas Hotel . . . was the luxury end of it. It charged more money. Once I got up enough courage to enter the Dumas. But a person showed up that was not good-looking at all, and informed me the charge would be $1 per minute. I took one more look at her and fled![21]

Historian Joseph Kinsey Howard described the cribs in Venus Alley in the early 1940s as "dingy, crude offices" for what had become a revolting, furtive business. The shabby cribs and their several hundred women were a far cry from the district at its prime. After Prohibition, the women moved in again, closing off Venus Alley with a board fence. Signs warned, "Men Under 21 Keep Out"—a grim reminder that boys working in the mines became men before they reached legal age. Public women stayed behind their blinds until after five o'clock, since the new high school was only several blocks away. But Anaconda's high school basketball teams eagerly anticipated the yearly games at Butte. Bus drivers dropped the boys off in the district to gawk, giving them ten minutes to get to the gym.

Despite periodic closures, a dozen fading parlor houses and brothels in Butte survived well into the mid-twentieth century. In January 1943, World War II brought

Iron plates and then a coat of stucco covered the outside of this crib's door and window at the back of the Dumas Hotel. Owner Rudy Giecek recently discovered this and several other cribs, closed since 1943. Photograph by Ellen Baumler.

another closure to Venus Alley and the women dispersed, leaving the rickety multistoried labyrinth of shabby, one-room "offices" abandoned. Cribs at the Dumas Hotel, including those at the back opening onto Venus Alley and those in the basement, closed as well. But along Mercury Street, the Dumas, the Windsor (later the Missoula), the Victoria, and the Royal—as well as an infamous house at 14 South Wyoming and others—continued to operate as they had during Prohibition, now under the flimsy guise of hotel or "furnished rooms." Such places never specified exactly what they furnished.

By the 1950s, Butte's former district was once more operating on a significant scale. Women again occupied some of the alley cribs, working independently, while madams employed women in the houses.[22] The Montana attorney general's office conducted surveys of prostitution in all counties in the 1950s. In March 1952, the survey found nine brothels open for business in Butte. Some of the working women, said one person interviewed, "are really old hags." Cab drivers received a commission for bringing business to the district, and women sat in the windows, tapping with rings, knitting needles, and other items at passersby. When asked why they did this, one Mercury Alley prostitute replied: "Guys like to be roped in. Some just get a bang from walking through here and getting called in. Maybe we don't get 'em on the first visit, but they sure come back. Besides, some guys . . . don't want to go into a joint until they see the girl they like. . . .

It's just like window shopping."[23]

In February 1953, the report concluded that Butte, Montana, was still one of the nation's "most wide open towns," attracting many patrons, including servicemen as well as civilians. Prices were $3 and $5. One cab driver offered this observation: "With all the miners here in Butte and the soldiers we get from other towns, the guys have to have some way to blow off steam, so the cops let the line run. . . . The girls don't bother anybody. The line is in an alley and nobody has any business going in there unless he wants a girl."[24]

Another explained that Butte had always been wide open, and always would be: "This is one town the blue noses can't crack. . . . Go over on East Mercury Street. You get anything you want. . . . If the front doors are closed, try the rear." Mercury Alley, or Venus Alley, received its final nickname at about this time. Butte's last madams knew the dark slum behind the Dumas as "Piss Alley."[25]

Monroe Frye, of *Esquire*, wrote of Butte prostitutes in 1953: "The girls range in age from jail bait to battle ax. . . . [They] sit and tap on the windows. They are ready for business around the clock." Frye named Butte one of the three "most wide-open towns" in the United States.[26] The *Esquire* article brought what many saw as unwanted and offensive national attention to Butte. City officials determined to clean up the district and did so in 1954, removing the unsightly alley structures. The days of "the line" had passed into legend, but the mines continued to operate in Butte and the women persisted, working out of the several remaining antique-filled, dilapidated houses. At the back of the Dumas, a heavy steel door with a small sliding window afforded a secret entrance, and steel plates covered the doors and windows of the alley-facing cribs as if they had never existed.

During the 1960s, Beverly Snodgrass bought the antique-filled, rundown Windsor Hotel at 9 East Mercury, a remnant, along with the Dumas, of the high-rolling 1890s. After a suspicious fire closed it down in 1968, Snodgrass went to the IRS and to the Washington offices of Montana senators Mike Mansfield and Lee Metcalf, claiming that local officials burned her out of her business for nonpayment of "protection" money. She claimed that she had been paying $700 a month to Butte police since 1963 and that uniformed policemen periodically demanded the services of her girls. Snodgrass paid her employees from her own pocket for these interludes. A local detective compiled a report for Snodgrass theorizing that although "many believe prostitution in Butte is controlled by some national syndicate, the syndicate is made up purely of local individuals, most of them so-called officials."[27]

Butte's mayor Tom Powers responded to the scandal, telling John Kuglin of the *Great Falls Tribune*, "The people of Butte want prostitution," and that "at least we're honest in Butte and admit we've got houses of prostitution."[28] Butte's respectable citizens cringed. In the course of Kuglin's seven-part series, the *Tribune* reported that several police officers took it upon themselves to close down Butte's three operating houses. Only the Dumas reopened.

Ruby Garrett bought the Dumas in 1971. As Snodgrass had previously maintained, Ruby also claimed that she bought silence from Butte police officers, costing her $200 to $300 a month. At that time, customers paid about $20 for the services of one of her several employees. A brutal assault and holdup in 1981 left Ruby pistol-whipped and traumatized. Publicity about the crime, an inside job set up by an employee, led federal officials to investigate Ruby's business. The IRS claimed she owed $83,000 in unpaid income taxes. Convicted, Ruby struck a plea bargain. She received a six-month sentence at a minimum-security facility in California, paid $10,000 in back taxes, and promised not to reopen. Friends gave her a going-away party and sent her off to do her time. Butte's long-lived red-light district came to an end. Coincidentally (or was it?), the mines in Butte closed for good that same year.[29]

Red-light Remnants

The Dumas Hotel, built in 1890, is Butte's only surviving parlor house. Unlike any other historic resource in the West, its artifacts and building sequences offer unprecedented interpretive opportunities spanning the period from 1890 to 1981. Antique dealer Rudy Giecek unwittingly stumbled on the Dumas in 1992. He happened by Ruby Garrett's "alley sale" and stopped to inquire about a pile of beds. They struck up a conversation. "I can't sell the Dumas for anything but a brothel," she said. "I'll burn it down before I let the IRS have it." So she gave it to Giecek, the only person who seemed interested in its history.[30] Giecek explored the basement and back rooms, which had been closed for forty years. He discovered the basement cribs as well as additional cribs, sealed like time capsules, at the back of the building.

Exploring the basement, Giecek found dozens of empty Butte Beer and grape brandy bottles, cigarette butts, matchbooks, old jars of petroleum jelly, dingy bedding, World War II–era calendars, vintage posters, a miner's carbide lamp, and petrified chewing gum painted over in the doorjambs and window frames. Unlike the classier upstairs rooms, which were equipped with corner sinks, the basement amenities included call buttons used to order drinks or summon help, a washbasin, and an occasional chamber pot.

Behind one side of the Dumas's basement cribs

Among the hundreds of artifacts found in the Dumas Hotel are these articles of the trade including a ten-minute timer, scrip the women used instead of cash, cigarettes, and alcohol. Photograph by Ellen Baumler.

and beyond the original boiler, Giecek found an isolated crib tucked under the stairway. It provided a tiny, dirt-floored "office" where someone eked out a living. Like the miners who worked underground, many public women did likewise. In 1990, when workers demolished the Copper Block at the corner of Wyoming and Galena streets, home base to the district's women for a century, they uncovered row after row of similar tiny subterranean cubicles.[31]

The original second-floor suites, with their

Elegant upstairs suites, where wealthy copper kings spent a fortune, featured a corner sink and numbered transoms. Photograph by Ellen Baumler.

The second floor retains its original configuration, arranged around an open balcony. Photograph by Ellen Baumler.

numbered transoms and corner sinks, and the later basement cribs illustrate the two extremes of the business. A close look at the first floor shows the transition from elegant parlor house to public door-window-door-window cribs. Heavy pocket doors, discovered hidden beneath 1950s paneling, once opened to grand spaces where staged soirees were preliminary to upstairs entertainment. The Dumas's architectural style is sometimes referred to as "Victorian Brothel," an inappropriate term. Although built expressly for prostitution, there is nothing in the building's original architecture to suggest this use. Patterned after standard rooming houses, like those elsewhere in Butte, it featured a central skylight, downstairs communal parlors, a dining room for entertaining, and private upstairs suites. The Dumas and other houses like it were designed to put the patron at ease in comfortable domestic spaces.

The post–Victorian era cribs of the 1910s are what make the building's use obvious and illustrate the change from high-end clients and a domestic environment to working-class customers in a public,

Conversion of grand first floor spaces to common cribs in the Dumas occurred circa 1916. Photograph by Ellen Baumler.

The wear pattern on the floor of this crib at the back of the Dumas Hotel illustrates how the business was conducted: soliciting at the window, left; negotiations at the door; then straight to the cot. Photograph by Ellen Baumler.

even marketlike, setting where customers could "window shop." Inspection of the first-floor woodwork reveals telltale differences in moldings, supporting the idea that conversion of this space to cribs for "window shopping" did not occur until early in the twentieth century, circa 1916. Orange shag carpeting, a pay phone, and red-orange paint on the trim are 1960s attempts at modernization. When Ruby Garrett was madam in the 1970s, latticework stretched across the open second-floor balcony to protect residents from the beer bottles and trash unruly patrons sometimes tossed upstairs. The back stairway, added so that madams could keep better track of patrons, long ago had replaced a grand central staircase. These richly historic layers are what make the Dumas unique.

Reminders of the past dot the former district, but few observers recognize or appreciate these remnants. Except for the Blue Range and the Dumas, other district buildings once housing brothels or cribs have long been converted to other uses and contain no trace of their lurid histories. Lest the town forget its past, in 1998 Butte artist Gloria Clark painted a mural on buildings at the west end of the block, depicting the district in the 1930s when the board fence enclosed it. Butte's Urban Revitalization Agency created a parking lot where Pleasant Alley and the Copper Block used to be, incorporating the building's wooden nameplate into the corner space and preserving the last remaining bricks of Venus Alley. Timeless metal figures, made by local high school shop students (to the consternation of some officials), walk the alley as men and women did for a century.

Clark's mural and the park proved prophetic, as the legacy of its famous tenderloin, unwanted by some, continued to haunt Butte. On the heels of the park's creation, Norma Jean Almodovar swept into town. The former Los Angeles cop and Beverly Hills call girl bought the Dumas as headquarters for her organization, the International Sex Workers Foundation for Art,

Culture, and Education (ISWFACE). She planned to restore the building as a museum of prostitution and sex workers' art. Giecek stayed on as manager and curator. The project brought Butte international press touting the Mining City's bawdy history. Almodovar, a retired prostitute, and Bob Butorovich, the former sheriff who had closed the Dumas in 1981, posed together amicably. It was a historic moment, and Almodovar pronounced Butte "whore friendly."[32]

Many residents were horrified. Mike Bowler, of the *Baltimore Sun*, covered the story on October 19, 1999, observing that some in Butte did not want to pay historical homage to prostitution. Retired insurance agent and civic activist Donald Ulrich summed it up: "We worked so hard to restore Butte's image, and then [Almodovar] plops down here without an invitation and says she wants to make Butte the sex capital of the world. It breaks my heart." In the end, Almodovar could not raise the necessary funding. A legal battle with Giecek over back wages ended in 2002, with Almodovar returning to California, no longer owner of the Dumas. This put Giecek back where he began, trying to save his building.[33]

Today, the Dumas is in a precarious state of deterioration. The basement has flooded, the leaking roof has caused structural damage, the stairway has collapsed, and the upper floor is inaccessible. However, the building has a new roof in progress thanks to a

A false floor with an entry in the wall, hidden behind a dresser, offered a hiding place during raids. Photograph by Ellen Baumler.

generous donor, and there is hope for its future.

While some would prefer to forget the tawdry side of Montana's colorful past, red-light districts were an integral part of Butte, Anaconda, and most other towns across the West. Anaconda has none of these remnant elements, making those that survive in Butte that much more significant. The bricks of Pleasant Alley, the Blue Range and its door-window-door-window facade, and the rare architectural layers of the Dumas Hotel are teaching tools that help interpret an important, often misunderstood chapter in the history of the American West.

1   Sanborn-Perris Fire Insurance Maps of Butte for 1884, 1888, and 1890 (New York: Sanborn-Perris Map Publishing Company).

2   Sanborn-Perris Fire Insurance Maps of Butte for 1884, 1888, and 1890; Sanborn-Perris Fire Insurance Maps of Anaconda for 1884, 1888, 1890, 1891, and 1896 (New York: Sanborn-Perris Map Publishing Company).

3   Compare, for example, the locations of Chinatowns in Butte, Helena, and Big Timber. In Helena in 1891, the Sanborn maps show a Chinese pharmacy and a Chinese physician located between cribs along Clore (now Park) Street. See also Ellen Baumler, "Devil's Perch: Prostitution from Suite to Cellar in Butte, Montana," *Montana The Magazine of Western History* 43 (Spring 1998): 4–21.

4   Robert R. Swartout, "From Kwangtung to the Big Sky: The Chinese Experience in Frontier Montana," in *The Montana Heritage: An Anthology of Historical Essays*, ed. Robert R. Swartout and Harry W.

Fritz (Helena: Montana Historical Society Press, 1992), 61–79.

5   Patrick F. Morris, *Anaconda, Montana: Copper Smelting Boom Town on the Western Frontier* (Bethesda, MD: Swann: 1997), 113–24.

6   Compare the footprints in the Sanborn maps of Butte's parlor houses along Mercury Street with Butte's many boardinghouses.

7   Dolores Hayden, *The Grand Domestic Revolution* (Cambridge, MA: MIT Press, 1985), 95. This may partly explain why, even today, some of Butte's historic lodging houses— even respectable ones—have been unfairly labeled as brothels.

8   For a description of the public and privates spaces in Helena's famed Montana Club, see Patty Dean, "Unique and Handsome: Cass Gilbert's Designs for the Montana Club," *Drumlummon Views* 1 (June 2006): 1–2, http://www.drumlummon.org/images/PDF-Spr-Sum06/DV_1-2_Dean.pdf (accessed October 31, 2008).

9   Mary Murphy, *Women on the Line*: *Prostitution in Butte, Montana, 1878–1917* (master's thesis, University of North Carolina, Raleigh, 1983), 62; Warren G. Davenport, *Butte and Montana beneath the X-Ray: Being a Collection of Editorials from the Files of the Butte X-Ray during the years 1907–08* (Butte, 1909), 39–40; Workers of the Writers' Program of the WPA in the State of Montana, *Copper Camp: The Lusty Story of Butte, Montana, the Richest Hill on Earth* (1943; reprint, Helena, MT: Riverbend, 2002), 190.

10   Matt J. Kelly, *Anaconda: Montana's Copper City* (Butte, MT: Soroptimist Club of Anaconda, 1983), 42; Morris, *Anaconda, Montana*, 198; *Anaconda Standard*, March 6, 1908.

11   *Anaconda Standard*, November 3, 1911.

12   *Butte Miner*, December 6, 1901. The *Butte Evening News*, May 10, 1905, defines the term *shady-go-naked* as underworld slang for an ulster, or long, loose overcoat.

13   See, for example, the dramatic story

of the stabbing of Mollie Quinn in the *Butte Miner*, May 21, 1907, and the shooting of Big Eva in the *Butte Miner*, May 14, 16, and 21, 1901.

[14] *Anaconda Standard,* September 24, 1894; *Butte Miner*, January 2, 1902.

[15] *Anaconda Standard,* February 26, 1902.

[16] *Butte Miner*, January 16, 1902; Morris, *Anaconda, Montana*, 198.

[17] *Butte Miner*, January 16 and 20, 1901; December 6 and 7, 1901; January 19, 1902.

[18] *Butte Miner*, January 20, 1902; *Butte Miner*, January 3, 1903.

[19] *Butte Daily Post,* January 14, 1916; Murphy, *Women on the Line*, 99; Bascom Johnson and Paul M. Kinsie, "Prostitution in the United States," *Journal of Social Hygiene* 19 (December 1933): 469.

[20] Author interview with Jerry Hanson, curator at the Deer Lodge County Historical Society, July 15, 2008; Polk City Directories for Anaconda, 1944–1956.

[21] Ray M. Wainwright, of Denver, Colorado, correspondence with the author, October 27, 1998.

[22] Sanborn Maps of Butte, 1951.

[23] Montana Attorney General, Report on Prostitution, September 1952, series 76, box 46, Montana State Archives, MHS Research Center, Helena.

[24] Montana Attorney General, Report on Prostitution, February 1953.

[25] Montana Attorney General, Report on Prostitution; Rudy Giecek, interview with author, September 17, 1996. Ruby Garrett knew the alley by this name.

[26] Monroe Frye, "The Three Last Wide-Open Towns," *Esquire* 47 (June 1953).

[27] *Great Falls Tribune*, October 13–18, 1968.

[28] (Butte) *Montana Standard*, February 22, 1991.

[29] (Butte) *Montana Standard*, June 23, 1982.

[30] Zena Beth McGlashan, *Tales of the Dumas*, promotional pamphlet (Butte, MT: n.p., 1995).

[31] Mark Reavis, Butte-Silver Bow Historic Preservation Officer, communication with the author, October 16, 1996.

[32] (Butte) *Montana Standard*, August 27, 1998.

[33] John LaFave, letter to the editor, (Butte) *Montana Standard*, February 18, 1999; *Baltimore Sun*, October 17, 1999; the court case and decision may be found at http://dli. mt.gov/hearings/decisions/2002/ whdec524_2001.htm (accessed July 31, 2008).

The Silver Bow Club of Butte: Architectural Gem in the Mining Metropolis

Patty Dean

Silver Bow Club, Butte, August 24, 2005. Photograph by Patty Dean.

On New Year's Eve 1907, when the Silver Bow Club, a private men's club on Butte's West Side, opened in its new quarters, its debut capped an extraordinary two years of record-breaking new construction for the Mining City. The erection of such multi-story commercial buildings as the State Savings Bank (designed by Cass Gilbert, perhaps America's best-known architect of the period), Phoenix/Symons Dry Goods Co. building, Hennessy's department store annex, cosmopolitan Napton and Leonard apartment buildings, and civic improvements had totaled three million dollars in 1906 alone. Vestiges of the city's rough-and-tumble mining-camp origins were fast disappearing. On December 12, 1906, the *Butte Miner* noted, "unsightly wooden houses in the business districts are rapidly being supplanted by modern blocks. Before many more months have passed it will be almost a matter of impossibility to find a wooden building in the principal commercial centers of Butte."

The completion of the Silver Bow Club manifested the city's ambitious expectations: "Any city," bragged the *Miner,* "that can boast of a club building such as is being erected . . . can well claim rank with the foremost in the country. . . . it [will be] worthy of classification with any metropolitan club." Founded by mining and capitalist pioneers in 1882 (copper king and future U.S. senator W. A. Clark was its first president), the Silver Bow Club Building Association incorporated in May 1905 to engage in real estate activities "for the purpose of erecting, constructing and maintaining thereon a building or buildings suitable for club house and business purposes." The club members capitalized the corporation for $50,000.

The club's two-lot site on West Granite and Alaska Streets was occupied by one of the "few remaining landmarks of the days of Butte as a mining camp," a one-story frame house with bay window, tucked between the two-story brick veneer storefront Albion Hotel and the cupola-roofed Silver Bow County Courthouse. In about 1876, "pioneer placer miner" Joel Ransom paid $10 for each of the two lots and lived in the small home until leaving for California to become a farmer and vineyard owner. Ransom's friend, copper baron Marcus Daly—and W. A. Clark rival—eventually purchased the property and transferred it to his Anaconda Copper Co. which, in turn, sold it to the Silver Bow Club. In the meantime, reported the *Miner,* the Robinsons, a vaudeville costumer and her popular dancing master husband, vacated the premises to make room for the forthcoming "ornament . . . a gem of architectural beauty."

Plans for the club's new quarters, prepared by Spokane architects Kirtland Cutter and Karl Gunnar Malmgren, arrived in the spring 1905 with a presentation drawing featured in the *Anaconda Standard.* The illustration depicted a boxy brick and stone Jacobean Revival building of five stories with Flemish gables nearly identical to their 1902–1904 Rainier Club in Seattle. (The firm also designed the Davenport Hotel in Spokane, Washington, and later, the Lewis Hotel or Lake McDonald Lodge in Glacier National Park among other landmarks.)

The Cutter-Malmgren design was not carried out, however, and Link and Haire, a new Montana

"Site of Silver Bow Club Building." Anaconda Standard, April 22, 1906. Courtesy Butte Silver Bow Public Archives, Butte.

partnership that was to be the Spokane firm's local associate, evidently came up with their own design. The forty-nine-year-old Charles S. Haire had trained as an architect in his native Ohio before moving West to Pocatello, Idaho, to work first as a Union Pacific draftsman and then, a year later, in the same position for the Great Northern Railway in Butte. Haire settled in Helena in 1889, serving first as draftsman and later an architect for the prolific real estate and construction company Wallace and Thornburgh before opening his own architectural office in about 1900. The thirty-six–year-old John G. Link had attended the Royal Academy in Lindau, Bavaria, became a naturalized U.S.

"New Home of the Silver Bow Club." Anaconda Standard, *May 22, 1906. Courtesy Montana Historical Society, Helena.*

citizen in Buffalo, New York, in 1887, and dedicated himself to further architectural study in Denver and St. Louis. Link was a new Billings resident in 1906 when Haire and he established their office in that city.

The firm already had other Butte projects underway from their Silver Bow Block office, working with Cass Gilbert associate George Carsley of Helena on copper king F. Augustus Heinze's State Savings Bank on Park and Main Streets and the four-story Ansonia apartment building on West Park Street.

With the frame house razed, the Albion Hotel was to be moved downhill nine blocks south to the corner of Montana and Aluminum Streets. The *Anaconda Standard* reported, "The brick work on the outside has been removed carefully, and when the frame inclosure [sic] shall reach its new location, the brick will be replaced. . . . All the furniture and fixtures will be left as they are when the moving is done. If the occupants care to do so, they can go to sleep at Granite and Alaska Streets and wake up at Montana and Aluminum. The moving of buildings has been brought down to such a fine art that it will not be necessary to chain anything down in the big building."

Unrelenting rains during much of June delayed new construction throughout the Copper Capital, postponing the move of the final two-story section of the Albion Hotel from the club site. But the excavation contractor was able to commence. The *Standard* noted, "Every team that possibly could be utilized in the space was started to work dragging away the surface dirt. . . . the contractor for moving . . . has not yet started on the work, but that is not interfering with the digging. . . . When this part [rear section] of the building is moved, the work of excavating for the foundation will be pushed along rapidly."

In the meantime, the Silver Bow Club Building Association had resolved to double its capital to $100,000, perhaps recognizing that Link and Haire's design of a five-story building with, in the words of the *Butte Miner*, "beautiful hardwood finishings, splendid

"The Foundations of the new Silver Bow Club." Anaconda Standard, *July 29,1906. Courtesy Butte Silver Bow Public Archives, Butte.*

Silver Bow Club presentation drawing, Link & Haire, Architects. Anaconda Standard, *September 2, 1906. Courtesy Montana Historical Society, Helena.*

interior decorations and excellent arrangement of clubrooms, reception rooms, dining halls, kitchen, ballroom and the like" would require more than the original $50,000 in capital. The *Miner* put the construction cost at $125,000. One of the Mining City's most long-lived contractors, Charles C. Goddard, was selected as the project's contractor. Goddard, a Wisconsin native, worked as a mason in Butte in the late 1890s but within a few years had started a contractor company, constructing the Thornton Hotel (1900) and Hirbour Block (1901), a proto-skyscraper.

One of Link and Haire's first buildings, the Silver Bow Club demonstrated their facility with a variety of architectural styles and elements. The building's exterior of pinkish-red pressed brick, possibly purchased from the Menomonie Hydraulic Pressed Brick Co. in Minneapolis, and buff sandstone quarried in Columbus, Montana, conveyed a solid yet pleasant appearance. Ornamenting the two-story main entrance were an iron and glass canopy trimmed with tabs of art glass suspended by chains linked from lions' mouths and a graceful grilled panel. The third story's recessed balcony

"The Miners Union Local #1 was built at 125 West Granite in 1906 to house the Silver Bow Club, an exclusive Butte businessmen's club," ca. 1980. Historic American Buildings Survey/Historic American Engineering Record (HAER MONT,47-BUT,1-70). Photograph by Jet Lowe.

Silver Bow Club, Butte, August 24, 2005. Photograph by Patty Dean.

with wrought iron railings was accented by two canted columns topped by stylized pegged capitals and, at each corner, quoins of alternating light and dark masonry that lightened mass without compromising density. The balcony's sandstone cornice with raised chevron elements featured three cartouches, the center with an entwined "SBC" and the flanking ones depicting a bow and club, a visual pun on the club's name and Butte's resident county. The top story's fenestration and decorative elements were of a more conventional nature in the Renaissance Revival style with bracketed eaves and a cornice topped by anthemions (now removed).

Accounts of the building's interior configuration indicate that the Link and Haire scheme did not differ substantially from those of Cutter and Malmgren and replicated the spatial and social hierarchies implicit in gentlemen's clubs since their origins in early eighteenth century London. A male "domesticity" had evolved from the leisurely conversation, gambling, and dining that had occurred in informal coffeehouse gatherings in the late 1600s, finding form in a townhouse design. The interior plan of the men's club presented strict physical, hierarchical, and social separations between men and women, "stranger" and member, and staff and member.

Such segregation began literally on the sidewalk outside the building, as there were restrictions as to who could use a particular entrance. The double-door main entrance facing West Granite Street was reached by climbing several sandstone stairs into a high-ceilinged vestibule and ascending more stairs to the elevated first floor where one could either continue his way through the reception hall to the club rooms if a member or, if not, be directed by club staff to, in the words of the *Anaconda Standard,* an "exquisite little room done in greens and browns," the stranger's room. The entryway to offices intended to be leased to the Butte Water Co. was a single door on the ground (basement) floor to the east of the main entrance. Finally, on the building's east side facing Alaska Street a double-door entrance, with a Ludovici-tiled overhang with its access to the Otis elevator, "affords privacy," the *Standard* reported, "to those who may wish to go to the club quarters on the second floor when the first floor is in use."

By the spring of 1907, the St. Paul firm of William A. French and Co. had been retained to provide the Club's interior decorations and furnishings. A native of Plainfield, New Jersey, William A. French had come to Minnesota at the age of twenty-three in 1887 and in 1900 opened a shop specializing in "decorations, draperies and special furniture" in downtown St. Paul. A 1903 advertisement noted: "Much of our furniture is made in our own shops and is faithfully copied from the best models of their respective periods…" French's clientele included railroad, mining, and timber magnates from Milwaukee to Seattle (including Charles Benton Power of Helena), and it is likely a number of Silver Bow Club members were familiar with his firm. In addition, Haire himself must have had a long-standing relationship with French as a letter he sent to French opened with the salutation, "My Dear French."

At the Silver Bow Club Building Association's September meeting, its trustees voted to pay French the $7,500 owed him for the decoration and furnishings of the club. Although very few photographs exist of

Advertisement for William A. French & Company, St. Paul showroom. The Western Architect, *August 1905. Courtesy of Minnesota Historical Society, St. Paul.*

the building's interior, extant features and historic textual descriptions convey the variety and artistry of its décor. Certain sections and levels of the building, however, were of a more utilitarian use and for specific persons. The basement housed resident servants' rooms, storerooms for wine and liquor, foodstuffs, and the vacuum heating plant. The club could not sustain itself on members' dues and expenditures alone and entered into a long-term lease with the Butte Water Company for a five-room office at the southeast corner of the building. The water company's superintendent, Eugene Carroll, a Silver Bow Club member, disclosed that "the beauty of it [his office's location in the Club building]

is that it connects by a private hall which leads to the dumb waiter and when his friends drop in to see him, there'll be no long waiting between drinks." The Water Co. remained in this location until it purchased the Montana Independent Telephone building directly across the street in 1918.

The second or main floor (that is, one floor above the basement level) contained the requisite kitchen and butler's pantry, main and private dining rooms, and a reception hall for lounging. The latter room retains much of its original ambiance with beamed ceiling and a massive mottled green-enamel-tiled fireplace dominating the north wall, flanked by doorways that once led to the large dining room. The fireplace surround featured at its center a large ceramic plaque finished identically to the surrounding tile and depicting a bow with arrow and club, once again alluding to the club's name, in bas-relief. Above the fireplace, the artistry of the French Co.'s decorators was evident with painted "frescoes" depicting a medieval English hunt scene. The room was furnished with Craftsman-style rockers, settees, and center tables, likely manufactured at French's new factory in St. Paul.

Similar paintings were installed above the double-swinging doors on either side of the fireplace that led into the main dining room about which the *Butte Miner* exclaimed: "no more beautiful room is contained in the building than this. Its [Oregon pine]

Silver Bow Club reception hall, Butte, February 22, 2006. Photograph by Patty Dean.

Silver Bow Club reception hall fireplace detail, Butte, February 22, 2006. Photograph by Patty Dean.

woodwork is green, showing the grain of the wood and is inlaid with broad red lines [of wood]. A wainscoting 7 ½ feet high extends around the [12-foot high] room. Above the wainscoting is a splendid hand-painted frieze, depicting mountain and pastoral scenery." Above the wainscoting, a plate rail ran all the way around the room with china closets enclosing two columns, likely steel posts, at the center of the room. Hanging light fixtures made of substantial Craftsman-style statuary bronze (a durable satin finish) and spherical glass shades reinforced the masculine aspect of both rooms.

Other major rooms on the second floor included

the private dining room (which could be used by ladies and was adjacent to an ivory gold reception area for their use) to the left of the main dining room. The dining room's wall covering of metallic Japanese leather and painted frieze depicted foliage and apples beneath a coved and beamed ceiling. One of two reading rooms or libraries—requisite in a gentlemen's club—occupied the southeast corner just off the reception hall and was decorated in an imitation oak with ivory plaster frieze and walls tinted a soft green.

The club's upper floors were accessible via a quarter-sawn oak staircase with curving banister or by birdcage Otis elevator in an area off to the right of the reception room. With such an arrangement, it was possible for members to enter the club through the Alaska Street east entrance and completely bypass the main floor, which, the *Anaconda Standard* reported, "when such festivities are in progress will give the bashful members a chance to slip in and slip out without anyone being the wiser." Another commodious lounging room contained a large tiled fireplace with a copper-studded hood, green-tinted woodwork, and wall coverings of a faux red Spanish leather and handpainted border. Venetian windows with art glass opened onto the balcony that overlooked West Granite Street below. Arched doorways at right and left opened into the second reading room/library with buff–colored walls with custom bookcases. A card room, with eight-foot

high wainscoting comprised of Spanish leather panels below a deep, hand-painted floral frieze, was at the other side of the lounging room as was a private card room with its frieze depicting a forest.

The bar room adjoining the card room presents some of the most intact elements found at the club today. The room's hand-painted frieze above deep paneled wainscoting depicts "all the grains and fruits which go to make up the festive cocktail. Luscious grapes clamber over lattice supports in the pictured scenes. . . . Directly overhead . . . the grape and fruit design of the frieze is reproduced in a ceiling panel in colored art glass, which shines resplendent and is reflected by numerous mirrors." A huge quarter-sawn oak panel on the back-bar inscribed with a Henry Aldrich rhyme reads: "If this be true as I do think/There are five reasons we should drink/Good friends, good wine and being dry/Or lest we shall be bye and bye/or any other reason why." (This same quote was featured in the 1915 log dining room and bar building at Kootenai Lodge "camp" on Swan Lake, owned jointly by Silver Bow Club members L. O. Evans and Cornelius Kelly. The original plans for this building document Spokane's Kirtland Cutter as its architect.)

To the east of the bar was the billiard room which was outfitted with six billiard tables (each illuminated with its own light), eleven-foot-high copper paneled wainscoting, and an Art Nouveau design frieze. The

Above: *Silver Bow Club bar room, Butte, February 22, 2006. Photograph by Patty Dean.*

Right: *Silver Bow Club bar room frieze detail, Butte, February 22, 2006. Photograph by Patty Dean.*

south end of the room still features an inglenook with two high-backed settles of faux pegged construction facing each other and a tiled fireplace with hammered copper hood and brick hearth.

The building's top story was configured for approximately twenty rooms for members with hot

Silver Bow Club billiard hall inglenook, Butte, February 22, 2006. Photograph by Patty Dean.

and cold water and adjacent bathrooms, and well-lit hallways. The club planned to lease most of the rooms to resident members, perhaps in recognition of Butte's housing shortage, while reserving a very few for out-of-town members.

Unfortunately, the New Year's wish the *Anaconda Standard* expressed in 1908 for Silver Bow Club members— "many years of delightful association in their new home"—was not to be. Although membership rolls numbered over 600 in 1912, the years following World War I with Prohibition, severely eroding copper prices, regressive economic conditions,

and fewer new club members to take the place of those who had died or moved away caused the remaining members to consider drastic action. Complicating any efforts was the discovery by the Building Association's officers that they had inexplicably failed to renew their corporate charter. The directors of the corporation became its trustees.

A year later, the trustees contracted with restaurateur Joseph Reau to "operate café, buffet and dormitory," paying him $7,500 annually for those services. They also leased the former Water Co. offices to the North Butte Mining Co. and took out a $50,000 six percent mortgage note held by the Monidah Trust Co. In October 1932, a proposed merger between the Butte Country Club and the Silver Bow Club failed, and the directors immediately ordered that the water and heating systems in the building be drained and shut off and the windows on the building's north and west sides be boarded up. The tenancy of the North Butte Mining Co. remained rent-free in exchange for protecting the property.

The Monidah Trust's agent and attorney, James E. Murray, began foreclosure proceedings while letters were mailed to members near and far owing money to the club and some furniture was sold to the Anaconda Copper Mining Co. By December 1932, the Monidah Trust Co. was granted a sheriff's deed for the property and the Silver Bow Club was formally discontinued.

Approximately twenty years later, the Silver Bow Club, that had once hosted and housed the wealthy and famous, became the Miners Union Club, a destination for the working man and his family. The Silver Bow Club embodied the Mining City's twentieth-century fortunes and misfortunes yet succeeded in its initial role by securing Butte's position as the metropolis of the Northern Rockies.

Sources

Anaconda Copper Mining Company Records, MC 169, Montana Historical Society, Helena.

Anaconda Standard

Butte Miner

Corning, Leavitt. *The Razoo,* St. Paul, 1902-1914, Minnesota Historical Society, St. Paul.

Dean, Patty. "Inspiration & Innovation: Early Twentieth Century Minnesota Furniture Designers and Manufacturers," unpublished paper, 1997.

Dean, Patty. "Unique & Handsome: Cass Gilbert's Designs for the Montana Club," *Drumlummon Views,* Spring/Summer, 2006, www.drumlummon.org/images/PDF-Spr-Sum06/DV_1-2_Dean.pdf

"Kootenai Camp," National Register of Historic Places nomination file, Montana State Historic Preservation Office, 1983.

Link and Haire, Architects, Records, MC 152, Montana Historical Society, Helena.

Shovers, Brian, et al. *Butte and Anaconda Revisited: An Overview of Early-Day Mining and Smelting in Montana,* prepared in cooperation with the Klepetko Chapter, Society for Industrial Archeology and Butte Historical Society, 1991.

Men in Hats
Mary Murphy

"Wear your hat with an air, with a dash, with a hey nonny nonny!"
—Dorothy Stote, *Men Too Wear Clothes*, 1939

Indiana Jones gave his to the Smithsonian. Rick Blaine strolled into the night at the beginning of a beautiful friendship topped with his. Dashiell Hammett wore one as, no doubt, did the Continental Op when he came to clean up Poisonville. Fedoras—those soft felt hats with a snap brim, a lengthwise crease at the crown, pinched at the sides for easy doffing—adorned the heads of the dashing, the dangerous, and the shady in the early part of the twentieth century. They were ubiquitous in Butte.

When the Farm Security Administration (FSA) photographers traversed Montana in the 1930s and early 1940s, they took a lot of pictures of men in hats. Until the 1960s, practically everyone wore a hat when in public. Women's hats spoke of their sense of fashion and their economic well-being. Men's hats spoke of their occupation and their urbanity, or lack thereof. Soft caps of wool, tweed, and serge with short visors were common everywhere for both men and boys, but when a man went to work, he commonly wore signature headgear. Ranchers and cowboys wore cowboy hats, dramatic symbols of the mythic West—too new and

Arthur Rothstein. Men in hats lounge in front of the Arcade Bar and Café, Butte, 1939. Courtesy Library of Congress, Prints & Photographs Division, FSA/OWI Collection (LC-USF33-003112-M4).

tidy a cowboy hat marked a dude. Some sheepshearers sported peculiar beanies, the kind of hat that in another world would signal a college freshman. Farmers and loggers snugged into warm wool hats with practical earflaps that could be pulled down as shields against the bitter Montana cold. Miners in Butte donned hard hats topped with lights when they went underground. But aboveground they wore fedoras.

Fedoras were urban. In 1902, the *New York Times* reported that the city was "thick" with the newly fashionable fedora. The style spread throughout the United States, dominating men's headgear from the 1920s through the 1940s. Butte men could walk into any of a dozen men's clothing stores in the 1920s and 1930s and purchase a fedora, or they could order one from the Montgomery Ward catalog for $2.45 plus 7 cents postage. It was the hat of choice for city men. By the 1920s, the fedora had also become associated with bootleggers, detectives, and newspaper reporters—the characters who would later dominate film noir, the characters who peopled the streets of Butte.

In the first half of the twentieth century, Butte was Montana's metropolis, a teeming, tumultuous, twenty-four-hour-a-day hive of hard work and hard play. Men and boys filled its streets. Newsboys hawked papers; delivery boys toted bundles of laundry and buckets of beer. Men marched purposefully on their way to work or to the lodge or union hall, and

Arthur Rothstein. Cowboys branding a calf during a roundup, Quarter Circle U Ranch near Birney, Montana, 1939. Courtesy Library of Congress, Prints & Photographs Division, FSA/OWI Collection (LC-USF33-003235- M1).

Arthur Rothstein. Dudes in town, Billings, Montana, 1939. Courtesy Library of Congress, Prints & Photographs Division, FSA/OWI Collection (LC-USF33-003092-M3).

they lounged on street corners, outside saloons and speakeasies, smoking, talking, ogling girls. It was the odd fellow who didn't wear a hat in his perambulations about the city.

FSA photographers Arthur Rothstein and Russell Lee caught the tail end of this Butte when they came to the city in 1939 and 1942. Assigned to document the Great Depression and the country's recovery, Rothstein and Lee found Butte fascinating.

Rothstein photographed the streets in 1939; Lee followed miners to work, home, and the union hall in 1942. Their photographs capture the seriousness of Butte men's work and the vitality of their street life. And they also portray their hats.

Arthur Rothstein. Men in hats and the Art Deco façade of the Board of Trade, Butte, 1939. Courtesy Library of Congress, Prints &
Photographs Division, FSA/OWI Collection (LC-USF33-003128-M4).

Russell Lee. Miner waiting to take the cage down into the mine, Butte, 1942. Courtesy Library of Congress, Prints & Photographs Division, FSA/OWI Collection (LC-YSW3-008150-D).

Russell Lee. John Herlihy, shift boss, Mountain Con Mine. Courtesy Library of Congress, Prints & Photographs Division, FSA/OWI Collection (LC-USW3- 008263-D).

Russell Lee. Playing cards in the Miners' Union Hall, Butte, 1942. Courtesy Library of Congress, Prints & Photographs Division, FSA/ OWI Collection (LC-USW3-009681-D).

Equestrian Oasis: The Anaconda Saddle Club

Kate Hampton

Driving west from the industrial town of Anaconda toward the Pintlar Mountains and their recreational riches—hot springs, skiing, hiking, fishing—Montana Highway 1 lazes its way through a low pine forest. In a clearing about two miles from town, grandstands unexpectedly rise around a small track and rodeo grounds, and an iron entrance gate announces the Anaconda Saddle Club (ASC). Neat rows of bright red stables crisply trimmed in white, together with an octagonal log clubhouse, present a rustic retreat and entice visitors and residents alike to investigate further. This local institution has been an important part of Anaconda's social and recreational world for more than sixty years.

Montana mining baron Marcus Daly founded Anaconda, Montana, in 1883 as the site of the Washoe Reduction Works, the smelting operation of his Anaconda Mining Company, and the town became home to a community of workers and laborers in related industries. Perhaps recognizing the need to provide recreation to keep the population happy and productive, Daly, the Anaconda Company, and the Anaconda community were progressive when it came to providing leisure outlets in the community for

The stables at the Anaconda Saddle Club, 2000. Courtesy Montana State Historic Preservation Office. Photo by Kate Hampton.

residents. A horse enthusiast himself, Daly oversaw the construction of a horse-racing track west of town in 1888 as well as several parks. The Anaconda community continued the tradition of investing in recreational outlets even after Daly's death in 1900, including the donation of a city block for the town's first urban park, the construction of athletic facilities, and other projects through the mid-twentieth century.[1]

As a result, Anaconda offered a wealth of recreational opportunities for townspeople and residents of the outlying area. The founding of the Anaconda

The ASC's octagonal log clubhouse, 2000. Courtesy Montana State Historic Preservation Office. Photo by Kate Hampton.

Saddle Club represented a continued commitment to the social health of the Anaconda community. Numerous local residents rallied behind the effort. The only complex of its kind in the Anaconda–Deer Lodge area, it stands as a tribute to rural recreation and social clubs and respects its historic tradition as it continues to serve Anaconda and the surrounding area.

In 1944, an active group of local horse enthusiasts gathered at Dr. Milo Snodgrass's West Valley barn and organized the ASC, which held monthly meetings at the Montana Hotel in Anaconda. By January 1945, the club's land committee purchased acreage west of town for the construction of a saddle club and horse-boarding facility. Martin "Abe" Nelson designed plans for the property, and within weeks of acquiring the land, ASC members began clearing away the brush and rocks in the field. The members solicited donations of building materials, which were scarce during and immediately after the end of World War II. Members also served as the construction crew on the project, erecting all of the buildings and structures on the site.[2]

Each phase of the construction was carefully planned to take advantage of the vision, skills, and aesthetic ideals of the club members. They chose a decidedly Rustic design, building on the function of the club and the recreational building trends of the early and mid-twentieth century. The "Rustic" style of architecture came to epitomize the favored architecture of western tourist destinations, such as dude ranches, during the 1900–1950 period.[3] Especially associated with wilderness tourist destinations, the Rustic Movement "was a natural outgrowth of a new romanticism about nature, about our country's western frontiers." Further, the style is generally characterized by "the use of native materials in proper scale" and "the avoidance of rigid, straight lines, and over-sophistication." Through these simple means, the style "gives the feeling of having been executed by pioneer craftsmen with limited hand tools," and when "successfully handled," it "thus achieves sympathy with natural surroundings, and with the past."[4]

Blending well with their scenic natural surroundings, Rustic buildings celebrated the pioneer days and frontier living with a great deal of nostalgia, much like western tourists themselves. Widespread reliance on log construction, therefore, was more than merely convenient in the heavily forested Mountain West; it expressed a philosophical statement that grew out of the ideological climate of the early twentieth century. "Real log cabins represented more than artful simplicity," Peter Schmidt has noted. "They expressed an attitude toward life itself."[5]

A log blacksmith shop, the first building completed at the ASC, served as the temporary headquarters and social center of the organization until the main clubhouse was finished in 1946. During the construction, tables were set up in the blacksmith shop and the club ladies brought home-cooked meals to serve to the workers. Later on, the main clubhouse offered a kitchen and separate clubroom for these entertainment purposes. The unusual octagonal design of the clubhouse not only was charming but also provided a large, welcoming space for club and community events. Almost every evening and every Sunday between the summer of 1945 and the fall of 1946, the 160 ASC members worked on the construction of the barns, clubhouse, and caretaker's house and garage. Local residents Jack Carraher, Clarence Weis, and Stuart Ainsley drew the plans for the horse barns, and in a tradition that carries on today as the club continues to grow, members were asked to purchase the materials for the stalls and to construct them according to club specifications. The result is a series of long, narrow barns, made up of stalls that are uniform in size, design, and color.[6]

Recognizing the fledgling complex's importance to the community, Deer Lodge County provided trucks and laborers to help complete the race and exercise track, now the site of the rodeo arena, east of the barns. One of the first projects on the site, the oval track and associated corrals and bucking chutes, was completed in 1945, and improvements continued through 1947. A public grand opening on September 22, 1946, celebrated the official opening of the ASC complex, though some construction work would continue into the next year. During the grand opening, a huge crowd, estimated at 1,500, enjoyed guided tours and a colt show. The same day, Martin Nelson acquired five additional acres of land west of the clubhouse for future expansion. In August 1947, the *Anaconda Standard* reported that the "individual barns . . . hold 66 horses, and [there is a] clubhouse, garage and caretakers house of milled log to match the clubhouse with a large bright kitchen, large living room, two bedrooms and a bath, and front and back porches."[7]

Longtime members Bess and Harold Levengood served as unofficial historians for the club from the time they joined in 1946. As early as the 1960s, Bess began to assemble scrapbooks memorializing the club's events; these scrapbooks are now housed at the local historical society. In an *Anaconda Leader* article celebrating the club's fiftieth anniversary, Bess related one of her favorite stories from the early days at the club, when many of the ladies were "green" riders:

Despite their inexperience, several of the ladies decided to go on a ride of their own. Bess had only been riding one month, and decided to take a "green" horse and add a pair of spurs to her outfit. As she came down in the saddle, her horse bucked her up in the air. She came back down in the saddle and he tossed her up again. Again, she came back down in the saddle and thought, "this isn't so bad." The horse gave her another toss, only this time he sidestepped. Bess hit the dirt. After she regained her breath, she and Ruth Nelson collapsed in laughter. About that time the other women showed up, each with a tale of woe to tell of their own disasters.[8]

The men had their own stories, including one about two men who owned a very large mule together: "Every Sunday these two would attempt to ride this mule, to the great amusement of everyone present. The mule always 'won the day and went to bed happy!'" Although the club sponsored rides and shows for specific groups, children always played a big part of the family activities at the ASC. A longtime tradition, the Little Britches Rodeo, began just after the rodeo grounds were built and included roping and riding calves.[9]

Through the years, the club has offered not only fun and frolic but also informative and practical equestrian care. The good work continues today as ASC provides workshops and clinics that educate the community in everything from trimming hooves to trailering to general horsemanship. The club still depends on the volunteerism of its members to maintain the property, combining work parties with swap meets and other fund-raisers to keep the club grounds inviting and functional.

Since the club settled into Anaconda's West Valley in 1945, it has served as a respected center of family activity, recreation, and quality promotion of horses. In a flurry of activity from 1945 through 1960, the ASC established itself as an important local institution, in keeping with the traditions of organized recreation in Anaconda. The clubhouse, barns, and other outbuildings are fine examples of Rustic architecture as constructed during the mid-to late 1940s. Collectively, these buildings are also a visually significant representation of equine-related facilities and evoke a connection with an earlier era. The club—well maintained and much loved by the community—continues to be a vital part of Anaconda. The traditions of volunteerism, quality horse care, and fun have been synonymous with the club for more than sixty years.

1   Kim Currie Morrison, "Historic and Architectural Resources of Anaconda, Montana Multiple Properties Documentation Form," 1992, Anaconda National Register of Historic Places Files, Montana State Historic Preservation Office, Helena.

2   Cindie Kalan-Green, "Anaconda Saddle Club," *Anaconda Leader,* May 1996.

3   For a discussion of the character-defining features of Rustic architecture, see William C. Tweed, Laura E. Soulliere, and Henry G. Law, *Rustic Architecture: 1916–1942,* National Park Service, Western Regional Office, Division of Cultural Management, February 1977), 1–3. For a comprehensive overview of the ideological and architectural influences that gave rise to the popular Rustic style in America, see Linda Flint McClelland, *Presenting Nature: The Historic Landscape Design of the National Park Service: 1916–1942* (Washington, DC: National Park Service, 1993).

4   Albert H. Good, *Park and Recreation Structures: Part I—Administration and Basic Service Facilities* (reprint of the 1938 edition published by the U.S. Department of the Interior, National Park Service; New York: Princeton Architectural Press, 1999), 5.

5   Peter J. Schmidt, *Back to Nature: The Arcadian Myth in Urban America* (New York: Oxford University Press, 1969), 168.

6   *Anaconda Standard* newspaper clippings, "Anaconda Saddle Club National Register of Historic Places Nomination File," Montana State Historic Preservation Office, Helena.

7   *Anaconda Standard*, August 18, 1947.

8   Cindie Kalan-Green, "Anaconda Saddle Club," *Anaconda Leader,* May 1996.

9   Kalan-Green, "Anaconda Saddle Club."

"Queer Spots In and About Butte": An Introduction

Patty Dean

In the spring of 1906, the *Anaconda Standard* initiated a new feature, "Queer Spots In and About Butte," in its hefty Sunday newspaper. Focusing its editorial eye on such topics as ethnic enclaves, landmarks, nearby natural wonders, and derelict industrial sites, among others, the series profiled a wide range of built environments and landscapes conceived to be "queer," that is, interesting and singular in early twentieth-century parlance.

While there was no introduction or fanfare announcing the series, it must have been conceived as a continuing feature, given its semi-weekly regularity, its placement at the coveted top of the page, and the distinctive artwork that accompanied the copy. A calligraphic "Queer Spots/In and/About Butte" banner stretched from page edge to edge, flanked by line drawings that often pertained directly to the story's topic.

In *Copper Chorus : Mining, Politics and the Montana Press, 1889–1959,* Dennis Swibold has observed that the *Anaconda Standard* "owed its existence to Marcus Daly's wealth, but editor John H. Durston made the paper excellent beyond its means." Durston's education (he possessed a Ph.D. from the University of Heidelberg) and vision drove the content and the appearance of the newspaper. Additionally, the *Standard* employed the most

advanced printing technologies available, and by the time "Queer Spots" first appeared, Swibold notes, "Montana's premier daily was in its prime, its popularity resting on its muscular news and feature sections."

This supremacy is evident with each "Queer Spots" feature, especially given the many non-stock photographs and drawings that accompany the dense writing. Story subjects that initially appeared to be of little interest—or even provoke a flicker of repulsion—for some readers seemed to especially intrigue the uncredited reporter who urged the reader to look beyond the surface. The tone of these stories is a blend of stereotypes, racism, and an acknowledgement of some quality indicative of their process toward Americanization.

Following is a listing of each "Queer Spot" feature with its publication date as well as four of the forty "Queer Spot" features—"The Assyrian Colony," "Chinatown," "The Chinese Gardens," and "The Cree Village"—together with contextual essays by scholars Benjamin Trigona-Harany, Christopher W. Merritt, and Nicholas Peterson Vrooman.

Queer Spots In and About Butte

No.	Date	Title/Subject
1	1906-03-18	Precipitating Plants [Langford, Boston & Montana at Meaderville, etc.]
2	1906-03-25	City & Water Supply
3	1906-04-01	Assyrian Colony
4	1906-04-08	[Street] Car Barns
5	1906-04-15	Recreation Spots [Nine Mile Canyon, Basin Creek Road, etc.)
6	1906-04-22	Dismantled Smelter [Parrot, Colorado, Bell & others]
7	1906-04-29	Butte's Powder Supply [stone powder storage houses east of Durant]
8	1906-05-06	Silver Bow Poor Farm
9	1906-05-13	Bluebird Mine & Mill
10	1906-05-20	Chinatown
11	1906-05-27	Cree Village
12	1906-06-03	Underground City [copper miners' environment]
13	1906-06-10	Silver Bow City [Crystal Springs]
14	1906-06-17	Burlington & Rocker
15	1906-06-24	Seen from the Car [route of the "Seeing Butte Observation Car"]
16	1906-07-01	Nine Mile Canyon

17	1906-07-08	Walkerville
18	1906-07-15	The Old Placer Field
19	1906-07-22	House in the Grove [Mr. & Mrs. E.S. Baxter's home & tree grove south of Butte]
20	1906-07-29	Fire Department
21	1906-08-05	Columbia Gardens
22	1906-08-12	Continental Divide & Woodville
23	1906-08-19	Studio of artist E. S. Paxson
24	1906-08-26	Crematory & City Dump [including photographs of Cree, "citizens of the dump"]
25	1906-09-02	Ore Bins [electric ore train at Bell, Original Mines, etc.]
26	1906-09-09	Highland City & Red Mountain City
27	1906-09-16	Railways ["old NP station", NP roundhouse, BA&P station, etc.]
28	1906-09-23	Grading Camp [Milwaukee Road grading camp between Butte & Whitehall]
29	1906-09-30	Playground [public & private, i.e., empty lots]
30	1906-10-07	Chinese Gardens [near Nine Mile & Basin Creek]
31	1906-10-14	Summer Camps [tent camping at various locales]
32	1906-10-21	Silver Bow Creek
33	1906-10-28	In the Silver Bow Canyon
34	1906-11-04	Stringtown & Butchertown [north of Walkerville]
35	1906-11-11	Glendale [home of Hecla Consolidated Mining & Milling]
36	1906-11-18	On Fleecer Mountain
37	1906-11-25	Woodville
38	1906-12-02	Brown's Gulch [behind Big Butte, Italian population]
39	1906-12-09	Police Station
40	1906-12-30	The Big Butte

No. 3 The Assyrian Colony
Anaconda Standard, April 1, 1906

Walk along East Park street any afternoon. When you reach the corner by the Clarence hotel turn south for half a block and you will see a number of frame houses in the alley, placed indiscriminately upon the ground for a distance of several hundred feet in an easterly direction. Continue your walk on to Mercury street and then go east half way through the block and you will be facing the Assyrian colony, one of the queerest of the queer spots in Butte. It is unique in its way and it is asserted on the best authority that it is the only colony of its kind in the United States.

Rival Factions

No accurate census of the Assyrian population of Butte is available, but it numbers close to 200 men, women and children. The business of the men, as a general rule, is scavenger work and several of the bosses have a number of teams and it is said are making money out of the distasteful work. Really there are two factions of the Assyrians in Butte and there is considerable business rivalry among them. John Paul is the leader of one clique and Shabin Ferris heads the other. Both have proved to be good business men and their followers trust them implicitly.

Quaint Homes

The houses which they occupy and which are shown in the several views on this page are among the most dilapidated and ramshackle affairs to be found in

THE ASSYRIAN COLONY

Butte. They are built in no regularity; they have no style or attempt at comfort. They are placed on the ground wherever the fancy of the owner dictated or he could get the ground to build upon. In nearly every case a stable is necessitated by the business of the occupant of the cabin and this stable is as disreputable looking as the house, more so carrying out the comparison of what the two structures should be. The wagons used necessarily cry aloud to the heavens, especially on a warm day, but they worry the Assyrians but little. They are brought as close to the houses as possible for convenience sake and allowed to stand all day long, the work being done during the night. Evidently the residents of the colony get used to it and like other industries, pay but little attention to the unusual conditions which surround the work.

Americanized

Taking matters around the colony, a visit to the place shows it to be but little different from any other section of town, judging from the outward appearances and excepting the conditions already named. Playing in the yards and vacant lots will be seen a number of dark-skinned and dark-eyed children. Their games will be the same as are played by other children of Butte, and if the stranger gazes too long or too earnestly at the spectacle he will be greeted by the cry of "rubber" or the query, "Do you see anything green about here?" Truth compels a person to answer no to this query, for the Assyrian colony is one of the bleakest and most barren spots in the Butte district. The women are apparently always busy with their housework, but it does not seem as if they accomplish much, still they are doing something. The children attend the public schools of Butte and it is said they are bright pupils, quick to learn and grasp the opportunities offered. However, the people are most clannish. They keep well within themselves. They do not mix with the other people of Butte and have few pleasures, such as attending theaters and other amusements. Their language is the only language spoken in the colony. Many of the men and nearly all of the women cannot understand a word of English, or at least they pretend they cannot when placed in a position where it is necessary for them to talk. The leaders are bright and quick to grasp a business point. The men who act as interpreters catch the meaning of their questioners quickly and faithfully. The members of the colony have some pleasures in their own houses; parties and dances such as were in vogue in their country thousands of years ago being still indulged in occasionally, and the fete days and dances of the mother country are never forgotten.

Ten Years Old

The colony has been in existence in Butte for about 10 years; away back in their country along the river Jordan, some of the Assyrians heard of the blessings of free America and one of them told the story of his emigration to a Standard man only a little while ago. His English was broken, but his talk was sincere. "I knew only in a __where I wanted to go," he said, "I only knew that America was a country thousands of miles away. I trusted to the agent of a steamship company whom was worthy of trust. Myself and my family, and my friends were there on the steamship together. After days of waiting and watching we sighted the shores of the new country. Eagerly we crowded to the rail to see the land which would give us our fortune someday. We landed and then we learned we had been deceived and instead of America we were in Brazil. We were without money. We did not want to stay in that land, which was little better than the home we left, so we worked day and night, our women and children slaved with us, and finally we had gotten enough coin together to resume our passage, and this time we made no mistake. We landed in New Orleans or Texas, I do not remember which, and finally we came to Butte. Here we have since lived. We have had our share of troubles and woes and have enjoyed prosperity. Almost every man had made some money. Someday we might go back to the old country for the ties are strong which draw us there. There we have no great prospects of the future, but it is still home. We could go back there and live like princes but it would not be America, as we know it too well. We would have no privileges like we have here; the rulers of the country would swallow up every cent of the money we brought home with us. They would nag at us and persecute us until we yielded and it would be necessary for us to come back to Butte and America and make another stake. Many of us are American citizens and I think the Assyrian colony in Butte will increase from year to year rather than diminish, for many of our people far away across the oceans know we are prospering and I look for them to come to Butte for this city is now known even in the center of Asia as a great place where gold can be earned by the work of the individual and where the customs of the fatherland are preserved in many respects."

Assyria

Assyria, the country that was called home by these strange people before they migrated to America and afterwards to Butte, is one of the oldest Asiatic states of history and is frequently referred to in the Old Testament as a dependence of Babylonia. At the time of its greatest power it covered an area of 75,000 square miles, bounded on the north by Armenia, the lower Zaab on the south, the Zagros Mountains on the east and the Euphrates on the west. The name of the country appears in Genesis, X. 2, and refers to a small country on the left bank of the Tigris. Ancient Assyria was a fertile country and the name was sometimes applied to the whole of Babylonia. The early history of the two countries is interlocked and the conditions of the one are closely related to the conditions of the other. The favorite amusement of the kings of ancient Assyria was lion hunting. According to Genesis, the Assyrians are descendants of Shem and emigrants from Babylon and her religion was also derived from the mother country, as well as its civilization.

Ancestry

A search of the records shows that the Assyrians were brave and warlike and were always aggressive during the ancient times. The Babylonian emigrants established Assyria about 2,000 years before Christ. The first Assyrian rulers of which history deals flourished in 1816 B.C. For the next 300 years nothing is known of the condition of Assyria. In the fifteenth century B.C. Assyria was involved in a war with Babylonia, then under the rule of the non-Semitic Kassites. War continued between the two countries for a long time with varying success, but Assyria finally became supreme, forcing Babylonia to become a vassal state. Between 705 and 681 B.C. Assyria reached the height of her power, King Esarhddon having by his conquests about that time added to his name the title of king of

THE FRONT ENTRANCE ~

upper and lower Egypt and Ethiopia. In 688 B.C. the decline of the Assyrian power began, Asshurbanipal being then king. In some respects his reign was most brilliant. It was a golden age of art and literature. The military spirit became comparatively dormant, although the town of Susa was conquered and destroyed. Taking advantage of the apathy shown by the Assyrians and their indulgence in the more peaceful occupations, induced by the awakening of art and literature, the nations which had been conquered awoke to their opportunities. They rose in their might. Their uprisings were rapid and persistent. Assyria was soon trembling in dismay and the downward path was soon reached. Their soldiers made a rally, repelled the attack of the Medes and Persians and it seemed as if they would regain some of their old-time glory. Then the invaders were in command of Phraortes and they were signally defeated. Seventeen years later the attack was repeated. Cyaxares, in union with Nabopolassar of Babylon, repeated the attack and won. Nineveh of the Assyrians fell and with the end of this battle the power of the Assyrians fell forever. And this was 608 years before Christianity came to the earth with the birth of Christ.

Changed Conditions

Of the later years of the Assyrian history, the books of reference deal but little. In company with many of the other states and provinces of Asia Minor and the Palestine country, the Assyrian have become subjects of the Turkish empire. Its territory is now limited to the valley and plains and mountains on the east side of the Jordan and the Dead Sea. Generally speaking, its area is mountainous, but by no means at a high altitude. Its people are oppressed and many of them are half wild. However, they are loath to leave their homes; they put up with almost any hardship for the privilege of living in peace upon the wild side hills, and the fact that the colony in Butte is said to be the only one of its kind

in the United States is cited as proof of the love these people have for the land which was once gloriously theirs 2,000 years before the Christian Era began.

School boys of years ago can remember the stirring song that was in their readers,

> "The Assyrian came down like a wolf on
> the fold,
> And his cohort was gleaming with silver
> and gold."

Then the story of the bravery of these bold old warriors was recounted until even the school boy was compelled to admire the sturdy men of old.

Tame Now

Now all of their war like spirit was vanished, especially among the Butte colony, although occasionally a fight will take place, and once in awhile they will get into court. The women are just as valiant as the men. Some of them are more so, for the records of a recent court case tell where a woman, over 70 years old, took a hand in a fight and held a man who was trying to run away while her son got a gun and shot him.

Take it all in all, while the Assyrians make fairly good citizens and attend strictly to their own businesses and fight only among themselves, they have gladly degenerated, and the Butte colony, although descendents of the men who helped make song and story with their deeds of valor in pre-Christian days, have had an awful fall and are now the scavengers of the greatest mining camp on earth and they are all making some little money from the business too.

Assyrian Colony of Butte
Benjamin Trigona-Harany

In the minds of most North Americans, the basic divisions of Christianity are quite simple—Catholic, Orthodox, and Protestant—but the Middle East is home to a myriad of other denominations with their own theologies, hierarchies, and traditions. The late eighteenth century saw the beginning of immigration to the United States by some of these Christians, bringing their peculiar religious practices and unintelligible languages with them. It is no surprise, then, that when a group of Arabic-speaking Maronites from the village of Hadchit in the mountains of Lebanon appeared in Butte, Montana, at the turn of the twentieth century, they should have been the subject of some mystery to the local residents. It is also not surprising that the *Anaconda Standard* should have confused the exact identity of these settlers when we consider the complexities of Middle Eastern Christianity.

At the beginning of the twentieth century, much of the Middle East was still part of the Ottoman Empire, a five-hundred-year-old state that would finally disintegrate at the end of the First World War. Determining the identities of individual Ottomans can be challenging in that the administrative system recorded only the religion of its citizens. Ottoman historians are therefore forced to rely on religion, names, and place of residence to determine the specific community to which individuals belonged, something which is very much an imperfect practice. The difficulties are compounded when researching immigrant communities since names are often obscured by imperfect transcription of other languages and the lack of information for place of birth other than "the Ottoman Empire" or, as it was often known, "Turkey." The case of Butte exemplifies this very problem: the turn-of-the-century censuses include names that are identifiably Armenian, Serb, and Arab.

The latter case is particularly problematic since Muslims, Christians, and Jews of various affiliations all would have been found using Arab names but in the *Anaconda Standard* they were described as "Assyrians." That this was an error is not surprising, though a short exploration of Middle Eastern Christianity is required to fully appreciate the problem at hand.

The theological differences among each group go back to the early centuries of the church when ecumenical councils seeking to establish the basic tenets of the faith resulted in deep splits between the official Christianity supported by the Roman Empire and beliefs that it considered heretical. Long before the schism that created Catholics and Orthodox out of a single church, the independent Church of the East (more often called the Nestorian Church) established itself in the fifth century inside what is today's Iraq.

This was followed shortly thereafter by a more serious split that saw separate Armenian, Coptic, and Syrian churches break away with a common theological position. For our purposes here, we can leave the Armenians in Asia Minor (Anatolia) and the Copts in Egypt aside and focus on the Syrian, better known as the Jacobite, Church.

The first point is that not all Christians in Syria followed the Jacobite Church in rejecting the Roman Empire's official doctrine. Those who remained loyal, the Melkites ("royalists"), later themselves split into separate Greek Orthodox and Catholic Churches after the Great Schism in 1054. These slowly became Arabized in the centuries following the Arab conquests of the Middle East and today constitute the majority of the Christian populations of Syria, Palestine, and Jordan. In Lebanon, the Maronites, a separate faction allied to the Catholic Church but with its own tradition, predominates.

The Jacobite Church established its theological center farther east in upper Mesopotamia, present-day southern Turkey. Although the Nestorian and Jacobite churches differed fundamentally in their Christian beliefs, they did share a common liturgical language, Syriac (a form of Aramaic). Modern dialects of Syriac are still spoken today in some parts of Turkey, Iraq, and Syria, but by the nineteenth century, many of these communities had adopted the predominant local language, be it Arabic, Turkish, Armenian, or Kurdish. They also often lived close to one another in Mesopotamia, although the Nestorians were generally situated farther east and the Jacobites farther west.

Like the Melkites, both churches experienced conversion to Catholicism; Nestorians who became Catholics are known as Chaldeans. It should be noted that Chaldeans are Catholics but not Roman Catholics, since they use Syriac as a liturgical language and have their own non-Latin rites and traditions. Today, they constitute by far the largest Christian group in Iraq, with their spiritual leader resident in Baghdad and a heavy concentration of their communities located in and around Mosul. By contrast, the Jacobite and Nestorian churches used to be centered in present-day Turkey, but after the First World War both relocated, the former to Damascus and the latter to Chicago.

In the nineteenth century, Protestant missionaries also arrived in the Ottoman Empire and Iran, and although the scale of conversion was much less than that to Catholicism, the American and British missionaries had a profound impact by introducing the notion that the Nestorians, Chaldeans, and Jacobites were all the descendants of the ancient Assyrians. Although almost all Nestorians and Chaldeans have embraced this identity, the Assyrian thesis is highly controversial today, with many Jacobites rejecting it outright.

Returning to Butte, we are confronted with the idea that the local Arabic-speaking population was an "Assyrian colony." This, however, may well be a misunderstanding by the author of the article in the *Anaconda Standard*. There was a natural confusion between immigrants from "Syria" and "Syrian Christians," but it must be remembered that most Christians from Syria were *not* Syrian Christians but, rather, Greek Orthodox, Catholic Melkites or Maronites, which is exactly who we know to have settled in Butte.

This does not, however, preclude the possibility that there were also Assyrians residing in Montana. Across the border, a group of Nestorian converts to Protestantism from western Iran had settled in Saskatchewan at the turn of the century, though they—along with Chaldeans and Jacobites—were to be found in their greatest numbers along the eastern seaboard and in California. It is entirely possible that the centuries-old religious discord among the various Middle Eastern Christian groups lay behind the emergence of the "two rival factions" in the small Butte community; certainly such "internal" disputes were a fact of life in the Ottoman Empire.

This one small case demonstrates how complex stories of immigrants to the United States may be hidden behind census records indicating birth in "Turkey" rather than "the Ottoman Empire." It also helps shed some light on the various Christian churches that still exist across the Middle East but that have also firmly established themselves across North America.

No. 10 *Chinatown*

Anaconda Standard, May 20, 1906

Every town of prominence in the West, with a few rare exceptions, has its Chinatown, picturesque or otherwise. Butte is strictly in line with the best of them and its Chinatown is considered one of the queer spots of the town. Not only are the habits and the customs of the people queer but queer people live among the Chinese as there are queer doings in the dark places of the town when the rest of the world is sleeping. Chinatown is located close to the business center of the town. Only a block away is busy Park street where thousands of people pass up and down the street every hour in the day. On West Galena, where Chinatown begins, the street is silent and it is but little frequented in comparison with its busier neighboring thoroughfare. But the Chinamen do not worry over these conditions. In fact, they seem to enjoy them and they much prefer to be left to their own devices and follow their own customs.

All Sorts

Butte's Chinatown is peculiar in many respects. Some fine-looking, two-story brick buildings are found upon its streets. Nestling by the side of these are often found frame shacks which are propped up from without and girded within to keep them from falling to pieces. The town has its stores and its own marts of

trade. There are gambling resorts, so it is said, where "fan tan" holds the attention of the Chinese sports, for the Chinese gambler is one of the greatest devotees of the game on earth. If you look for it and are among the initiated you can find a place where a quiet smoke can be had and dream away hours of bliss under the soothing influence of the pill which is rolled by deft hands of the Chinese attendant. It is said that there are underground palaces beneath some of the squalid structures which look so dingy and dirty to the casual passerby, and that these are fitted up with magnificent

and costly furnishings, but whether or not this is true cannot be proven, but it is still one of the traditions of the people below the line, and some say that its sacredness is reserved for only the swells among the Chinese populations.

The Joss House

Like every other town, the Chinese of Butte have their "joss" house. It is located on the corner of Mercury Street alley .... Its fittings are of the same order as in all of the joss houses of the country. The hall is quite a large one, but it has one peculiarity—it has no seats or pews. The particular joss to whom the temple belongs is represented by a picture which is displayed on the altar, which is carefully trimmed with artificial flowers, gilt paper and Chinese mottoes and prayers. Ornamental lanterns of various kinds are strewn around the room in seeming disarray, but every one placed with some particular end in view. An immense gong, a drum and tom-toms form a part of the equipment of the place and on the altar always a light is kept burning, this being one of the symbols of the religion. In still another quarter of the room is another never-failing light, which it is said is burned to keep the devils away, for the Chinese have a belief that the evil spirit is always present, and to placate him and keep him at a safe distance from the beliefs they love, this light is forever constantly kept lighted.

Chinese Politics

Time was in Montana when the keeper of the joss house was the greatest honor a Chinaman could earn, and many were the struggles made for this election. This event occurs at the conclusion of the celebration which follows the Chinese New Years. In times past, when the Chinese were more numerous in Montana, the Celestials were divided into factions or cliques, and these would line up against one another and in a struggle on an open field they would race for rings hurled into the air by the explosion of bombs. The side securing the greatest number of these rings chose the joss house keeper for the year.

Drawn by Gold

The discovery of placer gold first attracted the Chinese to Montana, and Butte, being primarily a placer camp, has had a Chinatown for fully 40 years. At first the Chinamen of Butte were laundrymen; then as the placer mines began "petering out" they were abandoned by the white men and taken up by the Chinamen. In this they made money, not such as would satisfy the white man but it was good wages for a yellow man, and from Silver Bow to Butte they worked the bars all along the creek until money could no longer be made. Then they invaded other fields of Butte, went into the restaurant business, the tailor business, acted as shoemakers and repairers, went after the laundry business strong and were the principal raisers of green vegetables and truck farming. Then came the agitation against the yellow man, the boycott which became famous the country over and which was carried to

the supreme court of the United States and wherein the Chinese won out, and have been since permitted to conduct their business in peace and without interference.

Noodles

It was not many years ago, comparatively speaking, that the people of Butte learned that Chinese noodles made good eating and as the trade developed a number of noodle parlors were opened in various parts of Chinatown. Almost from the beginning these were favored with a good patronage and from a little beginning the "noodle habit" has grown into a thing of large proportions and in a number of places in Chinatown can be found the sign "Noodle Parlor," the second floor of several brick buildings being fitted up for the serving of the viand, which is considered quite toothsome by many people of Butte. "Noodle parties" are common and society people pay the parlors visits almost nightly. Society people who turn up their noses at the faintest sign of contamination in their own homes climb the stairways of these places and amid surroundings which are not always the most pleasant, partake of the bowls of noodles or chop suey which are brought from the mysterious depths of the kitchen and placed before them piping hot, to be washed down with copious draughts of tea, made only as the Chinese understand how to make it and served

a standard stock in trade for every store. There are quaint designs in chinaware, decorated by Chinese artists, and although the picture may not have a meaning to the layman, every one spells a message of some kind, and its meaning is explained by the clerk when he makes the sale, and it is always found to be one which interests the purchaser. Dainty creations of silk are shown, handkerchiefs, scarfs, night robes, shawls being included. There are tiny shoes made in China, their composition being almost entirely of paper; there are jade stones set in all kinds of jewelry, which make cherished mementoes of the trip to Chinatown; lanterns and napkins of paper, confectionery and nuts prepared mysteriously, jars of preserves concocted in a manner known by no one save the Chinese, but which are declared to be delicious by all who have tasted them. Then there is the practical side of the store keeping the dainties which come from China, but whose uses are understood alone by the Chinese. Many of them, including edible birds' nests, dried fish of many kinds and others of which no white man can understand the makeup, are considered delicacies by the Chinese epicures, but to

generally without either sugar or cream. On crowded nights in these places society people touch elbows with the people of the lower world without comment or without noting the incongruity of the situation, for in a noodle parlor the conditions are democratic and all are welcome by the Chinese proprietors, providing they have the price and conduct themselves with propriety.

Merchants

Chinatown has its stores, and they are up to date and with obliging clerks, who understand English perfectly, and can drive a bargain or make a sale as intelligently as any white clerk who ever stood behind a counter. As a matter of course, curios form the uncultivated palate they are nauseating. Fair dealing marks the Chinese trader all of the time. They get a good price for their curios from sight-seers, but the sight-seers consider their mementoes of the trip are worthy of the price paid, and both are satisfied by the bargain made.

Industrious

As a general rule, the Chinese residents of Butte are peaceful and industrious. It is but seldom that they quarrel among themselves and the appearance of a Chinaman in court, save when he is arrested for indulging in his favorite pastime of smoking or having an opium joint in operation, is a rarity. Seldom it is that one is hailed before a magistrate for a disturbance, but at least one recent murder has been laid to the door of the Chinese of Butte and it has been pretty clearly proven that the charge is a true one, but the accused men are no longer members of Butte's Chinese colony. No matter what trouble a Chinaman gets into in Butte, he invariably sends for "Louey" and Louey comes to his assistance. If the charge is not a serious one, the Chinaman is allowed to go when Louey vouches for him, and it must be said to their credit that they have never violated this confidence and when the hour appointed for their appearance in court arrives they are there and Louey is with them to act as interpreter, help them out of their trouble

if it can be done and if not, to pay their fine, for it is not on record during recent times, at least, where a Chinaman served out his fine in jail.

Laundries

Chinese laundries are common in Butte and they are found in many sections of town, in addition to Chinatown. Nearly all of them have wagons and they drive from place to place collecting their laundry in the same manner as their white brothers. The greater part of their business is with families and they do a considerable part of the family washing of the town, making better rates than do the steam laundries. Truck gardening is another industry in which the Chinese of Butte are extensively engaged and they have a number of "farms" down on the flat below town. Butte's ability to get fresh vegetables from the California and southern markets has hurt this industry in recent years, but the China boys have stayed with it for years and have made money out of it, coming into the town in the early morning and driving from place to place among the residence parts of town and staying with the load until every vegetable is disposed of. Old timers of Butte can remember when the Chinese vegetable man came to town with a big basket load of vegetables suspended from a yoke which was carried on his shoulders. Before the days of a water system in Butte water was carried in the same manner, and in the days of placer mining the pay dirt was carried in the same manner from the bars to the rocker or sluice boxes, where it was washed and the values recovered.

Opium

Well authenticated reports say there are opium joints conducted in various parts of Chinatown and in the red light district by Chinese proprietors. Some of these are elegantly fitted up, while others are the vilest sort of hovels. Many of them are fitted up with the sole view of making a quick getaway, and as an officer stated on the witness stand some time ago, "They are just like rabbit warrens; there are a dozen or more trap doors in the sides of the buildings and when we made the raid those who were not too sleepy from the drug rolled over in their bunks, gave the side of the building a sharp kick and they were out in the alley to freedom before we realized they were getting away."

Queer Enough

Butte's Chinatown is queer and its people seem queer. Still, they have their place in the industrial and business world of Butte and all that they ask is to be allowed to live their lives as they see the way to live. They are becoming Americanized in many particulars, some of them are getting wealthy and they never burden the county with an unfortunate fellow; they care for their own people, have their own doctors, who are extensively patronized by Americans, enjoy their religion unmolested and pay their debts promptly. A Chinese mission is maintained and many of them attend Sunday school regularly. They are sagacious in making a business deal, welcome their visitors cordially when their great holiday, the new year's festival, comes around, contribute liberally to any good cause and were among the first in Butte to contribute when San Francisco's great disaster occurred.

Leaders

They have their leaders and listen to their counsel. They never bring a suit in court and are never sued. Their numbers are getting smaller year after year, for no Chinaman is allowed to come to America under their exclusion act and few are being raised in this country, especially in Butte. There are few Chinese families in Butte and the comforts of home are enjoyed by them, just as in American homes, so, take it all in all, the Chinese colony in Butte averages up well with other colonies for foreign birth and they are more peaceable than many, and while they cannot enjoy the privilege of American citizens, they make no protest against it and take everything as it comes and neither complain or whine.

No. 30 *The Chinese Gardens*

Anaconda Standard, October 7, 1906

Queer isn't it, that near Butte, despite all of the croakings and assertions that nothing can grow within miles of the smoke area, the most fertile acres in the state should exist? But that is strictly the case and they are found within a few miles of Butte on Basin creek and the Nine Mile. They are the Chinese gardens and are so cultivated that thousands of bushels of roots and other vegetables are raised every year from a few acres of land. And generally they are raised at a good profit too, one garden of 10 acres averaging $8,000 worth of produce every season.

Well Filled

Ye Dee is the owner of one of these gardens and it is located within a short distance of the Nine Mile house. He has 10 or 15 acres and it is cultivated to a high degree of perfection. Almost every available foot is seeded to some vegetable there being no field crops of any kind, unless potatoes be included in that class. Very few potatoes, however, are raised and these are all of the early varieties which can be shipped from the ranches of the surrounding valleys or else from a distance from warmer climates.

Model Gardeners

There is no more scientific or painstaking gardener in the world than the Chinese gardener. He is not much on making fancy or ornamental beds or patches, his desire being to bring every bit of his soil up to the highest degree of productiveness and he does it. He thoroughly understands fertilization and there is no

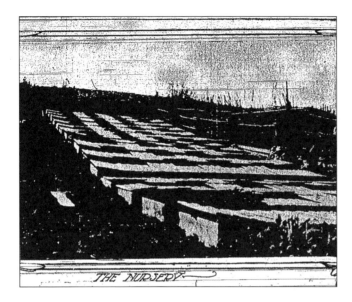

THE NURSERY

labor too irksome which will result in the betterment of the soil that he will overlook. In this climate the growing season is necessarily short and the gardeners take all advantage of it. At Ye Dee's place there is a warm, sandy side hill which has a southern exposure and at the same time not on a bleak north side hill. There he has a long row of hotbeds and cold frames. With the first indications that spring is on hand Ye Dee begins his preparations.

Ingenuity

He has none of the advantages of greenhouses, as have some of his American competitors, but he has a deal of ingenuity and by means of plenty of glass which gathers the heat of the sun from above and a fermenting bed of manure which gives heat from below and at the same time fertilized the soil, the early varieties of vegetables are forced to grow and are made ready for the market by the Chinese gardeners long before the snow has disappeared from the surrounding hills. At the same time cabbage, squash, cucumber and other seeds which produce plant life of a semi-tender nature are sown and by the time the spring passes and all danger or frost is passed they are transplanted and have a state which will start them on their way to maturity ahead of plants sown in the field or in the open garden.

Many Varieties

Almost every kind of vegetable is grown in the Chinese gardens near the city and to thoroughly appreciate them a person should visit them. The proprietors receive guests courteously, explain the varied vegetables they are raising and how they accomplish the work. However, none of the employees or the boss himself will stand for having their picture taken; they think it bad luck and will bring on sickness and misfortune. "The only way you can catch my boys," said Ye Dee, "is to sneak up on them and get them when they are not looking."

"Cannot we get your picture to go with your cabin?" said the *Standard* artists.

"No, no," was his quick response. "Not now. I

look too much like a Siwasm." And his naturally brown skin, tanned to an extreme by many hours spent in the garden under summer sun and rain and wind, told plainly that he was speaking the truth.

Seasonal Crops

Early vegetables first occupy the attention of the Chinese gardeners—radishes, onions and lettuce being first on the list. Then come various kinds of greens, early turnips and beets and peas. Later come new potatoes and then corn and carrots, with radishes, lettuce and onions always in the market, being planted at intervals throughout the entire season, they requiring but a few weeks to come to maturity.

The Gardeners

On an average each Chinese garden near Butte employs about eight men. "We have a great deal of trouble getting men who understand the work or who can work as we want them to," said Dee yesterday. "There is such a demand for laborers all over the country that it is almost impossible to get China boys to work in the gardens and I could use more than the seven men I now have to a good advantage if I could get them. It was not so long ago that we could get all of the men we wanted and did not have to pay them more than $25 or $30 per month. Now we pay $15 and $17, and even more and cannot get as many as we want at that

READY FOR MARKET

price. We board the men—give them plenty to eat of the things the Chinamen like for we go on the theory that no man can work unless he is well fed. The hours are longer than you white men enjoy, for we have to make the best of the season for it is never a long one."

The System

"The work is steady, but it is not hard and there is little of a strenuous nature to be undertaken. Wherever possible the soil is plowed for the first crop in the spring, but after that all of the cultivation is done by hand. Rotation in crops is practiced to a great extent among the gardeners, a plot of ground sown in one vegetable is sown in another season and in this manner the soil is not worn out. I have a 10 year lease on this ground and pay $500 a year for it. One year I made $1,000, but at other times I have not done so well. There are only a few days in the entire year when I am not busy. In the winter time I keep one or two men only and we get things in readiness for the coming season. Then we take matters a little easy, but the rest of the time we are on the move and make the best of the short season that the Butte district affords."

About eight months of the year constitute the gardening season of Butte and three of these are unprofitable, as the work is all of a dead nature preparing the ground in the spring, seeding it and waiting for the growing crop consumes two months and another month in the fall, cleaning up the ground, is lost for it is not directly productive, but the work has to be accomplished. During the five months when the harvest must be reaped there are few idle moments about the gardens, for something is being done all of the time. During the growing season the mornings are spent in the field, cultivating the different vegetables, irrigating them, weeding and hoeing. After the noon hour, generally, the vegetables intended for market the following day are gathered, placed in great baskets which are balanced on an old shovel handle or other pole and carried to the house by one of the laborers.

For Market

When all that is ready for market is gathered the laborers adjourn to the washing house, which is fitted up with a great wooden tank filled with water and through which a constant stream of cool, clear water passes. There the vegetables are washed, trimmed and assorted into bunches of a uniform size, tied up with wisps of straw and packed in other baskets to be placed in a cool place to await transportation to market. This part of the work is a most interesting one. The laborers carefully pick off all of the dead leaves from the onions, lettuce and radishes. Then the tops of the root vegetables are carefully trimmed off, a sharp butcher knife driven firmly into the top of the tank being the instrument used and when the bunches are spotless and free from all dirt, they are considered ready for market. With the other root vegetables, turnips, carrots, beets and the like equal care is taken, a brush being used to remove all traces of the soil before they are considered worthy of being sent to the market. The toil is laborious and painstaking, but the men go at it with a will and make a thorough job of it.

Every garden has a team or two and a vegetable wagon. Early in the morning, at daylight generally in the summer and fall, these teams leave the gardens, the wagons being loaded as high as they can be packed with fresh vegetables. Some of the gardeners peddle about town but the others dispose of their produce to Chinamen who live in the city and have regularly established routes. Some of the peddlers go on foot with the basket balanced between his shoulders, each side loaded with the different varieties of early vegetables which are raised near town. Generally they meet with a ready sale, for the prices are seldom, if ever, exorbitant and the quality always good. In the matter of getting their vegetables and garden truck in readiness for market, the Chinese have all of the white gardeners beaten, for the painstaking care they devote to washing the vegetables, grading them uniformly and neatly tying them into bundles, is far more pleasing to the eye and it makes it look to the housekeeper as if she were getting the worth of her money.

Not Smoke Farmers

Some years ago the greater majority of the Chinese gardeners were located just at the foot of the hill and across the railroad tracks in the flat below town. Here despite the fact that smelter fumes filled the valley nearly all the time and the fog of smoke and mist which used to accumulate from outside roasting and the crude smelter methods which prevailed during pioneer smelting days, the gardens thrived and seemed to do well in the "smoke belt" which enveloped Butte. There were no complaints made of blighted vegetation, for the gardens grew luxuriantly and the gardeners prospered. However, with the growth of Butte the ground became more valuable for its possibility and desirability as a residence section and now the site of

many of the old gardens is covered with homes and well surveyed streets. For that reason the Chinese gardeners were compelled to seek another location and they went out to Basin creek and the Nine Mile, where they have since made their home and tilled the soil industriously and profitably.

Economical Irrigation

In the matter of getting great results from a little water there is no gardener in the world who can excel the Chinaman who understands his business. Give him a tiny stream of water, it doesn't have to be much more than enough to keep a pipe one inch in diameter filled regularly, and he will cultivate an acre of ground and make it fruitful—in fact, make a good living off of it and lay a little money away to await the time he goes back to the home county either in the flesh or in the spirit—for all Chinamen live in the belief that their bones will find a last resting place in China, and many work to the end that they may make a little fortune and return home to live in affluence.

Nothing Wasted

But to return to the irrigation methods. The gardeners take advantage of every drop of water; none of it goes to waste, night and day, especially when the supply is limited. Along the line of the ditch which carried the water from the spring or stream to the

WHERE THE GARDENERS LIVE

gardens deep holes are sunk every rod or so and in the garden at the head of nearly every bed the same procedure is followed. These form miniature reservoirs and they are kept constantly filled, the melting snows of the early spring first filling them with flood water and later the stream or spring is used as a supply, the reservoirs being drawn upon when the hot suns of the summer dry up the water sources.

All Systematic

There is no indiscriminate irrigation, no flooding of a field and allowing the water to go to waste below, but every bed is carefully sprinkled, every row of vegetables is given just the proper amount of water and no more. The Chinese are as painstaking with their irrigation as with the rest of the gardening. They will carry water for hundreds of yards, two big buckets being balanced to the yoke which fits to their shoulders, if necessary, and there is no complaint made. They will raise a crop if it is possible for any one to do so and the night time is just the same as the daytime to them, when it comes to save a crop or enhance the value of their garden, for they have been known to carry water all night long in places where water is scarce, to use on their garden, in this manner taking advantage of the flow of water which comes down the little streams after the sun, which has licked it up during the daytime, has sunk behind the hills. Fortunately these conditions do not prevail in the Butte distinct, for there is plenty of water for the gardeners, but they husband it just the same, their natural distaste to seeing it go to waste being bred in their bones.

The Chinaman is a natural gardener and go where you will through the country, wherever you find a bunch of Chinamen working in a placer digging or engaged in other occupations, there you will find a garden. It may be a tiny one but it will be cultivated carefully and the Chinese workmen will always have something green to eat upon their tables as long as the growing season lasts.

The Chinese in Montana
Christopher W. Merritt

During the mid-nineteenth century, thousands of Chinese citizens came to the United States seeking their fortune on Gam San, or "Gold Mountain." These immigrants, largely poor farmers from the south of China, were fleeing an economically depressed country that was in the midst of a civil war. However, many wished to return home after they made enough money to support the families they had left behind. Once in America, some Chinese workers fulfilled their dreams quickly and returned to China as wealthy men; however, hundreds more toiled in various industries, barely earning subsistence wages. Thousands of Chinese workers helped construct the transcontinental railroad, established fishing industries along the western coast, engaged in hard-rock and placer mining, entered manufacturing positions in urban centers, and started hundreds of businesses throughout the country.

The thousands of Chinese immigrants who came to Montana in search of economic security indelibly etched their imprint on the vast landscape of the Treasure State. According to historian Robert Swartout, the Chinese "played a crucial part in transforming Montana from a primitive, isolated patchwork of localities into an increasingly sophisticated, urbanized, and economically prosperous society."[1] By providing the bulk of the labor to Montana's first railroad systems in the 1880s and helping to prolong the vitality of many mining districts through dedicated and painstaking labor, Chinese immigrants were integral in shaping modern Montana. Unfortunately, most of these contributions have been lost within the written pages of Montana history and the state's collective memory, and Chinese heritage has yet to be incorporated into local identity in most communities.

By the early 1860s, large Chinese populations existed in Idaho, Oregon, Colorado, Wyoming, and California. With news of gold strikes along Grasshopper Creek and Alder Gulch in the mid-1860s, Montana began to see its first influx of Chinese immigrants. It appears that the first Chinese immigrants to Montana probably settled near the mining settlements of Bannack and Virginia City during the early 1860s. These first immigrants were largely placer miners, according to the 1870 federal census, though some ran laundry and restaurant businesses. Until 1869, most of the Chinese in the state were based in Bannack, Virginia City, and Helena, with minor populations near Drummond and Butte.

With restrictive federal immigration legislation and declining mining opportunities, the Chinese began to consolidate to large urban Chinatowns in the late 1870s and 1880s. Butte was one location that the Chinese began to congregate, and by 1890 the city boasted the largest Chinatown in the state. Butte's Chinatown contained dozens of businesses, including restaurants, laundries, herbal and chiropractic doctors' offices, brothels, and stores catering to both Chinese and non-Chinese patrons. In 1906, the *Anaconda Standard* featured two Chinese stories in its "Queer Spots In and Around Butte" feature, one focused on Chinatown, and the second on a large Chinese-owned garden complex. Butte residents viewed the Chinese, with their unique cultural activities and exotic language and customs, as a strange and sometimes unwelcome addition to their community. By the 1930s, most of the Chinese who had once called Butte home had left for larger Chinatowns in San Francisco and Seattle; a rare few even returned to their homeland in China. The Wah Chong Tai Company building, located on Mercury Street in downtown Butte, now home to the Mai Wah Society, is one of just a handful of standing reminders to Chinese immigrants across the landscape of modern Montana.

A complete understanding of Chinese influence on Montana may never be accomplished, but through a recent increase in historical research and archaeological endeavors across the state, Montanans may be now realizing the true depth of their contributions. Stories on the Chinese like those featured in "Queer Spots In and Around Butte" are a rare remnant of this forgotten page in Montana's history and provide a personal glimpse into these immigrants' lives.

1   Robert R. Swartout Jr., "Kwangtung to Big Sky: The Chinese in Montana, 1864–1900," *Montana the Magazine of Western History* 38, no. 1 (1988):42–53, quote at 53.

No. 11 The Cree Village
Anaconda Standard, May 27, 1906

Among the "queer spots" in the vicinity of Butte the Cree Indian village must occupy a place of decided interest. Most Butte people going for a drive out on the flat give the Cree Indian camp a wide berth, seeing little that is likely to prove of interest in the representatives of the "noble red men" who have fixed their habitation near Butte. But the Crees, dirty, ragged and poor though they may be, are nevertheless an interesting people.

As you drive along the road past the cemeteries toward the east, stretching out toward the city dump lies one of the camps. For the most part it is made up of common wall tents, eight or ten in number, but several conical tepees can also generally be seen. Another camp of the Crees is located a little farther south, up a short distance on the side of Timbered butte [sic]. Here there are not more than four or five tents. One or two families may occupy a tent, and as the Indians are constantly coming and going, it is almost impossible to ascertain their exact numbers; probably 50 would not be far out of the way.

Not Clean

These homes are not very imposing from the outside, surrounded as most of them are by piles of bones, rubbish and filth, and often the interior is even less inviting. Some of the people have a faint idea of cleanliness, while others are dirty in the extreme. The ground is generally covered with old pieces of carpet, oilcloth or blankets, and close to the walls are packed the blankets for sleeping and the clothing. From the poles may hang moccasins or meat in the process of drying. In the wall tent there is always a stove or something which answers the purpose of a stove. It may be an old metal wash tub or something of the kind, and it is always furnished with a stovepipe. In the tepee there is no stove but a tripod crane from which a kettle is suspended. There is no stovepipe; the flaps are so arranged that the smoke draws out of the top of the tepee.

In The Tepee

The half of the tent nearest the door belongs to the women and children, the far side always being reserved for the men. This custom is pretty generally observed by all Indians. When entering the tent, if you are a man, you are greeted with "Os-tum-pe-to-ge" (Come back inside). Should you come at meal time, you would find the whole family sitting on the floor around the fire with tin plates in their hands and a cup of tea beside them. Their spread is not varied; boiled meat is the principal dish at all meals; it may be beef, calf's head or fish. The bread is usually cooked in a frying pan and eaten without butter. They all have good appetites and seem to enjoy their food.

Holidays

If your visit happens to be on New Year's day or during some other celebration, the Crees would have out their holiday goods. The tea would be replaced by beer and plenty of it. The rest of the meal would likely consist chiefly of dried blueberries cooked with meat, making a greasy, unsavory mixture of which the Indians are very fond. The berries are kept in a sack made of the entire skin of a very young calf, looking when filled with the berries, like a toy dog stuffed with sawdust. Some of the children, on these occasions, may be seen sticking their fingers in a jar of jam and licking them off like a bear cub.

Civilization

Some of the Crees are good Indians and get drunk only twice in the year—New Year's day and the Fourth of July. Others are not so good and are drunk about all the time. But these are in the minority. They have no trouble whatever in obtaining liquor whenever they want it, notwithstanding the strict laws prohibiting the sale of liquor to Indians.

Cree Attire

As a rule the Crees dress in "store clothes" and almost everything they have is of white man's manufacture. In the fall they lay in a supply of buckskin, most of which is made into moccasins which are often worn out before the next hunting season opens, and so you will find many of the Indians wearing shoes. They generally keep a pair or two of beaded moccasins, which they reserve for festal occasions. A few of the older men, however, still cling to the leggings, breech cloth and blanket. Most of them have Indian "togs" which they keep carefully wrapped up and wear only as their Sunday best, not, however, to go to church in. The women wear calico dresses, moccasins and blanket; baby boards are not used. The mother leans over, lifts the baby onto her back and then draws the blanket tightly around their backs. Thus the child is held very securely in a fairly comfortable position. Occasionally one may see a "buck" who is condescending enough to tote his offspring around squaw fashion.

Fashions

The men as a rule wear their hair long and braided, the front hair being combed straight back and tied, not parted, as with the Sioux and Crows. The children in general wear anything they can get. On a cold winter's day, when the ground is covered with snow, little boys and girls are to be seen clothed only in calico shirts and dresses, barefooted, playing around and apparently enjoying themselves as much as the bundled-up white children.

Peculiarities

Like all plains Indians, the Cree is fond of horses, and unless he is very poor, he will have five or six head. He also generally owns a wagon and numerous dogs. The dogs are used for various purposes. The Indian does not, as the white man is reported to do, turn his extra dogs through the sausage machine, but he turns them into soup. The squaw puts them to another use. She hitches them to the travois and is often seen returning from the dump, the dog patiently trotting along under the weight of the load. The dog travois was the primitive vehicle of the plains tribes, while in the far North the sledges play an important part.

Pagan Customs

Although the Crees are nominally members of the Catholic church, many of them are in reality pagans, especially the old women, who are very conservative and the last to surrender old customs and the superstitious beliefs of their heathen ancestors. Many of the old dances, songs and ceremonies are still retained. It is not uncommon to find in the fireplaces within the tents a little pile of ashes and a few pieces of sweet grass remaining unconsumed which have been burned as incense for a sweet savor to the spirits.

Fear The Camera

It is not an easy matter to secure photographs of the Crees. Many object to being photographed, thinking that it takes vitality from them and they are more liable to die. While pointing the camera at one of the tents old Mrs. Lo came out and protested so vigorously that the camera had to be turned in another direction. She would not even allow her dog to be taken, because as the old man who interpreted put it: "She say if the dog taken, he dead. Damn fool, he got to dead some time anyway; can't always life." One old Indian on being photographed crossed himself devoutly several times.

The Modern Chase

The Montana Cree, as did his wild ancestors, gets his living by hunting, but in a different manner. Instead of making for the woods or mountains he generally heads for the city dump, slaughter houses or the back doors of hotels and restaurants. As he is a good hunter, patient and wary, he rarely goes home empty handed. If he is especially energetic he may haul firewood into Butte, which he sells for $5 a load. Some money is made

by selling beadwork and curios, but perhaps the chief industry is preparing and selling "buffalo horns." Lo goes to the slaughter house, picks out some good, symmetrical cows' horns, takes them to his tent, fully polishes and mounts them on a board covered with plush. Then he goes to Butte and sells them. Many easterners buy the horns to send to friends who have not been so fortunate as to travel west and see "real buffalo horns."

Casino

Another chief occupation of the Cree is playing casino, or, as he calls it "sweep." He is very fond of this game and will play for hours at a stretch. He also plays checkers with men and boards of his own manufacture, 16 men each being used instead of 12, and in other details the game differs from the white man's game. Another game, purely Indian, is called "o-shan-noh" (bones). Two Indians face each other, having in each hand a piece of bone about two and one-half inches long by three-quarters of an inch wide, one being plain and the other wrapped around the middle with a rag. One of the men passes the bones back and forth quickly through his hands while the other tries to guess which hand contains the plain bone. Thus taking turns they keep up their guessing until one player loses all his stake. Each man has his retainers, who occupy the space back of him and generally keep up an incessant chanting while the game is in progress.

The Cree names all have meanings. They call Butte "spiet-e-now" or "spiet-e-now-ow-tan-now," meaning "high hill." The word for Anaconda is "wah-sah-has-kaw," meaning "valley in the mountains." Deer Lodge is called "ki-poh-ho-to-we-kah-nik." Americans are called "zie-chu-mo-ko-mon," meaning "big knives," the name arising from the swords used by the United States cavalry. Their word for Indian is "ne-he-o-wok."

Although considered ignorant, the Crees have an alphabet of their own and a written language in which books are printed and which nearly all the men and

A COUPLE OF YOUNGSTERS—

older boys can read. They also carry on correspondence among themselves, although they may not be able to read or write English. Only the older Indians know sign language, the younger generation taking little or no interest in the old ways.

Frequent Guests

The Crees are not the only Indians who visit Butte; they come occasionally from all directions, Shoshones, Flatheads, Bannacks, Chippewas and others. But the Crees are the only ones who are with us the year round.

The Montana Crees must not be taken as the best type of their race. They are but a small band of renegades, fugitives from the Canadian government, having left their reservation for various reasons. Land troubles with the government and the agents are given among the reasons and the Crees also say that they cannot make a living in Canada so easily as here. They don't like the agents who make the work too hard. Perhaps the chief cause of their first wandering was the Riel rebellion. After that rebellion many of the Crees moved over into the United States, where they have been homeless wanderers ever since. They have often been rounded up and sent back to Canada, but only to cross the border to this country once more.

From Canada

The main body of the Crees live in Canada, and they are much superior to their relatives in the United States. They make their living chiefly by hunting, trapping and fishing for the Hudson Bay company. The more southern bands do some farming and cattle raising. Altogether the Crees in their various branches number in the neighborhood of 15,000.

Butte's Crees may be reckoned among its most peaceable inhabitants, and in general it may be said of the Crees that they are a peaceable, law-abiding people. Their progress towards civilization is slow. They are almost entirely self-supporting, receiving little or no aid from the government, but while they engage so extensively in hunting and fishing, little advance can be expected. When these resources for a livelihood have been exhausted they will be forced to settle down, cultivate lands, care for their cattle and learn to walk the white man's road.

Sun Dance in Silver Bow:
Urban Indian Poverty in the Shadow of the Richest Hill on Earth

Nicholas Peterson Vrooman

1: Piyak

It's midsummer, just past dawn. You walk out into the first rays of sun. All that's on your mind is your responsibility for the couple of hundred folks stirring about. You've led your charges over the last two months from Great Falls to Havre, down to Helena, and now here. Some have horses, but most walk. Wagons are few; tipis, wall tents, and what minimal goods there are among you are hauled on travois—just as in the old days. In this place, you truly hope your decision will help ease the suffering of those with you. You look up the hill from where you're camped; you search all your languages for words to describe the scene, and only Cree makes sense. Yet your mother tongue falters; there is no vocabulary to speak such newness that surrounds you. Just old terms come to mind that name this place, terms from your father's stories of camping and hunting on this very hillside. In those days, your people ranged free from the North Saskatchewan to the Snake River and over to Red River. This was common hunting ground in the time of your youth.

This is the third time this summer you've asked your people to make this sacrifice, outside of time-

Cree camp, Butte area, Montana, 1906. Frank E. Peeso, photographer. Courtesy of the Glenbow Archives (Image No: NA-1431-14).

honored tradition. But you have a chance to put together enough goods and money to help them through the next few months. So, you agree to do it again, now here in Butte. Most of your band winters here, and perhaps by building this Medicine Lodge, holding this ceremony in this place, the newcomers will understand a little more and not be so hard on your people. Perhaps, if you pray hard enough, even the mercy of Gishay Manitou will shine upon you and the misery will all go away.

The crowd is amassing. You pull yourself together. OK, here you go. *Meowasin. Paypiitegway.* All's good. Come on in . . .

Imassiise, Little Bear, son of Mistahimaskwa, Big Bear, ca.
1905. Photographer unknown. Courtesy of Archives and Special
Collections, Linderman Collection, The University of Montana
(Image No: 007(VIII):418).

Little Bear, our protagonist, knows that those who have pledged to dance are already exhausted, not only from the summer's travels but from the past couple of days' work in the woods gathering materials for constructing the Big Lodge. They are good and loyal people. They too hope for mercy. They walk out into the morning from the all-night sing, where they sang, smoked pipe, prayed, and blew on their eagle bone whistles from dusk to sunrise. One of them, an older man in skins, dressed beautifully with quill and beads, fringe hanging in sway, walks to the tip of a trimmed tree on the ground. He nestles himself into the top end of a twenty-some-foot aspen ritually chosen and hauled in from the surrounding forest. He settles securely amid the huge bundle of willow shoots and berry branches tied to the three-prong crotch that is the Eagle's Nest of the Thunder Pole. A rattle in his right hand, he sounds the eagle call and begins to sing.

A handful of men stand at the pole base. Two other fork-tipped lifting poles of equal length are firmly wedged beneath the crotch, with men at the butt ends. The three teams begin to push the tripod toward the man in the nest. Slowly, the center rises as apogee. The holy man straightens, extending upward, reaching to the heavens—rattling, singing—as the heel of the main pole is moved to the hole dug to receive its base. The lifting poles push the Thunder Pole fully erect. Rattle held high, the man's song calls the spirits of ancestors, and all of nature, to the people gathered. The Thunder Pole is wedged and tamped into place, solid as the key architectural element of this millennium-old yet ephemeral structure. Construction of a Medicine Lodge of the Nehiyaw Pwat has been performed once again, repeating the blend of belief, knowledge, tradition, and technology synthesized into one holistic human endeavor that ceremonially symbolizes the relationship of aboriginal humans to this very piece of earth and all that it comprises.[1]

A fire pit is dug close to the base, on the south side of the Thunder Pole. The fire-keeper brings coals from the last embers of the all-night-sing lodge, transferring the life flame and accumulated prayers to the Medicine Lodge. It will stay alight for the duration of the ceremony.

One fork-tipped aspen post as tall as a man's arms lifted high is planted in a hole directly to the north of the Thunder Pole at a radius length equal to the Eagle's Nest loft. Then, completing a circle around the Thunder Pole, twelve other similar uprights are set evenly. Crossbeam logs tie the posts together, securing a wall frame enclosing the inner space of the Thirsty Dance Lodge. Using bark-strip lashing, rafter poles are laid and sashed tight at the outer frame with the pole ends at the uprights; the tops are laid over one another to nestle and lock in the zenith of the center pole, tying the Medicine Lodge together as one solid structure.

Raising of Thunder Pole, Sun Dance Priest in Eagle's Nest, 1912. This is a Nehiyaw Pwat Thirsty Dance as it occurred in Montana's urban circumstance. Frank E. Peeso, photographer. Courtesy of Archives and Special Collections, Linderman Collection, The University of Montana (Image No: 007(VIII):225).

Aspen saplings are next propped against the frame of the outer wall, leaning against the bond-beam and filling in the space between the uprights to enclose the whole structure. The opening between the two uprights facing south remains uncovered, forming the entrance of the lodge.

Inside the lodge, a railing about waist high and about a body length in from the perimeter is constructed from stripped saplings, much like a smaller version of the outer wall. The fence has a second parallel tie running around its bottom. It is filled in with willow shoots woven to create a barrier and stall area in which the Sun Dancers reside throughout the ceremony, separated from the community seated around the inner part of the lodge. Colored prayer cloth is attached to stick rods and suspended as banners—spirit offerings—from the rafters. A bolt of red fabric is hung from the Thunder Pole, draping down to represent the flow of community lifeblood.

Every action and the smallest nuance in the construction of the lodge are imbued with sacramental meaning. The very act of "putting up" the lodge is itself a critical component of the ceremony. The Medicine Lodge is a palimpsest of the universe, a fleeting "woodhenge," where humans ritually enact their place in a world beyond their power to control.

The singers situate themselves inside the lodge to the northeast side of the Thunder Pole and begin. They beat a dry and stiff buffalo hide. Dancers line up. The medicine man—with lifted eagle wing fans entreating the heavens with caresses and with bone whistle rhythmically matching the beat of the buffalo hide—begins the procession. With right shoulders toward the lodge, the dancers encircle the exterior four times then enter, continuing in clockwise. Pipes and offerings are placed to the north end of the lodge, forming an altar, as the male dancers file past behind the rail and settle into their stalls on the sunset side of the lodge. The women do the same to the sunrise side of the lodge. The singers work the dancers. With every beat, the dancers, straight bodied, flex their knees in rhythm, blowing on their eagle bone whistles, beat by beat, breath by breath, hyperventilating, thirsting, fasting, and exhausting themselves to create a physical and mental condition within this ancient, time-refined ritual environment that sheds the peripheral and temporal, inducing a super-reality of infinite consciousness and an embodiment of eternal unified existence.

They dance because they have a purpose: to promise to behave in a certain way on behalf of their family, loved ones, and community. They dance to seal that promise through sacrificing all each one has in the end to give in the name of their love: their life energy, food and water, and the very flesh of their bodies. The sacrifice is to show the extent each is willing to go in seeking mercy—that their promise to fulfill their purpose may be attained. Thus begins four days of ritual giving, supplication, and sacrifice.

2: Nīso

This scene differs little from those occurring elsewhere, in distinctive tribal variation, across the northern plains, with elements of the ceremony dating back to the last ice age. The primary difference is that it's taking place in Butte, Montana, in 1894, with paying white spectators, who are titillated by witnessing the famous "torture" rites of the savage Plains Indians, literally in the shadow of the Richest Hill on Earth, at the foot of a brand-new, Victorian-era, Chicago/Pittsburgh hybrid–style, U.S. industrial revolution city then exploding from a mountainside in the remote Northern Rockies. The juxtaposition and irony of images is immense: a singular, fleeting Paleolithic ceremonial structure—whose central architectural element is a Thunder Pole and open hearth carrying prayers of hope and renewal in direct conduit to the heavens to create balance in nature—existing side by side with towering, mass-production brick smelter stacks spewing smoke skyward, billowing dreams of wealth, power, and dominion over the landscape in testament to human advancement in architecture and technology.

Two epochs framing the span of human history from the stone age to the industrial age pooled as one that summer of 1894 in Butte. The recombinant image also represents the distance in that human community at that time between the winners and the losers, the wealthiest and the most poverty stricken, the privileged and the dispossessed—the expanse between the American robber barons and Montana's first generation of homeless Indians. Although the ritual enactment was a spectacular entertainment for the whites, in no way does that remoteness between worlds lessen the meaning, significance, and value of the Medicine Lodge and the very real hope of those Sun Dancers that summer—or the power of the whites to dominate the existence of that community.

Today, here's the viewshed: Butte, Montana, out a mile and a half east of the current smelter, in the southeast part of town, close to where the old dump was, just over where the old racetrack used to sit.

Marcus Daly's racetrack was built in an area of Butte which is now a residential neighborhood south of the Berkeley Pit and the Weed Concentrator. The working class neighborhood that grew up around it actually became known as the Racetrack neighborhood. The location was east of Clark's Park (still there today) and generally between where the Greeley Elementary school and East Junior High School (Grand

Avenue) now stand. . . . It was close to what was known as Parrot Flat where . . . Indian camps were located.[2]

From there, looking back up the hill, "the Pit" and uptown are what you see; it is 115 years later, and the National Folk Festival is in Butte, highlighting in part Indian culture in Montana. How much has transpired can be recounted; how much has changed is a worthy question. In the Indian way, that Racetrack neighborhood, where the Sun Dance was held, remains forever sacred ground.

3: Nisto

In early 1900s, people from the eastern United States were fascinated with the "West" and the "Frontier Epic," which was already mythological as the origin story of America's birthing. A generation earlier, it had been Charlie Russell and Frank B. Linderman who came to Montana, embodying the boyish wonderment that fused Tom Sawyer and Huckleberry Finn as the archetype for any red-blooded American youth worth his salt to follow. This time, in 1905, it was a young Frank E. Peeso who moved from New York State to Butte to work in the mines as an engineer. Engineering was his job, but he chose Montana for other reasons. He sought Indians and their way of life. As a boy growing up in Syracuse, he had learned that

Smallboy family, Cree, Butte area, Montana, 1906. Front row, l-r: Maggie Smallboy; Paul Smallboy; John Smallboy; Bobtail or Chief Robert Smallboy, leader of Smallboy's Camp. Back row, l-r: Mary Smallboy; Marie Isobel (Coyote) Smallboy, wife of Peter (Pierre) Smallboy. Frank E. Peeso, photographer. Courtesy of the Glenbow Archives (Image No: NA-1431-9).

his community inhabited the ancestral homeland of the Onondaga Hodenesaunee (Fire Keepers of the Longhouse People). As a youngster, he had spent time with Onondaga. Later, he studied anthropology and American Indians at the University of Pennsylvania.[3] To the benefit of Montana history, Peeso also enjoyed photography. His images of Indians in Butte remain one of Montana's best records of the early years of the state's historic first urban Indian population.

Peeso wrote that Butte's Indians were Cree, and refugees from the Riel Rebellion in Canada.[4] They subsisted by "cutting wood, collecting horns from which they made novelties for sale, and making beaded moccasins and other items popular with the whites." Many spoke "pretty good English."[5] He recognized that they had "mixed to a considerable extent with the Assiniboin, Saulteaux [mixed Chippewa from Sault Ste. Marie] and French."[6] Although an amalgam of primarily Cree, Assiniboine, Chippewa, and Métis (known in the aboriginal world as the Nehiyaw Pwat, meaning Cree-Assiniboine), in Montana they also included related Kootenai, Nez Perce, and Shoshone and were all grouped together as "Cree" by non-Indian society.[7]

Butte's Cree were not an aboriginal circumstance unique to Silver Bow County or Montana. Rather, they were part of a broad swath of dispossessed fur trade–era refugees from various backgrounds who had been left out of the reconfiguration during the switch from aboriginal to Anglo society in both the American and Canadian West in the late nineteenth century. They were an unreconciled remnant aboriginal population from the preceding economic era of North American history and the Indian Wars, which excluded them from participating in the new economic era of resource extraction, agriculture, and mercantilism. In the lifetime of Little Bear, the acknowledged chief of those

Andrew Valler [Valier?], half-breed Cree with Kootenai wife and two children, ca. 1910. Photographer unknown. Courtesy of Archives and Special Collections, Linderman Collection, The University of Montana (Image No: 007(VIII):197).

Montana "Cree" bivouacked at Butte who were Sun Dancing for mercy, his people went from being part of one of the most formidable and wealthy aboriginal confederations on the continent to crashing as a culture, pitiful, penniless, and persecuted.

A scholar of Montana's mixed-blood peoples, Elizabeth Sperry, draws connections that show how broadly dispersed displaced peoples were in Montana at that time.

> Similar to the "Road Allowance" Métis settlements in Canada, many of the Métis, Cree and Chippewa in Montana survived at the fringe of white settlements on public or county land, or along the railroad right-of-way. These types of communities are illustrated by permanent settlements such as Hill 57 in Great Falls and Boushie Hill in East Glacier, but also include the temporary camps located near various towns throughout Montana. These temporary camps were utilized primarily during the winter months when travel was not practical and employment on farms and ranches was not available. Fringe settlements were located all along the Front Range and throughout the intermountain region near the communities of Garrison, Deer Lodge, Anaconda, and Butte. Fringe communities were also located near communities along the Highline, such as Havre and Wolf Point.[8]

Adding Missoula, Helena, and Billings to the scenario, this wider group of aboriginal people represents a third (concealed) sector of Montana's society, along with the dominant white community and the reservation-separated, federally overseen Indians. Known now as the Little Shell Tribe of Chippewa Indians, they remain that third class of Montana and U.S. citizens today, the remaining group that lingers outside any legitimate status as American citizens, unrecognized and homeless within their own traditional historic homeland. They are Montana's historic urban Indian community.

Today, most of America's four million Indians live in urban centers throughout the country. Unlike most other urban Indian communities, which arose as a consequence of the federal Indian policy era following World War II that was called Termination and Relocation, Montana's urban Indian communities are largely a consequence of a dispute between the United States and Canada following (strangely) the Minnesota Sioux Uprising of 1862. Many Dakota (Sioux) from that Minnesota resistance fled to Canada and were given sanctuary. The United States wanted them extradited and held on trial. Canada refused, giving them reserves instead. Canada also hesitated to extradite Sitting Bull and his band, who had fled there following the Battle of the Greasy Grass (Little Big Horn) in 1876. After the Riel Resistance in 1885, even when many Montana citizens petitioned the government to rid the state of these "Cree" renegades, the United States refused (initially) to deport the "Cree" back to Canada as a tit for tat.[9]

The notion of who "belonged" to either Canada or the United States is a false construct when applied to aboriginal peoples. The scheme of nation-states did not pertain to the aboriginal world but was superimposed on it by the Anglo federal governments. The Nehiyaw Pwat inhabited the Silver Bow country from the period of the Cree-backed Blackfeet war with the Shoshone (circa 1680–1825) to the Rocky Mountain fur trade following the Corps of Discovery (1806 to the 1840s) to the Hudson's Bay Company Fort Hall (1830s–1850s; now Pocatello), the Johnny Grant Métis Colony in the Deer Lodge Valley (1840s–1860s; now the Grant-Kohrs Ranch National Historic Site), and over to Fort Owen (1850s) in the Bitterroot Valley, and even included in the Stevens Blackfeet Treaty of 1855. The diagonal from Winnipeg to Saskatoon to Edmonton, with trails from each point down to Pocatello, were well-traveled routes, funneling Cree, Assiniboine, Chippewa, and Métis consistently back and forth. The collapse of the bison economy changed everything.

4: Niyo

The decade following the last herd in the Judith Basin (in 1882–83) and the trauma of cultural collapse, with nowhere to go and nothing to do, forced the excluded peoples to scavenge at the periphery of the newly forming white society. Slowly and then regularly, reports of Indians in Montana cities became recurring newsprint fodder, denigrating them in their poverty as contrasting proof of white superiority and privilege.

On November 28, 1892, a white rancher, Thomas O. Miles, wrote the Butte *Semi-weekly Inter-Mountain* to ask: "Why is it that we cannot get rid of these Cree Indians. About a year ago they were into camp near here and right on our range with some 160 to 200 head of horses." An early statement of protest in Butte, Cree horses were eating the hay that ranchers wanted to harvest. Miles wrote Governor J. K. Toole and talked with U.S. Attorney Elbert Weed and U.S. Senator T. C. Power, complaining for the need to send the Cree to Canada. "It would seem strange," wrote Miles, "that after a full and amicable agreement between the United States and Canadian authorities that these pests are still permitted to go where they please and Indians of the United States are . . . on a reservation."[10] U.S. Attorney Weed wrote to the secretaries of state and war, on behalf of Montana, about the "renegade Crees" in Silver Bow and Deer Lodge counties.

Their presence here is very offensive to all the settlers who are unfortunate enough to live in the vicinity of their camps. It is the habit of these renegade Indians to wantonly destroy all game, without regard to local laws or regulations, to steal stock of the settlers, and, generally subsist by larceny and plunder. They have no business whatever here, and should be immediately removed to the British Possessions, where they belong.

Weed went on to say that if the federal government did nothing, there would be "serious difficulty between them and the white settlers."[11] People didn't understand who the "Cree" were and how they came to such condition. Weren't all those of red races supposed to be set apart on reservations and kept from interfering with white communities? This was the first generation of white appropriators to take over the land of the aboriginals. They were not about to countenance social conscience in claiming their newly commandeered territory and its resources. Apartheid was surely the best way to protect Indians from trouble. With the complaint fresh in the thoughts of the editors and readers alike of the local newspaper, another piece was printed a week and a half later condemning the Cree for destroying game in the surrounding area.[12] A stone was cast into society's pond; its ripple continues to this day.

Cree band, horse with travois, moving through town [Butte?], ca. mid-1890s. Photographer unknown. Courtesy of Archives and Special Collections, Linderman Collection, The University of Montana (Image No: 007(VIII):222).

On May 8, 1893, scarlet fever hit the Cree camp in Butte, where about seventy people lived in lodges. The camp was quarantined, and scant provisions were brought to those confined. Anti-Cree sentiment trumped humanitarian morality and social services. Children died. Through the end of 1893, officials around the state actively petitioned the federal government to send the Cree north.[13]

What was occurring in Butte was also happening in Helena, Great Falls, and other Montana cities. With the overt push to rid Montana of the "Cree," the Nehiyaw Pwat started to organize and seek the advice of an attorney. They sought citizenship and a reservation of their own. The district attorney of Chouteau County made headlines saying that the Indians were "Not Desirable Citizens" and advising the "Clerk Not to Issue Any More First Papers to Crees." All further requests by the Indians for citizenship were denied. The impetus from the white community was nonaccommodation. Any energy spent on the Indian problem was intended to purge them from Montana.[14]

5: Niyānan

Destitution set in. Hunting in the nearby forests, selling trinkets, working odd jobs, and scavenging the discards of white communities weren't enough to sustain the Nehiyaw Pwat. Whether it was Chief Little Bear's idea, gained from his connection with his old cohort Michif leader Gabriel Dumont (who traveled with the Buffalo Bill Wild West Show as the Halfbreed military leader of the Northwest Rebellion), or that of white promoters, a public Sun Dance was scheduled for June 14–16, 1894, in Great Falls. The idea was to capitalize on the popularity and money-making formula of William Cody. The scheduled date fell during the traditional time for the annual renewal ceremony. Putting up a Medicine Lodge requires resources. The people needed the stabilizing effects of the Thirsty Dance to help offset the trauma they were living through. Charging admission would cover their costs while giving the whites a romanticized, albeit prurient, view into their lives. Little Bear also thought that if whites understood them more fully, life for his people would get better. The event was supported by the chamber of commerce.[15]

The promoters wanted to tour "the show" throughout Montana, copying the success of Buffalo Bill. Protestants went into an uproar. It would turn "loose several hundred idle, lazy, shiftless barbarians in the city and is a queer way of 'promoting its prosperity.'"[16] The governor, John E. Rickards, prohibited the event with an official proclamation. Little Bear and his band moved to Havre, where the ceremony was staged. Assiniboine and Gros Ventre from Forts Belknap and Peck, and other Nehiyaw Pwat from Canada, came to dance and support the ceremony; the local Anglo community attended as audience.[17]

Based on the publicity the episode generated, Helena decided—Great Falls controversy be dashed—that it wanted Little Bear's band to come to the capital and perform for the Fourth of July festivities at the Lewis and Clark County fairgrounds.[18] Little Bear was pleased to snub the governor in his hometown.[19] Helena's hit event was then desired by Butte.[20]

Performing at the Marcus Daly Park Racetrack in Butte that summer, Little Bear had to put survival before honor in agreeing to exploit the sacred ceremony of his people one more time for the entertainment of whites. As a true leader of his people, he had to give them hope. The only door open in the new world in which they found themselves following the disappearance of the buffalo was through engaging the white society; they had nothing of interest to offer the whites but the curiosity of their traditional culture. If they did this, *something* would happen that would again bring fulfillment; *some* good would come from it. He had to devise a way to avoid despair and to create a strategy that put volition and consequences in their own hands—hence the Sun Dance in Silver Bow, in the shadow of the Richest Hill on Earth.[21]

The purpose, promise, sacrifice, and plea for mercy of Little Bear's people did not curtail their ostracism and exploitation by whites. Even as the Progressive Era took hold, and worker's rights and social services began integrating into white industrial society, oppression of the Nehiyaw Pwat escalated.

Frank B. Linderman, the great Montana author, worked for a period as an assayer in Butte. Linderman initially met the Cree at the exact moment in 1886 when both he arrived in Montana and Little Bear's band entered the state in the Swan Valley following the Northwest Resistance and the Riel debacle. His books provide some of the Northwest's earliest record of Indian oral literature. He tells us that one day in 1895, while he was walking around the city,

just across the valley near the foothills I saw four Indian lodges, looking white against the brown background. The sight of them thrilled me more than anything I had lately seen. The day was fine. The mountaintops laid shadows upon the four lodges that seemed to belong to another world altogether. I walked to the camp, not guessing what Indians were there. Imagine my delight when I was greeted by my old friend, Muskegon, the Cree, who had told me so many tribal folk tales in the Flathead.

Times were growing hard for the Crees, he told me. Game in the open country was scarce. They had been gathering buffalo bones and selling polished buffalo horns in town. They were now working their way back to Flathead country, where there were many deer and elk in the forest. Muskegon looked dejected. His cloths, ragged portions of white men's apparel, seemed to have lowered both his morale and his personal appearance. He was a changed man. Yellow-face, another Cree friend who was in this camp, was more cheerful. However, he was a much younger man, and still wore leggings and breechclout. We visited for hours. They could not understand why I, as a hunter, came to be in Butte. And by the same token, I was at a loss to explain their presence so near the big mining camp. I did not then suspect that the wandering band of Crees and Chippewas, numbering about three hundred men, women, and children, to which these four lodges belonged, would someday become a charge of mine. However, when I went to work the next morning I saw that the four lodges were gone. Several years were to pass before I again saw a Cree.[22]

Linderman's allusion to those who "would someday become a charge" of his is a reference to his truly heroic work as the single most important Montanan to bring about a sea change for "vagabond" Indians of the state. But that story comes later in this narrative.

6: Nikotwāsik

The success of the 1894 Butte Sun Dance, as well as Helena's, became a promoter's dream. In 1895, two Montana businessmen created "Montana's Wild West Show." Little Bear's Cree were the attraction. They were "featured [as] the Cree Indians who had taken part in the Canadian Riel rebellion." The band was advertised as the "only people in the United States without a country."[23] Leaving Montana in April 1895, incredibly, the troupe played Joliet, Chicago, New York, and New Orleans. When they got to Cincinnati, their promoters, two wily and scurrilous characters from Helena named Beverage and Davenport, absconded with all the tour's proceeds and left the Cree stranded.[24] The band was actually camped across the river in Bellevue, Kentucky, when the scoundrels took off. Cincinnati felt for the plight of the Montana Cree. The famed Cincinnati Zoological Gardens invited the Cree to camp on their grounds until they could earn enough money to get back to Montana. In a picture almost too surreal to bear, our band, who had Sun Danced in Butte less than a year earlier, were now an exhibit next to the elephants, giraffes, and tigers at the Cincinnati Zoo. The Montana Cree were such a success at the zoo that a band of Sicangu Sioux was invited to follow as an exhibit, replacing the Cree when they left town.[25]

Over the year that a portion of Little Bear's band was on tour, white outrage toward Montana's first urban homeless class produced a hot political issue as increasingly vehement calls for how to get rid of the

CHAP. 175.—An Act Making provision for the deportation of refugee Canadian Cree Indians from the State of Montana and their delivery to the Canadian authorities.

May 13, 1896.

Be it enacted by the Senate and House of Representatives of the United States of America in Congress assembled, That there be, and is hereby, appropriated, out of any money in the Treasury not otherwise appropriated, the sum of five thousand dollars, or so much thereof as may be necessary, the same to be immediately available, to enable the President, by employment of the Army or otherwise, to deport from the State of Montana and deliver at the international boundary line to the Canadian authorities, all refugee Canadian Cree Indians in said State.

Approved, May 13, 1896.

Cree Indians. Appropriation for delivery to Canadian authorities.

The Cree Deportation Act of 1896. [27]

"Cree" mounted. Pressure from state authorities for the U.S. government to act caused an event that remains one of Montana's most shameful affairs.

While the Cree were yet a zoo exhibit in Cincinnati, the U.S. Congress fell to the pressure of Montana's businessmen and politicians, passing the Cree Deportation Act of 1896. The act fit neatly into the sense of Anglo exceptionalism, which at the time also included the more well-known Chinese Exclusion Act of 1896. Montana cities were bent on cleaning up their towns of left-over riffraff from the former Frontier Era.

The U.S. Census Bureau (in 1890) and Fredrick Jackson Turner (in 1893) had recently proclaimed the frontier to be over and America to be officially complete. Settling this land for Anglo America had been ugly business. Now that the job was done, it was time to sweep the remnants under the new-order social rug. The burgeoning American middle class was taking center stage, and blue-collar workers were being promised that industrial wealth would trickle down to them. A high-horse attitude toward those living at a city's dumps and feeding off its refuse held no compassion or attempt to understand the circumstance, condition, or why and wherefore of the Indians. To the contrary, it served to deeply separate the newcomers from the first peoples of Montana.

The demoralized Nehiyaw Pwat continued to disperse and circulate throughout Montana, forming other encampments in Missoula, Helena, Great Falls, Chinook, Glasgow, Augusta, Choteau, Dupuyer, Billings, and Lewistown. But Butte was home to the largest number of lodges, forty, representing between 160 and 240 people. Butte also possessed the strongest political sway. They would have their way. [26]

Before the ink was dry from signing the Cree Deportation Act, the U.S. Army out of Fort Assiniboine, near Havre, mobilized. As soon as those Cree in Cincinnati made it back to Havre later that spring of 1896, they faced an assault on their dignity and human rights. Beginning in June, and completing their task in August, a full complement of Buffalo Soldier cavalry, led by a young Lt. John J. Pershing, either shipped in cattle cars or herded well over five hundred "Crees" to Alberta, Canada. They were dispatched to reserves throughout the province. Many immediately snuck back across the border into Montana and hid out. To this day, at Hobbema, in Alberta, there remains a group of Nehiyaw Pwat called the Montana Band, descendents of that legacy.

The Cree Deportation Act was a pogrom of premeditated violence directed at destroying the way of life of the Nehiyaw Pwat in Montana. It took the form of a human cattle drive—an actual roundup and forced march—of these people to Canada. Other tribes were kept securely apart on reservations; Montana would not suffer Indians on the loose, especially those including among them mixed-bloods and half-breeds, the product of (in Victorian-era terms) a scorned lawless and immoral time in the nation's history.

Most of the deported Nehiyaw Pwat made it back to the state, hiding out in the coulees, draws, and canyons, mixing in with relatives on reservations, or continuing to press their luck around their old haunts, camping at the dumps, and forming refugee camps—including Moccasin Flat, Buckskin Flat, and Breedtown—around the state. That was the status quo for the next few years. White communities were resigned for the time being to this underclass.

7: Tipakohp

Some serious work to accommodate the difference between Indian and non-Indian society did occur. In 1900, Fort Shaw Indian School, west of Great Falls on the Sun River, brought its boys football team to Butte. The headlines declared: "Indians Saw the Town, The Boys of Butte Treated Them Nicely." Students at the Fort Shaw Indian School numbered about 330 at the time and came from Wyoming, Nevada, Idaho, and North Dakota, as well as Montana. The superintendent of the school, F. C. Campbell, provided what he believed to be constructive diplomacy in describing to the Butte community the benefits to white society for supporting Indian education. He said that it "was to their interests to have the Indian civilized and brought into the circle of citizenship, for then the vast acreage of the reservations will be thrown open to settlement and the education of the Indian will bring its own reward." Campbell's words had a dual significance: a true conviction in the benefits of education but also the self-serving interests of manipulating Indian society in order to acquire their land. Campbell promised to bring to Butte the following March the school's Indian band and mandolin club as proof of how Indians can be civilized.[28] It was easier to talk about the Indian problem with a group who was disciplined to conform to white standards, à la football, and who did not live at the margins of one's own community.

The local Indians did not receive the same consideration, however. Reservation Indians who went to school under the controlled obedience to white leadership were a horse of a different color from Indians encamped at the garbage pit on the edge of town. The following spring, Butte was mocking a wedding that "was celebrated with pomp at the city dump," as if it were discussing the upper-crust social registry. A derisive attitude toward the Nehiyaw Pwat Indians in Butte was exactly the social force that cultivated the marginalization of Indian people.

> The bride was given away by her grand aunt, who is a boarder at the offal pile at the slaughter house, and the best man was Jim Crow, the tin can collector of the band. The dame of honor carried a bouquet of mountain daisies and a gunny sack across her shoulders. The wedding feast was spread at the west end of the city dump and the menu contained evidences of several grand feeds in the city a week or more ago.
>
> Mr. and Mrs. Bull Horn will tour the southern part of the county in search of mavericks and recreation. The groom received a magnificent plug of tobacco from his friends of the Tripe club, and the bride was charmed with a presentation by her squaw friends of a pair of brass martingale rings [horse tack]. They will be at home at pile No. 47 on the city dump after Arbor day.[29]

The reality was, in fact, anything but humorous. The scene in Butte that April of 1901 was repeated in Helena, Great Falls, Missoula, and elsewhere around the state where bands of the Nehiyaw Pwat were isolated in smaller contingents for survival. No one dump pile or trinket and odd-job market could sustain the whole tribe in a single place. Elizabeth Sperry, in her valuable addition to the story of "Montana's Landless Indians," offers a succinct understanding of the issues involved.

> Survival in Montana depended upon a complex system of kin networks between diverse groups of Métis, Cree and Chippewa [i.e., Nehiyaw Pwat, including Assiniboine and other nonstatus Indians]. The historical processes of increasing white settlement, the formation of an international boundary line dividing the United States and Canada, the creation of Indian reservations, and the demise of bison herds required a

reorganization of the social, economic, and political activities of those who came to be known as Montana's Landless Indians. . . .

One element of landless Indian history in Montana is their utilization of city dumps and slaughterhouses. While this aspect of landless Indian history signifies the realities of their starvation and poverty, these areas provided items that were essential to the Indians' economic survival. Landless Indians utilized items discarded by the dominant society and transformed them into something they could use or resell. For instance, the "Cree camp stove" was constructed out of old washtubs, which was efficient because it was a commonly discarded object that was easy to find and they "threw heat well." The slaughterhouses were likely the source of cow horns, which landless Indians collected, polished, and sold to tourists in a variety of forms. This alertness to useable objects in their environment ensured the landless Indians' long-term economic viability and survival.[30]

The disparaging sentiment in Butte toward the nascent urban Indian population had festered for over a decade by that time. The local condition directly affected the larger political perception of Indian affairs

"Be It Ever So Humble, There's No Place Like Home." Cartoon caricature of Butte Cree Indian. Artist unknown. Courtesy of the Montana Historical Society Research Center. Published in Anaconda Standard, *May 12, 1901.*

nationally. On December 8, 1901, the *Anaconda Standard* wrote in critique of the federal Indian commissioner William Arthur Jones's statement that "the Indians must be made to recognize the dignity of labor." Once again, mockingly, the article challenged Jones to "by all means make the Indian recognize this particular brand of dignity when he meets it. There are the Crees, for instance; teach them the dignity of labor for starter. Let Commissioner Jones take the job himself and work at it until he has succeeded or wiped out the Crees. There will be a lot of Cree funerals."[31]

In other words, the opinion existed that bringing Butte's Indians into the fold of the American economy (to say nothing of the society as a whole) was a futile cause. What no one in white society recognized at the time was that urban Indians were in actuality already fulfilling a viable economic niche in the burgeoning new municipal centers of Montana, however demeaning. Sperry's work emphasizes a bias and makes clear that

> the various types of work Montana's landless Indians were involved in are often presented in culturally distancing terms [i.e., scavenging], and . . . much of what has been written about American Indian wage labor comes from the perspective of their unemployment or lack of paid work. While landless Indians worked as wage

laborers, small commodity producers, or sellers of crafts and other handiwork, these types of economic livelihoods have not been considered as actual work. For this reason, Native labor was often distanced from the larger economies in which it was nested, and was relegated to a world outside of the emerging dominant economy.[32]

Called, among many disparaging names, the "Ishmaelites of the Prairie" (referring to a descendent of Ishmael, the son Abraham sent away following the birth of Isaac—that is, Arabs), the Nehiyaw Pwat in Montana remained linked to Louis Riel and to a fear of rebelliousness still projected onto aboriginals that continued to threaten the guilt-ridden mind-set of both Anglo Canada and the United States. The Nehiyaw Pwat were perceived as

> refusing to accept the bounty of either nation [and] hovered around the borderline, living on stray cattle and whatever they can find loose on the prairie. The "range calf gone astray" is the particular prey of these gipsies of the Northwest. [The public was reminded that just a few years earlier the state made an attempt to] . . . deport these undesirable nomads to Canada. . . . Cree

Indians were rounded up from all over the state and escorted across the border, where they were expected to remain. . . . But they refused to be deported. . . . [T]hey swarmed back almost as soon as their escorts were out of sight. . . . Occasionally reports of their depredations are heard of, but the Cree question remains unsettled.[33]

This particular reportage in the local paper was really about assigning blame to a new outbreak of smallpox in Montana. The sentiment of the time was that whites were close to eradicating the disease but that the Cree made it impossible. "Thriving on filth," the account continues, "constantly moving from place to place, as a disseminator of disease he is a howling success. . . . That man will win the gratitude of the people who will make a satisfactory disposition of this vulture of the garbage pile, who breeds microbes and disturbance and refuses to be governed."[34] The Montana urban Indians had become the state's "untouchable" caste.

8: *Ayinānīw*

By 1902, there arose another call, supported in Butte, for the general deportation of Montana's Cree to Canada. The rationale this time was for the "protection of game and also for sanitary purposes. . . . There are 2,000 Cree Indians in the state and they slaughter as much game as is killed by all the white inhabitants, in addition to the loss and the great amount of trouble which they occasion the stockmen by their thieving and pilfering."[35] Wild game had evidently become the provenance of solely the white society.

A second grouping of Indians "wandering" Montana wasn't so easy to write off, however inaccurately, as Canadian. Although it made no difference to the white populace that wanted them all gone, they complicated matters for the government. When the roundup of 1896 occurred, many of the people herded told the officials repeatedly that they were neither Cree nor from Canada (although, aboriginally speaking, that is a moot point). While some protested that they were Shoshone, Nez Perce, and Kootenai, most of the people were of Chippewa heritage within the Nehiyaw Pwat, with a pathway into Montana that trailed back to the Turtle Mountains and Pembina in North Dakota.[36]

Little Shell was the leader of the Chippewa band in Montana. Although his people, too, had been well represented in Montana continually since the 1830s, as part of the larger Nehiyaw Pwat Confederacy, his group was closed out of the reservation negotiations back on the Turtle Mountains in 1892. This band was in reality a mixed Cree Assiniboine Chippewa Michif group of the Nehiyaw Pwat.[37] They roved mostly Montana's Hi-Line and North Dakota, sometimes hooked up with Little Bear's band. Little Shell and his band were back at Turtle Mountain in 1901 when he died. Stone Child, also known as Rocky Boy, assumed leadership of a portion of the band, which was forced to return to Montana because "the supplies intended for them especially designated, as now what is sent here [to Turtle Mountain] has to be divided among so many that it is impossible to give them the help which their condition requires."[38] Elizabeth Sperry ably recounts Rocky Boy's entrance to the scene.

> The earliest account of Rocky Boy's band occurred in 1902, when Flathead Agent William H. Smead discovered Rocky Boy's band living near Anaconda, Montana, with a large group of Indians Smead identified as "Canadian born Crees." In 1908, Indian Inspector Frank Churchill identified Rocky Boy's band as belonging to "the roving Indian group" in Montana, which also included Little Bear and his band of fifty persons and numerous other Indian groups living in the state. According to Churchill this landless Indian group lived throughout Montana in smaller groups, and while they had intermarried to a considerable extent they "knew very little about each other and the relationship existing between families."

This observation implies that these groups maintained a high level of social and geographical distinctiveness; however, rather than suggesting that the Indians lacked knowledge of each other, this observation could signify an effort among the various groups to conceal their interrelationship and/or Cree heritage from outsiders to avoid being deported to Canada or denied rights in the United States based upon a stigmatized "Canadian" Cree heritage.[39]

In actuality, the groups were closely interrelated. Little Bear was married to Rocky Boy's sister, and one wife of Little Bear's father, Big Bear, was a sister of Rocky Boy's wife.[40] The band had relatives among all the Nehiyaw Pwat tribes and bands across the Hi-Line. Yet the change in leadership created a huge confusion that yet muddies the story of who are the Little Shell Tribe in Montana and the process of federal recognition of the Little Shell to this day. The appearance of Rocky Boy's band has always been treated as if a whole new and separate band of Indians showed up in Montana. From the time Rocky Boy became leader of the Chippewa among the Nehiyaw Pwat in Montana, Chippewa Cree, as an amalgamated group, started to take on a new conception by whites. Little Bear's "Cree" and Rocky Boy's "Chippewa" became fused. The use of the term *Little Shell Band* disappeared until resurfacing in the late 1920s as the group taking form from which today's Little Shell are comprised.

One way the Butte community worked to manage the Indian population was by promoting the ideal they wanted the larger local Indian community to grasp. When, for example, Mrs. Harry Denny died on February 6, 1904, the paper took advantage of the fact by writing an article entitled "Death of a Good Indian . . . Mother of Nine Children, a Cree, Goes to the Happy Hunting Grounds." The article tells that Harry Denny and his wife

> were exceptions in the Cree tribe, for they had lived together quietly for many years, and always discountenanced the indiscriminant marriages which have been the rule among members of the tribe. They reared a family and all the children held their parents in high regard. Denny hauls wood and does odd jobs, and manages to provide for his children. . . . Two of the daughters are married and have been seen in the city often, both neatly garbed and one of them carrying a papoose on her back.[41]

The most interesting bit of information in this piece is the statement that, as of 1904, the Dennys had lived in Butte, albeit quietly, for many years. This strongly indicates at least a portion of the non-reservation-based Indian society was working to establish an ongoing permanent Indian community in Butte by that time.

9: Kīkā-mitātaht

Not missing a chance to prove the superiority of white society by denigrating the failure of the Indian, the Butte community claimed that the "Silver Bow Crees Fake[ed] [the] Sun Dance" of 1904. Pressures from the oppressive circumstances of the Indians caused a response to eliminate the "torture features of the original sun dance." It was held that year between Butte and Anaconda at a place called the "Hump." A year earlier, the Medicine Lodge had been erected south of Silver Bow. The report states that, "like the feeble old beast, they must, sooner or later, relinquish their grasp and become reconciled to the conditions which surround them and yield to the inevitable—the ancient sun dance is not popular with the renegade Crees and their allies, the half-breeds." Apparently, only the

> old bucks whose hearts throb at the sound of the tom-tom [whose] blood warms at the sight of their brothers in hideous array dancing in weird fashion, . . . in devilish glee [remained committed].

The half-breeds [Métis], and by the way, they are in the majority, do not favor the old custom. They counsel their blood relations to abandon it. The full-bloods heed them not. So there is a dance, a mere semblance of the ancient dance, and the half-breeds play cards and smoke in their tepees while the dance goes on. . . . There are about 100 in camp, and of that number there are at least 50 women and children, breeds, and 20 full-blood squaws and papooses. The others are Cree, Flathead, Chippewa and Lemhi [Nez Perce] bucks, with the Crees numbering two for one of the others. Chief Sitting Horse of the Cree squad managed the whole jumping match and he danced with only a breechclout on.[42]

It is valuable to continue with this particular newspaper account because of its observations of the actual dance. Although denigrating the event overall, the reporter did get certain structural parts correct in the description.

The others affected the costumes of the cowboy. The squaws wore calico dresses and red paint. When they entered the arena they tossed their blankets on the ground and disappeared behind a hedge of cottonwood boughs. The drum sounded and, each with a reed [eagle bone whistle] in his mouth, the dancers raised their heads above the hedge, shouting, and gradually drew themselves to an upright position. After rising by degrees to their full height they gave one shout in concert and the first movement was finished. Then they dropped out of sight behind the bushes, to rise again to the noise of the weird chant and the drum beat. A chief would exhort a bit, the drum and reeds would again split the air and the dance was resumed, and this is the way it went until the dancers got tired. Then another relay would take up the dance and so on till the chant of "Home Sweet Home" in sagebrush minor shivered the miniature sand dunes of the "Hump."[43]

The anonymous reporter goes on to tell that an "admission fee was charged whites at the pavilion entrance." He also comments that there would have been a larger crowd in attendance if the Sun Dance had been held closer to the city.

Fourteen miles away is too far to travel overland to witness such a sensationless spectacle. The horde that got together was made up of such coarse grafters as to be out of reach of the average visitor. They would not talk unless they got money for their pains. They would not impart a line of information without a tip and in order to make a photograph of one or a few a tip staggering in its size was demanded. Some had cow horns to sell, but the demand was discouragingly small. Some had beaded moccasins which were held at prohibitive figures. The English-speaking breeds were more persistent grafters than the full-bloods. The Crees are a shiftless lot, without ambition and pests this country wants to get rid of.

The congress will adjourn to-day and the Indians will return to their respective camps. The visiting tribes will return to their reservations and the Crees will come back to the city dump and be at home to anything handy that comes their way.[44]

Finally, with this full-blown front-page article complete with photographs, we see the bias of the reporter. He named the ceremony a fake because he wanted to see the blood and torture. And, while he states that the Crees are "without ambition," he is put off by the fact that they are using the ceremony as an entrepreneurial event to capture some economic benefit for their people.

The state's sentient newspaper, the *Anaconda Standard*, railed not just at the local Indian problem in its pages. Highly critical of the federal government's handling of the Indian question, on July 13, 1904, it ran another column ridiculing the U.S. commissioner of Indian affairs William A. Jones. This time it was for a "harebrained" idea of setting up an Indian agricultural school in the Prickly Pear Valley outside of Helena.

The Commissioner is said to have approved the Prickly Pear valley as a place in which to make his experiment. With the Flathead Indians on the west, the Crows on the east, the Blackfeet on the north and the Crees all around, to say nothing of the savages that infest Last Chance gulch when the legislature meets, it is doubtful if even the famed refinement of the metropolis of the Prickly Pear valley could permanently civilize the Indian.[45]

The editorial goes on to chastise Jones's logic on his choice for developing agriculture, stating that it is "extremely doubtful, if an Indian could be enthused over farming if he tried to raise crops in the Prickly Pear valley, 'a ____ ____ prairie that a grasshopper couldn't cross without packing rations.'"[46]

10: *Mitātaht*

The years 1905 and 1906 bring back to the fore Frank E. Peeso and the unique visual documents he created of Butte's early urban Indian community. There's Rosie Denny in front of her lodge. Jimushas, a Shoshoni with the Butte Cree, shows the relationship that exists to this day between Montana's Chippewa Cree and the Fort Hall Shoshoni and Bannock Tribe. Monais's image expresses the desire to maintain critical elements of his traditional culture through choosing to wear his hair and pieces of clothing Indian style. The hodgepodge of blankets and canvas tell of less than optimum materials for living quarters.

The group photo of Oschasemas (Old Boy), Osememas (Young Boy), Too-way, Wahwahkeekat, and Joe Little Pine give us a look at five young men in their twenties. They are the first generation to come of age following the defeat of aboriginal resistance to Anglo American and Canadian expansion. Even in the squalor of their poverty, they exhibit a sense of self-pride in their appearance and demeanor. Their identity remains intensely Indian. The picture of the children and dog with travois is exceptional. The image is the Butte dump, where the boy and girl forage the grounds freely. The boy is in Euro-American clothing; the girl wears moccasins. Their dog is remarkable not only for the ancient travois but for the breed. It is an aboriginal American dog. The camp itself is interesting for showing the mix of a wall tent with a woodstove next to a traditional lodge. Also notable is the placement of the domiciles, separated into singular private spaces rather than grouped in a communal circle. The social structure was changing.

Frank Peeso's image of Osememas and his mother (who was 105 at the time) shows a man with a strong bent toward the future and fitting into the new western society. His choice of identity is rural cowboy, not that of urban miner, which surrounded him in Butte.

The crowning Peeso photo is of Marie Isobel Smallboy and her children. Marie's husband was Pierre Smallboy. There is a story here that gives clues to the complexity of aboriginal relationships, revealing an insightful coupling of Montana to the wider culture region of aboriginal society.

Marie's grandfather was the famed Cree Chief Bobtail (Kiskayiwew). His brother was Chief Ermineskin (Sehkosowayanew). They were also known as, respectively, Alex Piche and Baptiste Piche (from Pichette, a *Canadien* at Fort Vermillion on the Saskatchewan River in 1809). They were mixbloods. Their bands were part of the Sahiya Xe Ya Bine (Mountain Cree People), referred to as Halfbreeds in Montana. They were deeply intermarried with the Salish, Pend'Oreille, and Kootenai. Marie's grandmother was Catherine Cardinal, a Cree

Group of Cree men, Butte area, Montana, 1906. L-R: Oschasemas, Old Boy; Osememas, Young Boy; Too-way; Wahwahkeekat; Joe Little Pine. Frank E. Peeso, photographer. Courtesy of the Glenbow Archives (Image No: NA-1431-10).

Rosie Denny, Cree, Butte area, Montana, 1906. Frank E. Peeso, photographer. Courtesy of the Glenbow Archives (Image No: NA-1431-1).

Cree children and dog travois at the dump, Butte area, Montana, 1906. Frank E. Peeso, photographer. Courtesy of the Glenbow Archives (Image No: NA-1431-11).

Osememas and his mother, Cree, Butte area, Montana, ca. 1910. Called Young Boy in English, he died in 1945. His mother was 105 at the time of the picture. Frank E. Peeso, photographer. Courtesy of the Glenbow Archives (Image No: NA-1431-8).

Bobtail or Chief Small Boy, Cree, Butte area, Montana, 1906. Frank E. Peeso, photographer. Courtesy of the Glenbow Archives (Image No: NA-1431-4).

Indians near Butte. 1900." An amateur photographer shot this picture from his wagon seat. Photographer note on the negative's original envelope. John Babtist, photographer. Courtesy of Thomas Robinson, Historic Photo Archives, Portland, OR.

Métis (from Joseph Cardinal, her grandfather, also a *Canadien* at Fort Vermillion in 1809). Her aunt Josephte Cardinal married Antoine Blondion (Fair-haired), son of the Chippewa Chief Mukatai (Powder), who was the brother of the Mistahimusqua (better known as Big Bear, who became a chief of the Cree), the father of Little Bear, and the leader of the Butte "Cree." Big Bear's predecessor was Chief Broken Arm (Maskipitoon), the man who signed the Stevens Treaty of 1855 at the mouth of the Judith River. So Marie was

a cousin to Little Bear. Her lineage shows the deep connectedness to Montana of the Butte band camped at the dump in 1906.[47]

Following her experience in Butte, Marie took her family back to more Cree-centered territory. The eldest boy in the picture, Bobtail (named after his great grandfather), grew up to become chief of the Ermineskin Band of Cree, who settled with the Montana Band, at Hobbema, Alberta, following their removal from Montana in 1896. Bobtail's life, and his Butte residency, culminates this story.

The next year, in early June of 1907, Anaconda was the site of the Nehiyaw Pwat's annual Sun Dance. Indians came from all over Montana and Idaho. There were around "200 braves and innumerable squaws and papooses" camped between Anaconda and Warm Springs on the William Fairweather Ranch. It was called a "Swell Affair" with the Indians "All In Gorgeous Toggery." Chief Rocky Boy led the "performance," while "visiting palefaces enjoy the scene. . . . The braves, smeared with paint and wrapped in bright blankets, circle about the lodge, uttering piercing yells. They keep up the performance until they fall exhausted. They never get out of their war togs from the beginning to the end of the dance."[48]

As in 1894, when the first documented Sun Dance was in held in Butte, the notion of Indians performing a spectacle that allowed outsiders to have access to the

Cree head chiefs at Hobbema, Alberta, ca. 1920. L-R: Ermineskin, (Ermineskin band); Charles Rabbit (Montana band); Joe Samson (Samson band). Ermineskin was the great-uncle of Marie Smallboy. Bobtail grew up to become chief of the Ermineskin band. Photographer unknown. Courtesy of the Glenbow Archives (Image No: NA-1223-21).

titillating, risky, savage, and arcane (though thoroughly controlled environment) was acceptable for the white community. Being spectators at an event where images of a mythic noble savage played out was very different from living daily with Indians in abject poverty.

Just two weeks later, a "tramp band" of about a hundred "Crees, Lemhis [Nez Percé], and Chippewas" were ordered by the Silver Bow County sheriff to get out of Butte. They were camped by the slaughterhouses on the south side of town for several weeks, being a "dirty nuisance to the people of the southern section of the city." He gave them "two sleeps" to pack it up and move on, threatening to kill their dogs, scatter their horses, and confiscate their provisions if they weren't gone.[49]

II: Piyakosāp

By 1912, the tenor of the discourse was changing. When Rocky Boy's band was placed on the grounds of Fort Harrison in Helena to winter over, the special dispatch to the Butte newspaper used the term "homeless" to describe the Indians. The account reported: "There are 700 homeless Indians in Montana, divided into small bands, which are eking out an existence in camps near the larger cities." Quoting Major A. E. MacFatridge, the agent in charge, the white community received a new message and context for how to make sense of urban Indians. "The Crees are not bad fellows," said MacFatridge. "The younger members are anxious and willing to work. They do not like to be dependent upon government charity, nor do they wish to lead a nomadic life." There was now compassion toward Indians in the voice of white authority. And for the Indians, a new generation had come of age, and they did not want the life of their parents. Somehow they had to find a way to engage the larger society. A new conversation began.[50]

Little Bear negotiations for decommissioned Fort Assiniboine (Rocky Boy's Reservation), Placer Hotel, Helena, 1915. L–r, Little Bear, Kinnewash, William Boles (Publisher of the Great Falls Tribune), U.S. Secretary of the Interior Frank K. Lane, Jim Denny, Other Person, interpreter Pat Raspberry (LaFromboise), and Frank B. Linderman. Photographer unknown. Courtesy of Archives and Special Collections, Linderman Collection, The University of Montana (Image No: 007(VIII):48).

The following year, Frank B. Linderman, at the time acclaimed as the only white man to have been adopted into the Cree tribe, began working fervently for a reservation for his Cree family. Linderman set up a meeting in Helena with U.S. Secretary of the Interior Franklin K. Lane. He had the support of William M. Boles, the publisher of the *Great Falls Tribune*. The conversation took place at the Placer Hotel. Little

Bear told the secretary that "God was taking care of us all right until the white man came and took the responsibility off His hands. Last winter our wives and our children lived on dogs and the carcasses of frozen horses to keep from starving."[51] Not shy in the face of power, Little Bear made his proposal. It was for a portion of the decommissioned Fort Assiniboine to be turned over to his people as their homeland in Montana. It was a good idea.

The following spring, Little Bear explained to folks in Butte that

> my people need much; they need a home. We are not Canadians—we fought with Riel and we lost, but we came from the states of this country; some are Chippewas, some are Nez Perces, some are Shoshones, only some Crees. The Cree Indian came first to Montana with the Assiniboines away long ago; my father [Big Bear] was a Cree that lived on the Snake River [in Idaho] with Moose and Two Horns, and they came here—in Butte—long ago when we hunt buffalo and deer here on this hill, where now these big mines send black smoke to kill the game and the birds.[52]

A year and a half later (in 1916), a reservation was carved out of the southern edge of Fort Assiniboine for Montana's landless Indians. But Little Bear was right. His people had been part of the Silver Bow environs since the early eighteenth century. And they're still there today. Not all of them moved to the newly established Rocky Boy's Reservation. Some of the "Crees" had already established their own family niche that proved sufficient for them to stay in Butte. But that was the end of Sun Dances in Butte and in Montana's urban culturescape.

In 1881, Little Bear's father, Big Bear, the great Nehiyaw Pwat chief, was with his people in Montana as the buffalo were on their last pasture in the Judith Basin. It was before the Northwest Resistance and Louis Riel's martyrdom; in fact, Riel was also living in the Judith at the time. Big Bear did not take treaty with Canada. He was secure in his people's right to be in the Judith Basin, along the Missouri Breaks, and across Montana, reinforced by the knowing

> that someone from his nation had signed a treaty with the Americans in 1855. This chief, named Eyes in the Front and Back [aka Maskepetoon, or Broken Arm], had even travelled to Washington to see the Great Father [Andrew Jackson in 1831] and to receive presents from him. . . . Big Bear also learned that Maj. John Young, the officer currently in charge of the huge Indian

reservation that occupied most of northern Montana, was sympathetic to his people. He considered the eastern part of the reservation to belong to the Gros Ventre, Assiniboines, Crees, River Crows and Sioux.[53]

Big Bear still believed in the validity of his predecessor Broken Arm's role in the Blackfoot Treaty of 1855, when the United States first made a pact with the Upper Missouri tribes, including the Nehiyaw Pwat. Also, in 1881, the U.S. military yet held interpretation of that treaty as a continuing legal document.

By the time Little Bear assumed leadership of his father's band in Montana in 1886 following the Riel tragedy, things changed—hence this story of the first generation of urban Indian poverty in Butte and other Montana cities. Yet eventually, after much travail, Little Bear and his band, along with their relatives in the Little Shell/Rocky Boy's band, finally came to rest in 1916 on a reservation within their traditional historic homeland in the Bear's Paw Mountains of north-central Montana.

12: Nīsosāp

But not all of the Nehiyaw Pwat in Montana were accommodated by the creation of the Rocky Boy's Reservation. Some are known today as the Gopher Clan of the Rocky Boy Chippewa Band, a distinct group that became separated from the larger settlement of Rocky

Boy's Reservation in 1916. They are centered in Great Falls. The other group is organized as the Little Shell Tribe, who are recognized by the State of Montana but not by the federal government. They still suffer from the stigma that a portion of their citizenry is "Canadian" and doesn't "qualify"; that they are not (as Nehiyaw Pwat Michif) in fact "Indian" enough and can't satisfy the criteria as a historically cohesive and distinct group of aboriginal people to be eligible as a tribe for federal recognition. These people continue to reside, as they long have, in Butte, Helena, and Great Falls, along the Front Range, in Lewistown, across the Hi-Line, and in numerous other communities throughout Montana. They are Montana's historic urban Indian population, part of Montana's urban landscape from the inception of city-culture in the state.

After World War II and the Termination and Relocation federal policy era, many tribal citizens from reservation-based Indian nations made their way into Montana's cities. Since the late 1940s and continuing today, representatives of all of Montana's tribal nations comprise an additional population within the urban Indian community. In the past generation, a third sector of Indians, highly educated and working in professional occupations, came to Montana cities from Indian country throughout America. More than a third of Montana's total Indian population lives in the state's urban areas.[54] Yet the presence of the historic urban

Indian groups of "landless Indians" in this geography, and their relationship to all the aboriginal peoples in this territory, is deeper and predates the nation-states of Canada and the United States of America in belonging to this land.

The importance of the early urban Indian experience in Butte cannot be overstated for Indian country. The story of one of Butte's early urban Indian residents plays out to this day with profound significance. In camp at the dump, Little Bear told many times the story of his father and their people camping on that very Butte hillside before the white people came, when all life was natural. Among Little Bear's audience was a young boy just the right age. He really listened. His imagination took hold, and the depth of meaning in Little Bear's words reached his core. That boy was Bobtail, son of Marie Smallboy, pictured with his brothers and sisters that 1906 day in Butte. For Peeso there must have been something else that stood out with that young boy, for he also had him pose singularly.

That image, in retrospect, holds incredible prescience. Of his siblings, Bobtail is the one still dressed in traditional Indian style. After moving from Butte with his family to the Bear Hills (now known as Hobbema) to be closer to relatives, he grew to become chief of the Ermineskin Band. By 1968, so disheartened with the continual suffering of his people and the increase in substance abuse and social deterioration, he led his people off the government reserve, walking away from modern life, and trekked into the isolated Rockies to set up a traditional tribal community. It became known as Smallboy's Camp. There he washed away the devastation of a century, rejuvenated the Sun Dance of his youth and the full ceremonial calendar, and taught his people to hunt, forage, and again speak their native language. No more garbage dumps. No more cast-offs. No more middlemen between his people and the Creator.

Chief Bobtail Smallboy, a boy of old Butte, is a magnificent and legendary hero to aboriginal peoples across the continent. His story continues to resonate as a proactive model of how a group of people can reclaim their lives in the face of a larger society out of balance with nature. Smallboy's Camp survives to this day. Looking at Frank Peeso's boyhood photo of him in Butte—in which he can't be more than twelve years old—he emanates a determination, steadfastness, and pride that are already deeply set. He will not suffer the indignity of dominant society's poverty. He will not be a victim.

Remembering the story of Little Bear's father, Big Bear, camping on the same Butte mountainside with his people as Otchipemsu'uk (they who own themselves), in contrast to the *unśika* (pitiful) camp at the Butte dump where the story was told, Bobtail found a way to embody again the wealth of culture that was his heritage and to offer it, once more, to his people. He would stand atop the Thunder Pole singing down the heavens, creating the condition of mercy for his people. He learned that resolve in Butte. Just as the American Indian population hit its nadir of 250,000 souls, a plummet from 20 million people at the beginning of mass European immigration, we see the astounding strength and beautiful obstinacy of Bobtail's stance as a boy in that ageless and awe-inspiring image. A greater legacy of the Butte dump than anyone ever imagined, that boy understood the poverty, there in the shadow of the Richest Hill on Earth, and made his promise. His purpose would be fulfilled. In the compost of that Butte refuse pile, a seed of renewal and hope for aboriginal people was sown.

1   The Nehiyaw Pwat is an aboriginal confederacy comprised of primarily the Cree, Assiniboine, Chippewa, and Métis. The confederacy is a multiethnic society bonded by intermarriage and deeply integrated culturally, economically, politically, and militarily.

2   George Everett, executive director, Mainstreet Uptown Butte, e-mail of October 29, 2008, on file with the author.

3   Olga W. Johnson, "Fred Peeso Collected Stories Related by Cree Indians," *Great Falls Tribune*, November 30, 1958, 16–17. See also F. E. Peeso, "The Cree Indians," *Museum Journal* (University of Pennsylvania) 3, no. 1 (March 1912): 50.

4   Also referred to as the Northwest Rebellion. From the aboriginal perspective, the conflict between aboriginal peoples and white businessmen and the Canadian government in 1884–85 was a resistance to invasion and occupation. The events of those years culminated at the Battle of Batoche and the trial of Louis Riel, a Montanan and U.S. citizen, for treason. He was hanged in Regina, Saskatchewan, in November 1885. Many aboriginal people fled for their lives from Canada to Montana and North Dakota following those events, to avoid the intense white retribution for their resistance.

5   Johnson, "Fred Peeso," 16.

6   Peeso, "The Cree Indians," 51.

7   Nicholas Vrooman, "Broken Arm: Cree Plenipo of the 19th Century Northern Plains," *Montana the Magazine of Western History* 58, no. 4 (Summer 2009), forthcoming.

8   J. Elizabeth Sperry, *Ethnogenesis of the Métis, Cree and Chippewa in Twentieth Century Montana* (master's thesis, University of Montana, 2007), 70. Copy given to the author by Ms. Sperry.

9   Raymond Gray, *The Cree Indians* (unpublished manuscript), WPA Federal Writers Project, 1941–42, 37, copy in author's possession.

10   Thomas O. Miles, letter to the editor, (Butte) *Semi-weekly Inter-mountain*, November 30, 1892. Cited in Gray, *The Cree Indians*, 16–17.

11   Gray, *The Cree Indians*, 150–51.

12   Gray, *The Cree Indians*, 17.

13   Gray, *The Cree Indians*, 17–18.

14   Gray, *The Cree Indians*,, 19–20. The attorney's name was John Hoffman.

15   Gray, *The Cree Indians*, 27–32. Also Sperry, *Ethnogenesis*, 40.

16   Gray, *The Cree Indians*, 30.

17   "They Danced," *Havre Advertiser*, June 21, 1894.

18   "Last of the Sun Dances," *Helena Daily Independent*, July 8, 1894.

19   Gray, *The Cree Indians*, 40.

20   Work Projects Administration, *Copper Camp* (Hastings House, NY: 1943), 101–3.

21   Jonathan Lear, *Radical Hope: Ethics in the Face of Cultural Devastation* (Cambridge, MA: Harvard University Press, 2006), 106.

22   Frank B. Linderman, *Montana Adventure: The Recollections of Frank B. Linderman* (Lincoln: University of Nebraska Press, 1968), 99–100.

23   Gray, *The Cree Indians*, 32.

24 Verne Dusenberry, *The Montana Cree* (Norman: University of Oklahoma Press, 1998), 36.

25 Susan Labry Meyn, "Who's Who: The 1896 Sicangu Sioux Visit to the Cincinnati Zoological Gardens," *Museum Anthropology* 16, no. 2 (June 1992): 21.

26 Gray, *The Cree Indians*, 6–8. Most lodges held four to six people per household.

27 *Statutes at Large of the United States of America from December 1895, to March 1897, and Recent Treaties, Conventions, and Executive Proclamations*, vol. 29 (Washington, DC: Government Printing Office, 1897), 117.

28 *Anaconda Standard*, December 9, 1900.

29 "Wedded on City Dump, Sad-Eyed Annie and Bull Horn Are One," *Anaconda Standard*, April 29, 1901.

30 Sperry, *Ethnogenesis*, 28, 38–39.

31 *Anaconda Standard*, December 8, 1901.

32 Sperry, *Ethnogenesis*, 38–39.

33 *Anaconda Standard*, June 16, 1901.

34 *Anaconda Standard*, June 16, 1901.

35 *Anaconda Standard*, February 6, 1902.

36 The moot point of this being that, in aboriginal terms, the true eco-division between culture regions was from Pembina to the Big Bend of the Missouri, to the confluence of the Yellowstone, and over to the Front Range of the Rockies, rather than the 49th parallel.

37 Gray, *The Cree Indians*, 223.

38 Gray, *The Cree Indians*, 169–72.

39 Sperry, *Ethnogenesis*, 94–95.

40 Gray, *The Cree Indians*, 161; see also Dusenberry, *The Montana Cree*, 40.

41 *Anaconda Standard*, February 7, 1904.

42 *Anaconda Standard*, June 26, 1904.

43 *Anaconda Standard*, June 26, 1904.

44 *Anaconda Standard*, June 26, 1904.

45 *Anaconda Standard*, July 13, 1904.

46 *Anaconda Standard*, July 13, 1904.

47 Heather Devine, "Aboriginal Naming Practices," *People Who Own Themselves* (Calgary: University of Calgary Press, 2004), http://www.ucalgary.ca/~hdevine/naming.htm. Also, Catherine Anne Cavanaugh, Michael Payne, Donald Grant Wetherell, eds., *Alberta Formed, Alberta Transformed* (Edmonton: University of Alberta Press, 2006), 241. And Joachim Fromhold, *The Western Plains Cree* (Norman: University of Oklahoma Press, forthcoming), ch. 2. Manuscript highlights given to the author by Dr. Fromhold.

48 *Anaconda Standard*, June 7, 1907.

49 *Anaconda Standard*, June 22, 1907.

50 *Anaconda Standard*, November 24, 1912. Even the title of the article, "Rocky Boy Band to Be Guests of Government," is an indicator of a sea change in attitude toward urban Indians.

51 Gray, *The Cree Indians*, 83.

52 "Sad Is the Story of the Crees," *Anaconda Standard*, March 30, 1913.

53 Hugh A. Dempsey, *Big Bear: The End of Freedom* (Lincoln: University of Nebraska Press, 1984), 102.

54 Seattle Indian Health Board/Urban Indian Health Institute, 2007, http://www.uihi.org/the-weaving-project.

Extra Tasty and Fried the Way You Like It!:
Butte's Historic Drive-in Restaurants

Jon Axline

Butte displays some stunning examples of late-nineteenth and early-twentieth-century architecture, but sometimes the least imposing building houses the best treasure. Just south of the junction of South Montana Avenue and Interstate 90 on Placer Street stands a white, two-story, vernacular Craftsman-style building with green trim and large picture windows; a menu attached to the wall is outlined by neon tubing, which also graces the eaves of the place. A neon sign and lighted star on the roof announce it as Matt's Place, a certifiable Montana treasure that hearkens back to a different time when, as one man grumbled, "people with cars are so lazy that they don't want to get out of them to eat."[1] In this particular case, though, you'd be crazy not to get out of the car and walk a few feet to eat inside. Everything about Matt's suggests the 1950s, the golden age of the drive-in restaurant in Montana.

Walking in the door of Matt's Place is like taking a step back in time. Not much has changed, including its menu, since it opened in 1931. More than seventy years ago, Butte residents enjoyed Matt's famous Nutburger, its better-than-sex French fries, and the milkshakes thick enough to walk on just as much as their descendants savor them today. Customers sit on stools around a short,

Matt's Place, a certifiable Montana treasure. Photograph by Jon Axline.

U-shaped Formica counter with chrome trim, which is presided over by a chrome-finished, backlit soda fountain and Coca-Cola dispenser from the early 1950s. The fountain is the center attraction for patrons fortunate to find a place to sit during the busy noon-hour rush. Knotty pine paneling that was installed in 1950 and two large backlit photographs of Montana scenery provide additional ambiance. Presiding over the lunch crowd is ninety-four-year old Mae Laurence, who went to work as a waitress for the establishment's first owner, Matt Korn, in 1936. Seven years later, in 1943, Mae and her late husband, Louis, purchased the business from Korn and moved into the second-floor apartment over the business. She's been there ever since, preserving the quality of the

DRIVE IN FOR THE
FINEST FOOD
in TOWN
"Matts Place"
OPEN NIGHTS
'Til 1 A.M.
Counter & Curb Service 11:30 A.M. 'Til 1 A.M.
MONTANA AT ROWE ROAD JUNCTION

Matt's Place ran this ad in the June 5, 1965 Montana Standard-Post. *Courtesy Montana Historical Society Research Center.*

place, its traditions, and the best food in Montana.[2]

Upon entering Matt's, the aroma of frying burgers, homemade French fries, the 1950s decor, and the excitement in the voices of the patrons make you want to try everything on the menu. The last time I had the great fortune to eat there, I wolfed down a hamburger with a fried egg on it and relished each and every French fry to the point where I wrapped some of them up in a napkin to take home to my wife; they didn't make it past Elk Park. To be honest, I don't think I've ever had a bad meal

in Butte, but Matt's was exceptional. If all the drive-in restaurants in Butte were this good, then no wonder the Mining City had so many of them back in the day.

The first modern drive-in restaurant in the United States opened in Dallas, Texas, in 1921. The Pig Stand was the first restaurant built specifically to serve meals to motorists in their cars. The roadside eatery was the brainchild of Dallas physician Reuben W. Jackson and entrepreneur Jessie Kirby. The restaurant was an immediate success, and the number of Pig Stands mushroomed throughout Texas. Although the drive-in restaurant was a Texas innovation, it reached its penultimate form in California and became strongly associated with the freewheeling lifestyle of that state's citizens.[3]

The relatively mild climate and informal Southern California lifestyle proved ideal for the drive-in restaurant. In 1922, Lawrence Frank, Joe Montgomery, and Walter Van deKamp opened the first California drive-in near Griffith Park in Los Angeles. The first Montgomery Country Inn was followed by the Tam O'Shanter, A & W, Big Boy, Carpenter's Sandwiches, and Chicken in the Rough automobile-oriented eateries. To attract customers and build a readily identifiable business, drive-ins began sporting whimsical and streamlined modern architectural designs that would characterize this type of business all over Southern California and eventually throughout the United States.

TAMALES

V. TRUZZOLINO

Genuine Chicken Hot Tamales

16 W MERCURY STREET

WHOLESALE AND RETAIL SUPPLIES

You will find these Tamales in all the leading business houses in the city

Phones: Ind. 5526;   Bell 717.

An advertisement for Truzzollino's famous tamales. From the 1909 Butte City Directory. Courtesy Montana Historical Society Research Center.

For many on the-go Texans and Californians, drive-ins ideally suited their lifestyles. Consequently, the number of drive-ins boomed, becoming a firmly entrenched part of the American popular culture. By 1927, drive-ins based on the California models had spread throughout the United States, catering to both regional and national tastes in food.

Interestingly, the first drive-ins catered mostly to families and offered a full-range of menu items tailored specifically to what middle-class families usually ate for dinner. Chicken and pork dinners were the primary fare, but all-American hamburgers were the hot menu items that drew many to the roadside eateries. It wasn't until the post–World War II years that drive-ins became indelibly associated with teenage cruisers—much to the chagrin of many of the establishments' owners.[4]

The appearance of the drive-in restaurant coincided with the rise of the American car culture after World War I. As Americans made the transition from the horse to the car, the switch opened the field to new businesses that catered specifically to motorists. In addition to the drive-in, other business opportunities included service stations, convenience stores, and tourist cabin camps, like those made famous in Frank Capra's classic 1934 Oscar-winning film *It Happened One Night*. Drive-in restaurants certainly filled a need and quickly became part of America's popular culture. Interestingly, in the days before the national franchise chains, drive-ins catered to local gastronomical tastes. In the South, roadside pig and fried chicken stands were popular, while in the Northeast motorists stopped to order cuisine popular in that region. It was in the West, though, that drive-ins became inextricably associated with hamburgers, hotdogs, chicken, French fries, and milk shakes. Montana's drive-ins did not buck the regional trend.

It is difficult to determine when the first drive-in restaurant opened in Montana, but Matt's was certainly among the first. Bud Ferrat operated a curb service near the Northern Pacific Railway depot in Helena in 1933. Billings may have had a drive-in, the Black & White Hamburger Stand, as early as 1932, while Missoula's first roadside eatery, the aptly named Drive-Inn, didn't appear until 1945. Before World War II, all of Montana's drive-ins were small, privately owned outfits, but after the war the roadside landscape changed dramatically. Some communities had mostly mom-and-pop drive-ins, whereas others were dominated by a fair number of franchise restaurants, especially in Billings, Great Falls, and Missoula.

I vividly remember Sandy's on Grand Avenue in Billings, with its brilliantly lighted space-age building design, as well as the Frostop's huge spinning root beer mug in Billings Heights. All of the restaurants featured an abundance of neon, lighted menu boards, and various styles of canopy roofs covering patrons' automobiles. Some restaurants, such as A & W, relied on speaker boxes at individual stalls; others had drive-up ramps, as at the Tenth Avenue South Burgermaster in Great Falls and Big Boy Drive-in on Broadwater in Billings; and at Matt's in Butte and Gertie's in Helena, carhops took orders and brought food out to the car.[5]

The Mining City, along with other Montana communities, has had a taste for takeaway food since at least the early 1900s. Considering the size and ethnicity of Butte's population, street vendors undoubtedly peddled food in the Uptown during the early twentieth century. In many communities, including Butte and Havre, tamales seemed to be a popular fast food. Interestingly, though, the tamale vendors were Italians and emigrants from the Middle East. In 1905, two businesses peddled tamales in uptown Butte, including Salvator Truzzolino on Mercury Street. By 1910, the number of tamale hawkers in Butte had grown to five, including Truzzolino, Shadad Khan, and Marif Khari.

Within a few years, however, Butte's eateries began to stretch south down Montana and Harrison avenues toward the highway, where a new, mobile clientele also demanded good food at a reasonable cost. Most of Butte's tourist camps and, later, motels were located south of Butte on Harrison and Montana avenues. Fortunately, Matt's Place was located on U.S. Highway 10 South just across the road from the Montana Tourist Park, which later became the Kozy Korner Motel. Other Butte drive-ins were also located near motels, which greatly benefited the already thriving businesses.

Matt's fulfilled a need in the new automobile age, and it appears to have been the first drive-in in 1933, but that fact can't be confirmed from the information provided in the city directories. By 1941, only one other restaurant, Whimpy's Palace, advertised itself as a drive-in. While drive-in restaurants and roadside stands were common on the West Coast and in the South in the 1930s, the craze didn't really hit Montana until the postwar years. By 1952, Butte had five drive-ins, including Matt's, Bill's (the renamed Whimpy's Palace), the Copper Hill, Kingsburgers, and Scotty's.

From there, the number of establishments steadily mushroomed, reaching a peak of eleven restaurants in 1966. Most of Butte's drive-ins were family or individually owned; other than A & W Root Beer

Drive-in, there were no franchise joints in the city. Most were located along Harrison Avenue, with others scattered on Montana Avenue, Placer Street (which was old U.S. Highway 10 until the construction of Interstate 90 in the early 1960s), and Front Street. They went by the colorful names of Copper Hill, Kingsburgers, Leon & Eddie's, Robie's In & Out, Merry Jane's, Sully's, and Tinkerbelle's, to name just a few. In 1939, Bill Sebena opened Whimpy's Palace at 2101 Harrison Avenue. He changed the name to Bill's Drive-in in the late 1940s and then went on to open other drive-ins in Three Forks and Manhattan. All of the Butte-based eateries depended on good home-cooked food, clean conditions, and friendly service to bring customers back again and again.

Besides Matt's, one other drive-in sparks a resonance in the memories of the people who patronized it: the Donnabelle Drive-In.[6] Owned by Butte entrepreneur Park Davis, the Donnabelle opened at 3301 Harrison Avenue in 1956. Like Matt's, it was a relatively small place, with two-thirds of the building occupied by the kitchen and the remaining space open for seating—a few tables and a counter. Hungry Butte residents drove up to the building on the Harrison side of the establishment and used an intercom to order food, perhaps one of the delicious hamburgers, a "killer milk shake," and French fries smothered in dark gravy, a favorite among teenagers in the Mining City. Davis and later owner Jeannie Davis hired youngsters to peel potatoes in the basement for the fries. One patron, Bob Lubick, remembers that the owners strove to create at the Donnabelle the same atmosphere as at Matt's Place. An advertisement in the March 2, 1958, *Montana Standard* boasted that "when it comes to food . . . all kinds of delicious food, the Donnabelle Drive-In is the place. Everything from tea to T-bones expertly boxed to go!" The roadside eatery also specialized in sandwiches and "acronized" chicken, with a sixteen-piece sack selling for only $3.50. By the late 1970s, the restaurant was owned by Jack Hanley and was the "Home of the Wottaburger."[7]

Unfortunately, by the 1980s, changes in family lifestyles that required faster food delivery, an increase in juvenile delinquency, and changes in food preparation technology contributed to a decline in the number of traditional drive-in restaurants. Some franchise companies, such as Sandy's, were absorbed by national fast food conglomerates, while others, such as Frostop, simply disappeared from the roadside landscape. The locally owned establishments fared a little better and were able to hold out longer against McDonald's, Burger King, and Hardee's. The number of drive-ins in Butte peaked in 1966 at eleven drive-ins, located mostly on Harrison Avenue. But a little over a decade later, there were only four still operating in the Mining City, including the venerable Matt's Place, the model for all the Butte drive-ins. Donnabelle's closed in 1977. In the late 1980s, I had the great fortune of becoming addicted to the barbecue beef sandwiches at the Red and White Dairy on South Montana across from the old Milwaukee Road Railroad depot. But, alas, by 1993 even it was gone.[8]

Today, Matt's Place is still open, serving the same excellent fare it always has. It is living history at its best. To step in the front door, plop down on a chrome-trimmed stool, and order anything from the menu is truly an experience, one that many have enjoyed over the years. Unlike the sterile interiors of McDonald's, Burger King, and Arby's and their assembly-line food, Matt's is a step back into a time when drive-ins were new, the food was excellent, and the customer service was genuine.

[1]   Michael Karl Witzel, *The American Drive-in* (Osceola, WI: Motorbooks International, 1994), 25.

[2]   Jon Axline and Ellen Baumler, Matt's Place (24SB624), National Register of Historic Places Nomination, March 29, 2001; Andrea McCormick, "Drive-in Serves Up Morsels of Yesterday," (Butte) *Montana Standard*, July 27, 1980.

[3]   Witzel, *American Drive-in*, 25–26; Jim Heiman, *Car Hops and Curb Service: A History of American Drive-in Restaurants, 1920–1960* (San Francisco: Chronicle, 1996), 12, 14, 16.

[4]   Witzel, *American Drive-in*, 73, 78–79; Heiman, *Car Hops*, 16, 17–18, 20, 104–7.

[5]   Ellen Baumler and Dave Shors, *Lost Places, Hidden Treasures: Rare Photographs of Helena, Montana* (Helena: Farcountry, 2002), 60; R. L. Polk and Co., Billings, Butte, Great Falls, and Missoula City Directories, 1930–1950, Montana Historical Society, Helena.

[6]   Polk, Butte City Directories, 1930–1980; Obituary: William J. "Bill" Sebena Sr., *Bozeman Daily Chronicle*, July 8, 2008.

[7]   Polk, Butte City Directories, 1956–1980; interview of Bub Lubick by Jon Axline, July 31, 2008; advertisements, (Butte) *Montana Standard*, July 4, 1957; March 2, 1958, February 11, 1977.

[8]   By the mid-1950s, the advent of the post–World War II youth culture and the youngsters' access to automobiles became a significant problem for owners of family-oriented drive-in restaurants. Teenagers hung out at drive-ins, took up valuable parking space, and didn't spend much money. Add to that situation litter, brawls, loud music, and cruising, and it took a toll on the drive-ins as families began to stay away and to patronize establishments that didn't cater as much to teens. Although the media suggests that the 1950s and 1960s were the golden age of the drive-in, the problems with teenagers and juvenile delinquency actually contributed to the decline of the drive-in. The vacuum left by the demise of those establishments was filled by McDonald's, Burger King, Arby's, and a host of other franchise places. Heiman, *Car Hops*, 104–10; Polk, Butte City Directories, 1960–2000.

Our Contributors

Jon Axline is the historian and interpretive markers coordinator at the Montana Department of Transportation. His work has taken him to all corners of the Treasure State in search of historic sites adjacent to the state's highways. Jon is the author of many articles on the state's history on a wide variety of subjects, ranging from dinosaurs to railroads, Montana jerks, and flying saucers. He is the author of *Conveniences Sorely Needed: Montana's Historic Highway Bridges* and the editor of the recently published *Montana's Historical Highway Markers*. He lives in Helena with his wife, Lisa, daughters, Kate and Kira, four cats, and two Corgis.

Matthew Basso is the Director of the American West Center and jointly appointed in History and Gender Studies at the University of Utah. He received his Ph.D. from the University of Minnesota's Program in American Studies in 2001 and his MA in history from The University of Montana in 1996. He has taught in various roles at both those universities as well as in the U.S. Army while serving in Germany during the Gulf War. Prior to his stint in uniform he spent four glorious years at Vassar College where his keen interest in gendered relations of power was born.

He is currently working on a book project on Montana's World War II home front that will be published by the University of Chicago Press. In 2001 Routledge published his co-edited volume, *Across the Great Divide: Cultures of Manhood in the U.S. West*. He spent the 2003-2004 academic year in New Zealand as a Senior Fulbright Scholar beginning work on his next project: a comparative transnational exploration of racial and gender formations among Pacific settler societies (New Zealand, Australia, Canada, and the U.S.). At the American West Center—www.awc.utah.edu—he oversees a number of public history projects including: the Utah American Indian Digital Archive, the Utah Indian Curriculum Project, the Digital Pacific Archive Project, and the Westerns of the World Film Festival.

Ellen Baumler received her Ph.D. from the University of Kansas in English, Classics, and History and has been the interpretive historian at the Montana Historical Society since 1992. She has authored dozens of articles and several books, among them *Beyond Spirit Tailings*, honored with an Award of Merit from the American Association for State and Local History. Ellen is also the editor of *Girl from the Gulches: The Story of Mary Ronan*, a 2004 Finalist Award winner of the Willa Literary Awards. Her most recent book, *Dark Spaces: Montana's Historic Penitentiary at Deer Lodge*, is an illustrated documentary featuring the contemporary work of photographer J. M. Cooper.

Joeann Daley, founder of the Copper Village Art Center in Anaconda, is currently resident artist at Dominican High School, Whitefish Bay, Wisconsin, where she has her etching studio, Studio San Domenico. She has been a practicing printmaker for over thirty years and has exhibited in the United States, eastern and western Europe, and South America. She has done artist residencies in New York, Montana, Wisconsin, Illinois, and Italy. She has taught grade through college and adult classes. A past member of the Montana Arts Council, Joeann has had experience as an arts administrator and a speaker at local, regional and national conferences of art and religion. Years of Europan travel and studying and living in Italy have enriched her life experience as well as her art.

Patty Dean received her A.B. in history from Carroll College and an M.A. in History Museum Studies from the Cooperstown Graduate Program/State University of New York. In the early 1980s, she was Curator of Collections at the Montana Historical Society and later founding curator of the Arkansas Arts Center Decorative Arts Museum in Little Rock. Patty worked at the Minnesota Historical Society in St. Paul for sixteen years, first as Museum Collections Manager and later as Supervisory Curator.

As an independent public historian in Helena, Montana, from 2005–2008, she was adjunct faculty for the history and music departments at Carroll College and a historian for the Montana Historical Society's "Identifying African-Americans in Montana Heritage Resources" project.

Since December 2008, she has been the Curator of History for the Montana Historical Society. Patty has served as a board/commission member for the Montana Preservation Alliance, Drumlummon Institute, Helena/Lewis & Clark County Historic Preservation Commission, and the Montana Heritage Commission.

Butte native **Edwin Dobb** is a fourth-generation descendant of Cornish tin miners and Irish copper miners. A former magazine editor, Dobb has been an independent writer for almost twenty years. National publications he's written for include *The New York Times Magazine* and *Harper's*, where he's been a contributor since 1996. Dobb is the co-writer and co-producer of *Butte, America*, a feature-length documentary film produced by Bozeman-based Rattlesnake Productions. Since 2000, Dobb has been a periodic visiting lecturer at the U.C. Berkeley Graduate School of Journalism, where he teaches creative nonfiction. He divides his time between his home in East Walkerville and various elsewheres.

Ron Fischer was raised in Anaconda. His dad worked for the Anaconda Mining Company, and his mom worked at the State Hospital in Warm Springs. He earned a teaching degree from Western Montana and started teaching high school in Butte. The University of Montana would send out writers like Bill Kittredge and Rick DeMarinis to do summer workshops. They liked Ron's writing, thought he showed promise, and urged him to get into the MFA program at The University of Montana while Dick Hugo was still teaching there. He did. In grad school, he received a $5,000 award for a short story, "Borders and Anaconda Streets." His play *A Dance on Crumbling Earth*, a musical about a miners strike in 1930s Butte, won a centennial playwriting contest and was performed in Butte. His collection of short stories called *Journeys Into Open Country* won the Montana Arts Council's First Book award in 1992. Ron went on to get his doctorate at Idaho State University. He is now Associate Professor of English at Minot State University, Minot, North Dakota.

Kate Hampton joined the staff of the Montana Preservation Alliance in July 2008 to head up the Montana's Most Endangered Places program. Kate has a master's degree in western U.S. history from The University of Montana and a bachelor's degree in history from Towson State University. Prior to coming to MPA, Kate was the National Register of Historic Places Coordinator at the State Historic Preservation Office within the Montana Historical Society for eight years. She was also an intern and, later, full-time employee at Historical Research Associates in Missoula, where she worked on historical research and cultural resource management projects throughout the United States. She assisted in and managed the inventory and evaluation of properties for eligibility in the National Register, including field survey and photographic documentation. Kate also conducted research and authored reports on projects related to historical/legal issues between Native American tribes, state governments, and the federal government.

Mary S. Hoffschwelle teaches American history at Middle Tennessee State University. Her interest in the Aesthetic and Arts and Crafts movements began when she was Curator of the Original Governor's Mansion for the Montana Historical Society in 1981–1985. More recently her research on the material culture of reform has focused on the rural South and African American schools, including *The Rosenwald Schools of the American South* (University Press of Florida, 2006).

Chere Jiusto is Executive Director of the Montana Preservation Alliance, Montana's statewide nonprofit group dedicated to preservation of Montana's historic places, heritage, and culture. Based in Helena, MPA conducts outreach on community preservation, threatened sites, heritage education, and places of cultural significance. Chere came to MPA by way of the Montana Historical Society where she was Curator of History with the museum and later served as the National Register coordinator and community preservation historian with the State Historic Preservation Office. Throughout her career, she has worked with members of Montana's urban, rural, and tribal communities to preserve Montana's traditional heritage and cultural landscapes.

Chere's publications include *Montana Mainstreets, Vol. 4: A Guide to Historic Hamilton* and *The Heart of Helena: A Historical Overview.* She is also a ceramic artist and co-author of *A Ceramic Continuum: Fifty Years of the Archie Bray Influence* (University of Washington Press/Holter Museum of Art, 2001).

Dale Martin teaches history at Montana State University at Bozeman. He grew up in the Seattle area, attended Washington State University, spent years in field work in archaeology and history, and currently pursues interests in the history and technology of railways, metals and mining, and the First World War.

Christopher W. Merritt received a B.A. in Anthropology from The University of Montana, and a M.S. in Industrial Archaeology from Michigan Technological University. He is currently pursuing a Ph.D. in Cultural Heritage Studies at The University of Montana. Chris' dissertation research is focused on understanding the role that the Chinese played in Montana history by combining archaeology and history. He has already led archaeological investigations of Chinese sites around the state including Big Timber's Chinatown and Cedar Creek Mining District near Superior and is currently partnered with the U.S. Forest Service to produce a synthesis of that agency's Chinese cultural resources in Montana and Idaho.

John Mihelich is an associate professor at the University of Idaho, where he teaches anthropology, sociology, and American studies. Dr. Mihelich's research focuses on American culture and explores questions about the intersections of community, class, and religion. Along with ongoing research on the mining community of Butte, Montana, Mihelich's research areas include young adults and religion, material and popular culture, labor and economic ideology, and critical theory.

Mary Murphy is the Michael P. Malone Professor of History at Montana State University, Bozeman.

She is the author of *Mining Cultures: Men, Women and Leisure in Butte, 1914-41* and *Hope in Hard Times: New Deal Photographs of Montana* as well as numerous articles on the history of women in the American West.

Fredric Quivik is a consulting historian of technology, currently living in Philadelphia, Pennsylvania. He often works as an expert witness in Superfund and related environmental litigation. During the years 1977–1990, he and his wife, Melinda, lived in Butte, where he was an active member of the Butte Historical Society (BHS). As a volunteer with the BHS, he helped organize the Historic American Engineering Record project in 1979 that led to creation of the Urban Revitalization Agency; he helped Bill Walker establish the Butte-Silver Bow Public Archives; he organized the survey of historic buildings and structures in the Butte National Historic Landmark; and with Mark Fiege and Dennis Glick he wrote the Butte-Anaconda Historical Park System Master Plan. The Clark Fork Superfund case, embracing Butte and Anaconda, was the first Superfund case on which he worked as an expert.

Dennice Scanlon was born and grew up in Butte on the East Side. Her family moved to Butte's West Side when the Berkeley Pit expanded and swallowed up the old neighborhoods. She moved to Anaconda in 1972 where she taught school—both high school and elementary. In 1984, she received her MFA from The University of Montana. Dennice retired from teaching in 2007 after thirty-five years. Her poem, "The Difference in Effects of Temperature Depending on Geographical Location East or West of the Continental Divide: A Letter" (reprinted here) has also appeared in *The Last Best Place: A Montana Anthology* and *Circle of Women: An Anthology of Contemporary Western Women Writers*.

Brian Shovers has been a Reference Historian and is currently the Library Manager at the Montana Historical Society Research Center, where he has worked since 1993. Shovers lived in Butte during the 1980s, allowing him the opportunity to work on the 1984 architectural inventory of the Landmark District; to complete his Masters thesis on the influence of technology on working conditions in the Butte underground; and to edit a journal of Butte history entitled *The Speculator*. He is president of the Montana chapter of the Society for Industrial Archaeology and spends his free time watching birds and touring abandoned mines and smelters.

In 2002, **Benjamin Trigona-Harany** graduated with a B.Sc. from Simon Fraser University in Vancouver,

British Columbia. He has just completed his M.A. in Ottoman history at Boğaziçi University in Istanbul, having written on the newspapers published by Syriac Christians in the Ottoman Empire prior to World War I. Currently he is preparing his thesis for publication and working on translations of the early Syriac publications in the Ottoman Empire and the United States.

Nicholas Peterson Vrooman has been working as a cultural specialist since the 1970s. He was the first State Folklorist of North Dakota, the Dakota Field Representative for ArtsMidwest (a regional consortium of state arts agencies), second State Folklorist for Montana, Nevada State Folklorist for Indian Traditional Arts, Program Director of Educational Talent Search in Indian Country for the Montana Office of the Commissioner of Higher Education, visiting professor of Native American Studies at The University of Montana, and proprietor of Northern Plains Folklife Resources. Vrooman created the Indian Traditional Arts Residency and Master/Apprenticeship Programs for the North Dakota Council on the Arts and the Montana Arts Council. Through the 1980s and 1990s, he was intimately involved in the development of the Northern Plains Indian Art Market.

Nicholas has served as consultant to the Smithsonian National Museum of the American Indian, the Festival of American Folklife on the Mall, the Métis National Council of Canada, and the National Folk Festival. He's worked with tribal peoples throughout the American and Canadian West to produce sound recordings, documentary films, performances, publications, conferences, ceremonies, and festivals highlighting Aboriginal culture.

Photographer **Lisa Wareham** can be seen lurking in the alleys and abandoned buildings of Butte, Montana. But you probably won't see her walking. Instead you'll see her standing on the nearest dumpster or squatting low to the ground for the best angle for her next daily photo. Lisa has been capturing images of Butte every day since April of 2008 for her online project www.ButteDailyPhoto.com. Her images emphasize exaggerated angles and tiny details of the historic city. Besides photographing Butte, she spends long hours in her studio creating advertising images and photographing people. Those images can be viewed at lisawareham.com.

Lisa graduated from the University of Idaho in 2007 with a degree in Public Relations. While at college she worked for her school newspaper for three years as a photographer and reporter. It was there she fell in love with photography. After graduation she realized she wanted to pursue her passion of photography. She applied to the Rocky Mountain School of Photography's summer and digital intensive programs and completed them in 2007. Her technical education is the basis for her photos, but her creative vision is what brings her work to life.

Carroll Van West is a professor of history and director of the Center for Historic Preservation at Middle Tennessee State University and of the National Park Service's Tennessee Civil War National Heritage Area. He worked on the Montana State Historic Preservation Plan in 1984–1985 and has written *A Traveler's Companion of Montana History* (1986) and *Capitalism on the Frontier: The Transformation of Billings and the Yellowstone Valley in the 19th Century* (1993).

Trained as a painter and sculptor, **Roger Whitacre** began working full-time as a photographer in 1970. His first major account was a series of public relations photographs for the Colorado National Bank, which led to doing photographs for the Denver Symphony Orchestra for nearly ten years. In the early years of his career, most of Roger's work entailed photographing commercial real estate for publications & brochures.

At the same time, he began taking photographs for Historic Denver, Inc., which evolved into a focus on historic buildings, including HABS & HAER documentation photography. His prints have been published in sixteen books over the past thirty years and his works have been exhibited at the Colorado State Capitol, Colorado National Bank, Denver National Bank, and *Buildings Reborn,* a Smithsonian Institution traveling exhibition. Roger makes his home in Denver, Colorado.

Pat Williams is Montana's former Congressman, having served nine terms in the U.S. House of Representatives from 1979 to 1997. Pat, a native of Butte, has been a classroom teacher beginning in Butte and Helena where he taught sixth graders, a guest lecturer in colleges throughout the nation, and currently teaches graduate studies at The University of Montana. Pat is also a columnist for newspapers in the West and provides a regular commentary on Montana Public Radio.

DRUMLUMMON
INSTITUTE

RELIES ON YOUR GENEROUS SUPPORT!

To make a donation
in support of

DRUMLUMMON INSTITUTE
A Montana Nonprofit Corporation
with Federal 501 (c) (3) Tax Status

&

Drumlummon Views,
The Online Journal of Montana Arts & Culture

Please Make Your Check Payable to
DRUMLUMMON INSTITUTE

&

· mail to

DRUMLUMMON INSTITUTE
402 Dearborn Avenue #3
Helena, Mt 59601

Join Us Today!

The **Montana Preservation Alliance** (MPA) saves and protects Montana's historic places, traditional landscapes, and cultural heritage. We are the only statewide, not-for-profit organization working at the grassroots level to provide Montanans with the resources necessary to preserve our state's unique history and culture.

Your tax-deductible MPA membership will help support our efforts to preserve the best of Montana's history and heritage for the future. Members receive a one-year subscription to our quarterly preservation newsletter, *Preservation Montana,* notices of upcoming events, updates on statewide preservation issues, and discount admission to workshops throughout the year.

Please make checks payable to: Montana Preservation Alliance, 120 Reeder's Alley, Helena, MT 59601

For more information call 406.457.2822, email Christine@preservemontana.org, or write MPA, 120 Reeder's Alley, Helena, MT 59601. **Visit MPA on the web at www.preservemontana.org**